Butterworths **Tolley**
LexisNexis™

Members of the LexisNexis Group worldwide

United Kingdom	Butterworths Tolley, a Division of Reed Elsevier (UK) Ltd, 2 Addiscombe Road, CROYDON CR9 5AF
Argentina	Abeledo Perrot, Jurisprudencia Argentina and Depalma, BUENOS AIRES
Australia	Butterworths, a Division of Reed International Books Australia Pty Ltd, CHATSWOOD, New South Wales
Austria	ARD Betriebsdienst and Verlag Orac, VIENNA
Canada	Butterworths Canada Ltd, MARKHAM, Ontario
Chile	Publitecsa and Conosur Ltda, SANTIAGO DE CHILE
Czech Republic	Orac sro, PRAGUE
France	Editions du Juris-Classeur SA, PARIS
Hong Kong	Butterworths Asia (Hong Kong), HONG KONG
Hungary	Hvg Orac, BUDAPEST
India	Butterworths India, NEW DELHI
Ireland	Butterworths (Ireland) Ltd, DUBLIN
Italy	Giuffré, MILAN
Malaysia	Malayan Law Journal Sdn Bhd, KUALA LUMPUR
New Zealand	Butterworths of New Zealand, WELLINGTON
Poland	Wydawnictwa Prawnicze PWN, WARSAW
Singapore	Butterworths Asia, SINGAPORE
South Africa	Butterworths Publishers (Pty) Ltd, DURBAN
Switzerland	Stämpfli Verlag AG, BERNE
USA	LexisNexis, DAYTON, Ohio

© Reed Elsevier (UK) Ltd 2001 except:
Chapters 1 and 2 © Jackie Le Poidevin 2001
Chapter 4 and Appendix 4 © Bernard Williams Associates 2001
Chapter 10 © Louis Wustemann 2001
Appendix 3 © Landwell (Solicitors) Ltd 2001

A CIP Catalogue record for this book is available from the British Library.

ISBN 0 75450 230 9

Typeset by Columns Design Ltd, Reading, England
Printed and bound in Great Britian by Cromwell Press

Visit Butterworths LexisNexis *direct* at www.butterworths.com

Foreword

It is a great pleasure for me to write a brief foreword to this excellent handbook on facilities management.

Facilities managment now plays such an important part in the day-to-day running of a business that it is often difficult to keep abreast of all the technicalities of the law, not to mention the financial and practical implications of – for example – rising energy costs. This handbook, which combines practical best practice tips – including, I am pleased to see, business continuity – with advice on complying with the law, offers a veritable encyclopedia on facilities management issues which will undoubtedly be of substantial help to all facilities professionals, from the small businessman right through to those working for large companies.

I am sure readers will find many helpful tips within its pages and I congratulate the authors for making so much information available in such a useful and readable format.

Christopher W Rust
Chairman, Facilities Management Association

Contents

2 Employment Law

3 Property Law

BUSINESS ISSUES

4 Financial Management

5 Business Continuity

Contents

6 Outsourcing

7 Transport policies

8 Communications

THE BUILT ENVIRONMENT

9 Workplace Facilities

Contents

10 Space Design and Management

11 Access and Security

Contents

12 Maintenance and Repair

About the Authors

Amanda Benham has practised in the City as a solicitor for 16 years, specialising in landlord and tenant law and estates' management, and is the leader of the real estate practice in Landwell, the associated law firm of PricewaterhouseCoopers. She is a frequent contributor to property publications and regularly lectures to the property industry.
amanda.benham@uk.landwellglobal.com

Frank Booty is editor of *Facilities Management*, and a contributor to other market-leading titles and books in the fields of business, IT and networking and manufacturing. An award-winning journalist, he has also devised and chaired many conferences in the facilities management market.
fbooty@compuserve.com

Connel Bottom is a facilities management consultant with Bernard Williams Associates, specialising in facilities cost and performance benchmarking/modelling for corporate occupiers and service providers within the UK and Europe.
connel.bottom@bwasssoc.co.uk

Nick Croft is a real estate consultant at PricewaterhouseCoopers specialising in valuation advice for both occupiers and investors within the UK and abroad.
nicholas.h.croft@uk.pwcglobal.com

Nick Edwards is a solicitor with Landwell, the associated law firm of PricewaterhouseCoopers. He coordinates Landwell's real estate publications and advises businesses in the insurance and investment sector on facilities management and premises issues.
nicholas.edwards@uk.landwellglobal.com

Jackie Le Poidevin is a writer and editor on journals specialising in employment law and workplace health and safety. She also compiles the legal section of *Facilities Management*.
jlpoidevin@aol.com

Chris Taylor is a specialist editor and writer on management, and the issues and concerns which affect business today.
ct@clara.net

Louis Wustemann is a writer and consultant on facilities and employment matters. He is former editor of *Flexible Working* magazine and is general editor of the IRS Handbook *Flexible Working – Policy and Practice*.
lw@sivill.demon.co.uk

Acknowledgements

The publishers wish to express their thanks to:

Pat Anderson
Richard Armitage
Mike Bateman
Jane Bell
Nicola Coote
Ken Coules
Christopher Eskell
Martyn Gilbert
Janice Hunter
Janet Kelly
Maureen Moody
Simon Napper
Lucy Ponting
Phil Roberts
Valerie Taplin
Richard Tinson
Roger Tompsett
Vilnis Vesma
Roger Woodward

Introduction

The world of facilities management has changed dramatically over the past 10 years. From relatively humble beginnings, the job of facilities manager now encompasses a wide range of complex and challenging roles, often across entire estates. In a definition issued by NHS Estates in 1996, facilities management is described as "the practice of coordinating the physical workplace with the people and work of an organisation". And that really is just the starting point.

Facilities managers today may well have to run a department responsible for everything from risk assessments to gas supply, from preparing tendering documents to managing IT systems and car parks. They are usually in the unenviable position of having to request funds for functions unconnected to the core business of the company, which are nevertheless essential.

Aims of the book

The goal of this book is to provide information and guidance for facilities managers, allowing readers quick and easy access to the answers to their most pressing questions. Its aim is not to offer a conclusive definition of the role of the facilities manager, which is constantly developing, but to help those working within the facilities function to develop strategies for succeeding in an increasingly high-tech and global marketplace.

Who will find the book helpful?

Individual facilities managers and estates managers in all sizes of companies should benefit from this book. But so, also, will independent suppliers, architects, surveyors, lawyers, space planners, human resources staff and building services engineers who need an insight into the facilities universe.

Keeping abreast of the law

Clearly, not falling foul of the law is a major concern for facilities managers. The main areas of legislation in the sector are health and safety, employment and property law, each of which is covered by a separate chapter within this book. The laws and regulations regarding health and safety and employment in particular are fast moving and wide-ranging. Facilities managers need to cope with the needs of office workers for ergonomic workstations, access for

1

the disabled and the demands of TUPE, to name just a few of the areas covered here in the form of practical and actionable advice.

Running a business

Managing the facilities function can be like running a business in itself. Setting and meeting budget targets, cutting costs and making savings have been challenging tasks for facilities managers for some time. The business issues section guides readers through the demands of contract management and the outsourcing process. It also offers up-to-date information on communications and IT, where the combination of a shrinking world and fast-developing technology mean facilities managers need to know exactly what they can – and can afford to – invest in. Private investments and partnership – with huge implications for facilities managers – are on the increase and there is an ever-pressing need for business continuity arrangements in case of communications breakdown and other disasters. These are also fully explored.

Managing the built environment

Facilities professionals are responsible for an extraordinary array of workplace facilities. The procurement of utilities, the management of waste, the installing of integrated security systems, the purchase of office furniture and the costing of cleaning and catering functions are just some of the challenges facing facilities managers. This section of the handbook offers best practice information and advice on these issues.

Future challenges

The future workplace will bring with it a number of distinct priorities. More attempts to make flexible working a reality are likely – requiring improved IT and communications infrastructures. The expansion of a 24×7 work culture will necessitate non-stop support facilities – with consequent outsourcing, contract and health and safety considerations needing to be taken into account. PPP (public/private partnerships) and economic pressures will push facilities professionals towards more benchmarking, more cost benefit analysis and more performance measurement.

Facilities for businesses in the future will have to be more flexible and more streamlined than ever before. Managers will need to exploit growing communication opportunities and facilitate an ever-widening range of support services.

The challenges are mounting – this book can help you meet them.

Legal Issues

Legal Issues

1 Health and Safety Law

Jackie Le Poidevin

Prosecutions under criminal law and compensation under civil law are the tip of the iceberg when it comes to working out what poor health and safety costs employers. HSE studies suggest that for every pound in costs covered by employers' liability insurance, organisations must pay between another £8 to £36 in uninsured costs. The message is that safe, healthy workplaces save money, not only in obvious ways such as reducing absenteeism, but by making organisations more efficient and productive. By improving workplace design and ensuring workstations are ergonomically suited to the individual worker, for example, facilities managers play a crucial role in this process of improving staff morale and well-being.

The 1995 HSE survey of self-reported work-related illness estimated that two million employees were made ill by their work that year, of whom 721 000 left their jobs; 672,000 took no time off; and 624,000 took off 18 million working days between them. The CBI has estimated that the annual cost of absenteeism to UK plc is £10 billion, rising to £20 billion if indirect costs are counted.

As for accidents, in 2000/2001, 295 people were killed at work, and there were 27,935 major injuries. HSE estimated in 1996 that injuries cost UK

Cost of poor health and safety

Costs imposed by ill health and accidents include:

- sick pay
- lost production
- damaged equipment and materials
- extra administration
- losing skilled staff
- training replacement staff
- increased insurance premiums
- loss of staff morale
- bad publicity (which may put off job candidates and investors)
- compensation, fines and court costs

businesses £0.9 billion a year, illnesses £1.6 billion, and non-injury accidents between £1.4 billion and £4.5 billion. The total represents 4–8% of companies' gross trading profits.

Enforcement

The cornerstone of health and safety legislation is the *Health and Safety at Work etc Act 1974 (HSW Act)*. It is an 'enabling' Act, under which detailed regulations on particular work-related risks are made.

These regulations are supported by Approved Codes of Practice (ACoPs) and guidance. ACoPs have a special legal status like the Highway Code. If a court proves an organisation failed to comply with a revelant ACoP, it will be found guilty unless it demonstrates it complied with the law in another way. Following guidance is not compulsory and employers are free to take other action. But by following it, they will usually be doing enough to comply with the law.

The HSC and the HSE

The Health and Safety Commission (HSC) is the agency which has overall responsibility for developing workplace health and safety and deciding on new legislation to lay before Parliament. Its commissioners are drawn from employers' organisations, trade unions and local authorities. Its executive arm is the Health and Safety Executive (HSE). Both agencies are independent of the Government, although they are responsible to the Secretary of State for Environment, Food and Rural Affairs.

Responsibility for enforcing the law is shared between the HSE and local authorities. HSE inspects factories, chemical firms and construction sites, while local authority environmental health officers inspect offices, shops, warehouses, hotels and leisure sites. Inspectors may issue an improvement notice if they find a breach of statutory duty, or a prohibition notice stopping an activity which involves a risk of serious injury.

Regulations

Modern health and safety law in the UK is 'goal-setting' rather than prescriptive. The responsibility is on employers actively to apply these broad legal principles to suit their particular organisation, rather than following fixed rules which may not be appropriate to their circumstances.

Health and Safety at Work etc Act 1974 (HSW Act)

The *HSW Act* imposes a duty of care on employers, employees and suppliers.

Employers' duties (section 2)

Employers should, "so far as is reasonably practicable", ensure the health, safety and welfare at work of all employees by:

- providing safe equipment and working practices
- ensuring safe handling, storage and transportation of goods and substances
- providing information, training and supervision
- providing a safe place of work with safe access and egress
- providing a safe working environment and facilities

Safety policy (section 2(3))

Organisations with five or more employees must:

- prepare a written health and safety policy, listing the hazards present in the workplace
- provide details of arrangements for carrying out the policy
- make employees aware of the policy and arrangements
- update the policy as necessary

Duties to non-employees (section 3)

Employers should ensure "so far as is reasonably practicable" that they do not put anyone not in their employment (such as members of the public, contractors and agency staff) at risk from their activities. This duty can extend to trespassers, so facilities managers need to ensure that high-risk workplaces have adequate security and fencing.

"So far as is reasonably practicable" means that if the cost of removing a risk (in terms of time and trouble as well as financial cost) outweighs the possible benefit to employees and the public, an employer does not have to act. The burden of proof rests with the employer, meaning that, if prosecuted, it has to prove why a safety measure was not reasonably practicable.

Suppliers' duties (section 6)

Those who design, manufacture, import or supply goods or substances for use at work must ensure they are safe when used properly, and provide instructions on how to use them safely.

Employees' duties (section 7)

Employees must:

- take reasonable care for their own health and safety and that of anyone else affected by their work
- cooperate with their employer in ensuring it meets its legal obligations (by wearing personal protective equipment (PPE) or reporting accidents, for example)

Personal liability (section 37)

Company directors and managers may be personally liable for a health and safety offence committed with their consent or connivance. They face being fined and disqualified from being a director for up to two years.

A successful health and safety policy

Under the *HSW Act*, employers must prepare in writing:

- a statement of their general policy on their employees' health and safety at work
- the organisation of the policy
- the arrangements for carrying out the policy

Policies are normally divided into three sections to meet these three demands.

1. The statement of intent

This involves a general statement of good intent, and a commitment to comply with relevant legislation. Many employers extend their policies to the health and safety of others affected by their activities, such as contractors and the public. To demonstrate commitment from the top, the statement should be signed by the chairperson or chief executive.

2. Organisational responsibilities

This section shows how the organisation will put its good intentions into practice and which responsibilities those at different levels in the management structure will hold. The section might cover:

- making adequate resources available to implement the policy
- setting health and safety objectives
- developing suitable procedures and safe systems

- delegating specific responsibilities
- monitoring people's effectiveness in carrying out their responsibilities
- monitoring workplace standards
- feeding concerns up through the organisation

3. Arrangements

The policy need not contain all the organisation's health and safety arrangements, but should state where they can be found, such as in a separate health and safety manual or within various procedural documents. Topics which may require detailed arrangements include:

- operational procedures
- training
- personal protective equipment
- inspection programmes
- accident and investigation arrangements
- fire and emergency procedures
- first aid
- occupational health
- control of contractors and visitors
- consultation with employees
- audits of health and safety arrangements

Employees must be aware of the policy and their own responsibilities. They may be given their own copy, or the policy might be displayed around the workplace. Detailed briefings and induction training may be necessary for some arrangements.

Employers should revise their policies as often "as may be appropriate". Larger employers are likely to need to arrange for formal review and, where necessary, for revision to take place on a regular basis (by way of an ISO 9000 procedure, for example). Dating the policy document is an important part of this process.

The 'six-pack'

The 'six-pack' consists of six key sets of regulations introduced together in 1992. Some have, however, since been updated.

Management of Health and Safety at Work Regulations 1999 (Management Regulations)

The *Management Regulations* make explicit many of the duties contained in the *HSW Act*. They require employers to:

- make a "suitable and sufficient" assessment of the risks to employees (including, specifically, young people and pregnant women) and others affected by their work activities

- plan, organise, control, monitor and review health and safety arrangements

- record the assessment's significant findings and the health and safety arrangements, if five or more people are employed

- appoint "competent persons" to help apply health and safety law – since 1999, these are preferably to be employees, not outside consultants

- inform employees (and the parents of employed children) of workplace risks, control measures, and procedures in the event of serious and imminent danger

- provide adequate health and safety training

- provide health surveillance where the risk assessment shows it is needed

- arrange contacts with external services where necessary for first aid, emergency medical care and rescue work (a requirement introduced in 1999)

See RISK ASSESSMENT, PP16–19, for detailed information on conducting a risk assessment.

Workplace (Health, Safety and Welfare) Regulations 1992 (Workplace Regulations)

Employers and others with any control over the workplace (such as landlords) must ensure the workplace, equipment and devices listed in the Regulations are maintained in efficient working order and good repair. These Regulations govern much of the responsibility which facilities managers have for ensuring that the work premises are clean, comfortable, well lit, well ventilated and well organised. Specifically, employers must ensure:

- enclosed workplaces are ventilated by sufficient fresh or purified air

- a reasonable temperature is maintained

- there is suitable and sufficient lighting, especially natural light

- workplaces, furniture, furnishings and fittings are clean

- there is sufficient floor area and headroom
- workstations and seating are suitable for the person and the job
- floors are level, not slippery, effectively drained, and kept free from obstruction, and staircases have handrails
- risks from falls or falling objects are removed or controlled, with fences and covers for tanks and pits
- glazing is protected against breakage and marked so it can be seen
- windows and skylights can be cleaned, opened, and left open safely
- traffic routes are marked and organised so that pedestrians and vehicles can circulate safely
- doors, gates, escalators and moving walkways are safely constructed and safe to use
- enough toilets and washing facilities are provided, which are accessible, ventilated, lit and clean
- an adequate supply of wholesome drinking water is provided
- facilities are provided for storing and changing clothes
- facilities for resting and eating meals are provided, with suitable arrangements for non-smokers and pregnant women

Health and Safety (Display Screen Equipment) Regulations 1992 (DSE Regulations)

Employers must assess the risks to "habitual" users or operators of computer monitors and reduce them to the lowest level reasonably practicable. "Users" are employees, whereas operators are self-employed people or "temps". Habitual monitor users:

- use them continuously for an hour or more a day
- depend on them to do the job
- have no discretion over their use

Employers must also ensure:

- new workstations meet minimum legal requirements
- users take breaks from their monitor or change activities regularly (a five to 10-minute break every hour is better than 15 minutes every two hours)
- on request, employees receive free regular sight tests and corrective glasses
- employees receive adequate training and information

Manual Handling Operations Regulations 1992

Manual handling is the transporting or supporting of a load by hand or bodily force, including lifting, putting down, pushing, pulling, carrying or moving. Employers' duties are to:

- avoid the manual handling operation if reasonably practicable, by redesigning the task to avoid moving the load or by automating the process

- conduct a further risk assessment, if eliminating the risks is not possible, and reduce the risk of injury to the lowest level reasonably practicable

- provide employees with indications and, where practicable, precise information on the weight of each load and its heaviest side

Provision and Use of Work Equipment Regulations 1998 (PUWER)

Employers must ensure all work equipment (such as tools, photocopiers, vehicles, manufacturing plant) is:

- suitable for its intended use

- safe to use, maintained in a safe condition and, in some cases, inspected for safety by a competent person

- used only by trained personnel

- accompanied by suitable safety devices (such as guards, warnings, stop buttons)

- used according to a safe system of work (such as maintaining machinery when it is shut down, for example)

Some further points:

- If employees provide their own equipment, or work from home, the employer must ensure it complies with *PUWER*.

- *PUWER* does not apply to equipment used by members of the public (such as compressed air equipment on garage forecourts), although the *HSW Act* will apply.

- Mobile equipment (such as forklift trucks) meant to carry people must be suitable for the purpose, and employers must minimise the risk of it rolling over.

- Power presses and their guard devices must be thoroughly examined at specified intervals, inspected daily for safety, and records kept.

Personal Protective Equipment at Work Regulations 1992 (PPE Regulations)

Employers must:

- assess whether personal protective equipment (PPE) (such as face masks, fall-arresting equipment, gloves) is suitable and provide it to employees exposed to risks not adequately controlled by other means
- ensure items of PPE worn together are compatible
- ensure PPE is maintained in efficient working order and good repair
- provide storage for PPE that is not in use – if the PPE is contaminated, this must be separate from ordinary clothing
- provide information and training on the risks the PPE will limit, and how to use and maintain the PPE
- ensure the PPE is properly used

Other key regulations

Confined Spaces Regulations 1997

The main duties under these Regulations are:

- to avoid entry to confined spaces – by having work done from the outside, for example
- if entry to a confined space is unavoidable, to follow a safe system of work
- to put in place adequate emergency arrangements before the work starts

Construction (Design and Management) Regulations 1994 (CDM Regulations)

The *CDM Regulations* apply to construction work lasting more than 30 days or involving more than 500 person days of work. They require the client to ensure (via its planning supervisor) that its principal contractor is competent to handle the building project safely. It also imposes duties on the project's designer.

- The client must appoint a planning supervisor and principal contractor (it may appoint itself to both roles, provided it is competent); be satisfied they are competent and have adequate resources to fulfil their duties; pass information relevant to health and safety to them; and ensure there is an adequate health and safety plan before construction begins.

- The planning supervisor must notify HSE of the project, and ensure a health and safety file is prepared listing foreseeable risks to contractors.

- The principal contractor must ensure cooperation between contractors, ensure contractors comply with the health and safety plan and promptly provide the planning supervisor with information needed in the health and safety file.

- The designer must ensure its designs prevent at source foreseeable risks to affected persons (builders, cleaners, building occupiers). The *CDM (Amendment) Regulations 2000* ensure the requirements still apply if designers' employees prepare a design on their behalf.

A revised ACoP was due at the end of 2001.[1]

Control of Asbestos at Work Regulations 2001 (CAW Regulations)

The revised *CAW Regulations* were due to become law in 2001. They will place an explicit duty on people in control of premises to:

- take reasonable steps to locate materials likely to contain asbestos
- assume that any material contains asbestos unless there is evidence that it does not
- keep an up-to-date written record of the location of these materials
- monitor the condition of these materials
- assess the risk of exposure from asbestos and presumed-asbestos materials
- prepare and implement a management plan to control these risks

Control of Substances Hazardous to Health Regulations 1999 (COSHH)

Employers must:

- make a suitable and sufficient assessment of health risks to employees exposed to hazardous substances
- in order of preference, prevent exposure, control exposure, or provide PPE
- provide health surveillance for exposed employees
- keep exposed employees' health records for 40 years

Electricity at Work Regulations 1989

Employers must ensure:

- electrical systems are constructed and maintained to prevent danger

- use and maintenance of systems, and work near systems, is safe
- protective equipment is suitable and properly maintained and used

Health and Safety (Consultation with Employees) Regulations 1996

Employers must:

- consult employees on the introduction of any measure or new technology which substantially affects their health and safety
- consult employees either directly or through elected representatives
- provide elected representatives with training, paid time off and other facilities reasonably required

There are proposals to consolidate these Regulations with the *Safety Representatives and Safety Committees Regulations* (see P16).

Health and Safety (First Aid) Regulations 1981

Employers must provide:

- adequate and appropriate first aid facilities
- either qualified first aiders (the ACoP suggests one first aider for every 50 employees)
- or, in low-risk or small workplaces, an "appointed person" to take charge in an emergency

Health and Safety (Information for Employees) Regulations 1989

Employers must display an HSE information poster or provide each employee with an HSE leaflet. New versions of both have been in use since 1 July 2000.

Health and Safety (Safety Signs and Signals) Regulations 1996

Employers must:

- provide warning signs if they cannot avoid a risk by other means
- train employees in the meaning of safety signs

Lifting Operations and Lifting Equipment Regulations 1998 (LOLER)

These Regulations supplement *PUWER* and apply to equipment such as cranes, goods lifts, forklift trucks, mobile elevating work platforms, hoists and ropes. Employers must ensure:

- lifting equipment has adequate strength and stability

- lifting equipment is positioned and installed to make the risk of the equipment or load falling or hitting a person as low as reasonably practicable
- lifting equipment is marked with its safe working load
- equipment for lifting people does not present a risk of them being crushed or trapped or of them falling
- any operation involving lifting equipment is properly planned by a competent person, and properly supervised and executed

Noise at Work Regulations 1989

Employers must:

- reduce the risk of hearing damage to the lowest level reasonably practicable
- where noise cannot be further reduced, provide ear protection if personal daily noise exposures are 90dB or more (or on request at levels of 85–90dB)

Reporting of Injuries, Diseases and Dangerous Occurrences Regulations 1995 (RIDDOR)

Employers must:

- notify HSE of a death or serious injury immediately
- send a report form within 10 days if a person is absent following a work injury for more than three consecutive days or if there is a "dangerous occurrence"
- notify HSE if a person suffers a work-related disease (such as carpal tunnel syndrome, hand-arm vibration syndrome, legionellosis, dermatitis, asthma or asbestos-related diseases)

Safety Representatives and Safety Committees Regulations 1977

Trade unions may appoint employees as safety representatives with the right to:
- be consulted by the employer on health and safety
- carry out investigations and inspections
- have paid time off to perform their duties and attend training

Risk assessment

HSE has produced an ACoP and guidance to the *Management Regulations,*[2] as well as a *Five steps to risk assessment* guide.[3] According to its own definitions:

- "a **risk assessment** is nothing more than a careful examination of what, in your work, could cause harm to people, so that you can weigh up whether you have taken enough precautions or should do more to prevent harm"
- "a **hazard** means anything that can cause harm (such as chemicals, electricity, working from ladders)"
- "**risk** is the chance, high or low, that somebody will be harmed by the hazard"

Spotting hazards

Ways of identifying hazards include asking employees or their safety representatives what risks they have noticed; consulting accident and ill-health records, suppliers' manuals, the trade press, relevant legislation and guidance; or seeking advice from consultants.

Typical hazards to watch for include:
- physical hazards (such as poorly guarded machinery, mezzanine floors, slipping/tripping hazards, vehicles, poor electrical wiring, fire hazards)
- hazardous substances (such as chemicals, dust, fumes)
- a hazardous work environment (such as noise, poor ventilation, bad lighting, hot or cold workplaces)
- psychological hazards (such as stress, long hours, shiftwork)
- ergonomic hazards (such as repetitive work, lifting)

Who might be harmed?

Those at risk might be:
- employees (office, operational and maintenance staff, for example)
- contractors (cleaners and security guards, for example)
- members of the public and volunteers
- young and inexperienced workers
- new and expectant mothers
- staff with disabilities
- home, lone and mobile workers

Risks may increase at certain times of day, such as after dark or during busy periods.

Controlling the risks

It is important to consider whether existing precautions:

- meet legal requirements
- comply with industry standards
- represent good practice
- reduce risks as far as reasonably practicable

If not, an action plan will be necessary, categorising remaining risks as high, medium or low risk. Priority should go to those measures which will protect the whole workplace. The aim is to eliminate hazards altogether (by not using a hazardous substance, for example) or, if this is not possible, to control risks, in order of preference, by:

- combating risks at source (for example, if steps are slippery, treating them is better than displaying a warning sign)
- preventing access to the hazard (for example, by installing machine guards, using permits to work which restrict access to authorised staff, isolating a dusty area)
- organising work to reduce exposure to the hazard (by rearranging work patterns to reduce stress, for example)
- issuing personal protective equipment (PPE)
- providing welfare facilities (such as washing facilities to remove contamination)

Taking advantage of technical advances can make work processes safer and more efficient. It is also crucial to provide relevant training and information to staff, and in shared workplaces, to swap information with other firms on site.

Recording the findings

Generally speaking, organisations with five or more employees must write down their risk assessment. The document can make cross-references to the health and safety policy and other relevant paperwork, rather than repeating everything. An inspector or union safety representative may ask to see the risk assessment, or it may provide evidence in the event of a personal injury claim.

Reviewing and revising

Most health and safety legislation requires employers to review the risk assessment, and revise it as necessary, if it is "no longer valid or there has been a significant change". Hazardous substance and asbestos assessments must, however, be reviewed "regularly", and HSE guidance states that this is good practice for any risk assessment. Significant changes which might make the risk assessment out of date could include bringing in new machines, substances or procedures.

"Suitable and sufficient"

The *Management Regulations* require risk assessments to be "suitable and sufficient". This means:

- allocating appropriate resources
- making the level of detail proportionate to the risk – overcomplicated assessments of simple hazards are not required
- anticipating "foreseeable" risks
- ensuring consultants have sufficient understanding of particular work activities
- adapting any "model" assessment to the actual work situation
- drawing up a timetable for implementing short, medium and long-term controls
- reviewing non-routine activities such as maintenance, cleaning, loading and unloading vehicles, changes in production cycles and emergencies
- reviewing off-site activities, such as homeworking
- complying with specific regulations – though repeating assessments is not necessary
- addressing what actually happens in the workplace, not what the works manual says should happen

---

HSE's *Five steps to risk assessment*

1. Look for the hazards.
2. Decide who might be harmed, and how.
3. Weigh up the risks and decide whether existing precautions are adequate or more needs to be done.
4. Record your findings.
5. Review your assessment and revise it if necessary.

Criminal sanctions

Most breaches of health and safety laws are heard in the magistrates' courts, where a maximum fine of £20,000 for breaches of sections 2–6 of the *HSW Act* can be imposed. For most other offences, the maximum is £5,000. Magistrates can, however, refer cases to the Crown Court for a trial by jury, where fines are unlimited. Defendants can also ask for their case to be heard by a jury.

Campaigners have been arguing for many years that many of the fines imposed, especially by magistrates, are inadequate. In the construction industry, for example, where workers are six times more likely to be killed than in any other industry, there were 41 prosecutions in 1999 for fatal accidents. The average fine in these cases (including those heard in the Crown Court) was £15,661, and in 13 cases the fine was less than £1,000.

Penalties in the Crown Court have, however, been increasing, especially since the Court of Appeal's judgment in the *Howe*[4] case in 1998. This laid out sentencing guidelines, including that:

- the level of fine should reflect the gravity of the offence, the degree of risk, and whether it was an isolated offence

- aggravating factors include whether the defendant failed to heed warnings, deliberately flouted health and safety legislation for financial gain, and whether a fatality occurred

- mitigating factors include a prompt guilty plea, taking steps to remedy health and safety failures, and a good safety record

Since *Howe*, there have been some well-publicised seven-figure fines, including:

- £1.5 million under section 3(1) of the *HSW Act* against Great Western Trains for the Southall crash, plus £680,000 costs

- a total of £1.2 million against Balfour Beatty Civil Engineering and its tunnelling subcontractor, Geoconsult, following the Heathrow rail link tunnel collapse, plus £100,000 costs each, even though the incident was a 'near miss' and no one was injured

- a total of £1.7 million against Port Ramsgate, two construction and design firms and Lloyds Register of Shipping (which carried out inspection work), plus costs of nearly £250,000, following the collapse of a walkway which killed six people

Facilities managers should note that even though Balfour Beatty and Port Ramsgate contracted out the work which led to the incidents, they were still held accountable under health and safety law, being fined £700,000 and £500,000 respectively. See MANAGING CONTRACTORS, P48 for more on this issue.

The Crown Court can order imprisonment of up to two years for contravention of an improvement or prohibition notice, and failure to have an asbestos removal licence. The first person to receive a custodial sentence – of three months – was Roy Hill in 1996, followed by a nine-month sentence for Paul Evans. Both men breached the asbestos licensing regime.

Revitalising strategy

In its document *Revitalising Health and Safety*,[5] the Government laid out an action plan to make health and safety penalties tougher across the board. The plan includes:

- making prison sentences (in Crown Court and magistrates' courts) and maximum £20,000 fines (in magistrates' courts) possible under most health and safety legislation
- considering 'innovative' penalties, such as fines linked to turnover, stopping bonuses, suspending managers without pay or compulsory health and safety training
- publicly naming and shaming companies convicted of offences

Directors' responsibilities

In July 2001, the HSC introduced new guidance on directors' responsibilities for health and safety.[6] The original proposal for a more formal 'code' was dropped after criticisms that its legal status would be ambiguous.

The first four action points in the guidance are uncontroversial, reflecting existing best practice. They state:

- "The board needs to accept formally and publicly its collective role in providing health and safety leadership in its organisation."
- "Each member of the board needs to accept their individual role in providing health and safety leadership for their organisation."
- "The board needs to ensure that all board decisions reflect its health and safety intentions... it is particularly important that the health and safety ramifications of investment in new plant, premises, processes or products are taken into account."
- "The board needs to recognise its role in engaging the active participation of workers in improving health and safety."

It is the fifth and final action point for which business leaders have reserved their fire. It states: "The HSC recommends that boards appoint one of their number to be the 'health and safety director'." The use of the word "recommends" suggests some hasty watering down, but business representatives remain concerned at the potential for one individual to become a scapegoat in the event of an accident.

There are two main concerns. First, the Government could still use its forthcoming safety bill (see below) to introduce a more onerous, legal requirement to appoint a health and safety director. Second, when the new corporate killing law is passed (again, see below), a health and safety director could face imprisonment in the event of a workplace fatality.

According to a British Safety Council survey, 40% of firms feared directors would leave rather than risk liability for accidents. Others said they would intentionally appoint an easily replaceable 'fall guy' as health and safety director to avoid culpability themselves.

New legislation expected

The new penalties will require legislation, and the Government is expected to introduce a wide-ranging safety bill, being hailed as the most significant development since the *HSW Act*.

Corporate killing

Also expected is legislation making it easier to convict organisations of corporate killing, provided their conduct falls "far below what could reasonably be expected". Under existing legislation, an organisation can only be guilty of manslaughter if a culpable individual can be identified, who acted as its "directing mind". This meant that large companies with complex management structures escaped punishment for incidents like the Herald of Free Enterprise ferry disaster, King's Cross fire and Southall rail crash.

Under Home Office proposals for a new law,[7] juries would only need evidence of a general management failing that contributed to the death, in order to convict the company of corporate killing. Moreover, directors who "substantially contribute" to a corporate killing crime could be jailed or temporarily disqualified.

Other developments expected shortly, including revised asbestos regulations, a smoking ACoP and revisions to the Construction (Design and Management) ACoP are considered in the relevant sections of this chapter.

Civil compensation

An employee, contractor or member of the public who has been injured or made ill as a result of a negligent employer's act or omission can bring a claim for compensation. This is based on the common law concept that every member of society owes a duty of care towards others. Employers may also be "vicariously liable" for an accident caused by one of their employees during the course of their employment.

Civil actions must commence within three years of the claimant finding out about their injury or illness. Claimants can receive damages for a number of losses, including loss of earnings, pain and suffering, medical expenses and disfigurement. Employers, in turn, have a number of defences available. They can argue contributory negligence, which means the injured person contributed to the accident, for example by ignoring safety rules. Or they can argue that the injuries were not reasonably foreseeable.

The *Civil Procedure Rules 1998* introduced measures to speed up claims, including a 'fast track' system for claims up to £15,000. In practice, most claims are settled out of court by the employer's insurers. Employers are required to have insurance against such claims under the *Employers' Liability (Compulsory Insurance) Act 1969*.

In 2000, TUC figures show the unions secured £320 million in compensation for members injured or made ill at work – an average of £6,000 for each of the 54,650 cases pursued.

Promoting occupational health

Section 2 of the *HSW Act* provides that employers have a duty of care to ensure the health, safety and welfare at work of all employees. The following sections offer guidance to the facilities manager on how to comply with this duty.

Avoiding back pain

Back pain is the commonest source of workplace ill health. The causes include poorly designed workstations which encourage poor posture, and lifting and carrying of loads (manual handling).

More than one-third of serious workplace injuries reported each year are manual handling-related, and most of these are back injuries. Employers lose 10 million working days a year to musculoskeletal disorders, half of these to back pain. Many injuries are cumulative, in other words a number of apparently insignificant problems build up over a period of time until the effects become serious.

The best way to prevent injuries is to avoid the need for lifting and carrying in the first place by reorganising the task or automating the handling process. If mechanisation is chosen, facilities managers will need to ensure new risks are not imported. For example, lifting equipment will need to be properly maintained, or forklift trucks will need to be kept away from pedestrians.

Low-tech handling aids like trolleys may provide a simple solution. But all aids should be readily accessible or they will not be used, and employees must receive training in their use.

Risk assessment

HSE's manual handling guidance advises employers to assess four problem areas when considering how to make lifting and carrying safer. These are:

- the way the task is done
- the working environment
- the load itself
- the people doing the lifting

Facilities managers will play a key role in reducing risk in the first two of these areas (see MANUAL HANDLING CHECKLIST, P26). Changes to the task and the environment will often also increase efficiency and productivity.

The task

- Change the layout of the task – by storing loads at waist height, for example. Store only lighter loads, or those handled infrequently, higher or lower.
- Eliminate obstacles which the worker has to reach over or into, such as poorly placed pallets or excessively deep containers.
- Avoid employees having to lift loads from the floor while seated.
- Although a swivel-action seat will reduce the need to twist, bear in mind that a chair on castors might move accidentally.
- Ensure the relative height of seats and work surfaces is well matched.
- Consider using two or more people to handle an awkward load.
- Maintain all handling equipment and personal protective equipment (PPE) (such as gloves or safety footwear) properly.
- Improve the work routine – through self-pacing or job rotation, for example.

The environment

- Remove space constraints, such as narrow gangways, doorways and working areas. Ensure there is enough floorspace and headroom, and think about the positioning of fixtures.

- Ensure floors are flat, well maintained and properly drained. Clear spillages away promptly, and consider slip-resistant flooring.

- Avoid manual handling activities on more than one level. If this is unavoidable, ensure there is a gentle slope or, failing that, well-positioned and properly maintained steps. Working surfaces should, where possible, be level with each other.

- Provide a comfortable environment, avoiding extremes of temperature, high humidity and poor ventilation.

- Provide sufficient well-directed light.

The load

- Consider making loads lighter, smaller, easier to grasp, more stable or less damaging to hold.

The individual

- Consider whether individuals are at particular risk of injury, because they are pregnant or have a history or back, knee or hip problems, for example.

- Provide information and training on manual handling injury risks and good handling techniques. But remember that training workers is not a substitute for well-designed systems and workplaces.

Preventing WRULDs

Work-related upper limb disorders (WRULDs), sometimes known as RSI (repetitive strain injuries) are injuries to muscles, tendons or nerves, especially in the hands, wrists, elbows or shoulders. Specific WRULDs include tenosynovitis, carpal tunnel syndrome and epicondylitis (tennis elbow). But the courts have also awarded damages to employees suffering from diffuse RSI – that is, a collection of symptoms which do not constitute a medically recognised injury. Repetitive tasks like keyboard work, assembly line work and packing are common causes.

As with avoiding manual handling injuries, facilities managers have a responsibility to improve equipment and the layout of work areas. But such

Manual handling checklist

1. The tasks

Do they involve:

- holding or manipulating loads at distance from trunk?
- unsatisfactory bodily movement or posture, especially:
  - twisting the trunk?
  - stooping?
  - reaching upwards?
- excessive movement of loads, especially:
  - excessive lifting or lowering distances?
  - excessive carrying distances?
  - excessive pushing or pulling of loads?
  - risk of sudden movement of loads?
  - frequent or prolonged physical effort?
  - insufficient rest or recovery periods?
  - a rate of work imposed by a process?

2. The loads

Are they:

- heavy?
- bulky or unwieldy?
- difficult to grasp?
- unstable, or with contents likely to shift?
- sharp, hot or otherwise potentially damaging?

3. The working environment

Are there:

- space constraints preventing good posture?
- uneven, slippery or unstable floors?
- variations in level of floors or work surfaces?
- extremes of temperature or humidity?
- poor lighting conditions?

4. Individual capability

Does the job:

- require unusual strength, height, etc?
- create a hazard to those who might reasonably be considered to be pregnant or to have a health problem?
- require special information or training for its safe performance?

5. Other factors

Is movement or posture hindered by personal protective equipment or by clothing?

Source: *Manual Handling Operations Regulations 1992 – guidance on Regulations*, HSE Books

measures will only be effective if carried out in conjunction with fundamental changes to the way in which work is organised, for example, by allowing workers to take a break from repetitive work.

Risk assessment

Employees may be at risk of developing WRULDs if:

- the work involves:
    - awkward hand, arm, wrist or shoulder movements
    - rapid repetitive movements
    - prolonged physical pressure, such as gripping or squeezing
    - a prolonged uncomfortable position
    - few breaks
    - lack of variety
    - long hours
    - a fast work rate (to keep up with a conveyor, for example)
- tools and equipment are:
    - too heavy
    - an uncomfortable shape
    - vibrating or noisy
    - designed for men but used by women
- workstations are:
    - the wrong height for the individuals using them
    - not adjustable
    - noisy, cold, or have other adverse conditions
    - badly lit

Solutions

Ways to reduce the risk of WRULDs occurring include:

- redesigning workstations and equipment, by, for example:
    - reducing the reaching required
    - moving controls
    - making conditions less cramped
    - providing adjustable chairs, footrests, etc
    - improving lighting and cutting out glare, to prevent users sitting awkwardly
- redesigning tool handles, keeping tools sharp and lubricated, replacing hand tools with power versions, avoiding high vibration tools

- changing the method of work
- allowing self-pacing
- introducing rest breaks and variety of tasks
- training workers, including new staff or those using new equipment or working methods, in warning symptoms of WRULDs, good posture and safe working practices

Computer workstations

Computer workstations must meet a number of ergonomic standards laid out in a schedule to the *DSE Regulations* to avoid user strain. In order to comply, HSE has developed a risk assessment checklist in its booklet *VDUs: an easy guide to the Regulations*.[8] This includes the following questions:

- Is the display screen image clear?
  - Are the characters readable?
  - Is the image flicker-free?
  - Are the brightness and contrast adjustable?
  - Does the screen swivel and tilt?
  - Is the screen free from glare and reflections?
- Is the keyboard comfortable?
  - Is the keyboard tiltable?
  - Is there enough space to rest hands in front of the keyboard?
  - Is the keyboard glare-free?
  - Are the characters on the keys easily readable?
- Does the furniture fit the work and the user?
  - Is the work surface large enough?
  - Is the work surface free of glare and reflections?
  - Is the chair stable?
  - Do the adjustment mechanisms work?
  - Is the user comfortable?
- Is the environment around the workstation risk-free?
  - Is there enough room to change position and vary movement?
  - Are the levels of light, heat and noise comfortable?
  - Does the air feel comfortable?
- Is the software user-friendly?

Seating

Adjustable chairs are essential to combat musculoskeletal disorders such as back pain and WRULDs. When choosing or assessing seating, it is important to consider the individual's needs, the type of work and the size of the workstation. HSE guidance, *Seating at work*,[9] suggests ensuring:

- the chair is comfortable for the intended period of use
- the back is properly supported
- there is sufficient padding
- the seat and back height are adjustable and the backrest tilts
- armrests (if required) allow enough arm movement and allow the individual to get close enough to the desk
- footrests are supplied if necessary
- the chair meets special user requirements (pregnant women and disabled employees, for example, may have special needs)
- the chair meets special task requirements
- the adjustment mechanisms are well maintained

Midland Bank: the cost of WRULDs

- In 1999, the Court of Appeal ordered Midland Bank to pay damages of between £8,036 and £15,233 to each of five former data encoders, who it found were suffering from fibro-myalgia despite showing no objective physical symptoms. Interestingly for facilities managers, the court did not uphold the claimants' criticisms of their desk design, apart from uncomfortable keypads. Nor did it matter that their chairs were not easily adjustable, because they had found a way around it. In this case, the organisation of the work – particularly speed targets and the lack of any opportunity to stretch or move around – was the main culprit.

- In 1997, the Court of Appeal awarded a Midland Bank secretary, Michelle Mulligan, £155,000 for tenosynovitis, caused by the bank's failure to assess her work posture, provide breaks, or warn her of the risks of WRULDs. It had also increased her work pressure.

- In 1989, the Midland agreed an out-of-court settlement of £45,000 with another secretary, Pauline Bernard, who also had tenosynovitis.

Reducing noise

Under the *Noise at Work Regulations*, employees' daily exposure to noise must not exceed the equivalent of 90dB – roughly equivalent to heavy street traffic – received continuously over eight hours. Engineered solutions are preferable, and ear protectors are a last resort only.

Even in workplaces where sound levels are unlikely to reach 90dB, the *DSE Regulations* state that noise should not be distracting or disturb people trying to talk. Although the main concerns are hearing loss and tinnitus (a permanent 'ringing' in the ears), continual noise can also cause stress.

Both short bursts of loud noise and long-term exposure to lower noise levels can damage the inner ear. HSE figures suggest that 1.3 million employees in the UK are exposed to dangerous levels of noise.

As well as manufacturing environments, call centres and open-plan offices can be unexpectedly noisy. Indeed, HSE found that 41% of call centre operators have to raise their voices when communicating with people at a normal talking distance.

Control measures

HSE recommends controlling noise exposure by:

- designing workplaces for low noise emission – for example, using absorption materials to limit reflected sound; segregating noisy equipment from occupied areas
- engineering controls – for example, cushioning impacts in a yard where unloading takes place by fitting a rubber surface; using damping methods; mounting machines to prevent vibration; fitting silencers; using 'active noise control' to cancel out one sound with another
- modifying noise transmission paths – for example, enclosing machines; providing screens, barriers, walls and noise refuges; increasing the distance between employees and the noise source
- substituting noisy equipment or processes with quieter alternatives – for example, replacing compressed air tools with hydraulic equipment
- maintaining equipment and replacing worn parts
- changing working methods – for example, reducing exposure times through job rotation

For best practice advice on how to design noise transmission out of the workplace, see WORKPLACE FACILITIES: MINIMISING NOISE THROUGH DESIGN, P325.

Asbestos-related diseases

Asbestos kills over 3,000 people in the UK every year, one-quarter of whom have been employed in the building industry. By 2020, 10,000 people a year are predicted to die from asbestos-related diseases, which would make asbestos the biggest single killer of men under 65 years old.

Although all three types of asbestos have now been banned, the substance remains in many buildings constructed between 1950 and 1980, especially those with steel frames or boilers with thermal insulation. Those most at risk of contracting mesothelioma, an incurable and fatal cancer, are those involved in demolition, maintenance and refurbishment work (including plumbers, electricians and carpenters), and other contractors working nearby when asbestos fibres are released into the air. Others who may disturb asbestos are contractors installing computers, fire alarms, window blinds and telecommunications systems. Employees present when the asbestos is disturbed could also be exposed, and they could carry fibres home on their clothes.

There is no safe level of exposure, and repeated low-level exposure can also cause asbestos-related diseases. It takes 15–60 years for the symptoms of mesothelioma, asbestosis of the lungs, or asbestos-related lung cancer to appear.

The most common uses of asbestos, listed in order of how likely they are to release dust if disturbed, are:

- sprayed coatings and asbestos insulation used for fire protection, pipes and boilers, thermal and acoustic insulation
- insulating boards used for fire protection to doors, cladding on walls and ceilings, partitioning and ceiling tiles
- asbestos cement used for roofing, wall panels, pipes and water tanks

Surveys and logs

The amended *CAW Regulations 2001* are to formalise existing good practice. In effect, facilities managers will need to ensure their premises are surveyed for asbestos as a matter of course, rather than waiting until asbestos is accidently exposed. Current HSE guidance[10] already advises taking a proactive approach, recommending that employers identify the material's:

- location
- form (lagging, ceiling tiles, partition board, and so forth)
- condition
- type (blue, brown, or white asbestos)

The guidance recommends consulting the leaseholder, architects or original building plans to find out if and where asbestos was used. It may be necessary to bring in accredited personnel to analyse samples. If asbestos is present, the risk of fibres being released must be assessed.

Leaving asbestos in place

If asbestos is in good condition and not likely to be either damaged or worked on, HSE recommends:

- leaving it in place and logging where it is (mark it on building plans and/or set up a register)

- warning contractors that some undiscovered asbestos could still be present elsewhere
- making a note of safe materials which could be mistaken for asbestos
- labelling asbestos materials with a warning sign
- ensuring contractors know where asbestos is and its condition
- conducting regular re-inspections

Repair and removal

Depending on how poor its condition is, asbestos may need to be:

- repaired, sealed or enclosed, then logged following the above steps, or
- removed

In either case, HSE-licensed contractors must carry out the work. They must double-bag the waste, clearly label it and dispose of it at a licensed site.

Duty to contractors and employees

HSE warns that during asbestos repair or removal work, employers should ensure contractors

do:

- understand the health risks of asbestos exposure
- keep unnecessary personnel away
- take care not to create dust
- keep the material wet whenever possible
- wear a suitable respirator and protective clothing
- clean up with a vacuum cleaner complying with *BS 5415* (type 'H')

do not:

- break up large pieces of asbestos materials
- use power tools – this creates dust
- expose workers who are not protected
- take protective clothing home to wash

Legionellosis

Legionellosis is a group of diseases caused by legionella bacteria found in water. The bacteria occur in natural water supplies, but hot and cold water systems, air conditioning systems and cooling towers offer better breeding grounds. The most serious of the diseases is Legionnaires' disease, a type of pneumonia. HSE figures reveal 200–250 cases of Legionnaires' disease a year, but it believes there is under-reporting. About half these cases are linked to foreign travel.

Legionnaires' disease

Legionnaires' disease:

- kills around 12% of sufferers
- mainly affects people aged between 40 and 70
- affects three times more men than women
- is most likely to affect smokers, alcoholics, people with diabetes, cancer, chronic respiratory or kidney disease, or those on renal dialysis or immuno-suppressant drugs
- is caused by susceptible individuals inhaling water droplets contaminated with legionella bacteria
- is not believed to be transmitted by drinking water containing legionella bacteria, or by person to person transmission
- produces symptoms two to 10 days after infection, including chills, high fever, headache or muscle pain followed by a dry cough, and in extreme cases, pneumonia
- has broken out in or near large building complexes such as hotels, hospitals, offices and factories

Legal duties

Legislation relevant to controlling legionellosis includes *COSHH* and the *Notification of Cooling Towers and Evaporative Condensers Regulations 1992*. The latter require those in control of work premises to notify the local authority or HSE in writing of any cooling towers and evaporative condensers, including any being decommissioned or dismantled. Other places that can harbour bacteria include showers, taps, water softeners, humidifiers, calorifiers and pipework.

HSE's legionella ACOP[11] states that the duty holder "is required to have access to competent help" to assess whether there is a risk of the disease occurring. The accompanying guidance adds that whether it uses its own personnel, or a consultancy or water treatment company, the duty holder should ensure they are trained and have the necessary equipment. The duty holder should also appoint a manager or director with day-to-day responsibility for controlling the risk of legionellosis – in practice, this may be the facilities manager.

In mid-1999, the British Association for Chemical Specialities (BACS) and the Water Management Society (WMS) formulated a Recommended Code of Conduct for service providers. It offers advice to organisations, individuals or sub-contractors who provide services for controlling legionella bacteria in industrial or commercial premises. It is important for facilities managers to understand the code so they can measure their current or prospective service provider against its guidelines. They should also ask service providers whether they have signed up to the code. The code covers six areas: allocation of responsibilities; training and competence of personnel; control measures; communication and management; record-keeping; and reviews.

Designing out legionellosis

Ideally, health and safety in any environment is designed in at the start. Where facilities managers have input in the design of a new building or a refurbishment, they should ensure the following design criteria are applied to hot and cold water systems:

- ensure storage cisterns and calorifiers are the correct size for their intended use
- do not site cold water tanks in a warm part of the building
- ensure pipework is as short and direct as possible
- ensure adequate insulation of pipes and tanks
- use materials that do not encourage the growth of legionella
- protect against contamination by, for instance, fitting storage tanks with lids

Risk assessment and control

To minimise the risk of contamination in existing installations, HSE guidance recommends carrying out a site survey of complex premises, including an asset register of plant, pumps, strainers and so on, and an up-to-date diagram of the system. Some factors to consider include:

- the water source (is it mains water?)
- possible sources of contamination before the water reaches the cooling tower or cold water tank
- the system's normal characteristics
- reasonably foreseeable but abnormal operating conditions (such as breakdowns)

Measures to control the risk of disease include:

- controlling the release of water spray (such as the aerosol created by a cooling tower or shower)

- avoiding water temperatures of 20–45°C, which allow bacteria to proliferate
- avoiding water stagnation, which encourages biofilm to grow
- avoiding materials in the system such as sludge, scale, rust, algae and organic matter which harbour or provide nutrients for bacteria
- keeping the system clean to avoid sediments
- using water treatment programmes
- ensuring the system operates correctly and is well maintained

Routine monitoring of water systems is necessary, and the guidance suggests this should take place at least weekly. Testing of water quality and monitoring numbers of general bacteria are also important. But HSE suggests testing only for legionella bacteria is technically difficult, and the results difficult to interpret. The guidance states: "A negative result is no guarantee that legionella bacteria are not present. Conversely, a positive result may not indicate a failure of controls as legionella are present in almost all natural water sources."

If it is suspected that a user of the building has contracted legionellosis, HSE must be consulted immediately. Facilities managers should then involve senior management and take steps to identify the source of the infection and deal with any contamination as soon as possible.

Improving well-being

Sceptics may still doubt that 'sick' buildings really make people ill. But at the very least, problems like poor air quality, passive smoking, flickering lights and fluctuating temperatures undoubtedly reduce employees' well-being and productivity. Moreover, the *Workplace Regulations* impose a legal duty to look after employees' welfare.

Sick building syndrome

The World Health Organisation (WHO) has recognised sick building syndrome (SBS) since 1982. HSE estimates that 30–50% of new or recently refurbished buildings cause some form of SBS. In the worst cases, 85% of occupants may suffer symptoms.

Symptoms

Symptoms are flu-like and include skin problems, breathing problems (sore throats, coughs, blocked noses, sinusitis), muscle and joint aches (stiff shoulders, back ache), and neurological disorders (tiredness, headaches, digestion problems). The symptoms will be much more common than average among workers in a particular building, and will reduce or disappear during weekends and holidays.

At-risk buildings

According to WHO, buildings most at risk of SBS are likely to date from the 1960s or later and have:

- open-plan offices
- a low level of user control over ventilation, heating and lighting
- lighting with high glare or flicker
- air conditioning with cooling capacity
- lots of soft furnishings
- lots of open storage
- synthetic furniture, carpets and paint
- poor maintenance and repair
- insufficient cleaning
- high temperatures or large temperature variations
- very low or high humidity
- indoor air pollutants (ozone from photocopiers and laser printers, chemicals released from carpet adhesive, tobacco smoke)
- airborne dust or fibres
- computers

Solutions

Bucking the trend for open-plan offices, WHO recommends no more than 10 workstations in any room. Other problems may be resolved through maintaining air conditioning systems, replacing old photocopiers and laser printers, replacing fluorescent lights, and better cleaning. Since cleaning chemicals may themselves cause problems, however, the best solution is redesigning workplaces to be low maintenance.

Photocopiers

Well-maintained, modern photocopiers are rarely a health hazard. But if they are used frequently or there are a number of machines, there could be problems with noise, dry heat, and the release of ozone. The best solution is to place equipment in a separate room with separate ventilation. It is important to follow the manufacturer's recommendations for siting, cleaning and maintaining the machines, as well as following the precautions in the material safety data sheets for toner and other chemicals.

There should also be clear guidance on when it is safe for employees – with the appropriate training and information – to carry out repairs (such as clearing simple paper jams), and when a technician should be called. Modern equipment should turn off automatically when opened, but turning it off at the wall first is a simple safety precaution.

Lighting

Poor lighting can cause eyestrain, headaches, SBS and fatigue, as well as accidents (see TOWARDS A SAFE WORKPLACE: PREVENTING SLIPS AND TRIPS, P43).

Lighting risk assessment

- Is emergency lighting adequate?
- Are desk lamps provided?
- Are light fittings regularly cleaned?
- Are lamps replaced regularly (after about 7,000 hours' use)?
- Are desks placed at right angles to windows to prevent glare?
- Are fluorescent light strips covered with a diffuser?
- Are windows fitted with blinds or curtains?
- Are walls, ceilings and furniture decorated in light, matt colours (to increase the level of light and reduce glare)?
- Is there a source of natural light?
- Are there any dark, unlit areas?

Source: *Office health and safety – a guide to risk prevention*, UNISON

The ACoP to the *Workplace Regulations* states that:
- lights should be of a type and so positioned as to avoid glare
- lights should be repaired and cleaned to ensure effectiveness
- windows should be cleaned regularly
- local lighting should be provided as necessary

The legislation also requires:
- an average illuminance for a whole work area of 200Lx (lux) with a minimum for any individual work position of 100Lx

- the location of lights and associated fittings should not cause a hazard, with employees able to find light switches easily

In practice, generally accepted levels for offices are 400–500Lx at desk level, rising to 700Lx or more in specialist areas, such as architects' offices, where sharp focus is needed. Where each work task is individually lit and the area around the task is lit to a lower illuminance, as in local lighting in an office, the maximum ratio of illuminances of working area to adjacent area should be 5:1. Ambient lighting in common areas such as stairwells and lobbies may be considerably less powerful than for offices, down to 20Lx or less.

Natural light

Unlike some European countries, the UK has no legal requirement that workers should have access to natural light. But the tradition of placing offices for senior staff round the edges of a floor, making daylight access a privilege of managers and leaving those in open-plan cut off from natural light, is now widely challenged, and the recommended minimum ratio of artificial light to natural light at any long-term work setting is 1:5.

For best practice advice on workplace lighting, see WORKPLACE FACILITIES: LIGHTING, PP338–348.

Air quality

Temperature

The ACoP to the *Workplace Regulations* says that work rooms should normally be at least 16°C, or 13°C for work involving "severe physical efforts". There is no legally enforceable maximum temperature, but the ACoP says "all reasonable steps should be taken to achieve a comfortable temperature". It is rare for temperatures to be so extreme that they cause serious illness (like heat stroke or hypothermia), but less severe temperature problems can cause discomfort, loss of concentration, tiredness, irritability and SBS.

The Chartered Institution of Building Services Engineers recommends the following temperatures:

- heavy work in factories: 13°C
- light work in factories: 16°C
- hospital wards and shops: 18°C
- offices and dining rooms: 20°C

The *international standard for office environments ISO 7730–1984* recommends an operative temperature range of 20–24°C with a variation of less than 3°C between head and ankle height. Radiators fitted with thermostats produce least complaint from office occupants of any heating system (probably because it allows for a degree of user control), but many larger office blocks (especially those built in the years following the energy crisis of the 1970s) have sealed windows and centrally controlled systems.

Uncomfortably hot workplaces can be tackled by:

- providing air conditioning or fans
- ensuring windows can be opened
- shading windows with blinds
- siting workstations away from direct sunlight or hot areas
- insulating hot pipes
- providing a free supply of drinking water
- giving employees breaks to cool down
- introducing more flexible hours to avoid the worst effects of working in exceptionally high temperatures

Thermometers should also be provided for monitoring temperatures.

In intentionally cold workplaces, such as those preparing food, it will be necessary to provide a warm working station using localised heating, draught exclusion and so on. Catering areas could be particularly hot and humid, and fume extraction and extractor or circulation fans will be necessary. Air inlets must be carefully sited to allow air movement in all parts of the kitchen.

Ventilation

The *Workplace Regulations* require enclosed workplaces to be ventilated by "a sufficient quantity of fresh or purified air". The recommended minimum airflow is five litres per second, though eight litres per second is a safer minimum to prevent complaints of airlessness. Care needs to be taken to ensure that ventilation does not cause draughts.

Humidity

The *DSE Regulations*, in section 3(g) of the schedule, state that "an adequate level of humidity shall be established and maintained" in offices where there are visual display unit (VDU) users. To comply with the legislation, employers need to monitor humidity constantly, to ascertain whether adequate levels are being provided. It is also important for employers to recognise any dry heat symptoms being experienced by staff, in order to identify whether any problems need to be addressed to ensure staff health and comfort. For advice on humidity levels and monitoring, see WORKPLACE FACILITIES: MAINTAINING ADEQUATE HUMIDITY, PP318–321.

Passive smoking

In 1998, a government scientific committee found that long-term passive smoking could increase the risk of lung cancer by 30–40% and cause heart disease. HSC has presented a draft ACoP on workplace smoking to ministers for approval. This requires employers, in order of preference, to:

- ban smoking if reasonably practicable
- permit smoking in designated rooms
- provide smoking and non-smoking areas
- provide adequate ventilation
- reduce the time employees are exposed to smoke

Particular account must be taken of employees more susceptible to the effects of tobacco smoke, such as those who suffer from asthma, chronic bronchitis and respiratory diseases.

The ACoP will formalise existing HSE guidance on passive smoking. This says that non-smoking should be regarded as the norm in enclosed

---

Passive smoking case law

Ill-health awards

Two Stockport Metropolitan Borough Council employees have received awards for passive smoking at work:

- In 1995, Beryl Roe received £25,000 after retiring on ill-health grounds, suffering eye, nose, throat and bronchial hypersensitivity. The council had shut down the ventilation system in her office.
- In 1993, Veronica Bland received £15,000 after developing chronic bronchitis.

No right to smoke at work

In the 1992 case of *Dryden v Greater Glasgow Health Board*, Ms Dryden, a smoker, resigned and claimed constructive dismissal three days into a smoking ban. The Employment Appeal Tribunal decided she had no contractual right to smoke at work. It found the employer had introduced the non-smoking policy for a legitimate purpose, consulted employees, given notice of its plans and offered assistance and counselling to give up smoking.

workplaces, with special provision made for smoking, rather than vice-versa. It also warns employers to consult employees before drawing up a smoking policy, and to give them at least three months before a ban takes effect. It also recommends that employers provide assistance and counselling to employees trying to quit smoking.

In buildings with mechanical ventilation, HSE says employers should consider discharging air from smoking areas separately rather than allowing it to enter the recirculation system. If this is not reasonably practicable, the recirculated air should be brought up to an appropriate standard by suitable decontamination systems. Tobacco smoke building up in the workplace is a sure sign that the ventilation system is inadequate.

Best practice advice on maintaining good indoor air quality is covered in WORKPLACE FACILITIES: **HVAC, PP311–321**.

Stress

After carrying out a public consultation exercise, the HSC has shied away from introducing a stress ACoP, fearing that there is currently no clear way to measure employers' management of the issue. Nevertheless, employers have a legal duty under the *HSW Act* to ensure the workplace is healthy, and this applies to psychological as well as physical health.

Employees can also bring a common law claim against a negligent employer, and there have been several well-publicised out-of-court settlements for stress. These include £203,000 to the warden of a travellers' site, and £200,000 to a council employee who had a breakdown after alleged management bullying. In court, claimants have had a harder time, needing to prove that:

- they have a recognised psychiatric disorder
- the risk of psychological injury was reasonably foreseeable
- the employer's negligence caused the injury

More worrying for employers than a possible court case is the price of stress in terms of absenteeism and under-performance. Stress is second only to musculoskeletal disorders as a reported cause of absence from work in the UK. Research by the TUC shows that over 12 million people complain about stress at work. HSE figures suggest five million people, representing one-fifth of workers, suffer from such high work-related stress that it causes them serious mental and physical health problems.

Causes and prevention

The main culprits are work overload, unreasonable targets, poor management habits, bullying and long hours. The causes, in other words, are organisational – staff may have too little control over their work, or work relationships may be poor. The work may be repetitive, there may be too little or too much to do, or staff may be under or overqualified. Some staff may have difficulty balancing their work and home lives. Facilities managers can help to tackle these problems in their own staff through:

- taking stress seriously, rather than seeing it as an individual weakness
- allowing staff to plan and organise their own jobs, and contribute ideas
- being supportive, involving staff and communicating well with them
- avoiding bullying, racist or sexist attitudes
- giving staff the opportunity to develop their skills
- changing the way work is done – by introducing job rotation, more variety or responsibility, for example
- giving staff clear objectives
- giving warning of urgent jobs
- increasing flexibility – introducing flexible working hours or working from home, for example

Personal counselling may have a role to play in mopping up the after-effects of stress. But it should be used in conjunction with improvements in work design which will both attack the root causes of the problem and improve the performance of the organisation.

Stressful buildings

Facilities managers also have a responsibility to ensure that the working environment does not cause stress. Building users often complain about issues like:

- poor artificial lighting, lack of daylight and glare
- poor temperature control, particularly over-cooling
- draughts, poor ventilation and poor air quality
- windows which must not be opened
- noise and overcrowding
- uncomfortable workstations
- lack of control over their own environment
- poor response from building managers

These problems can all lead to stress and under-performance. They affect users of both open-plan buildings and buildings divided into large shared rooms. The former may be unhappy that the main circulation route through the building passes through their space. The latter may complain of overcrowding and inequitable distribution of space.

However, facilities managers cannot, on their own, solve their organisation's stress problems. As stated above, the real causes are overwhelmingly working methods and the company's culture. Commitment is needed at all levels of the organisation to resolve these issues.

Violence

Violence to employees encompasses everything from bank robbery, vandalism, hostage-taking and bombing, to the aggression displayed daily by members of the public in places like hospital waiting rooms, job centres and train stations. The risk to staff is two-fold – they may be physically injured, or they may be affected psychologically either following an actual attack or after being threatened. For detailed information about violence in the workplace and measures to combat it, see ACCESS AND SECURITY, PP379–383.

Towards a safe workplace

Preventing slips and trips

Slips and trips cause one-quarter to one-third of major accidents at work, or about 5,500–6,000 such accidents a year.

HSE has published guidance, *Slips and trips*,[12] which contains much useful advice for facilities managers. It recommends:

- getting workplace conditions right in the first place, for example, by selecting the right flooring and lighting, planning routes and avoiding overcrowding
- keeping areas free of obstructions
- checking flooring regularly for holes, cracks, loose mats, and so on
- using the correct cleaning methods to avoid slippery residues building up
- carrying out cleaning and maintenance after hours, or if this is not possible, using signs to warn people about wet floors, providing alternative routes, and avoiding trailing cables
- organising work and machinery to avoid spills, and cleaning up or fencing off any that do occur immediately

- positioning electrical equipment to avoid trailing cables, and using covers to fix cables down

- providing safety footwear free of charge to employees if floors are unavoidably wet or dusty (there are no British Standards for slip resistance, but the HSE guidance includes advice on shoe sole materials)

- keeping lights working, clean and free of obstructions, ensuring they do not dazzle, and providing extra lighting at stairs and slopes

- providing handrails, treads and floor markings on slopes or changes of level, and doormats between wet and dry areas

Flooring

Cost and looks should not be the only concerns when choosing flooring. Suitability for the location and the demands that will be made on the surface are also important. The HSE guidance states that "there is no need to put up with a slippery smooth floor because it is more hygienic or easier to clean". There are devices for measuring slipperiness, but HSE warns that the resulting 'friction values' must be interpreted with caution because workplaces differ so widely.

There are also floor treatments to reduce slipping – concrete can be abraded or chemically treated, there are coatings containing abrasive particles, and adhesive strips or squares. Some treatments may need regular reapplying.

Flooring needs to be laid by competent people, and kept clean and in good condition to maintain slip-resistance and prevent curling edges or lifting. Different flooring surfaces and certain spills may need different kinds of cleaning.

Employers' liability: case example

An occupational therapist, Alison Hockaday, received a £600,000 negotiated settlement from her employers, Durham Health Authority, in December 1999, after part of her right leg had to be amputated. She injured her knee in 1986, slipping on wet leaves on the entrance steps of the Winterton Hospital. She was left using a walking stick, but returned to work. In March 1990, she slipped on a wet floor at the hospital, fracturing her ankle, and in 1997 her leg had to be amputated below the knee. The health authority was found liable in court for the first accident, and did not contest the second claim.

Equipment

Heavy plant or humble ladder, photocopier or forklift truck, the risk from all work equipment must be as low as possible.

HSE's guidance leaflet, *Using work equipment safely*, advises employers to ensure that:

- new and temporary workers (who may lack experience), people who have changed departments, those with difficulties (such as impaired mobility), and cleaning and maintenance staff are properly trained and supervised
- guards and safety devices are convenient to use, not easily overridden, made from appropriate materials, and allow the machine to be cleaned safely
- control switches are clearly marked and carefully sited
- the type of power supply, (electric, hydraulic or pneumatic) is considered – each has different risks
- hand tools are not worn, the handles are not split, and there are enough tools to avoid employees improvising with something else
- routine checks are made, preventative maintenance is carried out where appropriate, and manufacturers' instructions are followed
- equipment can be safely maintained and repaired:
  - machines should be disconnected and not moving or hot
  - mobile equipment should have the engine off and brake on
  - flammable substances must be cleaned away
  - isolating valves must be locked off
  - equipment which could fall needs support

Practical examples

The guidance leaflet gives the following examples of risks arising from one of the commonest pieces of workplace equipment, the ladder. Risks include:

- ladders not being securely placed and fixed
- climbing with loads
- overreaching or overbalancing
- ladders being used when other equipment would be safer
- the use of poorly maintained or faulty ladders

Many accidents involving ladders happen during work lasting 30 minutes or less. They are often used for short jobs when it would be safer to use other equipment, for example mobile tower scaffolds. If facilities managers maintain equipment well, and ensure employees and contractors use the correct equipment for the job, this can significantly reduce the risk of accidents.

The GMB union has developed health and safety guidance for cleaners, which includes a case study about a group of women using heavy industrial buffing machines to clean floors. The case study demonstrates that work equipment can lead to occupational health problems as well as accidents. The women's union safety representative raised problems such as back and arm pain and numbness in the fingers with their employer, who:

- provided training in safe lifting
- provided thick gloves to minimise the effects of vibration
- increased the amount of manual cleaning
- introduced job rotation

Using the machines less not only solved the problems the cleaners had raised, it also reduced the number of slip and trip accidents.

Vehicles

Accidents involving vehicles at the workplace kill around 70 people a year and maim 1,000 more. Reversing vehicles are a particular hazard, causing one-quarter of such deaths. The accidents involve cars, vans, trucks and other mobile equipment. People can be injured by being knocked down, falling from vehicles, being struck by a falling load or vehicles overturning.

Under regulation 17(1) of the *Workplace Regulations*, every workplace must (so far as is reasonably practicable) be so organised that pedestrians and vehicles can circulate in a safe manner. Under regulation 17(2), traffic routes in a workplace must be suitable for the persons or vehicles using them, sufficient in number, in suitable positions and of sufficient size. Under regulation 17(3)(4):

- pedestrians or vehicles must be able to use traffic routes without endangering those at work
- there must be sufficient separation of traffic routes from doors and gates and between vehicle and pedestrian traffic routes
- where vehicles and pedestrians do use the same traffic routes, there must be sufficient space between them
- where necessary, all traffic routes must be suitably indicated

Work vehicles also count as work equipment for the purposes of *PUWER*. Regulation 5 says that they must:

- be constructed and adapted to suit their purpose
- be selected so as to avoid risks to the health and safety of persons where the vehicles are to be used
- only be used for the operations specified and under suitable conditions

Regulation 6 says work equipment, including vehicles, must be maintained in an efficient state, in efficient working order and in good repair. Vehicles must be provided with safety features (a reversing alarm, seat belts, lights, and so on). Under the *Management Regulations*, drivers must be trained for the job and supervised if necessary. Contractors also need to know the site rules, so that they can carry out loading and unloading safely.

Safe traffic routes

Facilities managers have a particular responsibility to ensure that the layout of the workplace does not create risks, either from work vehicles or private cars. Safety measures could include:

- creating pedestrian areas, including safe crossings and barriers if necessary
- providing enough designated parking places to avoid stopping in unsafe locations
- ensuring traffic routes are wide enough, well constructed and maintained, avoid blind bends and are free of obstructions
- increasing visibility for drivers and pedestrians
- providing road markings, signs, road humps and mirrors as required
- redesigning the workplace to remove the need for reversing, by introducing a one-way system, for example
- if reversing cannot be eliminated, ensuring there is enough space for vehicles to reverse and minimising the distance they have to reverse

HSE guides on vehicle safety provide further information.[13]

Maintenance and repair

Facilities managers will generally delegate maintenance and repair work on the premises to outside contractors. They cannot, however, delegate their health and safety duties in the event of death, injury or accidental exposure to asbestos or another hazardous substance.

Contractors have duties too, but if their employees are injured on your premises, or using your equipment, you could be liable. Equally, contractors may import risks onto your normally safe premises, putting your employees at risk and exposing you to possible legal action if you fail to take preventative measures.

Managing contractors

Many large firms keep a list of contractors whom they prefer to use, and who meet their safety criteria. Those who want to make it onto the list may have to undergo an audit on their own premises or while doing work on another site. The qualifications of their sub-contractors are also likely to be checked. Successful bidders for a contract will be asked to draw up a safety plan for the work, which may include targets and a contractual requirement for continuous improvement.

During the work, the employer should monitor the contractors' performance and investigate incidents and near misses. Typically, large firms will expect their contractors to meet the same safety standards as their own employees, to avoid differences across their site. They may set up safety competitions for the various contractors on site, or circulate details of each contractor's performance. Poor performance will, at best, lead to the contractor's removal from the 'preferred' list. At worst, the contractor may be dismissed before the end of the contract and have to pay for a replacement.

Legal duty to contractors

The principle that organisations retain responsibility for the safety of contractors working on their premises was established in the *Associated Octel* case, heard in the House of Lords in November 1996. There have been much higher fines, and much worse incidents, as the figures at the start of this chapter showed. But for facilities managers the lessons are salutary.

The case involved a maintenance job in a confined space, in which a contractor's employee was injured because he used the wrong equipment. The man, Mr Cuthbert, was repairing a tank lining at Octel's Ellesmere Port chemical plant, which was shut for maintenance. He was working by an electric bulb inside the tank, cleaning the lining with acetone. The acetone was in an old paint bucket which he had retrieved from a rubbish bin. The open container allowed the acetone to give off highly flammable fumes. The light bulb broke, and there was a flash fire in which Mr Cuthbert was badly burned.

Octel was prosecuted under section 3(1) of the *HSW Act*. This states:

"It shall be the duty of every employer to conduct his undertaking in such a way as to ensure, so far as is reasonably practicable, that persons not in

---

Five steps to managing contractors' health and safety

1. Planning
   - define the job
   - identify hazards
   - assess risks
   - eliminate and reduce risks
   - specify health and safety conditions
   - discuss with contractor

2. Choosing a contractor
   - check contractor is competent for the job (ask questions, get evidence)
   - discuss the job, the site and site rules
   - obtain a safety method statement
   - decide if sub-contracting is acceptable and will be safe

3. Managing contractors on site
   - ensure contractors sign in and out
   - name a site contact
   - reinforce health and safety information and site rules

4. Keeping a check
   - assess how much contact with contractors is needed
   - is the job going as planned?
   - is the contractor working safely and as agreed?
   - have there been any incidents?
   - have there been changes in personnel?
   - are any special arrangements required?

5. Reviewing the work
   - how effective was the planning?
   - how did the contractor perform?
   - record the findings

Source: *Managing contractors*, HSE Books[14]

---

his employment who may be affected thereby are not thereby exposed to risks to their health or safety."

Octel claimed Mr Cuthbert's injury was not caused by Octel conducting its undertaking within the meaning of section 3(1). Cleaning the tank was part of the contractor's undertaking, and Octel had no right to control how its independent contractors worked.

LIVERPOOL JOHN MOORES UNIVERSITY
LEARNING SERVICES

Why is the employer liable?

The House of Lords rejected the company's argument. In Lord Hoffman's words: "The tank was part of Octel's plant. The work formed part of a maintenance programme planned by Octel. The men who did the work, although employed by an independent contractor, were almost permanently integrated into Octel's larger operations. They worked under the 'permit to work' system [having to obtain authorisation before every job from Octel's engineers]. Octel provided their safety equipment and lighting."

In this case, he found it was clear that having the tank repaired was part of Associated Octel's undertaking. But he pointed out that in other situations "there will also be ancillary activities such as obtaining supplies, making deliveries, cleaning, maintenance and repairs which may give rise to more difficulty".

He gave some useful examples of an employer's duty: "If he has a repair shop as a part of his plant, that is an ancillary part of his undertaking. Likewise, as in this case, if he has independent contractors to do cleaning or repairs on his own premises, as an activity integrated with the general conduct of his business." Other activities though, which are completely separate from an employer's business, such as "the cleaning of the office curtains at the dry cleaners, the repair of the sales manager's car in the garage [and] maintenance work on machinery returned to the manufacturer's factory" would not form part of its undertaking. Thus: "The place where the activity takes place will in the normal case be very important; possibly decisive."

Working at a height

One of the biggest risks during maintenance and repair work is falling from a height. Facilities managers need to ensure that contractors have a number of safeguards in place, including:

- edge protection around openings, holes and roofs
- guard rails and toe boards of the right height on scaffolding and work platforms
- base plates on scaffolding uprights, with all ledgers, braces and struts in position and the structure secured to the building
- warnings or barriers to stop people using an unfinished scaffold
- protection from moving equipment and falling materials
- weekly, recorded inspections of scaffolds, hoists, cranes, and so forth
- using trained, competent staff

Roof work is particularly hazardous, and additional precautions include:

- avoiding anyone going on the roof – is cleaning just for cosmetic purposes really necessary?
- not allowing your own employees to 'take a quick look' at a problem
- displaying warning signs about fragile roofs and skylights, particularly at access points
- providing barriers or covers for fragile roof materials
- providing safety nets or harnesses if edge protection and secure work platforms are not possible
- excluding people from the area beneath roof work or protecting them from falling debris
- not allowing work in bad weather conditions

Further information is available in HSE's guides on construction work[15] and roof work.[16]

Confined spaces

Fifteen people a year, on average, are killed doing work in a confined space or trying to rescue someone trapped in one.

Regulation 1(2) of the *Confined Spaces Regulations 1997* defines a confined space as "any place, including any chamber, tank, vat, silo, pit, trench, pipe, sewer, flue, well or other similar space in which, by virtue of its enclosed nature, there arises a reasonably foreseeable specified risk". Some areas may, for example, become confined during construction or modification work. Risks can arise from lack of oxygen, chemical residues, dangerous gases, leaks, heat, fire, or use of machinery (which may create dust or cause an electric shock).

Under section 2 of the *HSW Act*, employers also owe their employees a duty to provide and maintain safe means of access to and egress from places of work. This duty extends to the workforce of other contractors. Regulation 4 of the *Confined Spaces Regulations* prohibits a person from entering a confined space to carry out work for any purpose where it is reasonably practicable to carry out the work by other means.

In practice, this means that employers should identify another way to do the work, for example by using a remote camera for inspection, or tools that can be used from outside. If entry is necessary, risk control measures include:

- appointing a supervisor
- ensuring workers have suitable training and experience, and are medically fit

- isolating hazardous machinery or pipework
- cleaning chemical residues before entering
- providing ventilation
- testing the air
- providing non-sparking or low-voltage tools and protected lighting as appropriate
- providing breathing apparatus if necessary
- preparing emergency arrangements, including how to raise the alarm
- providing lifelines
- having a safe communication system
- having a 'permit to work' system

Fire safety

According to Home Office statistics, 27 people died in 1998 and just over 1,700 were injured in fires in commercial premises. Employers or those who have "control" of a workplace are required to carry out a fire risk assessment. This includes people who through a contract or tenancy have an obligation in relation to the maintenance, repair or safety of a workplace.

The legal requirement to conduct a risk assessment is contained within both *The Management of Health and Safety at Work Regulations 1999* and *The Fire Precautions (Workplace) Regulations 1997* (amended in 1999). Whereas, previously, the enforcing authority inspected the premises, then produced a report detailing what had to be changed or improved, it is now entirely the employer's own responsibility to find out how to comply with the legislation.

It is a criminal offence to place one or more employees at risk of death or serious injury by failing to comply with the *Fire Regulations*. It is also a criminal offence to fail to comply with an enforcement or prohibition notice.

Fire certificates

In addition, the *Fire Precautions Act 1971* imposes requirements upon occupiers of premises, as distinct from the requirements upon them as employers or persons who "control" the workplace. The Act requires "designated" premises to apply for a fire certificate from the local fire authority, which will prescribe in detail what they are required to do to comply. This does not exempt them from also having to carry out a risk assessment.

Designated premises are factories, offices, shops and railway premises in which more than 20 persons are at work at any one time, or more than 10 persons work at any one time higher than the ground floor. Occupiers are required to:

- keep the certificate in the relevant building

- maintain the fire safety provisions in their premises and any other conditions imposed, precisely as detailed in the certificate

- give notice to the fire authority before making any material extensions or structural alteration to the premises

- give notice to the fire authority before making any material alteration to the internal layout of the premises or to the layout of furniture or equipment

If you are unsure whether or not your proposals constitute "material" change, it is good practice to consult your local fire safety officer for advice on the matter.

In addition, the *Fire Certificates (Special Premises) Regulations 1976* apply to premises which operate hazardous processes or manufacture or store specified hazardous materials in quantities which pose a significant risk.

Risk assessment

It is important to carry out a fire risk assessment appropriate to the particular workplace. It is also good practice to involve staff in the process, as they may have identified a potential fire risk of which people higher up the organisation may not be aware.

The two most important questions to ask are:

- How likely is it for a fire to start in my workplace?

- How easy is it for employees, and other people who may be affected, to escape to a place of safety in the event of a fire?

In larger workplaces, it is good policy to carry out a separate inspection for each significantly different section, area or department. The whole of the workplace should be taken into account, including any outdoor areas and any rooms or parts of buildings which are not currently in use.

If the workplace has been subject to previous approvals by the various enforcing authorities for other fire safety, licensing or building legislation, you are still required to carry out an assessment of your fire precautions under the *Fire Regulations*. However, if there has been no significant change in the workplace, for example, in the number of employees or the activities which they undertake, it is unlikely that any significant additional fire precautions will have to be provided.

If you do propose to make changes to your fire precautions as a result of carrying out a fire risk assessment, these must not conflict with the controls imposed by other legislation. If in any doubt, you are advised to consult a fire safety officer from your local fire service.

If other employers share your premises, your organisation has a responsibility to ensure that they are made aware of any significant risks and any action you have taken to reduce that risk. Under the *Management Regulations*, you are also required to cooperate with other employers who share your workplace to enable them to discharge their responsibilities under the *Fire Regulations*. In addition, you should take all reasonable steps to coordinate your fire safety measures with those of any other employers who may share your workplace.

The 'five steps' approach

The Home Office publication *Fire safety – An employer's guide* advocates extending HSE's five steps approach to risk assessment to fire safety. The five steps are:

1: Identify fire hazards

Potential fire hazards in the workplace will include potential sources of ignition, sources of fuel and any hazards associated with the processes carried out in the workplace.

2: Identify the location of people at significant risk in case of fire

This step needs to take into account not only employees, but other people who may be in the premises, such as customers, members of the public, visitors, and contractors. The special needs of any disabled staff and visitors must also be considered. There may be parts of the premises where people are more at risk than others.

3: Evaluate the risks

This step involves deciding whether existing fire precautions are adequate, or whether improvements are required to remove the hazard or to control the risk. It is necessary to look at any existing fire safety measures provided in terms of:

- the control of ignition and fuel sources
- fire detection and fire warning systems
- means of escape
- means of fighting fire
- maintenance and testing of fire precautions
- fire safety training for employees

The nature of the risk evaluation will depend very much on the nature of the workplace and the work activities carried out.

4: Record findings and action taken

Regulation 3(6) of the *Management Regulations* requires organisations which employ five or more people to record the significant findings of the assessment and any group of employees identified as being especially at risk. Under regulation 10, there is a legal requirement to provide employees with "comprehensive and relevant information". This means telling employees or their representatives about the risk assessment findings, and perhaps making the formal risk assessment report available to them on request.

5: Keep assessment under review

It is good practice to carry out an annual review of the workplace to ensure that no new risks have developed as a result of, for example, changes to work processes, machinery, substances or the number of people likely to be present in the workplace. There should also be a re-assessment of the workplace if you have carried out alterations or extensions, as they may have affected the fire precautions previously provided.

Means of escape

Once people are aware of a fire, they should be able to proceed safely along a recognisable escape route to a place of safety. In order to achieve this, it may be necessary to protect the route by using fire-resisting construction. The means of escape is likely to be satisfactory if your workplace is fairly modern and has had building regulation approval, or if it has been found satisfactory following a recent inspection by the fire authority (and in each case you have not carried out any significant material or structural alterations or made any change to the use of the workplace). However, you should still carry out a risk assessment to ensure that the means of escape remain adequate. If, as a result of the risk assessment, you propose making any changes to the means of escape, you should consult the fire authority (in Scotland you must seek the agreement of the building control authority) before making any changes.

When assessing the adequacy of the means of escape, you will need to take into account:

- the findings of the fire risk assessment
- the size of the workplace, its construction, layout, contents and the number and width of the available escape routes
- the workplace activity, where people may be situated in the workplace and what they may be doing when a fire occurs
- the number of people who may be present, and their familiarity with the workplace
- individuals' ability to escape without assistance

In some cases, it may be necessary to provide additional means of escape or to improve the fire protection of existing escape routes. If, having carried out your risk assessment, you think this might be the case in your workplace, consult the fire authority and, where necessary, your local building control officer before carrying out any alterations.

Home Office guidance

The Home Office guidance states that:

- Other than in small workplaces, or from some rooms of low or normal fire risk, there should normally be alternative means of escape from all parts of the workplace.
- Routes which provide means of escape in one direction only (from a dead end) should be avoided wherever possible as this could mean that people have to move towards a fire in order to escape.
- Each escape route should be independent of any other and arranged so that people can move away from a fire in order to escape.
- Escape routes should always lead to a place of safety; they should also be wide enough for the number of occupants and should not normally reduce in width.
- Routes and exits should be available for use and kept clear of obstruction at all times.

The time for people to reach a place of safety should include the time it takes them to react to a fire warning. This will depend on a number of factors including:

- what they are likely to be doing when the alarm is raised
- what they may have to do before starting to escape (turn off machinery, help other people)

- their knowledge of the building and the training they have received about the routine to be followed in the event of fire

Where necessary, these can be checked by carrying out a practice drill.

To ensure that the time available for escape is reasonable, the length of the escape route from any occupied part of the workplace to the exit should not exceed:

- where more than one route is provided, 25m for a high fire-risk area and 60m for a low fire-risk area
- where only a single escape route is provided, 12m for a high fire-risk area and 45 metres for a low fire-risk area

The guidance goes on:

- A doorway of no less than 750mm in width is suitable for up to 40 people per minute (where doors are likely to be used by wheelchair users the doorway should be at least 800mm wide).
- A doorway of no less than 1m in width is suitable for up to 80 people per minute.
- Where more than 80 people per minute are expected to use a door, the minimum doorway width should be increased by 75mm for each additional group of 15 people.
- For the purposes of calculating whether the existing exit doorways are suitable for the numbers using them, you should assume that the largest exit door from any part of the workplace may be unavailable for use; the remaining doorways should be capable of providing a satisfactory means of escape for everyone present.

Emergency lighting

Generally, in premises which have a daytime occupancy only, emergency lighting will only be necessary when there is insufficient natural light for people to make their way out of a building safely if the primary lighting should fail. The need for escape lighting is greater in buildings where visitors are present who are unfamiliar with the building.

Emergency escape and fire exit signs are necessary to indicate any emergency exit doors and routes which are not in common use.

Emergency exits

Under regulation 5 of the *Fire Regulations*:

- Routes to emergency exits and the exits themselves must be kept clear at all times.

- Emergency doors must open in the direction of escape.

- Sliding or revolving doors must not be used for exits specifically intended as emergency exits.

- Emergency doors must not be so locked or fastened that they cannot be easily and immediately opened by any person who may need to use them in an emergency.

Fire notices

Notices giving clear and concise instructions on the action to be followed in case of fire should be prominently displayed throughout the workplace. It is also important to include a designated assembly point in the notices.

Fire equipment

Where necessary, the *Fire Regulations* require the provision and maintenance of appropriate fire-fighting equipment, fire detectors and alarms. In determining what is appropriate fire-fighting equipment, account must be taken of:

- the dimensions and use of the buildings at the workplace

- the equipment they contain

- the physical and chemical properties of the substances likely to be present

- the maximum number of people present at any one time

Fire detection and fire warning systems, emergency lighting (including torches) and fire-fighting equipment should be checked weekly. There also needs be an annual full check and test carried out by a competent service engineer.

Staff responsibilities

An effective system for ensuring that the fire safety message is spread throughout an organisation is to cascade the responsibility through all staff levels by appointing floor, department or section fire marshals. The basis of this system is that the fire marshals are given a higher level of fire safety training than the average member of staff in order to look after a designated part of the premises.

Their role should be to check for hazards and potential fire risks within their area. They must check that fire safety equipment is working and in place, and be responsible for organising the evacuation of staff, the public and visitors, in the event of a fire alarm. This should include a final sweep of their designated area to ensure that everyone is out and to report accordingly to the person in charge of the assembly point.

It is not necessary for all staff to receive the same high level of training. This would be inappropriate and unmanageable. It is however necessary to ensure that all staff know:

- the location and use of escape routes
- the location of their assembly point
- how to use fire equipment provided
- how to summon the fire service

Fire risk assessment checklist

Escape routes

- Are main and emergency stairways protected by self-closing fire doors?
- Is the emergency route clearly sign posted?
- Are there any 'dead end' conditions where escape is possible in one direction only?
- Are all escape routes clear of obstructions?
- Are all exit doors unobstructed externally?
- Are there enough exits?
- Are exit doors free to open at all times (not locked)?
- Are fire doors fitted with 'fire door – keep shut' signs, and is this instruction followed?

Fire defence equipment

- Is the fire alarm system satisfactory for the risk?
- Will it meet current legal requirements?
- Are the fire alarm, hydrants, fire extinguishers/hose reels, sprinklers and emergency lighting maintained by qualified people? Is maintenance recorded in a log book?
- Is the fire alarm tested weekly?
- Does the fire alarm have automatic fire detectors in corridors, stairways and risk rooms?
- Are routine checks made to ensure equipment has not been obscured, moved or damaged?

Work equipment and furnishings

- Are all items of portable electrical equipment inspected regularly and fitted with correctly rated fuses?

- Is the wiring of electrical installations inspected periodically by a competent electrical engineer?
- Is the use of extension leads and multi-point adapters kept to a minimum?
- Are flexible electrical leads run in safe places where they will not be easily damaged?
- Is upholstery in good condition?

Cleanliness and tidiness

- Are staff encouraged to tidy their personal workplaces?
- Are the premises kept clear of combustible waste?
- Are metal bins with closely fitting lids available for waste such as floor sweepings?
- Are separate, clearly labelled containers provided for waste and special hazards – such as flammable liquids, paint rags, oily rags?
- Are waste containers removed from the building at the end of each working day or more frequently if necessary?
- Is waste awaiting disposal put in a safe place which is not accessible to the public?
- Is the burning of waste on site prohibited?
- Are cupboards, lift shafts, spaces under benches, gratings, conveyor belts and similar places kept free from dust and the accumulation of rubbish?
- Are pipes, beams, trusses, ledges, ducting and electrical fittings regularly cleaned?
- Are areas in and around the building kept free from accumulated packaging materials and pallets?
- Are metal lockers provided for employees' clothing?

Storage

- Are fire doors, exits, fire equipment and fire notices kept unobstructed?
- Are storage areas accessible to fire fighters?
- Are stack sizes kept as small as possible?
- Are there adequate gangways between stacks?
- Are stacks stable?
- Are stocks of material arranged so that sprinkler heads and fire detectors are not impeded and are the required clearances beneath this equipment maintained?

- Are excessive quantities of stock avoided?
- Is access to storage areas restricted to those who need to be there?
- Is stock kept well clear of light fixtures and hot service pipes?
- Are storage areas inspected regularly and at the end of the working day?

Maintenance of buildings

- Is every point of entry to the site and building secure against intruders?
- After close down of operations are all doors, windows and gates checked and secure?
- Is the building regularly inspected for damage to windows, roof and walls?
- Are the grounds surrounding the premises kept free of combustible vegetation by regular grass cutting and scrub clearance?
- Are all outside contractors supervised while on the premises and their work authorised by 'permit to work' schemes?

Heating and lighting

- Are there restrictions on using unauthorised heaters?
- Are combustible materials at a safe distance from appliances and flues?
- Is care taken that no materials are left on heaters?
- Are portable heaters securely guarded and placed where they cannot be knocked over or ignite combustibles?
- Are goods kept clear of lighting equipment?

Smoking

- Is smoking prohibited in all but designated 'smoking' areas?
- Are non-smoking rules strictly enforced?
- Where smoking is permitted are there enough ashtrays (as distinct from waste bins)?

Staff training

- Are new staff instructed in fire procedures and shown the fire escape routes on their first day at work?
- Are fire action notices posted throughout the workplace?
- Are there trained fire marshals?

- Is there a designated fire assembly point?
- Have staff had the opportunity to operate a fire extinguisher?
- Do staff know how to deal with the disabled, the public and visitors in the event of an evacuation?

Action plan

- Do you have a prioritised action plan for remedial measures following an assessment?

Flexible working

An employee's workplace is not always fixed. Some employees may work from home some or all of the time, or hotdesk around the office. Others may visit clients, spend a large amount of time travelling, work alone or work in a remote place. Employers have a duty to assess the risks associated with all these working conditions.

Homeworking

Employers may need to visit – and revisit – homeworkers to check their working conditions. It is important to remember that:

- Not only the employee, but also their children could be harmed – by trailing cables or dangerous substances, for example.
- The employer is responsible for maintaining any electrical equipment (normally a computer and printer) which it provides.
- The employee needs training in the safe use of equipment provided (the need to take regular breaks from computer work, for example).
- The employer must ensure the workstation and seating are correctly adjusted, the screen is positioned to avoid reflections, there is suitable lighting, and there is enough space to work comfortably.
- First aid provisions may be necessary.
- New or expectant mothers may be particularly at risk from some types of work.
- Some employees find working alone stressful – regular meetings, support or social events may help.
- Employees may work from home only occasionally, using their home furniture and lighting – if so, they will need advice.

It could be useful to incorporate health and safety into the homeworker's employment contract, requiring them to maintain a separate, designated work area at home. Also, although the employer is responsible for assessing homeworking conditions, it is helpful to give homeworkers their own checklist to display as a good practice reminder.

Hotdesking

To avoid WRULDs, workstations used by more than one person (including part-timers, jobsharers and shiftworkers) will have to be easily adjustable. Employees will also need training on the importance of actually making the adjustments.

Employees may need a mobile cart to store their work, in which case the principles of good manual handling will apply (for example, avoiding the need to wheel the cart further than necessary and avoiding obstacles). Finally, although a recent HSE-funded study found hotdeskers were not more stressed than their 'traditional' colleagues, it found it was important to consult employees before introducing new ways of working.

Laptops

Portable computers are covered by the *DSE Regulations* if they are used for more than an hour at a time. As well as the risks associated with any computer or monitor, there are problems associated with carrying round heavy, valuable equipment, and using cramped keyboards and screens in awkward locations (for example, wedged against the car steering wheel or on the passenger seat during a traffic jam).

An HSE-commissioned study on the safety of portable computers found that fewer than half the organisations contacted had any guidance or policy at all on using laptops, and most of them had started to get complaints from laptop users about health and safety. The researchers, System Concepts, went on to recommend:

- buying laptops with as large a keyboard and screen as possible, while keeping the weight down to 3kg at most
- supplying employees with rucksack-style laptop bags – they distribute the weight better and give away the contents less easily to would-be muggers
- checking the weight of transformers, cables, and so forth
- choosing a machine with long battery life, so transformers and cables can be left behind
- ensuring it is possible to attach a separate monitor, keyboard and/or mouse to a docking station for prolonged use

Homeworkers' checklist

Eyesight

- Take frequent mini-breaks by looking away from the screen and documents, preferably out of the window.
- Take a 10-minute break at least once an hour and leave the room – a short walk outside to lengthen the optical focus is ideal.
- Get your eyes tested regularly.
- If eyes regularly feel sore seek advice.
- Don't work in poor light or glare.

Strain injuries

- If you change your workstation set-up after it has been health and safety checked, either self-assess it within the company guidelines or ask your supervisor to do another check.
- Take frequent mini-breaks, stretch and gently exercise fingers, wrists, arms, shoulders and neck.
- Take a 10-minute break at least once an hour, leave the room, and carry out another activity.
- Take fresh air and exercise at least once a day.
- Keep work surfaces uncluttered – don't let paperwork and files build up over time, and keep plenty of space for keyboard, mouse and documents.
- Don't store boxes under the desk where they may cramp legs and feet.
- Recognise warning signs such as tiredness, sore eyes, headache or soreness, tension or numbness in hands, arms, neck, back or shoulders. If in doubt seek advice.

Posture

- Always use a good, ergonomic office chair.
- Remember to sit up straight with your back supported by your chair.
- Ensure your screen is close enough to see without leaning forward.
- If you need a footrest, use it.

Electricity

- Don't use multi-socket plugs or extension leads without first consulting your manager.
- Don't put drinks or vases of flowers on computer equipment.

Fire

- Storage of documents and reference material may constitute a fire hazard. Keep a fire extinguisher in the work area and ensure the smoke alarm is in working order.

- encouraging employees to restrict the use of laptops in non-ideal locations, and use docking stations where possible

Driving

HSE does not, at the moment, treat road accidents as work-related. But a consultation paper by the Government's work-related road safety task group proposes making employers liable for crashes caused by employees spending too long at the wheel or trying to meet impossible deadlines. Research suggests 800–1,000 of the 3,500 road deaths each year involve cars driven for work. The Government has set itself a target of reducing deaths and accidents on the road by 40% in 10 years.

Research commissioned by the former Department of the Environment, Transport and the Regions in 2000 found that tiredness caused around one in 10 road accidents. It advised stopping for 15 minutes after every two hours of driving – but not on the hard shoulder. RoSPA (the Royal Society for the Prevention of Accidents), which has been campaigning on the issue, advises employers to assess the risk of road accidents in the same way as they assess risks on site.

Mobile phones

In 1999, the Highway Code was amended to warn drivers never to use handheld mobile phones or microphones while driving. Hands-free kits, too, are "likely to distract your attention from the road". The police can bring prosecutions for causing death by dangerous driving, driving without due care and attention, or failing to have proper control of a vehicle.

A number of drivers have already been imprisoned following accidents involving mobile phone use. RoSPA estimates at least 15 deaths have been caused by drivers using mobile phones, including two using hands-free kits. It wants company health and safety policies to ban employees from using mobile phones while driving, encouraging them to pick up messages when they have stopped the car instead.

Evidence on whether mobile phone emissions are safe, even when using a hands-free kit, remains inconclusive. They do cause a slight warming of the brain, but the long-term effects of this are unknown. One option is to advise employees to make short, essential calls only, and to use land lines whenever possible.

The advantages of mobile phones should not be forgotten. For lone workers, those visiting clients at home or those on the move, they offer invaluable personal protection.

Lone working

Lone workers may include:

- those working outside normal office hours, such as maintenance, cleaning and security staff
- mobile workers, such as sales reps, estate agents, social workers, postal workers, painters and decorators
- homeworkers

There is no express legislation prohibiting lone working, but the normal rules on risk assessment apply. The assessment may show an activity is too dangerous to be carried out alone (such as lifting a heavy load or visiting a violent client at home) or without supervision (such as working in a confined space). The risk assessment should consider not only normal working conditions but emergencies.

Lone workers may need extra training or experience to cope in an emergency or to deal with aggression. Their employers need to set limits on what they can and cannot do on their own. There needs to be a system for them to report to base and for the employer to take action if they fail to do so. Lone workers need access to first aid facilities, and mobile workers will need their own first aid kit.

Environmental protection

There is, of course, a legal regime for prosecuting firms which accidentally or intentionally pollute the air, water or land during their industrial processes. But for facilities managers, the important new development in environmental law is the scrutiny under which every aspect of every company's environmental performance is starting to come. The regime is subtler – if you forget to turn the lights off at the end of the day, you will not end up in a courtroom, but you will feel the financial effects when your tax bill arrives. So whereas energy efficiency has, until recently, been a matter of choice, it is now starting to be regulated. There is also pressure to report on environmental performance, so that energy wasters will find it harder to conceal their poor record (see WORKPLACE FACILITIES: ENVIRONMENTAL MEASURING AND REPORTING, PP302–304).

Climate Change Levy

In 1997, the UK Government committed the country to substantially reducing greenhouse gas emissions such as carbon dioxide and methane by 2010.

Non-domestic energy use is one of the Government's main targets, and businesses are feeling the effect as the first fuel bills arrive containing the Climate Change Levy (CCL). The levy works by charging businesses and public sector organisations an extra sum on their fuel bills for every kilowatt hour (kWh) of electricity, coal, natural gas and liquid petroleum gas they use. In other words, unlike VAT, which is charged on the cash value of goods and services provided, the CCL is based on the energy value of the fuel supplied. This means that getting a cheaper supply will not reduce the amount of tax payable. Load management – moving energy-thirsty activities to periods of lower cost electricity – will be similarly ineffective at reducing the amount to be paid.

Levy rates

The rates of the CCL for 2001–02 are as follows:

Fuel	Rate
Electricity[17]	0.43p/kWh
Gas	0.15p/kWh
Liquid Petroleum Gas	0.96p/kg
Others (including coal and coke)	1.17p/kg
Source: Customs and Excise	

Exemptions

The CCL is not to be applied across the board; for example, the following will be exempt:

- small users and charities who pay VAT on fuel at 5%
- fuels used by the transport sector
- fuels used for energy generation
- oils already subject to excise duty
- electricity generated from new renewable sources such as solar and wind power
- fuels used jointly as a feed-stock and an energy source within the same process, for example coke in steel-making
- electricity used in electrolysis processes, for instance, the chlor-alkali process, or primary aluminium smelting
- fuel used by good quality combined heat and power (CHP) schemes as certified by the Quality Assurance Programme (CHPQA), a voluntary programme which has developed a universal method to assess, monitor and certify the quality of CHP

CHP exemptions, allowances and discounts

CHP schemes which combine heat and power production can achieve energy efficiencies of 60–80% or more, compared with 30–50% from more conventional forms of electricity generation and heat-only boilers. This gives CHP a key role in cutting energy costs and reducing carbon emissions and is why the Government is using the levy exemption to encourage its use.

For the year 2001/02, purchasers of certain types of approved energy-saving equipment will qualify for a 100% first year capital allowance. The list of equipment qualifying for an 'enhanced' capital allowance (ECA) includes: CHP plant, boilers, motors, variable speed drives, lighting systems, refrigeration equipment, pipe insulation and thermal screens. Perhaps surprisingly, building management systems are not included, apart from lighting controls. Energy-efficiency grants will also be made available.

The Government estimates that over 90% of existing CHP schemes could qualify for levy exemption for their whole electrical output, while the remainder will be eligible for a proportional exemption.

The Government is also offsetting the levy by an 0.3% cut in employers' National Insurance Contribution (NIC). It says that this, together with support for energy-efficiency measures such as ECAs, will enable it to recycle all the revenues of the levy back to business.

A key issue that everyone should be aware of is that, for individual organisations, there is no connection between the two sides of the treasury equation. The NIC reductions will occur regardless of how much levy liability an organisation has, and the ECAs and the energy-efficiency grants will not depend on how much tax is paid. There is no link between these measures.

Negotiated agreements on discounts

Those industries which, because of their nature, are high users of energy would face potentially crippling charges if the full levy were applied, so the Government is making it possible for them to claim discounts. Trade associations from 10 major energy-intensive sectors and around 20 smaller sectors are working with the Government to agree targets for improving energy-efficiency or reducing carbon emissions. The 10 major players are: aluminium, cement, ceramics, chemicals, food and drink, foundries, glass, non-ferrous metals, paper, and steel. If targets are agreed which meet the Government's criteria they will be able to claim discounts of 80% against the levy.

For best practice guidance on reducing emissions and levy costs, see WORKPLACE FACILITIES: REDUCING EMISSIONS AND COSTS, PP300–302.

Building Regulations

At a time of increasing concern about the contribution of energy production and consumption to climate change, it is inevitable that building performance should come under the spotlight. Buildings are responsible for about half the UK's carbon dioxide emissions and there is great scope for reducing this figure.

The operation of building engineering services, such as space heating, domestic hot water, mechanical ventilation, air conditioning and lighting, cause carbon dioxide emissions amounting to 46% of the national total (27% from housing and 19% from non-domestic buildings). This adds up to about 235 million tonnes of carbon dioxide per year according to government estimates – or about 63.5 million tonnes of carbon per year (MtC/year).

Revised Building Regulations

In 1998, the Government announced a review of the *Building Regulations* for England and Wales, last amended in 1991. The then Department of the Environment, Transport and the Regions issued a consultation document in 2000. The changes were expected to be made in August 2001 and to come into effect in early 2002. The accompanying Approved Document L, *Conservation of fuel and power*, which sets out ways of meeting the technical requirements, will be split into two parts: L1 for domestic buildings, and L2 for non-domestic buildings.

One of the most important changes will be the extension of the Regulations to work on existing buildings. "At present, the *Building Regulations* only apply to proposed alteration work if the works affect structural safety, means of escape, resistance to fire, access and facilities for the fire service or access and facilities for disabled people," says the consultation document. The Government now says that: "In order to capture appropriate work in the building stock however (but to avoid minor or emergency repair work), the definition of controlled service or fitting is being extended. The new definition includes a service or fitting in relation to which Part L of Schedule 1 imposes a requirement. This will mean that replacement windows, doors and rooflights and replacement building services installations will need to comply with Part L. For dwellings, this has been limited to apply only to windows and glazed doors and boilers with their associated controls."

It is expected that the new Regulations will be implemented in two main stages. Stage 1A, including new fabric insulation standards, together with requirements for improved heating, lighting, air conditioning and mechanical ventilation efficiency, is to be introduced within six months of the formal amendment of the *Building Regulations*. Further improvements, mainly those that require a longer lead-in time, would come into force in early 2003 – this is Stage 1B.

The consultation document also envisages other dates for additional regulations. Stage 2 measures are those "where more time is needed to ensure there are no technical, market availability or building control enforcement reasons that would make the proposals unacceptable." Stage 2 would be implemented about a year after stage 1B and might include such items as an energy rating scheme for windows.

Measures being considered under stage 3 are those requiring parliamentary time to amend the *Building Act*. The Government believes this would probably not be achieved before 2005. Finally, the next full revision of the *Building Regulations* is scheduled for 2008.

The new Regulations, as represented by stages 1A and 1B, are expected to deliver energy savings of 1.32MtC/year. Some in the construction industry have been criticising the cost of introducing the new measures, but government estimates suggest these will not greatly increase the cost of buildings (see Table 1).

Carbon dioxide emissions from dwellings built to the proposed standards would be about one-quarter less than average current practice, according to the Government. For other buildings the reduction is expected to be in the range of 20% (for naturally ventilated buildings) to 30% (air conditioned ones).

Table 1: Summary of prospective extra costs for non-domestic buildings

Possible outcome	First phase proposals with effect from 2002 only	Second phase proposals with effect from 2004 only
Naturally ventilated non-domestic buildings	£7/sq m	£10/sq m
Air conditioned and mechanically ventilated non-domestic buildings (mean stimate)	£4.80/sq m	NA

Improved window standards

Among the new standards for all buildings are improved window standards. Double glazing has been commonplace in many buildings for some time. However the new standards are likely to require that all replacement windows are fitted with low-emissivity glass as well, if the target insulation performance is to be reached.

The consultation document does allow certain exceptions – for example in the case of "conservation work and other situations where the existing window design needs to be maintained". Any exemptions will need to be clearly spelled out, however, to avoid unintended loopholes.

Effect of the changes

One practical consequence of the changes will be that a contractor will now have to demonstrate to the building control officer that, in the case of a non-domestic building, it can properly commission a building including all its different systems. It will now be possible for buildings to be delivered to their users in a fully functioning, efficient state. In the past, buildings may have taken months – or even longer – to come up to their proper performance levels.

Energy metering

The Regulations will also introduce the need for energy metering in non-domestic buildings. This will be among the first tranche of measures to be introduced. It will mean that facilities managers will be able to see where their energy is going and take action.

One of the most radical suggestions concerns the replacement of heating systems, but this applies to domestic boilers only. Any new domestic boiler will have to have a minimum efficiency of 75% – a significant improvement on the current average.

Development in Scotland

A consultation paper, *Improving Building Standards*, has been issued by the Scottish Executive. This covers the whole scope of building control in the country. Responses to this consultation paper will form the first part of a review process. There will then be a second consultation on the resulting proposals. The second paper will outline proposals on how to improve – or if necessary completely reform – the building control system through a new Act of the Scottish Parliament.

The conservation of fuel and power is already covered in the *Technical Standards*, but there is now a real need, says the Executive, to raise the specifications in an attempt to reduce energy consumption. There is an ongoing process of examining how the *Technical Standards* could be amended to encourage improved energy efficiency and, as a result, reduce carbon dioxide emissions.

Key changes to the Building Regulations

- Virtually all building work – whether for new build, refurbishment or alteration – will be subject to the energy-efficiency provisions of the Regulations.

- There will be an increase in the insulation performance required of buildings. This is to be implemented in two phases: six months and 24 months after amendment of the Regulations.

- The heating system chosen will affect the fabric performance standards required of a building – the better the heating system, the more flexibility over fabric performance.

- A reduction in leakage of both heat and air will be required.

- Pipe and duct insulation levels will be increased.

- New performance standards to prevent solar overheating will be introduced.

- There will be new performance standards for boiler efficiency.

- There will be new performance standards for heating and hot water systems.

- New performance standards for certain types of lighting in offices, industrial and storage buildings will be set.

- A display lighting performance standard will be introduced.

- Buildings (or parts of buildings) where more than 200 sq m of space is served by air conditioning or mechanical ventilation will have to meet new standards. Offices will be assessed under a Carbon Performance Index (CPI).

- Buildings with more than 1,000 sq m of floor area will have to demonstrate that their 'as built' performance matches the approved designs.

- Installers will have to show they have commissioned heating, hot water, ventilation, air conditioning and lighting systems in accordance with good practice guides from CIBSE or BSRIA.

- Energy metering and sub-metering will have to be installed in buildings to allow owners and tenants to monitor energy consumption of the main building services.

- Information will have to be provided to occupiers on how to operate and maintain the building services to sustain efficient energy performance.

References

1. The draft is at *www.hse.gov.uk/new/index.htm.*
2. ISBN 0-7176-2488-9
3. IND(G)132L
4. *R v Howe & Son (Engineers) Ltd,* Court of Appeal case no. 97/101/Y3, 6 November 1998
5. The *Revitalising Health and Safety* plan is at *www.open.gov.uk/hse/hsehome.htm.*
6. *Directors' Responsibilities for Health and Safety,* see *www.hse.gov.uk/pubns/indg343.pdf*
7. The *Involuntary Homicide* consultation paper is at *www.homeoffice.gov.uk/index.htm.*
8. HS(G)90
9. HS(G)57
10. IND(G)223(L)
11. ISBN 0-7176-1772-6
12. HS(G)155
13. Including HS(G)136, IND(G)199(L) and IND(G)148(L)
14. ISBN 0717-61196-5
15. HS(G)150
16. HS(G)33 and IND(G)284
17. Excluding that generated from 'new' renewable sources (except large-scale hydro) and by good quality CHP

2 Employment Law

Jackie Le Poidevin

The New Labour Government's first term (1997–2001) saw sweeping changes to employment rights. Some legislation, like the *Working Time Regulations 1998*, was required to be implemented under European law. Other changes, like enhanced maternity provisions, were the result of the Government's Fairness at Work proposals.

Some of the more difficult decisions, such as amending the law on transfers of undertakings were, however, put off until after the 2001 general election. This chapter looks largely at the first wave of employment law reforms under Labour, and the legislation due to take effect in their second term in office.

Flexible working

Reforms

The reforms are an attempt to enshrine the right to flexible working in law. The key message for facilities managers is that flexible working is not just about where employees work – whether from home, or hotdesking around an open-plan office. Changes to the built environment will be worth little if they are not accompanied by a change in culture that allows employees – both men and women – to balance their work with the needs of their family, to reduce their stress levels, and to find time to develop their creativity. Facilities managers need to take a combined approach with other departments, such as human resources, if flexible working initiatives are to succeed.

One way in which the reforms acknowledge the importance of flexible working is that many of the new laws apply to the new breed of 'workers' as well as traditional 'employees'. Section 230 of the *Employment Rights Act 1996* defines a worker as an individual who has entered into a contract of employment or any other contract, whether express or implied, which undertakes to "perform personally any work or services for another party to the contract whose status is not by virtue of the contract that of a client of customer". This includes individuals such as IT contractors who are not genuinely self-employed, but who work under a personal service contract. It will also cover some casual or temporary agency workers, and other 'atypical' workers. Facilities managers will need to clarify the employment status of any contract or agency workers to whom they have outsourced work in the light of the ongoing changes in legislation.

There are also new laws and proposals on protecting part-time workers, employees on fixed-term contracts and agency workers. These mean that employers will find it harder to use so-called 'flexible working' practices to avoid giving staff basic rights. The aim is to ensure that new ways of working offer genuine advantages to staff as well as businesses.

Working time

The *European Working Time Directive* was officially introduced as a piece of health and safety legislation, to reduce the risk of ill-health caused by overly long working hours. The Labour Government, however, transposed it into UK law with the promise, in its *Fairness at Work* white paper, that the legislation "will enable people to balance better their work and home lives".

Organisations which allow employees to work flexible hours or from home will need to keep track of their hours to ensure they comply with the working time legislation. Alternatively, they can ask employees to opt out of the minimum requirements. But this could be bad for homeworkers' stress levels and ultimate productivity, since it can be difficult for them to know when to draw a line under their work each day.

The *Working Time Regulations 1998* provide that:

- Workers' maximum working week must average 48 hours, normally calculated over a 'reference period' of 17 weeks.

- Workers can choose to sign a written agreement that they will work more than the 48-hour limit – this is an 'opt-out'.

- Workers who opt out can cancel the agreement provided they give the employer at least seven days' notice, or longer (up to three months) if this has been agreed.

- The Regulations define working time as time when an individual is "working, at his employer's disposal and carrying out his activity or duties" – this includes travel which is part of the job, working lunches and job-related training.

- Working time does not include commuting time, lunch breaks, or non-job-related evening classes or day-release courses.

Rest periods

Workers required to work more than six hours continuously are entitled to a 20-minute rest break. The employer can decide the exact timing, but the break should be during the six-hour period, not at the beginning or end or it. According to the Department for Trade and Industry (DTI), "employers

> ## Case law
>
> On 3 October 2000, the European Court of Justice (ECJ) made a ruling on the status of 'on-call' time. The case[1] was brought by a doctors' union, although it could be relevant to other sectors, such as the security industry. The court found that if a worker is required to be on call at their place of work, this will count as working time. When the worker is on call at home or elsewhere, and free to pursue leisure activities or spend time with their family, this is not working time for the purposes of the Directive.

must make sure that workers *can* take their rest, but are not required to make sure they *do* take their rest."

Young workers are entitled to a rest break of 30 minutes if required to work for any continuous period of more than four and a half hours. This entitlement can be changed in exceptional circumstances, in which case the young worker should receive "compensatory rest" within three weeks (see EXCEPTIONS TO THE REGULATIONS: AGREEMENTS, P77).

Annual leave

The Regulations currently state that all workers who have worked continuously for the same employer for at least 13 weeks are entitled to four weeks' annual leave. In June 2001, however, the ECJ ruled that the 13-week qualifying period was contrary to the *Working Time Directive*.

The legal challenge was brought by BECTU, the broadcasting and entertainment union, most of whose members work on short-term contracts of less than 13 weeks. But the decision will also affect sectors such as catering, security and cleaning, where short-term contracts are common.

The Government has issued a consultation document on removing the service requirement, proposing instead a system of accrual in the first year of employment. This will give workers one-twelfth of their annual entitlement each month, rounded up or down to the nearest full day. So, an entitlement to four weeks' leave (20 days) will work out at 1.66 days a month, which will be rounded up to two days.

The four-week entitlement includes bank holidays – there is no statutory right for bank holidays to be granted as leave. Employers can specify the times that workers take their leave – for example, over Christmas. Workers must give the employer notice that they want to take leave. When their employment terminates, they have the right to be paid for any leave not taken.

Nightworkers

Facilities managers who employ in-house or external security personnel may need to be aware of the provisions on nightworking (but see also EXCEPTIONS TO THE REGULATIONS: SPECIAL CIRCUMSTANCES, P78). The Regulations define a nightworker as someone who works at least three hours a night "as a normal course". Such workers should not work more than eight hours daily on average. There has been a court ruling that an individual who worked nights for one-third of their working time was a nightworker.

Night time is normally between 11pm and 6am, although workers and employers may agree to vary this. If they do, night must be at least seven hours long and include midnight to 5am.

Where a nightworker's work involves special hazards or heavy physical or mental strain, there is an absolute limit of eight hours on their working time each day – this is not an average.

Employers must also offer nightworkers a free health assessment before they start working nights and on a regular basis thereafter, usually annually. Workers do not have to take up the offer. If the worker suffers from problems which are caused or made worse by nightwork, the employer should transfer them to day work if possible. New and expectant mothers and young workers should receive special consideration.

Exceptions to the Regulations

According to DTI guidance,[2] there are four types of exceptions where parts of the Regulations may not apply.

1. Agreements

Workers can agree with their employer to vary nightwork limits and the right to rest periods and rest breaks, in return for "compensatory rest". They may also agree to extend the reference period for calculating hours worked up to 52 weeks.

The compensatory rest provision allows workers to take their total weekly rest of 90 hours in a different pattern to that set out in the Regulations. The principle is that everyone gets their entitlement in the end, although some rest may come slightly later than normal.

These agreements can be made by collective agreement (between the employer and a trade union) or by a workforce agreement, usually made with elected representatives of the workforce. If a worker has any part of their conditions determined by a collective agreement they cannot be subject to a workforce agreement. A workforce agreement can apply to the whole workforce or to a group of workers.

2. Special circumstances

The nightwork limits and the right to rest periods and rest breaks do not apply where:

- workers work far away from where they live and want to work longer hours over fewer days to complete a task more quickly
- workers constantly have to work in different places making it difficult to work to a set pattern
- the work involves security or surveillance to protect property or individuals
- the job requires round-the-clock staffing or there are busy seasonal peak periods
- an emergency occurs

In these cases, the reference period for the weekly working time limit is extended from 17 to 26 weeks, and workers are entitled to compensatory rest.

3. Unmeasured working time

Apart from the entitlement to paid annual leave, the Regulations do not apply if a worker can decide how long they work – for example, a senior manager or director. The Regulations state that a worker falls into this category if "the duration of his working time is not measured or predetermined, or can be determined by the worker himself".

4. Partly unmeasured working time

This exception refers to workers who have an element of their working time pre-determined, but otherwise decide how long they actually work. The guidance states: "Additional hours which the worker chooses to do without being required to by his employer do not count as working time; therefore, this exception is restricted to those that have the capacity to choose how long they work. The key factor for this exception is worker choice without detriment."

This exception does not apply to:

- working time which is hourly paid
- prescribed hours of work
- situations where the worker works under close supervision
- any time where a worker is expressly required to work, for example to attend meetings
- any time which a worker is implicitly required to work, for example because of possible detriment if the worker refuses

So if a facilities manager willingly chooses to work longer hours without recompense on their own initiative, they may. But if they feel pressured to work unpaid overtime because the company culture demands it, the company is in breach of the Regulations.

Record-keeping

The requirements for record-keeping under the Regulations are that employers:

- must keep records that show they are complying with the weekly working time limit
- do not have to keep a running total of how much time workers work on average each week; rather the method of monitoring depends on particular contracts and work patterns
- need only make occasional checks of workers who work standard hours which are unlikely to reach the 48-hour threshold
- must keep an up-to-date record of which workers have opted out of the Regulations, but not of their hours
- must keep a record of when each named nightworker had a health assessment and the result
- must keep records for two years
- do not need to record rest breaks, days off or annual leave

Enforcement

Enforcement of the *Working Time Regulations* is split between different authorities. The Health and Safety Executive (HSE) and local authority environmental health departments enforce the weekly limits on working hours. The employment tribunals enforce the entitlement to rest and leave.

Part-time workers

The *Part-time Workers (Prevention of Less Favourable Treatment) Regulations 2000* implement the European Framework Directive on part-time working. The Regulations allow part-time workers to bring a compensation claim if they have been treated less favourably, on a pro-rata basis, than a comparable full-time worker. This right applies both to the terms of the part-timer's contract, and "to any other detriment by any act, or deliberate failure to act" by the employer. The right applies to workers, not just employees.

Previously, part-timers, 80% of whom in the UK are women, had to prove indirect discrimination under the *Sex Discrimination Act 1975 (SDA)* in order to win damages for unfair treatment.

Comparable full-timers

Part-timers can only prove less favourable treatment if they can compare themselves to another actual worker (a 'comparator'). Under the *SDA* and the *Race Relations Act 1976*, the comparator can be hypothetical. A comparable full-time worker must:

- be on the same type of contract as the part-timer

- do broadly similar work

- have similar qualifications, skills and experience

- work for the same employer at the same establishment, or if there is no available comparator there, work for the same employer at a different establishment

The Regulations list six different types of contract. The effect is that, for example, a part-time worker on a fixed-term contract may only compare their situation to that of a full-time worker on a fixed-term contract. They may not compare themselves to a full-time employee on a fixed-term contract, nor to a full-time worker on a different kind of contract.

This has led to complaints by the trade unions that many of the part-timers with the worst terms and conditions, such as cleaners, are excluded from protection because there are no equivalent full-timers present.

A part-timer who switches to full-time work or returns part time to the same level of job within 12 months – for example, a maternity returnee – can compare their new position to their old one. They can, in other words, be their own comparator.

Pro-rata principle

Part-timers are entitled to the same pay, sickness and maternity pay, access to pensions, training, leave and redundancy selection criteria as full-time workers, calculated on a pro-rata basis. Employers should ignore part-time status when they make promotion decisions or give bonuses, shift allowances or unsociable hours payments. They should ensure that training, assessments and so on are arranged so that part-timers can attend. Excluding part-timers from profit-sharing or share option schemes will normally be unlawful.

The guidance to the Regulations acknowledges that it may be difficult to grant a proportionate share of some benefits, such as health cover, company cars, permanent health insurance, subsidised mortgages and staff discounts – you either get them or you don't. But the guidance states it will not be enough for employers to argue they could not provide the benefits pro rata. The decision not to provide them must be objectively justified.

Some employment law practitioners advocate calculating the value of the benefit in question and providing the cash equivalent. Alternatively, part-timers might be allowed to contribute towards the benefit themselves, or the employer might allocate points to all benefits, allowing staff to choose which ones they want.

The Regulations do permit one area of difference between part-timers and full-timers. Part-time workers are not entitled to full-timers' overtime rates until they have exceeded the normal full-time hours.

Justification

The employer can defend less favourable treatment of part-timers by arguing that it was objectively justified. Drawing from sex, race and disability discrimination case law, this is likely to mean that the employer must have a legitimate business objective for the less favourable treatment, and must have chosen reasonably necessary means of achieving this objective.

Remedies

Part-time staff who believe that their rights have been breached may ask their employer, in writing, why they have been treated less favourably. The employer must respond, again in writing, within 21 days. The aim is to give both parties the chance to resolve their disagreement without having to go to a tribunal.

However, if the employee does bring tribunal proceedings, the employer's written statement may be used as evidence. If the employer fails to provide a written statement, the tribunal is entitled to infer that the individual's rights were infringed.

The worker must bring the complaint within three months of their rights being breached. The tribunal may:

- award unlimited compensation
- make a declaration of each party's rights
- recommend that the employer takes action to remedy the fault within a specified period

In practice, employees may prefer to bring an indirect sex discrimination claim, because they may receive an award for injury to feelings. This is specifically excluded from the *Part-time Workers Regulations*.

The Regulations also protect part-timers from being either dismissed or subjected to a detriment because they sought to use their rights.

Regulatory guidance

The Regulations offer protection to individuals after they start to work part-time. They do not require employers to give part-time work to those who ask for it. The Government has, however, set up a task force to look at the issue of granting requests for part-time status (see FLEXIBLE WORKING, P89). The guidance to the *Part-time Workers Regulations* also encourages employers to offer part-time work.

Guidance to the Part-time Workers Regulations

To facilitate requests to work part time, employers should:

- review whether any vacant posts could be done part time
- consider, when asked by a potential part-timer, whether part-time arrangements can fulfil that position's requirements
- maximise the range of posts at all levels designated as suitable for part-timers or jobsharers
- take requests to jobshare seriously and, in larger organisations, maintain a database of those interested in jobsharing
- take requests to change to part-time work seriously, and explore with workers, if possible, how to bring about this change
- consider having a procedure to discuss with full-time workers whether they wish to change to part-time work
- review how they advertise their vacancies
- communicate with staff representatives on part-time issues

Fixed-term contracts

Around 7% of the UK workforce are employed on fixed-term contracts. EU member states were required to implement the Directive on fixed-term work by 10 July 2001. The UK missed this deadline because of its June 2001 general election, or, as the Government put it, because of "particular problems with implementation in the UK", which it failed to specify. The Government has not announced a new implementation date, but it has completed its consultation exercise on fixed-term work.

The title of the Regulations, the draft *Fixed-Term Employees (Prevention of Less Favourable Treatment) Regulations 2001*[3] gives two clues to their contents. Firstly, they mirror the similarly named regulations protecting part-timers. Secondly, unlike the *Part-time Workers Regulations*, they apply, in draft form at least, to the narrower category of 'employees', rather than the more inclusive 'workers'. This means that self-employed and agency workers are not included.

The draft defines a fixed-term contract as being one of the following:

- It is made for a specific term which is fixed in advance.
- It ends automatically when a particular task is completed.
- It ends with a specified event (which is not reaching the retirement age).

The Regulations create a right for employees on fixed-term contracts:

- not to be treated less favourably than a comparable permanent employee
- not to be subjected to detrimental treatment as a result of any act or deliberate failure to act by the employer

Employees on fixed-term contracts will be entitled to the same terms in their employment contract as comparable permanent employees, apart from pay and occupational pension terms. The employer can, however, defend its actions if they were objectively justified. The definition of a comparable employee mirrors that used in the *Part-time Workers Regulations* (PART-TIME WORKERS: COMPARABLE FULL-TIMERS, P80).

The same problems will arise in giving certain benefits to fixed-term employees as occur under the pro-rata principle for apportioning part-timers' benefits. Private healthcare and car leases, for example, may only be renewable annually.

The draft Regulations propose a right for fixed-term employees to receive information about any suitable permanent vacancies at their place of work.

They also suggest that individuals employed for four or more years on one fixed-term contract or an unbroken series of contracts should automatically become permanent employees. This would not apply to any period of employment before the Regulations take effect. Employers would, moreover, be able to argue that a series of fixed-term contracts was objectively justified.

The Government is also considering whether to abolish the practice of fixed-term employees waiving their right to claim statutory redundancy payments (see UNFAIR DISMISSAL, P107).

Agency workers

The draft *Conduct of Employment Agencies and Employment Businesses Regulations* were due to become law in the autumn of 2001. Under the *Employment Agencies Act 1973*, an employment business which hires out temporary staff is the employer of those staff. But an employment agency, in contrast, simply finds work for individuals, who go on to be employed by the hirer.

The rules are not, however, operating effectively, and temporary workers have regularly been provided on an agency basis. This means that they work for a succession of different employers, rather than for a single employment business, so that they fail to accrue the year's continuous service upon which many employment rights depend. There has also been confusion about who the employer is in various situations, and whether agency staff are employees or workers for the purposes of employment legislation.

The problems were highlighted in a recent case, *Montgomery v Johnson Underwood*.[4] Mrs Montgomery tried to claim compensation for unfair dismissal when her contract was terminated, only to be told by the Court of Appeal that she was employed by no one, neither her agency nor her hirer, and therefore had no one she could sue.

Agency workers do have some employment rights. The *Employment Relations Act 1999* gives them the right to be accompanied at a disciplinary or grievance hearing. They are protected from discrimination. They are, also, protected under the *National Minimum Wage Act 1998* and the *Working Time Regulations 1998*.

The proposed employment agency Regulations aim to clarify the status of agency workers. Agencies will have to make clear whether they are an employment business or an employment agency, and who the worker's employer is.

Family-friendly legislation

The Government keeps returning to the issue of how to enable both fathers and mothers to balance their work and family lives better. The *Maternity and Parental Leave Regulations* came into force on 15 December 1999. Barely a year later, on 7 December 2000, the Government published a green paper, *Work and parents: competitiveness and choice*, suggesting a further wave of family-friendly, flexible working initiatives. Since the end of the consultation period in March 2001, the Government has made a series of announcements with further details of how it plans to implement the green paper proposals. These changes will require primary legislation when parliamentary time permits.

Maternity leave

The *Maternity and Parental Leave Regulations 1999* entitle women to 18 weeks' ordinary maternity leave (paid), beginning no earlier than 11 weeks before the expected week of childbirth (EWC). Employees with one year's service can also take additional unpaid leave to a total of 40 weeks, or 29 weeks after childbirth. Although, previously, the employment contract continued during maternity leave, a new clause was inserted into the *Employment Rights Act 1996*, explicitly giving women the right to return on terms and conditions no less favourable than would otherwise have been the case.

The Regulations also introduced simplified notice requirements. Women no longer risk losing their job if they do not inform their employers when they intend to return to work – in fact, they are no longer obliged to inform their employers of their intention to return from additional leave at all, unless the employer specifically requests them to do so. If the employer does request notification, this must:

- be in writing
- warn of the consequences of failing to respond
- explain how to calculate the end of the leave period

The employee has 21 days to reply. If she fails to do so, she may face disciplinary action, but she no longer loses her right to return to work.

Previously, women who were ill when they were due to return from maternity leave could be dismissed after four weeks' sickness absence. In 1998, the Court of Appeal ruled that maternity leavers should not lose their right to return if they became ill. The 1999 Regulations clarified the situation by stating that ordinary contractual relations resume at the end of the additional leave period. So a woman off sick at the end of her leave will be treated like any other employee on sick leave.

The Regulations also expressly state that employees on ordinary maternity leave are entitled to all their normal terms and conditions, except remuneration. Remuneration is defined as "wages or salary".

In addition, the Regulations give women a new right not to suffer a detriment as a result of relying on these rights. Previously, they needed to prove sex discrimination before they could bring a successful tribunal claim. Also, dismissal on grounds of pregnancy, childbirth or maternity leave became automatically unfair.

Green paper maternity proposals

The green paper looked at ways to enhance these new rights, for example by:

- extending unpaid maternity leave so that women can stay at home for a year in total
- allowing the mother and father to share any extension of the unpaid maternity leave
- increasing the flat rate of maternity pay
- increasing the period for receipt of maternity pay to 26 weeks
- complete repayment of statutory maternity pay for small and medium employers
- payment of statutory maternity pay direct to mothers, rather than through the employer
- simplification of existing maternity rights

These proposals have now been firmed up following announcements that:

- From April 2003, women will be entitled to 26 weeks' paid ordinary maternity leave.
- From April 2003, women will be entitled to a further 26 weeks' unpaid additional maternity leave, bringing the total leave entitlement to one year.
- The flat rate of statutory maternity pay and maternity allowance will rise from the current £60.20 a week to £75 a week from April 2002 and £100 from April 2003.
- Women who have 26 weeks' service with their employer will be entitled to both paid and unpaid leave (currently only women with a year's service qualify for the additional unpaid leave).
- Twenty-six weeks will be used to calculate women's average weekly earnings for the purposes of statutory maternity pay (this is currently eight weeks).

- Around 60% of firms paying statutory maternity pay will be able to reclaim their costs in full, plus compensation for administering maternity pay, from April 2002.

- Existing 21 days' notice requirements for returning early from leave or changing the start date will be extended to four weeks.

- Notification arrangements will be harmonised on one date, the 15th week before the EWC – the 'notification week'.

During the new 'notification week', a woman must tell her employer she is pregnant, her EWC and the planned start date for her maternity leave. The employer must acknowledge this in writing during the notification week, make clear to the employee that she is expected to return to work at the end of the leave, and what this date is.

Parental leave

The *Maternity and Parental Leave Regulations* introduced 13 weeks' unpaid parental leave for each parent per child aged under five or per child adopted for under five years. Employees must have a year's continuous service, and must requalify when they change employers, taking the balance of their entitlement only.

Employees must give 21 days' notice of the leave dates, or of the EWC in the case of fathers taking birth leave. The employer cannot postpone birth leave, but may postpone other leave for up to six months where "the operation of its business would be unduly disrupted". The request for leave need not be written, and the employer must respond within seven days.

Employees must, according to the Regulations, take the leave in blocks or multiples of a week, to a maximum of four weeks a year. It would, however, probably be a breach of the Directive actually to deduct a whole week's leave from an employee who only took off part of a week.

Employees returning from parental leave of four weeks or less are entitled to their same job back. Those taking longer leave are entitled to terms and conditions no less favourable. If an employer unreasonably postpones or prevents parental leave, the employee may complain within three months to an employment tribunal, which may award unlimited compensation.

The new entitlements were controversial when they were first introduced, because they applied only to parents of children born after 15 December 1999. The TUC, advised by the Prime Minister's wife, Cherie Booth, challenged this limitation, and the question was referred to the ECJ. The

European Commission delivered a reasoned opinion that the provision is an incorrect transposition of the *Parental Leave Directive*, and the Government has said it will extend parental leave to all parents of under-fives.

No date has been set for the amendments, although the Government has promised transitional arrangements for parents who have so far missed out. Also, parental leave for parents of children with disabilities will be increased from 13 to 18 weeks, to be taken up to the child's 18th birthday.

Paternity leave

The *Competitiveness and choice* green paper proposes a new right to two weeks' paid paternity leave. More details have since followed, including that paternity leave will commence in 2003, and the rate will be the same as statutory maternity pay – £100 a week. It must be taken as a single block within two months of the birth. As with maternity leave, fathers must have worked for one employer for 26 weeks, and give 15 weeks' notice.

Adoptive parents

Another green paper proposal, paid adoption leave, has also been confirmed and fleshed out in subsequent announcements. When a child is first placed with a family, one adoptive parent will be able to take six months' paid 'maternity' leave and six months' unpaid leave. The adoptive parents will be able to choose which one takes the 'maternity' leave, and the other parent will be entitled to two weeks' paid 'paternity' leave. The leave will be available for children adopted up to the age of 18.

Time off for dependants

The 1999 changes introduced a right to unpaid leave for family emergencies. The entitlement applies in the following situations:

- to provide assistance when a dependant falls ill, gives birth, is injured or is assaulted
- to make care arrangements for a dependant who is ill or injured
- to deal with the death of a dependant
- to deal with unexpected disruption to or the termination of arrangements for a dependant's care
- to deal with an unexpected incident during a son or daughter's education

Dependants are defined as a spouse, child, parent or person living in the same household (tenants, friends sharing a house, or same sex couples). The

Parental Leave Directive allowed member states to limit time off for dependants to a specified number of occasions or length of time, but the UK legislation is silent on this.

The *Competitiveness and choice* green paper went on to propose extending the right to take time off work to routine hospital appointments for dependants (as opposed to time off for emergencies).

Flexible working

The most radical proposals in the green paper were on flexible working. It suggested:

- the right for mothers who return early from maternity leave to work reduced hours for the remainder of that leave

- the right for fathers to work reduced hours until the end of maternity leave

- the right for both parents to work reduced hours, for as long as they choose, after the end of the maternity leave

The green paper further suggested that employers would be able to refuse a request to work part-time if granting the request would harm their business. They would need to set out their reasons, which could be used in court as evidence.

Just before the 2001 general election, the Government announced it was setting up a task force to advise it on giving parents the right to request to work flexible hours after the birth of a baby. The task force is examining what the consequences will be for employers who turn down such requests "in an unsatisfactory or unreasonable way". The then Secretary of State for Trade and Industry, Stephen Byers, said the right would "stop short of an automatic right to flexi-hours, and employers will not be under a legal obligation to grant the request".

Under existing law, a mother whose request to work part-time is refused may bring a claim of indirect sex discrimination under the *Sex Discrimination Act 1975*. The definition of indirect sex discrimination has recently been revised, making it easier for women to bring such a claim (see SEX DISCRIMINATION, P106).

TUPE

It is two decades since a law was introduced which ensures employees retain their jobs on the same terms and conditions when their business is taken over. The term 'outsourcing' had probably not even been coined, and despite a series of controversial court decisions, the law has failed to keep pace with the trend for contracting out non-core activities to specialist service providers. It remains unclear whether such outsourcing contracts are covered by the legislation.

The key right contained in the legislation is that dismissal in connection with a "relevant" transfer is unfair unless:

- an economic, technical or organisational reason entailing changes in the workforce was the main cause of the dismissal, and
- the employer acted reasonably in the circumstances in treating that reason as sufficient to justify dismissal

What constitutes a relevant transfer has, however, been the subject of much debate in the courts.

The European legislation governing business transfers is contained in the *Acquired Rights Directive*. This was implemented in the UK by the *Transfer of Undertakings (Protection of Employment) Regulations 1981 (TUPE)*. Following pressure from the UK, member states agreed amendments to the Directive in 1998.

The changes to the Directive, including a new definition of a business transfer, do not, however, clarify the position on outsourcing or address the inconsistencies in the case law. The Government's consultation paper on amending *TUPE* and implementing the changes to the *Acquired Rights Directive*, finally published on 10 September 2001, has therefore been eagerly awaited (see P90).

The *Süzen* decision

The case which sparked off the current round of debate over *TUPE* was heard in the ECJ in 1997. Ayse Süzen and seven other cleaners were employed by a company contracted to clean a school premises. The company lost its contract to a rival operation, which did not take on the cleaners.

Prior to the *Süzen* case,[5] the ECJ had used a test, established in a previous European case, *Spijkers*, which said that if an economic entity transferred, and maintained its identity in the process, *TUPE* applied (see opposite). In *Süzen*, the ECJ ruled that this test was not met, because there was "no concomitant transfer from one undertaking to the other of significant tangible or intangible assets or taking over by the new employer of a major part of the workforce, in terms of their numbers and skills". In other words, contract cleaning was a labour-intensive undertaking, with no other assets apart from its employees. These employees were not taken on, so there was no recognisable economic entity left to which the *Acquired Rights Directive* could apply.

The problem with this logic was that the whole point of the Directive is to protect employees from not being taken on, something it clearly failed to do in Ayse Süzen's case. The ECJ has confirmed this stance in subsequent cases, but the UK courts have repeatedly refused to accept the precedent.

UK case law

The first sign of the UK rebellion was the Court of Appeal's decision in *ECM*.[6] The Court of Appeal found that an incoming contractor had deliberately tried to escape its responsibilities under *TUPE* by exploiting the *Süzen* loophole. It had intentionally avoided taking on either assets or the existing workforce, and the court said it was entitled to take this motivation into account in reaching its decision. The court ruled that it could not allow a deliberate attempt to evade the law to succeed, and ruled that *TUPE* did apply.

In another noteworthy case, *RCO Support Services*,[7] the Employment Appeal Tribunal (EAT) found in favour of a group of cleaners who were dismissed when an NHS trust reorganised its business. The EAT said it was not sorry to have reached this decision. In labour-intensive areas such as cleaning and catering, where there are rarely any assets, contracting-out is common, it found. Any incoming contractor thinks it can avoid *TUPE* simply by not taking on the outgoing contractor's workforce. This not only jeopardises the

---

Spijkers test

In the *Spijkers*[8] case, the ECJ set out a number of factors which the courts should use to decide whether *TUPE* applies. These are:

- the type of undertaking
- whether tangible or intangible assets transferred
- whether employees transferred
- whether customers transferred
- how similar the activities carried on before and after the transfer were
- whether there was any suspension in activities

---

fundamental objective of *TUPE* – the protection of employees' acquired rights – it jeopardises them in relation to the most vulnerable people, those with simple and commonly available skills which incoming contractors can easily supply through others.

These are tough words, and facilities managers (when bringing outsourced services back in-house, for example) will want to avoid being on the receiving end of them in the courtroom.

In its latest decision on 22 June 2001, the Court of Appeal again found that *TUPE* did apply to a labour-intensive service, after the incoming contractor refused to take on the existing workforce. The case[9] is interesting for facilities managers because it concerned a change in security contractors.

ADI lost a contract in which it supplied nine security guards to a shopping centre. The shopping centre made certain facilities available to the guards, including closed circuit television (CCTV) and a control room. The new contractor was also allowed to use the facilities, but otherwise, no tangible assets transferred.

The new contractor approached the nine security guards with a view to hiring them, but changed its mind following a dispute over terms. It assigned different employees to the shopping centre, gave them different uniforms, and changed their job title to 'customer liaison officers'.

The Court of Appeal found that although no single factor should determine whether there was a *TUPE* transfer, in a labour-intensive undertaking where the service is substantially the same and performed in the same place for the same person, questions about why the incoming contractor failed to take on existing employees could tip the scales in the employees' favour.

It was clear that if the incoming contractor had taken on the nine guards, there would have been a relevant transfer. Consequently, if a court decided an incoming contractor had deliberately avoided *TUPE*, it should treat the case as if the existing employees had actually transferred.

Practical implications

Some legal commentators argue that the *Süzen* line of cases and the *ECM*, *RCO* and *ADI* line of cases are not, in reality, inconsistent. They are simply an application of the law to a different set of facts. But either way, the difficulty of predicting which way the courts will swing in their own particular case is bad news for service companies bidding to retain or take over a contract.

If *TUPE* applies, the new company will have to take on the old contractor's workforce on their existing terms and conditions, which may be different from those of the rest of its employees. The transferred employees' continuity of employment will remain unbroken, and they will be able to sue the new contractor over any disputes they had with their former employer. As long as a potential new contractor knows all of this, however, it can factor these costs into its bid – it is the legal uncertainty which is damaging.

If a contractor believes that *TUPE* does not apply, and that it does not have to take on the existing workforce and the accompanying liabilities, it can put in a lower bid in the hope of undercutting the current contractor and any other competitors. If it succeeds and is right, the former contractor will be left with no contract, all the employees and the associated redundancy costs. If it wins the tendering process but is legally in the wrong, it will face unfair dismissal claims from the sacked employees – and regardless of the ECJ rulings, the sympathies of the UK courts have tended to be with the employees. This means that making a non-*TUPE* bid remains a gamble, despite *Süzen*.

Amendments to TUPE

The Government's consultation paper on amending *TUPE*[10] begins by saying: "The Government considers that the *TUPE Regulations* are based on a positive principle – the coupling of flexibility for business with fairness for employees," but that the Regulations need to be made to work as effectively as possible.

It goes on: "The revised Directive gives for the first time an explicit definition of a transfer of an undertaking, intended to clarify the existing legal position without changing it. The Government proposes essentially to adopt this definition in the new Regulations. This alone, however, may be insufficient to address the problems that have arisen. The Government considers that there may be a case for taking further measures in two particular areas – transfers within public administration, and service provision changes – that have in the past been particularly frequent sources of confusion and dispute."

The Government goes on to propose that:
if:

- a service provision change is to take place and
- prior to the change, there are employees assigned to an organised grouping, the principal purpose of which is to perform the service activities in question specifically on behalf of the client concerned

then:

- the employees assigned to the organised grouping shall be treated in the same way as in cases where *TUPE* normally applies and

- the party with responsibility for provision of the service before the change shall be treated as the transferor and the party with responsibility for provision of the service after the change shall be treated as the transferee

This would, the Government suggests, ensure that "the Regulations applied comprehensively in relation to such cases, regardless of the particular facts" and "arguably increase the likelihood that, from the outset, all concerned normally knew where they stood". The party which takes on the responsibility for providing the service would become automatically responsible for the employees assigned to the organised grouping (whose continuity of employment would be preserved) and for any outstanding liabilities toward them.

Requirement to notify

There would also be a requirement on the transferor to notify the transferee of all such liabilities where they were or ought to be known about at the time of the transfer, and this could then be properly planned for and taken into account. An added advantage, the Government believes, is that this would help to ensure that contract bids were made on a comparable basis, and would remove a significant disincentive for potential bidders, particularly smaller firms, to become involved in service contracting.

The new clause is intended to ensure that the extended protection does not normally apply in cases where clients are buying in services 'off the shelf' in the same way as they might buy in goods – for example, the arrangement of conferences, printing work, consultancy advice or plumbing repairs.

The consultation paper goes on: "In cases where the arrangement between the client and the outside organisation entailed the provision not only of a service but also of goods, the extended protection would apply only where the former was the predominant aspect and the latter an ancillary one. Thus the extended protection would not normally apply where the arrangement entailed, say, the provision of computer equipment with associated IT advice or the provision of photocopiers with on-call maintenance support". But: "The extended protection *would* normally apply, by contrast, where the arrangement entailed, say, the provision of packaging materials in conjunction with a packing service or the provision of food and drink in conjunction with a catering service."

Drawbacks?

The Government then considers the drawbacks of this approach. These include the potential for contractors intentionally to avoid TUPE by redesigning services so that the activities are no longer essentially the same following a change of contractor, so that the definition of a "service provision change" is not met. The Government has, it says, "considered the possibility of introducing a general "anti-avoidance" provision to make such arrangements unlawful, but has decided on balance that this would be inappropriate, in part because the risks of stifling legitimate innovation in the pursuit of efficient and effective service provision outweigh the risks of abuse".

Further proposals

There are also proposals on:

- better protection of employees' occupational pension rights
- greater flexibility when applying *TUPE* to transfers of insolvent businesses, to make it more attractive for potential buyers to rescue those businesses
- clarifying the "economic, technical or organisational" defence
- introducing a legal requirement for the transferor to notify the transferee about the rights and obligations being transferred

Employee consultation

At the moment, UK employees have the right to be consulted in a limited number of situations. These are:

- if collective redundancies or a *TUPE* transfer are planned
- if any measure or new technology is introduced which substantially affects employees' health and safety (see HEALTH AND SAFETY LAW, PP5–72)
- if there is a European Works Council

The UK has, however, agreed to a European Directive on information and consultation which will enhance employees' rights in this area.

European Works Councils

The *European Works Council Directive* was implemented in the UK by the *Transnational Information and Consultation of Employees Regulations 1999*. They require undertakings or groups with at least 1,000 employees across the member states and at least 150 employees in each of two or more of those member states to set up European-level information and consultation procedures (usually through a European Works Council agreement).

Redundancies and transfers

The requirement to consult employees before making them redundant is contained in section 188 of the *Trade Union and Labour Relations (Consolidation) Act 1992*. The requirement to consult employees before the transfer of a business is contained in regulation 10 of *TUPE*. It is easy to confuse the two sets of requirements, so it is useful to summarise both here, even though *TUPE* is the bigger concern for facilities managers.

Amendments to the requirements came into effect on 28 July 1999. The main changes, according to DTI guidance[11] are:

- If employees who may be affected are represented by a trade union recognised for collective bargaining purposes, that union now has an automatic right to be informed and consulted over collective redundancies and transfers of undertakings; it may no longer be bypassed by the employer in favour of other employee representatives (although these may also be consulted if the employer so chooses).

- Explicit rules have been introduced for electing employee representatives where there is no recognised union (existing employee representatives may be consulted only if their remit and method of election is suitable).

- Where there is no recognised union and affected employees fail to elect representatives, having had a genuine opportunity to do so, the employer may fulfil its obligations by providing information direct to employees.

- Both union officials and non-union representatives have a right to reasonable paid time off for relevant training.

- Employees are protected against being unfairly dismissed or detrimentally treated for participating in an election of employee representatives.

- the amounts of compensation that employers may be required to pay if they fail to inform and consult have been increased and rationalised

For failing to inform and consult about collective redundancies, the maximum compensation per employee is 90 days' pay. For non-compliance over transfers of undertakings consultation, the maximum compensation is 13 weeks' pay. In cases involving both collective redundancies and a transfer of an undertaking, employees may receive both awards.

A collective redundancy is one where 20 or more employees are to be made redundant within a 90-day period. Employers are under no legal obligation to inform and consult representatives if fewer employees are to be dismissed. But the DTI warns they may face unfair dismissal claims if they fail to inform and consult individual employees who are to be dismissed.

"Affected" employees are not necessarily only those who face redundancy or a transfer to a new employer. If there is a dispute, it is for an employment tribunal to decide whether any particular employee or group of employees was affected in the light of all the facts.

Consultation about collective redundancies must begin in good time and at least:

- 30 days before the first dismissal if 20–99 employees are to be made redundant
- 90 days before the first dismissal if 100 or more employees are to be made redundant

Consultation about the transfer of a business must begin "in sufficient time", but *TUPE* sets out no specific time period.

On collective redundancy, the employer must consult, with a view to reaching agreement, on how to avoid the dismissals, reduce the number of employees affected, and mitigate the consequences of the dismissals. It should disclose:

- the reasons for the proposed dismissals
- the numbers and classes of employees whom it proposes dismissing
- the total number of employees of such description employed
- the proposed criteria for selecting employees for redundancy
- the proposed procedure and timescale for dismissing employees
- the proposed method for calculating redundancy payments

On the transfer of a business, the employer must inform the union or employee representatives:

- that the transfer is to take place and when
- the reasons for the transfer
- the legal, economic and social implications of the transfer
- the measures which the employer proposes taking in relation to the employees affected

Electing employee representatives

The amended rules on electing employee representatives where there is no recognised trade union are:

- The employer shall make reasonably practical arrangements to ensure that the election is fair.

- The employer shall determine how many representatives are to be elected so that there are enough to represent the interests of all the affected employees (bearing in mind the numbers and different categories of employees).

- The employer shall determine whether the representatives should represent all of the affected employees or particular categories of those employees.

- Before the election the employer shall determine the term of office as employee representatives so that it is long enough for relevant information to be given and consultations to be completed.

- The candidates for election as employee representatives are affected employees on the date of the election.

- No affected employee must be unreasonably excluded from standing for election.

- All affected employees on the date of the election are entitled to vote for employee representatives.

- The employees may vote for as many candidates as there are representatives to be elected to represent them.

- the election must be conducted so that:
    - so far as is reasonably practicable, those voting do so in secret
    - the votes given at the election are accurately counted

Selection for redundancy

The main cause of employees complaining to an employment tribunal is that they believe they were unfairly chosen for redundancy. The most easily understood way of choosing employees for redundancy is to use the 'last-in-first-out' method. But most employers prefer to use a range of criteria against which to 'mark' employees, which might include their attendance record, timekeeping, productivity (quality and quantity of work), their adaptability and the employer's future needs.

If challenged in a tribunal, the employer must be able to show it used a fair, consistent and objective selection procedure. Employers should avoid vague criteria such as 'attitude', which allow room for prejudice, and discriminatory criteria such as part-time working, pregnancy or trade union membership. They should also take care not to discriminate against disabled employees, whose attendance record, for example, might otherwise mark them out for redundancy.

A redundancy dismissal will also be unfair if the employer has failed to consider suitable alternative employment.

National Works Councils

Despite the existing consultation requirements, there have been a number of recent large-scale redundancies where employees have claimed that far from being involved in any debate about the company's problems, they barely received any warning that they were about to be sacked. When Marks & Spencer tried to dismiss 1,700 staff in its French stores in spring 2001, it gave them half an hour's warning before announcing the plans to the stock exchange. The French court successfully ordered Marks & Spencer to suspend the store closures, because it had not allowed employees time to negotiate. However, the 2,000 employees made redundant from Vauxhall in Luton in December 2000, the 6,000 steelworkers dismissed from Corus in Wales and Teeside in February 2001 and the 3,000 employees sacked at Motorola in Scotland in Spring 2001 were less fortunate.

The UK will, however, have to comply with a European Framework Directive on informing and consulting employees which the member states agreed on 11 June 2001. The UK dropped its opposition to the Directive after securing anything up to a nine-year exemption from the full effects. Member states are likely to adopt the Directive formally in early 2002, after which the UK will have three years to implement it. Different sized companies will then have to set up formal consultation procedures within a given time. Companies with over 150 employees are likely to have until 2007 to comply two years later (2009), and those employing more than 50 people will have another two years to implement the requirements (2011).

The Directive gives employees a right to be:

- informed about the economic situation of the undertaking for which they work
- informed and consulted about employment prospects
- informed and consulted with a view to reaching agreement about decisions likely to lead to substantial changes in work organisation or contractual relations, including redundancies and transfers

Information and consultation has to take place at an appropriate time and at the relevant level of management. Normally it will be done via employee representatives, defined according to national law and practice. The expectation is that, to avoid having to keep re-electing employee representatives every time there is a substantial change, employers will have to set up permanent National Works Councils along the lines of the existing European Works Councils.

The Directive is without prejudice to existing information and consultation requirements. This means that they do not override the provisions of the *European Works Councils Directive*, which are far more onerous, but affect only a small proportion of employers.

Discrimination laws

The main recent change to the laws on discrimination, and a key concern for facilities managers, was the introduction of the *Disability Discrimination Act 1995 (DDA)* under the last Conservative Government. It works differently from *the Sex Discrimination Act 1975 (SDA)* and the *Race Relations Act 1976 (RRA)*, because it does not include the concept of indirect discrimination or require claimants to compare their treatment to another actual or hypothetical employee (a "comparator") in order to prove their case.

The Disability Discrimination Act

The *DDA* imposes duties on employers, suppliers of goods and services and landlords. For the purposes of employment law, it defines "disability" as a physical or mental impairment which has a substantial and long-term adverse effect on a person's ability to carry out normal day-to-day activities. "Long-term" means the disability must last or be expected to last at least 12 months.

Normal day-to-day activities are those involving:

- mobility, dexterity or coordination
- continence
- ability to lift, carry or move everyday objects
- speech, hearing or eyesight
- memory or ability to concentrate, learn or understand
- perception of risk

An employer discriminates against a disabled person if, for a reason related to their disability, it treats them less favourably than other people, and it cannot show that this treatment is justified. Discrimination also occurs if the employer could make a "reasonable adjustment" to work arrangements or premises to accommodate a disabled person, and its failure to do so cannot be justified.

Discrimination may be justified in limited circumstances. For example, employers and service providers must not do anything that would endanger health and safety, although they can no longer use 'fire risk' as a blanket excuse for excluding disabled people from buildings. Nor does the *DDA* require them to do anything which would prevent them from complying with other legislation such as listed building regulations.

"Reasonable adjustments"

Facilities managers will be involved in making reasonable adjustments in so far as they involve changes to the premises and acquiring or modifying equipment. See HOW ACCESSIBLE ARE YOUR PREMISES?, P104, for examples of changes which might be necessary to accommodate either employees or members of the public who have a disability.

But facilities managers need to be aware that the responsibility for making adaptations does not rest solely with them. There are also many other adjustments which can be made to accommodate a disabled employee, which involve changing the way the work is organised. These include:

- allocating some of the disabled person's duties to someone else
- transferring the person to fill an existing vacancy
- altering the person's working hours
- assigning the person to a different place of work, such as their home
- allowing absences for rehabilitation, assessment or treatment
- giving training
- modifying instructions or reference manuals
- modifying assessment procedures
- providing a reader or interpreter
- providing supervision

In considering what is "reasonable", employers are entitled to take into account:

- how far making the adjustment would prevent the effect of the disability
- how practicable it is to make the adjustment
- the financial costs of the adjustment and the scale of the disruption
- their resources
- the availability of financial or other assistance

The Government's assessment of the cost of complying with the *DDA* assumed that the average cost of making an adjustment at recruitment stage would be £200, and that ongoing costs would be minimal. Grants may be available to make adaptations to the workplace or provide special equipment.

The duty to make reasonable adjustments to physical features of premises applies only to your own premises. There is no duty to make adjustments to a disabled worker's own home, even if they work from there, nor to other premises which the person may visit during their work.

There is no qualifying period of time that a disabled person must have worked to be eligible for rights under the *DDA*. Indeed, a number of compensation claims have involved candidates applying for jobs who were not provided with suitable conditions during their interview. But employees of small firms (currently defined as those employing fewer than 15 employees) are presently excluded from protection.

Building alterations

Part III of the *DDA* makes it unlawful for those providing goods, facilities or services to the public and those selling, letting or managing premises to discriminate against disabled people in certain circumstances. There is no exemption for small businesses from this provision.

Leasing premises

If your organisation rents its premises, the lease may impose conditions which prevent certain alterations. In this case, the *DDA* overrides the terms of the lease. The organisation should write to the landlord asking for permission to make the alteration in order to comply with the duty of reasonable adjustment. You do not have to make the alteration until the landlord has given permission. The landlord must reply within 21 days or within a longer time if reasonable. The landlord cannot unreasonably withhold consent for an alteration, but may attach reasonable conditions. Those selling or renting property do not have to make adjustments to the property to make it accessible – that is the job of the tenant or buyer.

If a disabled person brings a discrimination claim, the employer can ask the tribunal to call the landlord as a party to the proceedings. The tribunal will then decide whether the landlord has unreasonably withheld consent for or imposed unreasonable conditions on making alterations. If the tribunal orders the landlord to pay compensation, it cannot require the employer to do so as well. But it can authorise the employer to carry out a specified alteration.

Public access

Those providing a service to members of the public have until 2004 to comply fully with the *DDA*. Specifically:

- Since December 1996, it has been unlawful for service providers to treat disabled people less favourably.

- Since 1 October 1999, service providers have had to make reasonable adjustments for disabled people, such as providing extra help or making changes to the way they provide their services.

- From October 2004, service providers will have to consider making reasonable adjustments to the physical features of their premises to overcome physical barriers to access.

Remedies

People with disabilities who believe they have been subjected to discrimination may complain to an employment tribunal within three months of the act complained of. The tribunal can:

- make a declaration of each party's rights

- order the employer to pay compensation

- recommend that the employer take action to remedy the problem (by making a reasonable adjustment, for example) within a specified period

If the employer fails to follow a tribunal recommendation without reasonable justification, the tribunal can award compensation, or increase an existing award. Compensation is unlimited, and ran into six figures even in one of the earliest disability discrimination cases, *British Sugar v Kirker*.[12] The damages can include an award for injury to feelings.

In line with the *SDA* and the *RRA*, the *DDA* makes employers vicariously liable for discriminatory acts by employees carried out in the course of their employment. This is unless the employer can prove it took reasonably practicable steps to prevent the employee doing such acts.

Contract workers

Again like the *SDA* and the *RRA*, the *DDA* outlaws discrimination by those who hire contract workers. Facilities managers who contract work out to a disabled person or someone who becomes disabled must not discriminate:

- in the terms on which they allow the worker to do the work

- by not allowing the worker to do or continue to do the work

- in the way they give the worker access to benefits or by refusing to give access to benefits
- by subjecting the worker to any other detriment

The hiring organisation must include contract workers in the count of their employees for the purposes of determining whether the small firms' exemption applies under the *DDA*.

Disability Rights Commission

The Disability Rights Commission came into operation in April 2000. It has a role similar to that of the Equal Opportunities Commission and Commission for Racial Equality.

Equal Treatment Directive

In 2000, member states agreed the *Equal Treatment Framework Directive*, which will harmonise anti-discrimination legislation across Europe. Member states have until 2 December 2003 to introduce legislation prohibiting discrimination in employment on the grounds of sexual orientation, race or religion. By 2 December 2006, they must have legislation to prevent disability and age discrimination (the UK negotiated this extension to the

---

How accessible are your premises?

- Are there disabled parking spaces with space for a wheelchair alongside a car?
- Are signs clearly written?
- Is there a ramp to the entrance?
- Are steps provided with a handrail, good lighting and clearly marked edges?
- Are glass doors marked for visibility, and are there handles at the correct height?
- Is there an induction loop in the reception area, and is the reception desk the right height?
- Are walkways free of obstructions?
- Are entrance doors wide enough?
- Is seating height adjustable?
- If telephones are fixed on the wall, can they be reached? Are minicoms provided?
- Are flashing and audible alarms provided? Are personal vibrating alarms provided for disabled employees?

original deadline). The Directive complements a second Directive on race discrimination, which member states must implement by 19 July 2003.

Under the *Equal Treatment Directive*, the UK will have to remove the small employer exemption in the *DDA*. Also, the police and various other public services will no longer be exempt from the *DDA*, although it will not have to apply to the armed forces. This will bring organisations employing some seven million workers within the legislation.

In all areas, the *Equal Treatment Directive* does allow employers to discriminate if there is a "genuine occupational requirement". On age discrimination, there are further defences that will allow employers to have different wages or different qualification requirements for younger or older workers. A mandatory retirement age is not considered age discrimination.

The earliest major change expected as a result of the Directive is the introduction of UK legislation banning discrimination on grounds of sexual orientation. Pressure is growing on the Government to act quickly because of incompatibility between the *Human Rights Act 1998* and the lack of protection from discrimination for gay and lesbian workers. This was highlighted by a controversial Scottish ruling in 2000 on the dismissal of a gay RAF serviceman, Mr MacDonald, by the Ministry of Defence.[13]

The Scottish Employment Appeal Tribunal ruled that the meaning of 'sex' in the *SDA* was ambiguous, entitling it to interpret the Act in accordance with the *European Convention on Human Rights*, so as to bar discrimination on grounds of sexual orientation. In June 2001, the Court of Session (Scotland's equivalent of the Court of Appeal), overturned this decision, pointing out that 'sex' clearly means gender, not sexual orientation. But only two judges agreed on this – the third sided with the EAT judge, leaving a split of opinion that only the new legislation can resolve.

There was a similar 2:1 split in a subsequent UK Court of Appeal decision, in which it was found that a lesbian teacher was not protected under the *SDA*.[14]

In the areas of sex and race discrimination, the two European Directives are expected to have little impact in the UK. The *SDA* and *RRA* already provide protection from discrimination, which, generally, exceeds the Directives' minimum requirements.

Equal pay

One area of sex discrimination law where the Government has issued proposals for change, however, is the *Equal Pay Act 1970*. Women earn, on average, 18% less than their male counterparts, and the aim of the proposals is to simplify and speed up claims for equal pay.

The main proposed change is to backdate any shortfall in earnings to six years. At the moment, successful claimants may only receive two years' worth of earnings arrears when they have been underpaid. Employees will still have to bring their claim within six months of the end of their employment.

Sex discrimination

Moreover, on 12 October, the *Sex Discrimination (Indirect Discrimination and Burden of Proof) Regulations 2001* were introduced. These implement the *Burden of Proof Directive* which member states agreed in 1997.

One of the changes that the Regulations introduce is a reversal in the burden of proof in sex discrimination cases so that it lies with the employer. At the moment, the legal burden is technically on the claimant to prove that their treatment was discriminatory.

In practice, however, the amendment does little but confirm what UK case law has already established. In *King v The Great Britain-China Centre*,[15] the Court of Appeal ruled that where the employer is unable to explain a difference in treatment, it is open to the tribunal to infer that the treatment was discriminatory. The case was concerned with race discrimination, but the ruling on the burden of proof has been applied to sex discrimination cases by analogy.

Of greater significance is the new definition of indirect sex discrimination set out in the Regulations. The old definition said that an employee could prove indirect sex discrimination if they had to comply with a "requirement or condition" with which fewer women than men (or men than women) could comply. Under the new definition, employees have to show there was a "provision, criterion or practice" with which fewer women than men (or men than women) could comply. They no longer have to prove that they themselves were unable to comply, just that there is a generally detrimental effect on one sex.

For example, a woman may claim indirect sex discrimination because her employer has refused her request to return to work part-time following maternity leave. At the moment, she has to prove that her employer's attitude amounts to a "requirement" to work full-time, and that she personally cannot comply with this requirement. When city worker Aisling Sykes brought such a claim, she failed, because her employer showed that she was paid enough to afford a nanny.

Now, the woman merely needs to prove that there is a general 'practice' against part-time working, and that this is detrimental to women generally because of their family commitments.

Unfair dismissal

Before the introduction of the *Employment Relations Act 1999*, employees had to have worked continuously for two years for the same employer before they had the right to claim unfair dismissal. The maximum award they could claim was £12,000.

The Act reduced the service requirement to one year and raised the maximum compensatory award to £50,000. It also index-linked the award, which now stands at £51,700. The changes mean not only that more people are entitled to bring a claim, but also that it is more worthwhile to bring a claim, especially for higher earners. The Government has stated its intention to reduce the qualifying period further, to six months' continuous employment.

The Act also abolished the practice of those employed on fixed-term contracts of a year or more waiving their right to claim unfair dismissal. The waivers had been intended to prevent workers suing their employer for ending their contract when it expired. But the Government was concerned that unscrupulous employers were denying individuals their employment rights by forcing them into a series of short-term contracts. Waiving rights to redundancy payments remains lawful, although there are proposals to stop this practice too.

Automatic unfair dismissal

Employment tribunals will rule that a dismissal was automatically unfair if the employee was sacked:

- for exposing poor health and safety (protected under section 100 of the *Employment Rights Act 1996*)
- for maternity-related reasons
- for asserting a statutory right
- as part of a redundancy exercise for any of the above reasons
- for being a member of a trade union, or participating in union activities
- for having a spent conviction or failing to disclose it
- as part of a *TUPE* transfer
- for refusing to work on Sundays (shopworkers only)
- for blowing the whistle on fraud, malpractice or dangerous practice in breach of the *Public Interest Disclosure Act 1998*

- acting as a companion during a disciplinary or grievance hearing

The *Employment Relations Act* additionally made it automatically unfair to dismiss an employee for a reason connected with:

- parental leave
- pregnancy and childbirth
- ordinary, compulsory or additional maternity leave
- time off for domestic reasons
- participation in the first eight weeks of industrial action
- acting as a companion during a disciplinary or grievance hearing

In most of these situations, the employee does not need to have been employed for a year before bringing a claim.

Workplace surveillance

Used properly, e-mail and the internet are a real asset to businesses, allowing employees to communicate rapidly with clients and carry out research online. Used improperly (to forward jokes, games and indecent photographs, for example), they can not only affect productivity, but expose the employer to legal action. These problems explain the growing popularity of monitoring employees' e-mail and internet use, and the introduction of laws aimed at ensuring such surveillance does not infringe employees' right to privacy.

Surveys suggest that 72% of pornographic sites are viewed during working hours, 56% of employees shop online at work, and 90% of economic computer crime is committed by employees. In September 2000, Orange dismissed 45 people for circulating pornography, and the previous July, Dow Chemicals dismissed 50 workers and disciplined 200 more for the same reason. In 1999, the New York Times fired 23 employees for spreading offensive e-mails, and Xerox have sacked 40 staff for spending too long surfing the web.

Nevertheless, employees have a right to privacy when they use telecommunications systems, as the Alison Halford case[16] showed in 1997. Ms Halford, a senior police officer, alleged her private work telephone was tapped without her knowledge. The European Court of Human Rights found this breached her right under article 8 of the *European Convention of Human Rights* to respect for private and family life, home and correspondence.

At the end of 2000, the Government and regulators introduced various controls that seek to resolve the conflict between employers' need to protect their interests through electronic surveillance and employees' right to privacy. But much of the legislation has been introduced piecemeal and there appear to be inherent legal conflicts.

Why monitor?

There are a number of reasons why employers are keen to monitor e-mail and internet use. These include the following legal issues and concerns:

- Employees may inadvertently form binding contracts through e-mail – the tone may be chatty, but an e-mail's legal effect is the same as a formal letter.

- Carelessly worded e-mails could be defamatory or libellous – in a well-publicised case,[17] Norwich Union was sued after two of its employees exchanged defamatory e-mails about Western Provident, and reportedly settled for £450 000.

- Downloading or disseminating copyright material (as an e-mail attachment, for example) could lead to intellectual property disputes.

- Employers could face criminal charges if employees download pornography or hack into external computer systems.

- Employers might be vicariously liable for e-mails or downloads that harass fellow employees. In *Morse v Future Reality*,[18] a woman employee who shared a room with men who downloaded explicit material from the internet resigned and claimed sex discrimination. Her employer was found liable because it was aware of the men's behaviour and failed to prevent it.

- Employees could hack into their employer's confidential database, putting it in breach of the seventh data protection principle (ensuring data remains secure).

- Employers may commit a breach of confidence if an employee forwards on confidential material e-mailed by a client – or employers may face their own trade secrets or confidential information being disclosed.

- Employers can be liable for unlicensed software on their system, downloaded by employees.

- Monitoring how long employees spend typing may be useful for health and safety purposes, to prevent repetitive strain injury.

RIP to privacy?

In October 2000, the Government introduced the *Regulation of Investigatory Powers Act (RIPA)*. This restricts employers from intercepting employees' e-mails and telephone calls unless they believe both employees and the other party to the communication have agreed. What constitutes reasonable grounds for believing that consent has been given is not, however, entirely clear.

On 24 October 2000, the Government tried to clear up the confusion by bringing in extra Regulations under the Act. These are the *Telecommunications (Lawful Business Practice) (Interception of Communications) Regulations*. These allow employers more scope to monitor employees' communications, provided they meet all the following three criteria:

- the communication being monitored must be made in the course of business
- the employer must have taken all reasonable efforts to inform employees about the monitoring (there is no requirement to inform the party with whom they are communicating)
- the monitoring must be for one of the lawful purposes set out in the Regulations, including:
  - to establish facts relevant to the business
  - to ascertain employees' compliance with the law and self-regulatory policies or procedures
  - to ascertain whether employees are meeting the organisation's standards
  - to prevent or detect crime
  - to investigate or detect unauthorised use of the telecommunications system
  - to ensure the system's effective operation

Organisations may also monitor (but not record) communications without consent in order to:

- determine whether or not communications are business-related
- monitor communications to a confidential support helpline

An employer who routinely monitors e-mail traffic to ensure the system is used for business purposes only will act within the Regulations. Employers also do not need to obtain the prior consent of both senders and recipients. They are simply required to make all reasonable efforts to inform them that the messages may be monitored.

Laws on privacy

There is no privacy law as such in the UK. Employers who believe that the Regulations give them a green light to snoop on staff may, however, be in for a shock. There is an implied term of mutual trust and confidence in all employment contracts, which controls, to some extent, the behaviour which employees should reasonably have to endure.

In addition, there is the *Human Rights Act 1998*, which took effect on 2 October 2000. This enshrines article 8 (see WORKPLACE SURVEILLANCE, P108) in UK law, and blanket monitoring of phone calls, e-mails and internet use could violate this right. The Act is directly enforceable only against public bodies, but private companies are also likely to be affected. This is because the courts are public authorities, and have to interpret any ambiguities in the law in accordance with the Act. So they could declare *RIPA* incompatible with the human rights convention, which would put pressure on (although not oblige) the Government to change the legislation.

Private companies might feel the effects of the *Human Rights Act* more directly if they dismiss an employee and, for example, want to use an abusive e-mail to defend their decision before an employment tribunal. If the employee can show the e-mail was obtained in breach of their human rights, the tribunal may not allow the evidence, destroying the employer's justification for the dismissal.

Employers can, however, justify intrusion into private and family life if their reasons were to protect the rights and freedoms of others. So, for example, they can defend surveillance by citing their right not to have employees wasting their time at work, or the right of other employees not to receive offensive e-mails.

Personal data code

Finally, the Information Commissioner (formerly known as the Data Protection Commissioner) has drafted a Code of Practice on the use of personal data in employer/employee relationships[19] (see DRAFT DATA PROTECTION CODE, P112). She supports much tighter restrictions on corporate electronic eavesdropping than the *Lawful Business Practice Regulations* provide for. The draft code states that routine monitoring of business communications may unfairly "intrude on an employee's privacy or autonomy".

The draft code expressly states that it was prepared before the final amendments to the *Lawful Business Practice Regulations* were available. Some legal experts are confident that the ultimate version of the code will take account of, and be consistent with, those Regulations. However, the Information Commissioner has so far refused to back down on the issue, and a final version of the code has yet to be agreed.

It is also important to note that the *Data Protection Act 1998* itself requires employers to:

- process data fairly and lawfully (first data protection principle)
- obtain personal data for a lawful purpose and not to process it in a manner incompatible with that purpose (second data protection principle)

These principles apply regardless of the *Lawful Business Practice Regulations*.

Draft data protection code

E-mail monitoring

The code states that:

- Employers should monitor e-mail traffic rather than the content of specific e-mails to determine whether they are business-related.
- Where it is necessary to monitor the content of e-mails (for virus detection purposes, for example), employers should use an automated process.
- In the case of external e-mails, employers must at all times consider the privacy of the non-employee party to the communication and any third party referred to in the message.
- Under no circumstances should an employer open an e-mail that is clearly personal.

Internet monitoring

The code states that:

- Any monitoring must be a proportionate response to the risk faced by the employer. It is better to use monitoring to prevent rather than to detect misuse.
- The employer should not monitor the sites visited if it can achieve the business purpose for which it undertakes the monitoring by simply recording the time an employee spends on the internet.
- If the purpose of the monitoring is to detect the downloading of pornography, any information obtained should be disregarded unless it poses a significant risk to the employer. In assessing the results, the employer must take account of the ease with which websites can be visited accidentally.

There is, moreover, the threat of legal challenge against the Government. Both the TUC and the civil rights organisation Liberty claim the *Lawful Business Practice Regulations* breach the *Human Rights Act*. The European Commission's Information Commissioner is also investigating four possible breaches of European law.

Practical considerations

Whatever the legislation permits employers to do, there are sensible business reasons for avoiding blanket monitoring. Not only will Orwellian surveillance tactics be bad for industrial relations, but the logistics of tracking every employee's every communication are mind-boggling.

Similarly, the simplest policy from a legal viewpoint might be an outright ban on personal calls, e-mails and internet use. This may cut down on the employer's areas of vulnerability, but will disillusion existing staff and deter prospective employees. The problem is not, however, entirely new. Employers are used to dealing with personal use of the telephone, and a policy which expands on this, allowing limited and reasonable use of the system, including e-mail and the internet, is a sensible way forward.

Drawing up a policy

So rather than waiting for the authorities to sort themselves out, facilities managers should ensure they draw up clear guidelines for employees on using e-mail and the internet. In the event of abuse, these will allow the employer to dismiss the employee in accordance with the disciplinary procedure.

Employers cannot, however, change employees' existing contracts without their agreement. It is therefore important to make changes in a reasonable manner, and to explain why they are necessary.

The TUC suggests that an e-mail and internet policy should:

- warn users that e-mails may be electronically scanned for obscene, indecent, racist or illegal remarks
- allow for the occasional and reasonable personal use of e-mail, as long as this does not interfere with an employee's work
- give assurances that e-mails between union reps and members will not be monitored or read by managers
- remind employees that their e-mails may be checked by others at work if they are unexpectedly absent or have gone on leave without giving forwarding arrangements

Other measures which employment lawyers suggest include:

- ensuring that confidentiality statements and disclaimers are added to the bottom of any e-mail
- giving warnings where incoming e-mails may be monitored
- warning employees to treat e-mails to customers and suppliers as formal documents
- indicating an acceptable level of personal e-mail and internet use
- pointing out that computers and e-mail systems are company property
- warning staff about viruses and the danger of opening e-mail attachments from unknown senders
- banning all unauthorised software and explaining why this is the case
- obtaining express written consent from employees that their e-mails may be monitored – they cannot then later claim they were unaware of any policy
- encrypting confidential e-mails wherever possible
- warning employees against sending e-mails that criticise other organisations or harass individuals
- making employees aware of copyright rules
- clearly spelling out the disciplinary action that will follow any breach of the policy

As well as inserting clauses into employment contracts, it is also advisable to use on-screen warning messages when staff log on.

Disciplinary and grievance hearings

On 4 September 2000, a new right came into force for employees to be accompanied at disciplinary and grievance hearings. The right is set out in section 10 of the *Employment Relations Act 1999*. The employer must, if the worker makes a "reasonable" request, permit them to be accompanied by a single companion of their choice.

The companion is allowed to address the disciplinary or grievance hearing, but not to answer questions on the worker's behalf. They may, however, confer with the worker during the hearing.

A person is entitled to accompany the worker if they are:

- a trade union official as defined in sections 1 and 119 of the *Trade Union and Labour Relations (Consolidation) Act 1992*

- a trade union official whom the union has reasonably certified in writing has experience of or training in acting as a worker's companion
- another of the employer's workers

There is no qualifying period for enjoying the right to be accompanied.

A disciplinary hearing is one which could lead the employer to:
- administer a formal warning
- take some other action in respect of the worker
- confirm a warning issued or some other action taken

A grievance hearing is one which "concerns the performance of a duty by an employer in relation to a worker".

There is no right to be accompanied during an informal interview, although such an interview should be terminated if it becomes clear part-way through that formal action may be needed.

The employer must reschedule the hearing if:
- the chosen companion is not available at the employer's proposed time, and
- the worker proposes a reasonable alternative time within five days of the original date

A worker may complain to a tribunal if they were not allowed a chosen companion or to reschedule a hearing. The maximum compensation is two weeks' pay, currently capped at £230 a week. More seriously, the worker will almost certainly also claim that any dismissal following the disciplinary hearing was unfair.

Workers who act as companions are also protected from any detriment while seeking to exercise their right to accompany a fellow worker. If they are dismissed, the dismissal will automatically be unfair, regardless of their length of service.

Minimum wage

The *National Minimum Wage Act* was passed in 1998, and has been amended by subsequent secondary legislation. As of 1 October 2001, workers aged 22 and over must be paid at least £4.10 an hour, and workers aged 18–21 must receive a "development" rate of at least £3.50 an hour. From October 2002, the adult rate will be a minimum of £4.20 per hour, and the development rate will be a minimum of £3.60 per hour.

According to DTI guidance:[11]

- Employers will need to keep records to prove that they are paying the national minimum wage to their workers.

- Employers may be required by the worker, an Inland Revenue compliance officer, an employment tribunal or a civil court to produce evidence that they have paid the national minimum wage.

- If an employer fails to produce records to a worker on request, the worker may complain to an employment tribunal, which can impose a penalty.

- The burden of proof in a minimum wage dispute is on the employer, which must demonstrate to a tribunal or civil court that it has complied with the law.

- Where an employer has failed to pay the national minimum wage, compliance officers can require it to pay arrears by issuing an enforcement notice.

- If the employer fails to comply with the enforcement notice, compliance officers have the power to issue a penalty notice against the employer.

- It is a criminal offence to refuse to pay the national minimum wage, to obstruct compliance officers or not to keep proper records; fines for these offences can be up to £5,000.

Public interest disclosure

The *Public Interest Disclosure Act 1998* is more commonly known as the 'Whistleblowing' Act. It provides protection to workers who 'blow the whistle' on wrongdoing within their organisation. The Act was introduced following a series of disasters, such as the explosion on the Piper Alpha oil rig, and scandals, such as the collapse of BCCI, which might have been prevented if people with inside knowledge of the organisation had spoken out publicly.

A worker is protected if, acting in good faith, they reasonably believe their disclosure shows at least one of the following is happening now, has happened, or is likely to happen in the future:

- a criminal offence
- breach of a legal obligation
- a miscarriage of justice
- a danger to the health or safety of any individual
- damage to the environment

- deliberate covering up of information tending to show any of the above

They must make the disclosure:

- either to their employer, whether directly or through agreed procedures
- or to another person whom the worker reasonably believes to be solely or mainly responsible for dealing with such concerns (a "prescribed person")

So, for example, the worker might notify their trade union safety representative, the HSE or their local authority of a breach of health and safety regulations, or the Environment Agency of environmental risks.

There are different conditions attached, depending on whom the worker contacts. A disclosure to a legal adviser must be made in the course of obtaining legal advice. A disclosure can be made to a government minister (either directly or via a departmental official) if the worker is employed in a public body and acts in good faith.

If a failure is exceptionally serious, the worker may safely make a disclosure provided they act in good faith, do not act for personal gain, and reasonably believe the allegation is substantially true. But it must be reasonable for the worker to make the disclosure to the person chosen.

There are similar restrictions on a worker blowing the whistle publicly (to the media, for example) rather than informing their employer or a prescribed person. They may only go public if they fulfil the good faith, lack of personal gain and substantially true tests and also meet at least one of the following conditions:

- The worker reasonably believes they would be subjected to a detriment by their employer if they made the disclosure to the employer or a prescribed person.

- In the absence of an appropriate prescribed person, the worker reasonably believes that disclosure to the employer would result in the destruction or concealment of information about the wrongdoing.

- The worker has previously disclosed substantially the same information to their employer or a prescribed person.

Employees who are dismissed as a result of making a protected disclosure can claim unfair dismissal, while workers can claim they have been subjected to a detriment. If a tribunal upholds an unfair dismissal complaint, it will order re-instatement or re-employment, or the payment of compensation. If it upholds a complaint of being subjected to a detriment, it may order compensation.

References

1. *Sindicato de Médicos de Asistencia Publics (SIMAP) v Conselleria de Sanidad y Consumo de la Generalidad Valenciana,* case C-303/98

2. See *www.dti.gov.uk*

3. See *www.dti.gov.uk/er/fixed/*

4. *Montgomery v Johnson Underwood Ltd* [2001] IRLR 269

5. *Süzen v Zehnacker Gebäudereinigung GmbH Krankenhausservice* [1997] IRLR 255

6. *ECM (Vehicle Delivery Service) v Cox & Others* [1999] IRLR 559

7. *RCO Support Services & Aintree Hospital v Unison & Others* [2000] IRLR 624

8. *Spikjkers v Gebroeders Benedik Abbatoir CV & Another* [1986] ECR 1119

9. *ADI (UK) Ltd v Willer & others,* 22/6/01, CA (unreported)

10. See *www.dti.gov.uk/er/tupe/consult.htm* (consultation closes on 15 December 2001)

11. See the 'employment relations' section of the DTI website at *www.dti.gov.uk*

12. *British Sugar Plc v Kirker* [1998] IRLR 624

13. *Secretary of State for Defence v MacDonald* [2001] IRLR 431

14. *Pearce v The Governing Body of Mayfield School* [2001] EWCA Civ 1347

15. *King v The Great Britain-China Centre* [1991] IRLR 51

16. *Halford v United Kingdom* [1997] IRLR 471

17. *Western Provident v Norwich Union* [2000] (unreported)

18. *Morse v Future Reality Ltd* [1996] (unreported)

19. See *www.dataprotection.gov.uk*

Timetable for new employment legislation

Area of reform	Date of change	Summary
Fixed-term employees	10 July 2001 (delayed)	Deadline for introducing regulations preventing less favourable treatment of fixed-term employees
Sex discrimination	12 October 2001	Burden of proof shifts from claimant to employer; new definition of indirect sex discrimination
Equal pay claims	mid-July 2001	Underpaid workers can claim up to six years' backdated pay instead of the current two years
Minimum wage	October 2001	Increase in adult rate to £4.10 per hour and in development rate to £3.50 per hour
Employment agencies	autumn 2001	Draft Regulations requiring clearer contracts between agencies, job-seekers and hirers to be finalised
TUPE	15 December 2001	Consultation ends on reforms to transfers of undertakings legislation
Personal data code	December 2001	Draft Code of Practice on the use of personal data in the employment relationship to be finalised
Parental leave	no date announced	Parents of under-fives born before 15 December 1999 to receive 13 weeks' parental leave
Unfair dismissal	no date announced	Right to claim unfair dismissal to be extended to employees with six months' continuous service
Statutory maternity pay	April 2002	Statutory maternity pay to go up to £75 a week
Minimum wage	October 2002	Increase in adult rate to £4.20 and in development rate to £3.60
Maternity leave	April 2003	Statutory maternity pay to go up to £100 a week; women to receive 26 weeks' paid maternity leave and 26 weeks' unpaid leave
Paternity leave	2003	Fathers to receive two weeks' paid paternity leave
Adoption leave	2003	Adoptive parents to receive maternity and paternity leave
Race discrimination	19 July 2003	Deadline for implementing Directive on race and racial origins
Equal Treatment Directive	2 December 2003	Deadline for implementing sexual orientation and religion provisions
National Works Councils	2007	Employers of more than 150 people must comply with Information and Consultation Directive
Equal Treatment Directive	2 December 2006	Deadline for implementing age and disability provisions
National Works Councils	2009	Employers of 101–150 people must comply with Information and Consultation Directive
National Works Councils	2011	Employers of 51–100 people must comply with Information and Consultation Directive

3 Property Law

Amanda Benham, Nick Edwards and Nick Croft

Acquiring, selling and developing property for a company portfolio is a complex process. Company directors are increasingly calling on facilities managers to oversee this process and to report and advise on how to maximise the value of a property and minimise risks. Negotiating lease terms, ensuring any necessary planning permission is secured and procuring valuations all fall within the facilities manager's remit. A knowledge of the legal issues relevant to a company's portfolio is, therefore, a vital tool. It provides the facilities manager with a basis from which to navigate the complex legal processes encompassing property law, from acquisition and disposals, to planning, to liability for environmental clean-up – knowledge which will substantially impact on a company's costs.

Acquisition and disposal

This section is aimed at those wanting to acquire commercial property in England and Wales for their own use. It outlines the procedures involved and highlights particular considerations to be borne in mind. It does not deal with the ways in which an acquisition could be funded or structured.

Scotland and Northern Ireland have different legal systems, and local legal advice should be taken.

How is property owned?

Leasehold and freehold

Property in England and Wales is owned freehold or leasehold.

Freehold ownership is absolute. An owner of a freehold property owns it until disposal.

Leasehold ownership is limited in time. Leasehold is when an owner (a landlord or lessor) enters into a lease with a tenant or lessee to transfer the property to the tenant for a specified period of time (the term) in exchange for payment. The payment will either be a lump sum (a premium) or a periodic payment (rent) or a combination.

The tenant may also, subject again to the provision of the lease, create a further lease interest known as a sub-lease or underlease. This sub-lease must be for a shorter term than the original lease. In turn, further sub-leases can be created provided they are for shorter terms.

The system of land registration

The owner of a freehold or leasehold interest in land must be able to prove ownership or 'title'. Title either consists of documents of ownership (deeds) where title is unregistered, or a 'land certificate' where the title has been registered at the Land Registry. When title has been proved to the satisfaction of the Land Registry, the land is given a title number and a grade. Once title has been registered, a landowner need only show an official copy of the Land Registry entries as evidence of ownership. There are still parts of England and Wales which are unregistered.

Professional advisers – who does what

The estate agent

When no independent broker is involved, the seller's agent usually acts as the broker. The agent introduces prospective buyers and sellers, will show a prospective buyer around various properties and will often act as the go-between in the negotiations of the price and terms between the parties. In more substantial transactions the buyer may ask an agent to find a suitable property and to negotiate on its behalf. Offers should be made 'subject to contract' and 'subject to survey'. This means that the buyer will not be bound to buy the property if the result of the survey is not satisfactory or until the bargain struck between the parties has been properly and legally recorded and all relevant investigations made.

The surveyor

A surveyor will carry out a physical inspection of the property to check for structural or other physical problems. The survey result is sometimes used by the buyer to renegotiate its offer. A survey is not the same as a valuation. If a buyer obtains finance from a bank or other lending institution in connection with an acquisition, the bank will want to satisfy itself that the amount of the loan is sufficiently covered by the value of the property. It will therefore obtain a valuation. Unlike a survey, a valuation will not contain any detailed comments on the state of repair of the property or on any structural problems.

The solicitor

The buyer's solicitor will:

- negotiate and agree the terms of the contract by which the buyer agrees to buy the property (the first draft of the contract is usually prepared by the seller's solicitor)

- prepare the transfer document transferring the ownership of the property to the buyer

- negotiate and agree the terms of the lease, if a new lease is to be taken by the purchaser (again, the first draft of the lease is usually prepared by the landlord's solicitor)

- make all relevant title and other searches in order to build up a factual picture of the history and present status of the property

- arrange for exchange of contracts – this is when the matter becomes legally binding

- carry out 'completion' or 'closure'

- carry out registration and stamping formalities, following completion

Buying property

Buying property in England and Wales is a two-stage procedure.

The first stage ends in an exchange of contracts, when the parties enter into a legally binding agreement for the sale and purchase of the property, but have not paid the price or completed the transaction.

The second stage culminates in the formality of the purchase documents being signed and payment of the purchase price, at which point the transaction is said to have completed.

Exchange of contracts

The stage preceding the exchange of contracts is the most important. All legal issues must be settled and the buyer must be satisfied on all aspects of the transaction before exchange. All the searches and title investigations are done at this stage. Once contracts have been exchanged, the buyer cannot object to the terms of the contract or to anything about the title or the physical condition of the property. The contract is prepared in duplicate, a copy being signed by each party. The copies are then exchanged. It is at this stage that the buyer is committed to buy and the seller is committed to sell a specific property at a specific price. On exchange, a deposit of 10% of the purchase price is usually paid. If a buyer fails to complete through no fault of the seller, it risks losing the deposit.

On exchange of contracts, the 'beneficial' interest in the property is passed to the buyer, so it will need to insure the property from that date.

Completion

Legal title does not pass until completion of the transaction. It is traditional to have some period between exchange and completion, during which the buyer's solicitor will:

- carry out final searches
- make practical arrangements for collection and transmission of purchase monies
- prepare the transfer document which transfers title to the property to the buyer

The period between exchange and completion is flexible and may be for whatever period the parties agree, but is usually no more than four weeks.

On completion the balance of the purchase price is paid and thereafter the buyer owns the property. If the transaction needs to be registered at the Land Registry, this is done immediately following completion.

If the property is being purchased with borrowed money, the mortgage documentation is usually completed at the same time as the completion of the purchase.

Costs involved

Apart from the professional fees, the following taxes and statutory fees are payable when acquiring property in England and Wales:

Tax

Stamp duty

Stamp duty is payable on purchases of freehold and existing leasehold. The duty is normally paid by the buyer or the tenant and must be paid within one month of completion. Stamp duty is also payable upon the grant of a new lease and is calculated according to the amount of premium paid (if any), the annual rent and the length of the term. It is possible to mitigate stamp duty in appropriate situations. Advice should be taken early in the transaction. For details of the current UK rates, see FINANCIAL MANAGEMENT, P212.

Value added tax

The current full rate of value added tax (VAT) is 17.5%. Where the price or rent is subject to VAT, the seller or landlord must pay it to Customs and Excise, and will normally collect it from the buyer or tenant.

A person selling the freehold of a brand new building will usually need to charge VAT, although this can sometimes be avoided by taking a long lease at a premium instead.

This apart, a sale or lease will usually be subject to VAT only if the seller or landlord has 'opted to tax'. Once a person has opted to tax a building, then in general they are irrevocably obliged to charge VAT on rent received from tenants occupying it and on proceeds of sale from it. The main advantage of a person opting to tax a building is to enable them to reclaim from Customs and Excise the VAT charged on costs relating to the building, such as construction or refurbishment costs.

If VAT is charged on the purchase price or rent, the buyer or tenant may be able to reclaim it from Customs and Excise, depending on the use of the property. If it is used for a business which makes many exempt supplies (for example, as a bank or other financial business) all the VAT paid cannot be reclaimed, and so the VAT charge is a real cost for the buyer or tenant.

Many other businesses (for example, manufacturers and shops) can reclaim all or most of the VAT that they pay on costs. Unless the buyer negotiates to defer payment of VAT, the buyer or tenant will have a cash flow cost in paying VAT to the seller or landlord before recovering it from Customs and Excise. Where a buyer or tenant is entitled to reclaim, it can usually do so within one to four months. Exempt use of a property by a buyer within 10 years of its acquisition may oblige the buyer to repay to Customs and Excise some of the VAT reclaimed on the purchase price.

For a comprehensive list of these and other supplies liable to VAT, see FINANCIAL MANAGEMENT: VALUE ADDED TAX, PP209–212.

Other taxes

These include capital allowances (see FINANCIAL MANAGEMENT, P215), income tax and corporation tax.

Fees

Local land charges searches

There are various local authorities which maintain registers of planning and other matters affecting local properties. The buyer's solicitor will carry out a search at the local authority, for which a fee of around £150 is payable.

Land registry fees

In cases of dealings with registered land, a registration fee is payable. The fee is calculated on a sliding scale by reference to the acquisition value of the property, and currently runs from £40 for an acquisition of up to £40,000 to £800 for an acquisition of over £1 million. Fees are also payable upon first registration of previously unregistered land.

Other costs

Depending upon the location of the land and whether it is registered or unregistered, additional search fees will be payable. For example, a property may be in an area for which it is necessary to carry out a coal or other mining search. It will also be necessary to have a valuation carried out and often prudent to have a structural survey for which the surveyor will charge. Depending on the nature of the property to be bought, it may also be necessary to have an environmental audit carried out to assess whether the land is contaminated and potential liability for the costs of a clean-up of the land (see ENVIRONMENTAL MATTERS, PP152–154, for more on the law relating to contamination).

Acquisition for own use

Freehold or leasehold?

Before deciding whether to buy a freehold or a leasehold property, the buyer should analyse why and for what purpose the property is needed.

Generally speaking, a buyer with out-of-town site requirements needing to install plant and machinery that is not readily moveable will be more attracted to a freehold interest: there are fewer restrictions and the level of initial capital outlay is such that the buyer is looking for a long-term site. By contrast, the buyer requiring town centre office use may be better suited to a leasehold property at a market rent – that is, a lease of 25 years or less for little or no initial premium, but subject to an annual rent based on the market value of the building.

Traditionally, market rent leases were for terms of 20 or 25 years, with five-yearly rent reviews, usually on an upward only basis (see BUSINESS LEASES:

RENT REVIEW PROVISIONS, P130). In recent years, market forces have changed leasehold patterns, and it is now more usual for new leases to be granted for terms of 10 or 15 years and often for as little as five years. If the lease is for business purposes, the buyer as the tenant may have the right to renew the lease when it expires, subject to certain statutory restrictions (see BUSINESS LEASES: SECURITY OF TENURE, PP128–130 for more detail).

Leasehold: ongoing liability

A lease is essentially a contract between a landlord and a tenant. For leases granted before 1 January 1996, the rule is that the original tenant and the original landlord remain liable for their respective obligations under the lease for the duration of the lease term. This is the case even where the original tenant has sold its leasehold interest on to a new tenant, or where the original landlord has sold on its reversionary interest to a new landlord. This legal principle is known as 'privity of contract'. In practical terms, it means that where the original tenant has sold its interest to another who in turn fails to pay the rent, the landlord may seek payment of that rent from the original tenant. The original tenant is not free from its obligations even though it has parted with its interest in the property. The landlord is thus cushioned from the effects of tenant default by being able to look to the original tenant to meet the liability.

The *Landlord and Tenant (Covenants) Act 1995* (the *1995 Act*) has abolished original tenant liability in respect of 'new' leases, that is leases granted on or after 1 January 1996. The *1995 Act* provides that where a tenant sells its leasehold interest to the assignee, the selling-tenant is automatically released from further liability. There is an exception to this rule. A tenant will not be released if it has sold its lease without getting any requisite permission to do so from its landlord. Also, it is possible for a landlord to require a selling-tenant to give an 'authorised guarantee agreement' in respect of the buying-tenant's obligations under the lease. On a subsequent sale of the lease, this guarantee falls away.

The *1995 Act* means that a landlord loses the safety net that it had under the old principle of privity of contract. Landlords will need to be more concerned at the identity of proposed assignees. The *1995 Act* has given landlords greater power to control assignments, although such controls are in practice limited, not only by the relative bargaining strength of the landlord over that of the tenant, but also by the likely impact of restrictions in the lease on the next rent review. The more restrictive the lease, the lower the rent which can be demanded for a property. Both landlords and tenants favour continuing the recent trend towards much shorter lease terms and are wary of qualifications for assignment which are likely to have an adverse effect on future rent reviews.

The *1995 Act* also has implications for the landlord's liability. Although a tenant is generally automatically released from liability on a sale of the lease, the landlord is not automatically released from its liabilities on a sale of its reversionary interest. A landlord must request a release from the tenant. If the tenant refuses to give a release, the landlord may ask the court to grant one. If the court refuses, the landlord continues to be liable with the new landlord. If and when the new landlord chooses to sell its reversionary interest, the first landlord has a further opportunity to apply for a release.

Business leases

Businesses operate from the following types of premises:

- **freehold** – the occupier owns the premises outright for an unlimited length of time with few restrictions
- **leasehold** – the occupier has use of the premises for rent for a specified length of time
- **on licence** – the premises are used on flexible terms on a short-term basis

This section sets out the main provisions of a lease of business premises.

Parties

The lease specifies the names and addresses of the landlord, the tenant and any guarantor.

Premises let

The technical term for the premises let is 'demised premises'. Both parties should understand exactly what is being let. A lease sometimes refers to plans which outline the area let. If there are plans, they should be checked for accuracy.

Fixtures and fittings

Ownership of the plant and equipment in the premises is important, as someone has to maintain them. Also, the tenant might want to remove items when the lease expires. Sometimes items fixed to the premises by a tenant can become part of the premises, in which case the tenant is not entitled to remove them at the end of the lease, even though those items belong to it. If, however, the items were put there for the purpose of the tenant's trade and can be removed without causing irreparable damage to the premises, the tenant can remove them.

Rights granted

In order to make full use of the premises, the tenant will need rights over adjoining premises or land. These could include rights to use common parts in a building, such as lifts and car parking areas.

Exceptions and reservations

Just as the tenant requires to have rights over common parts, a landlord will want to be able to enter the tenant's premises in certain circumstances, for example to inspect the premises or to carry out repairs.

Term

This is the length of the lease. Traditionally, leases of business premises were long-term commitments, frequently of 25 years. Recently, much shorter leases have become more common. Sometimes the lease allows the tenant to end it at an earlier date than the contractual expiry. This is an 'option to break' or 'break clause'. If a lease contains such an option, it is important that the relevant date is diarised and a solicitor instructed well in advance of the exercise date so that the notice is dealt with properly and on time.

Security of tenure

Business leases are governed by a statutory code in the *Landlord and Tenant Act 1954* (*the 1954 Act*). Some business tenants enjoy 'security of tenure' – that is, the right to have a new lease granted when their current lease expires, subject to the following of a detailed notice and court procedure. The landlord can only deny this request in certain circumstances. It is, therefore, a valuable right. The following paragraphs provide only an introduction to this very complex subject.

The *1954 Act* applies to most leases where the property is occupied for the purposes of a business, unless the parties opt out of the *1954 Act* before the lease starts.

Termination

A lease protected by the *1954 Act* can only be determined by one of the methods prescribed by the *1954 Act*. These include notice given by the landlord or the tenant. A lease which is not determined by one of the methods set down in the *1954 Act* continues to run (despite expiry of the term) on the same terms until terminated by one of these methods.

Landlord's notice

A landlord's notice under the *1954 Act* must be in a special form and must specify a date (not earlier than the lease termination date and not less than six nor more than 12 months ahead) on which the lease is to end. The tenant must then notify the landlord whether or not it is willing to vacate the premises.

If the tenant wants a new lease, it must tell the landlord within two months of the landlord's notice and should make a special court application for a new tenancy, not less than two and not more than four months after the landlord's notice.

The landlord's grounds for opposing a new lease include:

- the tenant's failure to repair or pay rent, or its being in breach of other terms of the lease
- the landlord's intention to demolish or reconstruct the property
- the landlord requires possession for its own purposes

The time limits specified in the *1954 Act* for service of notices and applications to the court are strict and in general no extension of those limits is permitted.

Tenant's request for a new tenancy

A tenant's request for a new lease must be in a special form and must specify a date (not earlier than the lease termination date and not less than six nor more than 12 months ahead) for the start of the new lease. If the landlord wishes to object, it must tell the tenant within two months, stating on which statutory ground(s) it will rely. The tenant must then apply to the court for a new tenancy not less than two months and not more than four months from the service of its notice.

New lease

Unless the landlord can substantiate its objection to a new lease, a new lease must be granted. Usually this will be on similar terms to the previous one.

Compensation

If the landlord succeeds in obtaining vacant possession, based on a statutory ground which involves no fault on the part of the tenant, the tenant is entitled to compensation. In certain circumstances a tenant of business premises may also be entitled to compensation for improvements it carried out.

Rent

Rent control

There are no statutory limitations on the rent payable.

Payment of rent

The lease will specify the rent payable and when – usually quarterly or monthly. The 'usual quarter days' are 25 March, 24 June, 29 September and 25 December. Different days apply in Scotland. A landlord will generally issue a rent demand several days before rent is actually due and will expect payment to be made punctually and by banker's order. Rent is usually paid in advance, not arrears. For possible action to be taken by the landlord in the case of non-payment of rent, see P136.

Rent review provisions

Many leases contain rent review provisions. It is very common within the UK for leases to have provisions that protect the long-term investment of property from the landlord's point of view by enforcing 'upward only' rent reviews (meaning that the rent cannot fall).

Rent review provisions in leases can be complex. The dates for the reviews and the basis of the review are set out in the lease. Dates should be diarised and a solicitor and surveyor engaged to advise on the conduct of the review. The lease allows the landlord and the tenant to agree the new rent themselves for a certain period before the review date. If they cannot agree, the review can be referred to an independent surveyor to decide.

Rates and taxes

The tenant usually pays the rates and taxes imposed on the premises. A tenant pays VAT on its rent where the landlord has chosen to charge it (see VALUE ADDED TAX, P124).

Interest

Interest at a penal rate is payable on any late payments of rent and other sums due to the landlord under the lease.

Dealings

A lease will contain restrictions on a tenant disposing of its lease outright ('assignment'), sub-letting and sharing or disposing of occupation.

Assignment

A lease will usually say that the landlord's approval must be obtained for any assignment so that the landlord can be sure that the new tenant will be reliable. Usually, the landlord cannot take too long to give this approval and must not be unreasonable about it. The lease can impose conditions which must be met before assignment can take place.

Sub-letting

Similarly, a landlord will want to approve sub-lettings. Again, the landlord cannot take too long and must not be unreasonable.

Sharing occupation

A lease will usually contain restrictions with whom the tenant can share occupation, but it normally automatically permits sharing with companies which are in the same group as the tenant. Other forms of sharing normally require the landlord's prior approval.

Use

The lease will specify how and for what purposes the premises can be used, such as a shop or office. These restrictions can be enforced by an injunction (see also PLANNING: CONTRACTUALLY PERMITTED USE, P139).

Alterations

A tenant will often need to carry out alterations to the premises. The lease will set out what tenant's works are permitted or not. Most works will require the landlord's prior approval.

The lease will also allow the landlord to make the tenant 'reinstate' the premises at the end of the lease, undoing any work which it has done during the lease. A document called a 'schedule of dilapidations' is prepared and negotiated by the parties, setting out the work which needs to be done. Sometimes, specialist dilapidations surveyors need to be engaged.

When a landlord gives permission to a tenant to carry out works, the permission is often contained in a legal document called a 'licence for alterations'. It describes the works, attaching plans and specifications.

In certain circumstances, a tenant can claim compensation for improvements it has carried out to the premises during the leases, subject to a complicated notice procedure.

Repairs

The lease should set out clearly who is responsible for carrying out repairs to the premises. The definition of the premises actually let to the tenant is important. A tenant of an entire building will usually repair its entirety, at its expense. A tenant of part only of a building carries out internal repairs to its own premises and would contribute to the cost of repairing the whole building via a service charge.

New buildings

The tenant of a new building can find itself in the unenviable position of being required to make good 'inherent' or 'latent' defects in the design or construction of the building. Accordingly, when negotiating the terms of the lease of such a building, the tenant should:

- seek to shift liability for remedying inherent defects to the landlord
- require a duty of care agreement with the landlord's building contractor and professional team involved in the construction
- have the property surveyed and the plans and specifications reviewed by the tenant's advisers

Where these proposals are not acceptable to the landlord, it may be possible to agree a compromise – for example, that the landlord will rectify inherent defects which appear during a specified period of time. The landlord should also be prepared to agree to pursue its legal remedies in respect of inherent defects against third parties, wherever it is reasonable to do so.

Old buildings

An old building may not be in a state of complete repair but the lease will generally require the tenant to repair any defects which exist at the time of the lease. The tenant should have a survey to reveal any problems. Ideally, the landlord should remedy existing disrepair or compensate the tenant. Alternatively, it may be possible for the landlord and the tenant to agree a 'schedule of condition' (a detailed description of defects in the property accompanied by a set of photographs). The tenant's obligation could then say that the tenant will not be required to put the premises in any better condition than as evidenced by the schedule of condition.

Breach of repairing obligations

Where a tenant fails to repair, the landlord can either claim damages or, in limited circumstances, 'forfeit' (terminate) the lease. Alternatively, the landlord could enter the premises to carry out the repairs itself and claim the cost from the tenant.

Rights of access

The lease will allow the landlord to enter the premises let to inspect their condition, to carry out repairs where the tenant has failed to repair or to repair other parts of a building where such access is necessary. This is subject to the tenant being given advance notice and the landlord making good any damage caused.

Insurance

The lease will require either the landlord or the tenant (or both) to have various insurances. These relate to the premises, plate glass, plant, loss of rent and public liability. Consideration must be given as to which party should insure, whether the insurance should be in joint names and the sum for which and the risks against which the property should be insured. Where parts of a building are being let separately, the landlord insures the whole building and then seeks reimbursement from the tenants for the premiums.

The insurance should be repair on a full 'reinstatement basis' which means that the insurance cover should be sufficient to repair any damage or to rebuild.

What happens if the premises are damaged?

The tenant will be concerned with the following questions, which should be clearly covered by the terms of the lease:

- Does the rent cease to be payable until the damage is put right?
- Is there an obligation on one of the parties to reinstate?
- Are the costs of reinstatement covered by insurance?
- If reinstatement is prevented by factors which are outside the control of the parties, will the lease terminate and, if so, in what circumstances?
- If reinstatement does not take place and the destruction was caused by an insured risk, which party will own the insurance money?

Other financial considerations relating to insurance payable under the terms of a lease are covered in FINANCIAL MANAGEMENT: INSURANCE, P207.

Service charges

Service charges are payments made by a tenant, in addition to rent, to cover the cost of works and services. The amount payable may be fixed or variable according to the costs incurred.

Management arrangements

Either the landlord will carry out the management itself (with or without a managing agent) or pass it to a management company, which may be owned by the landlord, a third party or the tenants themselves.

The services

A tenant will be concerned to see the following services in most cases:

- repairs and maintenance of common areas
- redecoration
- provision of hot water, heating and lighting
- plant and machinery
- cleaning and refuse disposal
- employment of staff

Apportionment

The share of the landlord's total expenditure that will be reimbursed by a tenant will be a percentage or 'fair or due proportion' calculated by reference to the amount of space occupied or other factor.

Payment

The lease will require the tenant to make payments on account of service charge. There will then be a reconciliation procedure in the lease to deal with any difference between this provisional amount and the actual amount spent by the end of the year. Any shortfall is made up by the tenant and any over-payment is reimbursed or credited against future payments. The service charge accounts should be properly certificated by a suitably qualified surveyor or accountant.

Objections

The tenant will sometimes have the following objections relating to the service charge:

- that items have been included which should not have been

- that there has been a mistake in the calculations
- that the costs are excessive

The way to challenge the charges depends on the lease. Many leases rule out any challenge at all by providing that the surveyor's or accountant's certificate shall be final.

Reserve and sinking funds

A reserve fund is an 'expenditure equalisation fund' designed to avoid wide fluctuations in the amount of the service charges payable each year on account of relatively expensive and necessarily recurring items. As an alternative to asking tenants to pay every five years for expenditure such as the decoration of the exterior and the common parts of the building, the landlord makes an estimate of the likely costs in advance and collects this sum by five equal instalments over the years preceding the work.

A sinking fund is a replacement fund, by which a landlord aims to build up over many years a fund for the replacement of major items of plant and equipment, such as lifts and heating or air conditioning systems. The drawback for tenants is that these funds can be used to carry out improvements which ought to be carried out at the cost of the landlord rather than of the tenants.

A tenant will be concerned that reserve and sinking funds are kept separate from the landlord's own money to ensure that they do not form part of the landlord's assets on a bankruptcy or liquidation.

Options to terminate

A lease may contain an option for the parties or one of them to terminate the lease at a stated time or times, or on the happening of stated events before the contractual expiry date. This is known as an 'option to break' or 'option to terminate'.

Any matters which are made conditions to the exercise of an option must be very strictly observed. The notice exercising the option must be given within the specified period and any other conditions, such as having paid the rent and complied with the terms of the lease, must be observed. Even the most trifling breach can prevent the tenant from effectively exercising a break option.

Landlord's remedies for tenant breaches

Non-payment of rent

For failure to pay rent, the landlord may carry out the following:

- **Sue the tenant** – (or, if applicable, the tenant's guarantor or any previous tenant). Since 1 January 1996, a landlord can only recover arrears of rent from a previous tenant or guarantor of a previous tenant if it has first served an arrears notice on the previous tenant or guarantor specifying the amount to be claimed. That notice must be served within six months after the rent claimed first became due. Failure to serve the notice means that the rights of the landlord to recover the rent arrears is lost.

- **Seize the tenant's goods** – known as 'distraint'. The landlord may seize goods on the property equal to the value of the rent due (and costs incurred). This process is subject to restrictions and can only be used against goods belonging to the tenant.

- **Take rent from the deposit** – if applicable, the landlord may take the rent due from a tenant's deposit held and then, if necessary, take action in the courts against the tenant for reimbursement of the deposit fund.

- **Forfeit or terminate the lease** – in England and Wales, the tenant has certain statutory protections against forfeiture of its lease. The degree of protection varies depending upon the nature of the tenant's failure. This statutory protection is called 'relief from forfeiture'. Usually, the action is dropped if the tenant rectifies the breach.

Checklist: buying a business lease

A prospective purchaser of a lease of business premises should (in addition to the usual matters to be considered on a purchase) pay careful attention to:

- rent review
- repairing obligations
- service charges
- VAT implications
- whether the existing tenant is in breach of covenant giving the landlord the right to determine the lease
- the likelihood of a lease renewal being opposed by a landlord on other grounds, such as redevelopment
- provisions relating to dealings with the lease
- permitted use

Other breaches

For other breaches, the landlord may:

- if the lease permits it, remedy the breach itself and charge the tenant for the cost incurred
- forfeit or terminate the lease
- sue
- take action in the courts against the tenant (again, subject to certain statutory restrictions)

Planning

When companies assess their occupation requirements they rarely give high priority to planning issues. Are these companies running a high-risk strategy? What if a company occupies new premises, only to find that planning restrictions prevent it from operating from that site. Consider, for example, if:

- the planning permission which attaches to the site permits warehouse use but not offices in conjunction with the warehouse
- the company wants to add an extension but local planning policy is such that planning permission for this development will not be given by the local planning authority (LPA)

The company would have wasted capital expenditure on acquiring the site and may have committed to a long-term lease – a situation which will not find favour with the board of directors.

What could the facilities manager have done to protect that company's position before acquiring the property? What development projections should have been made?

This section looks at the key planning issues relating to the use and development of business premises.

The law

The *Town and Country Planning Act 1990* (the *1990 Act*) contains most of current legislation controlling the application of planning laws. The *1990 Act* has been amended by the *Planning and Compensation Act 1991 (PCA 1991)*. The effect of this is that certain amending provisions have been written into the *1990 Act*, whereas other provisions remain as standalone clauses in the *PCA 1991*.

When is planning permission required?

One of the questions most frequently asked by facilities managers is: do I need planning permission? To determine this it is necessary to establish whether what is proposed (building works or change of use) is classed as 'development' for the purposes of section 55 of the *1990 Act*. If the proposals do amount to development, then planning permission will be required.[1]

What is 'development'?

There are two classes of development:

- physical works carried out in, on, over or under land – usually grouped together as 'operational development'

- development relating to how land is used – classed as a 'material change of use'

Operational development

Any of the following will constitute development:

- **"Building operations"** – as defined in section 336 of the *1990 Act*, this includes "rebuilding, structural alterations or addition to buildings and other operations normally undertaken by a person carrying on business as a builder". Demolition works were later brought within the concept of building operations and this is discussed below (see DEMOLITION WORKS, P147).

- **"Engineering operations"** – as defined in section 336 of the *1990 Act*, this is generally interpreted to include operations usually undertaken by or calling for the skills of an engineer.

- **"Mining operations"** – this is not defined in the *1990 Act* but will include the removal of material of any description from a mineral working deposit.

- **"Other operations"** – this is a catch-all category enabling unclassified development works to be brought within the planning permission net. These are judged on a one-off basis and will include such things as installing protective grills on windows and raising the level of land by the addition of soil or other material. This is, then, a wide and potentially limitless category depending on the facts and circumstances of each case.

Use of land

A facilities manager is expected to deliver premises that operate in an efficient and commercially effective way. There must be no restriction affecting the use of the building which has a detrimental impact on the business. How then can facilities managers anticipate potential use problems? Firstly, they must understand the distinction between 'contractually permitted use' under a lease or similar arrangement and the 'lawful use' for planning purposes.

Contractually permitted use

Contractually permitted use is the use allowed under a contract such as a lease or licence. For example, a lease may permit the premises to be used for the purposes of high class offices. If the occupier uses the premises to run a shop then it will be in breach of the lease contract, even if the lawful use for planning purposes permits shop use.

Lawful use

Lawful use is the use permitted under planning legislation. The lawful use will override any use permitted under a lease or licence if they are inconsistent. For example, if shop use is prohibited for planning purposes and is permitted under the lease contract, the premises cannot lawfully be used as a shop.

Categories of lawful use are known as 'classes' of use. The classes of use are set out in the *Town and Country Planning (Use Classes) Order 1987* (the *1987 Order*). It consists of 16 classes of use arranged in four main parts (see APPENDIX 1).

Mention should also be made of uses which do not fall within the *1987 Order*. It is relatively easy to identify the lawfully permitted use for planning purposes by examining the LPA's records. However, some uses do not fall conveniently within the *1987 Order* and these are referred to as 'sui generis' uses. An example of a sui generis use would be where land is used for the purposes of overnight parking of large distribution lorries.

What is a 'material' change of use?

'Material' changes of use are a question of fact and degree. The change may be material because it constitutes a change in the *type* of use, or because it represents an increase in the *intensification* of a continuing use. The law determining what is a material change of use is not set in stone, although section 55 of the *1990 Act* does give guidance on which changes of use will constitute development:

No change of use

- use of land for agriculture or forestry; and
- uses falling within the same use class of the *1987 Order*

Material changes of use

- deposit of refuse or waste material on land
- use of external parts of the building not normally so used for the display of advertisements
- change of use class within the *1987 Order*

Does section 55 apply?

The process by which facilities managers can make decisions as to whether or not physical works or anticipated changes of use constitute development within the meaning of section 55 of the *1990 Act* is illustrated in Table 1 (see opposite). However, sometimes there will be grey areas, especially where changes of use are concerned. In such cases professional advice from a planning consultant or lawyer should be sought.

Listed buildings and conservation areas

Special controls apply if a property is a listed building or is situated within a conservation area. Listed building consent will be required for virtually all works carried out and a specialist consultant or architect should be involved at an early stage of any application process.

Conservation areas are designated as such to 'conserve' the appearance of the locality. Therefore, works to the exterior of a property in a conservation area will usually require planning permission even if they are of a minor nature. It must also be remembered that trees growing in a conservation area are protected by preservation orders. Any works of lopping, topping or cutting to a protected tree require consent from the LPA.

Understanding planning requirements

Building development projects should be worked around planning requirements so that, in a complex situation, a planning adviser or consultant can be employed at an early stage to advise on compliance and

Table 1: Do you require planning permission?

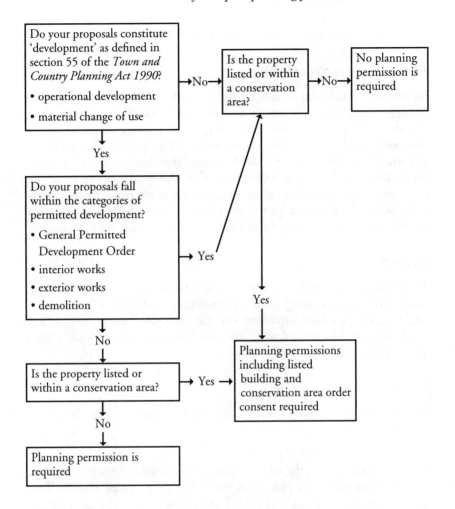

also to instigate and maintain a dialogue between the company and the planning authority.

A facilities manager who understands the planning process will be able to advise the board of directors in respect of any proposed expansion or refurbishment plans. The board can then factor the relevant information into the company's budget and time schedule.

It will also be useful to find out what planning permissions already exist in relation to a property and this can be done by asking the local authority or arranging for a solicitor to carry out a search of the authority's records.

Applying for planning permission

So, if planning permission is required, what is the next step? Is this the time to bring in professional advisers? What role will they play?

Architects/planning consultants

An architect or planning consultant will guide the facilities manager through the application process. Such an adviser is well placed to advise on local planning policy. They will have experience in interpreting the local development plans.[2] Planning decisions by LPAs are plan-led and it is important to interpret the development plan correctly. A planning application which is not consistent with the policy set out in the development plan is unlikely to succeed. Architects and planning consultants will also have local knowledge and previous dealings with the LPA. They will be able to streamline the application to give it the best chance of succeeding.

Solicitors

A solicitor can be involved in this process. Due diligence by way of a local search may reveal existing planning restrictions and adverse notices. The solicitor may also have confirmed the use class (see LAWFUL USE, P139). Legal advice will be needed to explain conditions and planning obligations attached to a planning permission.

Formulating the application

The following preliminary steps need to be taken in formulating the planning application:

- Clarify maps, diagrams and plans.

- Obtain copies of the relevant parts of the development plan and any other non-statutory plan which may affect the proposed development.

- Obtain an application form from the LPA, available free of charge. Each LPA produces its own form.

- Consider a pre-application discussion with the appropriate case officer. This is particularly important if the development proposals are not consistent with the development plan or other planning policy statement.

- Decide whether the application will be for full planning permission or 'outline' planning permission. Where the application is to erect a building, the applicant is entitled to apply for outline permission. In this case the application merely has to contain a description of the proposed development indicating its major features. An application for full planning permission will need to include full details of the proposed development. Full plans and elevations will need to be provided together with a considerable amount of detail setting out materials and construction methods.

Making the application

Table 2 illustrates the application process through to the planning decision.

Table 2: Planning application process

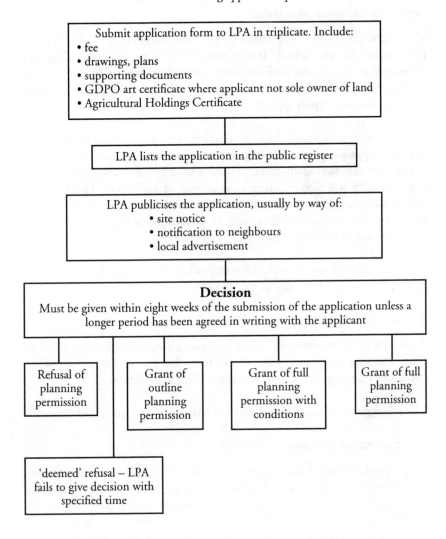

The planning application decision

The planning application will result in one of the following outcomes:

- refusal of planning permission
- failure to give a decision within specified time – a 'deemed' refusal
- grant of outline planning permission
- grant of full planning permission with conditions
- grant of full unconditional planning permission

Refusal of planning permission

If the LPA refuses planning permission it must state clearly in writing the full reasons for the refusal. If full reasons are not given, this does not necessarily invalidate the decision itself, but it does mean that the decision can be challenged by judicial review and the failure to give reasons could be taken into account upon appeal.

In reaching their decision, the LPA must take into account the provisions of the development plan and also any representations received following publication of the application. Listed building and conservation area considerations will also be taken into account if applicable. The LPA will also consider any other 'material' considerations – meaning considerations relevant to the application; they must be planning considerations and relate to the use and development of land.

There is a right of appeal to the Secretary of State. The appeal must be made within six months of the date of the decision.

A 'deemed' refusal

A deemed refusal is where an LPA fails to give a decision within the specified time. The specified time is eight weeks from the date of submission of the application, or longer if agreed in writing with the applicant.

There is right of appeal against a deemed refusal to the Secretary of State.

Grant of outline planning permission

By granting outline planning permission, an LPA is committed to allowing that development in principal, subject to approval of certain conditions. These conditions are known as 'reserved matters' and require subsequent approval from the LPA. They deal with the siting, design, external appearance, means of access and landscaping of the development. No further planning permission will be required when the development is commenced, subject to determination of the reserved matters. The outline permission cannot be revoked except on payment of compensation and additional conditions cannot be imposed over and above reserved matters.

Applications for approval of the reserved matters must be made within three years of the grant of the outline permission. The development approved by the outline permission must be commenced within five years of the grant of the permission or within two years of the approval of the reserved matters, whichever is the later.

Grant of full planning permission with conditions

The LPA may grant full planning permission but impose conditions. These conditions will relate to the development or use of any land under the control of the applicant, whether or not it is land in respect of which the application was made. The applicant can be required to remove buildings, to carry out additional works, to discontinue a particular use and to carry out subsequent reinstatement works if required. There are judicial restrictions upon the power to impose conditions to prevent these being abused by LPAs. These restrictions are intended to make sure that the conditions are:

- fairly and reasonably related to the development permitted

- not manifestly unreasonable

There is a right of appeal to the Secretary of State against the grant of planning permissions subject to conditions within six months of the notice of the decision.

Subject to appeal, development work authorised under a grant of full planning permission with conditions must be commenced within five years of the grant of the permission.

Obligations

A mention should also be made of the obligations which can be linked to the grant of planning permission and imposed under section 106 of the *1990 Act*. An LPA can impose additional obligations in return for granting planning permission. Take, for example, an application to develop a new supermarket. An LPA grants planning permission for the supermarket. In return for the LPA's consent, the developer agrees to build a new roundabout in the vicinity. This agreement would be contained in a section 106 agreement.

Grant of full unconditional planning permission

Full planning permission may be granted without conditions. Development works approved by the permission must be commenced within five years from the grant of permission.

Appeals

Only the applicant may appeal against a decision by an LPA, even if the applicant is not the owner of an interest in the land. Third parties, including the owner of an interest in the land who is not party to the application, have no right of appeal. In certain limited cases, a challenge to a planning decision may be brought by way of judicial review.

An appeal can be made in the following circumstances:

- refusal to grant planning permission

- grant of planning permissions subject to conditions to which the applicant objects

- refused approval of reserved matters on an outline permission

- refusal of application or grant of permission subject to conditions under section 73 or section 73(a) of the *1990 Act* (these sections allow an application to be made for the implementation of an existing planning permission – before it has expired – where the new applicant is seeking to implement that permission without the conditions originally imposed)

- failure to notify the applicant within the prescribed period – in other words, deemed refusal

In all these circumstances the applicant has a right of appeal to the Secretary of State within six months of the notice of a decision or failure to determine an application.

Challenging appeals to the Secretary of State

The validity of an appeal decision cannot be challenged in any legal proceedings. However, a 'person aggrieved' (section 288 of the *1990 Act*) may question the decision by appeal to the High Court if the decision was not within the powers of the *1990 Act* or if any relevant procedural requirements have not been complied with. Again, in certain limited cases an application for judicial review may be made.

Human Rights Act 1998

The *Human Rights Act 1998* came into force in the UK on 2 October 2000 and had an immediate impact upon domestic legislation. LPAs are now obliged to consider human rights issues when determining planning applications. In particular, the LPA must take into account the right not to be deprived of property (article 1) and the right to respect for private and family life (article 8). Facilities managers should remember that this will affect both their company's planning applications and also the ability of the company to object to the applications of third parties. Although a company is a corporate body rather than an individual, it is deemed to have rights protected by the *Human Rights Act 1998*.

When is planning permission not needed?

In certain circumstances planning permission is not required, even where the proposed works or change of use fall within section 55 of the *1990 Act*. These circumstances are usually referred to as 'permitted development'. It must be noted, however, that special rules apply to listed buildings and conservation areas. Professional advice should always be taken in these circumstances.

Permitted development includes:
- certain demolition works
- development permitted by the *Town and Country Planning (General Permitted Development) Order 1995*
- internal works
- certain external works

Demolition works

Demolition of buildings has been brought within the scope of development. Section 13 of the *PCA 1991* introduced a new section 55(1)(a) of the *1990 Act*. 'Building operations' now include "demolition of buildings; rebuilding; structural alteration of or addition to buildings…" Nevertheless, certain demolition works do not require planning permission.

Demolition works requiring planning permission
- demolition of part of a building

Demolition works not requiring planning permission
- demolition of a building smaller than 15 cubic metres

- demolition of any building (whatever the size) not being a dwelling house or adjoining a dwelling house

Town and Country Planning (GPD) Order 1995

The *Town and Country Planning (General Permitted Development) Order 1995 (GPDO)* permits certain types of development which would otherwise require planning permission. There are defined lists of permitted development set out in the schedules to the *GPDO*. Schedule 2 is of primary importance. This has 28 parts setting out descriptions of developments that can be carried out without the need for planning permission. The most important are:

- Part 2 – minor operations
- Part 3 – certain changes of use

These parts are set out in APPENDIX 2.

Internal works

Internal works which are not of a substantial nature involving major structural alterations do not usually require planning permission.

External works

External works which do not materially affect the external appearance of a building do not usually require planning permission. Again, what constitutes 'material' is a question of fact and degree. For the works to require planning permission, the change to the exterior must be capable of being seen by an observer outside the building. It must also materially affect the appearance of the building as a whole and not merely a part. The nature of the building must also be taken into account so that, for example, changes effected to a Georgian facade may have a greater visual impact than changes made to the external appearance of a factory. Special rules apply to signage and advertisements.

What if planning law is not complied with?

The facilities manager will now know that development works as defined in section 55 of the *1990 Act* will require planning permission unless it is permitted development. They will also know that operational development or a material change of use may have been undertaken in contravention of planning controls. If there is a breach of planning control, what action can be taken by an LPA? And what can the facilities manager do to protect the company's position?

The LPA will want to see that operational development and material changes of use have been undertaken within its planning district in a lawful way. In certain circumstances it may only need to view the exterior of the property. In other circumstances a more detailed inspection, including an internal inspection may be required and it will need to gain entry to do this. Having collected evidence of potential breaches of planning controls the LPA will then want to remedy the contravention. Not surprisingly, LPAs are given wide powers of inspection and enforcement for this purpose.

Power to enter and inspect

LPAs may authorise any person in writing to enter land at any reasonable hour without a warrant where there are 'reasonable grounds' for doing so. Where admission has been refused or if the matter is urgent the LPA may obtain a warrant to enter the property.

The sanction to any owner or occupier in these circumstances is that anyone who wilfully obstructs the person exercising a lawful right of entry is guilty of an offence.

The LPA can also compile evidence of a breach of planning control by using a Planning Contravention Notice (PCN) or a Breach of Condition Notice (BCN). A PCN is used to obtain information about any operations, use or activities being carried on at a property or on land. A BCN will be used primarily to establish whether or not conditions or limitations attached to an existing planning permission have been breached.

Enforcement action

An LPA has three options to enforce against a breach of planning control, namely: injunction, enforcement notices and stop notices.

Injunction

An injunction can be used to prevent an owner or occupier from carrying out activities which are being undertaken in breach of planning controls. Whether or not an injunction is granted is at the discretion of the court.

Enforcement notices

The LPA can also issue an enforcement notice. An enforcement notice must contain the following information:

- a statement of the alleged breach
- steps necessary to wholly or partly remedy the breach
- a statement of the effective date of the notice, being at least 28 days from service of the notice
- a statement of the time within which the steps specified to remedy the breach are to be carried out

Non-compliance with an enforcement notice makes the owner or occupier liable on summary conviction to a fine of up to £20,000 or, on indictment, an unlimited amount. The LPA also has the power, in addition to prosecuting, to rectify the breach itself and recover reasonable expenses from the owner or occupier.

Stop notice

A stop notice can be issued. As its title suggests, a stop notice requires an immediate halt to the activities causing the breach of planning control. This is a drastic step for an LPA to take and will only be used in very limited circumstances. A breach of a stop notice is subject to the same penalties as a breach of an enforcement notice. However, the LPA will always be aware that if a stop notice has been incorrectly served or is subsequently quashed by legal action or withdrawn, the LPA may become liable to pay substantial compensation. LPAs are often unwilling to expose themselves in this way.

Protection for owners and occupiers

Faced with the impressive armoury of enforcement sanctions available to LPAs, the owner or occupier of the land subject to enforcement proceedings may be able to protect itself by appealing against enforcement proceedings. However, a more attractive and effective option may be for the owner or occupier to 'regularise' its occupation of a property by applying for a certificate of lawful use or development.

Certificates of lawful use or development

Material changes of use and operative development are 'lawful' if no enforcement action can be taken. This will include where the time limit for commencing enforcement action has expired. Enforcement action cannot be taken in the following circumstances:

- where operational development carried out without planning permission has continued for a period of four years from the date on which the operations were substantially complete

- where any material change of use and any breach of condition or limitation attached to a planning permission has continued for a period of 10 years from the date of the change of use or breach

Facilities managers should remember that LPAs cannot impose further conditions when issuing a certificate of lawfulness. However, if, instead, an application is made for planning permission to regularise the existing use and development rather than an application for a certificate of lawfulness, this gives the LPA an opportunity to impose conditions.

Building Regulations

Often, little or no distinction is made between planning permission and Building Regulations. Although there is a degree of overlap in the sense that they must both be dealt with when carrying out building works, they are separate and distinct concepts. Planning permission deals with the obtaining of consent for the type or nature of work to be carried out. Building Regulations are necessary to ensure that the work is carried out with the correct materials and in accordance with appropriate health and safety laws.

The relevant Building Regulations are the *Building Regulations 1991*, the *Building Standards (Scotland) Regulations 1991*, and the *Building Regulations (Northern Ireland) 1994*. The 1991 rules have been amended by the *Building Regulations (Amendment)(No 2) Regulations 1999*. Building Regulations are covered in more detail in HEALTH AND SAFETY LAW: BUILDING REGULATIONS, PP69–72.

Complying with these Regulations does not represent any form of consent to works and is not a substitute for planning permission. They ensure that the methods and materials used are of an appropriate quality and that they meet all current industry standards.

A Buildings Regulations officer will be appointed by the local authority to inspect the works at various stages and must be notified before works commence. The officer will liaise with the various contractors to ensure that the works are compliant.

A certificate of satisfaction will be issued when the officer is satisfied that the works meet current industry standards. Conditions can be attached to the certificate and a final certificate will not be issued until these conditions have been met.

A fee is payable to the local authority. The level of the fee is calculated by reference to the cost of the works and the local authority will usually accept an estimated project cost as long as it is realistic. A final certificate will not be issued until the fee has been paid and the works completed to the officer's satisfaction.

Environmental matters

Environmental law – relating primarily to contaminated land – is a complex area of law. Little practical guidance can be given by examining individual statutory provisions. It is an area best dealt with on a case by case basis by an experienced environmental specialist, as the potential liabilities and remediation costs can be very high. Nevertheless, there are benefits in being well informed and facilities managers should be aware of the overall apportionment of responsibility for the clean-up of contaminated land.

The law

It is not easy to follow the relevant statutory enactments that deal with the clean-up of contaminated land. The *Environmental Protection Act 1990* (*1990 Act*) was the first serious attempt at introducing detailed statutory provisions controlling this. Further provisions dealing with remediation and apportionment of liability were introduced into the *1990 Act* by the *Environment Act 1995*.[4]

The provisions relating to the clean-up of contaminated land came into force on 1 April 2000. Note however, that the regime is retroactive in effect – the regime will apply irrespective of when the land is or was contaminated.

What is contaminated land?

Land is 'contaminated' if, as a result of the substances in, on or under it, there is:

- a resultant significant harm[5]
- a significant possibility of such harm occurring
- pollution or risk of pollution to water

Who is liable? – The 'polluter pays' principle

The polluter pays principle is a two-tiered system which requires the identification of an 'appropriate person' who will be liable for the remediation of the contaminated land. An appropriate person is either the person who:

(a) caused or knowingly permitted the land to become contaminated (the original polluter) – known as a class A appropriate person; or

(b) the owner or occupier of the land for the time being – a class B appropriate person.

The following chart illustrates this:

Local authority → identifies contaminated land

↓

remediation works enforced against class A appropriate person: 'polluter pays' principle

↓

if after reasonable enquiry class A appropriate person cannot be found

↓

remediation works enforced against class B appropriate person

Reducing liability for clean-up

Clearly, there is an obligation on facilities managers to ensure that no pollution is caused to a site during the period of their company's use of that site. However, they will also want to ensure that the risk of being held liable as a class B appropriate person is reduced. This means that they will want information about the environmental status of a property *before* that property is acquired for the company's portfolio. There is no public list or register of sites which may be contaminated. How then can the risks be quantified? The following options are available:

Desktop or phase I report

This involves a document-only analysis of the environmental aspects of a given site. Information for a phase I study is likely to be gathered by the following methods:

- specific enquiries of regulatory bodies
- specific enquiries of occupier
- researching planning history
- research title deeds and pre-registration documents

Physical survey or phase II report

The phase II report is more extensive and requires the taking and analysis of soil, water and other material samples from the site. The phase II survey is expensive, however, where the potential risks of contamination are perceived to be high (if, for example, the site has previously been used for a high risk use, such as storage of solvents or other chemicals), then the cost may well be justified in order to quantify the risks.

Occupiers' liability

Where an occupier acts or fails to act and by doing so creates a dangerous condition which later causes harm to a visitor using the premises, then the occupier may be liable under the provisions of the *Occupiers Liability Act 1957* (the *1957 Act*).

The grounds for making a claim against individuals or companies occupying or controlling premises are wide. They are an easy target, not least because it is widely thought that their insurers will step in to meet the claim. Potential litigants are also aware that it is very difficult for occupiers to show that they have acted as occupiers to the standard required by law.

Case study

Consider the following simple case study:

A company occupies office premises. The facilities manager has a strict cleaning and maintenance programme in operation. This involves polishing the client reception area to a highly polished finish. A client attends the offices, slips on the polished floor and is injured. Is the occupier of the office premises liable for a claim brought by the client because of this accident?

Is the claim valid?

The following key elements will determine the validity of the claim:

- Is the company an occupier?
- Has the accident occurred on 'premises' as defined in the *1957 Act*?
- Does the company owe a duty of care to the client?
- Has the company discharged the duty of care owed to the client?
- Can liability be excluded?

Is the company an occupier?

The rules of common law (determined by case law) define who is an 'occupier'.[6] Exclusive occupation of premises is not necessary. The test is whether a person has some degree of control associated with or arising from their presence and use of or activity in the premises; it is possible to have more than one occupier of premises. Consider the example given above in the following context:

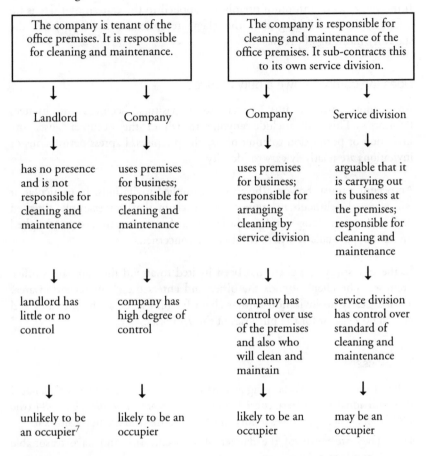

The company is tenant of the office premises. It is responsible for cleaning and maintenance.		The company is responsible for cleaning and maintenance of the office premises. It sub-contracts this to its own service division.	
↓	↓	↓	↓
Landlord	Company	Company	Service division
↓	↓	↓	↓
has no presence and is not responsible for cleaning and maintenance	uses premises for business; responsible for cleaning and maintenance	uses premises for business; responsible for arranging cleaning by service division	arguable that it is carrying out its business at the premises; responsible for cleaning and maintenance
↓	↓	↓	↓
landlord has little or no control	company has high degree of control	company has control over use of the premises and also who will clean and maintain	service division has control over standard of cleaning and maintenance
↓	↓	↓	↓
unlikely to be an occupier[7]	likely to be an occupier	likely to be an occupier	may be an occupier

In the example above, the company uses the premises for its business. It has control of the day-to-day running of the premises and is an occupier for the purposes of the *1957 Act*.

Did the accident occur on 'premises'?

Facilities managers will be forgiven for thinking that premises means only buildings from which a company operates. For the purposes of the *1957 Act*, 'premises' includes:

- any fixed or moveable structure
- any vessel, vehicle or aircraft

The definition is wide. Examples of what constitutes premises include scaffolding, ladders, grandstands, electric pylons and lifts.

If the *1957 Act* definition of premises is applied to the case study there is no difficulty in establishing that the client reception area falls within the statutory meaning of premises.

Does the company owe a duty of care?

An occupier owes a duty of care to its visitors, licensees and invitees ('visitors'). This will include anyone to whom the occupier gives any invitation or permission to enter or use the premises. Express permissions or invitations are relatively easy to identity.

An occupier must, however, be aware of implied invitations. In particular, it will always be difficult to argue against a claim that, for example, ungated pathways or a long-standing hole in a fence constitutes an implied invitation, particularly where children are concerned.[8]

In the case study, the client has been invited to attend the company's office premises. The client attends the office and enters the client reception area. This is clearly an invitation to that client for him to be at the premises and he will be a visitor for the purposes of the *1957 Act*.

Trespassers

What if the individual claiming against the occupier is not a visitor? What if that individual was a trespasser? Under the *Occupiers Liability Act 1984* (the *1984 Act*) an occupier owes a duty of care to those who are not visitors if:

- They are aware of the danger of a specific risk and have reasonable grounds to believe it exists.

- They know or have reasonable grounds to believe that the trespasser is in the vicinity of the danger or may come into the vicinity.

- The risk is one against which, in all the circumstances, they may reasonably be expected to offer the trespasser some protection.

Has the company discharged the duty?

The common duty of care owed by occupiers to visitors is a duty to take such care as is reasonable, taking account of all the circumstances. Visitors must be reasonably safe in using the premises for the purposes for which they were invited or permitted. As with any duty of care-based claims, such as a claim in the tort of negligence, the definition is legalistic and complex.

How then can the facilities manager judge whether or not the common duty of care has been discharged? Examine the case study – surely it is sufficient for the facilities manager to have a rigorous cleaning and maintenance programme in place? If a client slips on the highly polished entrance floor, does that client have a claim against the company as occupier under the *1957 Act*? Is this claim supported by case law? In determining whether or not the company has discharged its common duty of care as occupier to the client, the court will consider whether, in light of all the circumstances, the company has failed to achieve the standard of care required by the *1957 Act*. Again this is legalistic and unclear. Facilities managers should consider the following standard of care guidelines developed through case law:

- Children must be expected to show a lesser degree of safety awareness than adults.

- Visitors attending premises to perform their particular skill are expected to be prepared for special risks associated with that skill.

- Where the use of independent contractors gives rise to a claim based on the contractor's negligence, an occupier may satisfy the standard of care if it has acted reasonably in employing that contractor, believing the contractor to be competent.

A lesser standard of care is owed to trespassers under the *1984 Act*. The duty can be discharged if the occupier takes such care as is reasonable in all the circumstances to ensure that the trespasser does not suffer injury on the premises.

Can liability be excluded?

Consider the following in the context of the case study – the facilities manager arranges for the following warning sign to be placed in the reception area of the office premises:

N O T I C E

All visitors are asked to take care when entering the reception area. The floors are highly polished and very slippery, particularly when wet.

No liability for personal injury or damage to property is accepted by the company.

Does this warning discharge the company's common duty of care? Once again the legal rules are complicated. If a notice or warning sign is reasonable in all the circumstances and is sufficient to allow the visitor to avoid the danger then the occupier may well have satisfied the required standard of care. To return to the case study: the client is warned of the slippery floor by such a notice. Whilst they know that it is a potential hazard, they have no choice than to cross the floor in order to reach the reception desk. The company has created a danger which cannot be avoided. The notice does not discharge the common duty of care owed to the client.

On the basis that the warning about the slippery floor is insufficient to discharge the common duty of care, can the company rely on the exclusion of liability for loss or damage to personal injury or property contained in the notice? It is possible to limit or exclude liability in certain circumstances – if, for example, a visitor has agreed to such an exclusion, then in so far as loss or damage to property is concerned it would be effective. Such agreement could be formal – by means of signing a disclaimer, for example – but may also be implied. A trespasser, for example, who enters a premises uninvited, implies agreement to exclusion of liability. However, a decision to walk over a slippery floor to reach a reception desk does not constitute agreement on the visitor's part. Therefore, it is not possible to exclude liability for personal injury in these circumstances.

Knowing your portfolio and managing costs

There is no substitute for facilities managers knowing what properties are under their control. It is not enough merely to have details of the address. Building up a detailed set of information about the portfolio is time consuming and potentially costly. However, the advantages of doing this cannot be overemphasised. Consider how the facilities manager can add value to their role in the company and participate in board decisions in the following scenarios:

- The company's board of directors wants to rationalise that company's premises requirements. A good knowledge of the portfolio will enable the facilities manager to answer questions such as:
  - Which premises are not cost effective?
  - Can leases be terminated early without penalty?
  - Are there title or planning restrictions which may impact on the timing or value of an open market disposal?
- The board is seeking to diversify the company's business. The facilities manager can advise on whether any of the existing premises can be re-developed or undergo a change of use.
- Preliminary discussions are taking place with a potential purchaser of the company. The facilities manager can address issues which may have an impact on the price of the transaction, such as:
  - Can any of the properties be used in the negotiations?
  - Do any of them have unusual or special features?

- Do any of them have onerous restrictions which should be brought into the open at an early stage?

- Lawyers or other professional advisers have been instructed to act on a matter relating to a particular premises. The factual details such as the landlord's address and the agent's name are missing. Various deeds and documents are also missing. The lawyers spend a considerable amount of time collecting basic information, which increases their bill. Clearly, it would be more cost effective for a facilities manager to provide factual information to the lawyer or professional advisor rather than to pay the lawyer or professional adviser to collect that information. A transaction is also likely to run more smoothly if the lawyer or professional advisor is provided with all relevant background information at an early stage. A well-informed facilities manager can use their knowledge of the property and the potential problems of a transaction to negotiate a realistic fee structure with the lawyer and professional advisors.

Moreover, knowledge of any occupational and/or use restriction enables the facilities manager to formulate solutions.

Premises requirements are rarely at the core of a company's key business strategy. This is likely to mean that the facilities manager will have little support from the board of directors for any initiatives aimed at scheduling or collating factual information about the property portfolio. Nevertheless, a full knowledge of the portfolio will enable the facilities manager to enhance their position by providing key information at important stages of the negotiations, anticipating problems, offering solutions and achieving costs savings.

Key knowledge requirements

The key information which any facilities manager should know about the premises under his control should include the following:

- identification of property
- planning consents and restrictions
- title matters
- terms of occupation

The checklist set out in APPENDIX 3 offers guidance for collating this information.

Real estate valuation

The valuation of real estate is a broad topic, both in terms of the different categories of property and the methodology involved. It is difficult to envisage efficient real estate management without a clear understanding of the value of the assets and liabilities held. A valuation is an essential tool for considering opportunities to release capital, realise development gains and achieve cost savings.

Valuation theory is best left to the valuer; however, an awareness of valuation procedure is of relevance to the facilities manager. This section provides guidance on procuring valuations, and considers certain practical issues which impact on property value.

The regulatory framework

The provision of valuation advice within the UK is currently regulated by the Royal Institution of Chartered Surveyors' *Appraisal and Valuation Manual*, first published in September 1995 and better known as the 'red book'.

The 'red book'

The stipulations of the red book are mandatory for the majority of valuations, although certain categories of valuation are excluded. These include valuations undertaken in accordance with a statutory code, valuations prepared in the context of negotiations and those undertaken by an in-house valuer solely for use within its own organisation.

As key requirements of any valuation, the red book's specifications include:

- the need to agree the valuer's instructions in writing prior to issue of the valuation report
- the need to adopt the correct 'basis of valuation', appropriate to the purpose of the valuation
- the minimum content of valuation reports

Procuring valuations

When commissioning a valuation, it is important that both the client and the valuer have a clear understanding of the purpose of the valuation and the level of service required. This is unlikely to be achieved by a letter simply requesting a valuation of a given property for a specified fee, unless standard terms and conditions of engagement have already been agreed.

A more comprehensive definition of the task is normally required and the red book specifies the minimum level of detail needed. The main items that have to be agreed in writing before the final valuation report is issued include:

- the purpose of the valuation
- the address of the property and the legal interest to be valued, including the treatment of fixtures and fittings and plant and machinery normally regarded as part of the land and buildings

- the basis or bases of valuation
- any practicable assumptions to be made relative to the basis of valuation (for example, to take into account any change in the value of the property if planning permission for an alternative use is being sought and is likely to be granted)
- the date of valuation (this will have to be either before or at the date of the valuation report)
- any restrictions on how or what the valuer may do in the course of providing the service
- the requirements for obtaining the valuer's consent to publication of the report
- the limits of liability to parties other than the client
- the nature of information to be provided (such as title documentation, lease details, trading accounts, planning permissions) by the client/its advisers and the extent to which the valuer is to rely upon that information
- the treatment of environmental issues, such as land contamination
- the fee basis

It is always prudent when instructing a valuer to ensure that they have appropriate experience of the nature of the task, the category of property and the geographical location on which to base their opinion of value.

The purpose of the valuation

The purpose of the valuation and the nature of the property will determine the basis of valuation. The red book defines the accepted bases of valuation and amongst those most likely to be encountered in a facilities management context are:

- open market value
- existing use value
- depreciated replacement cost
- open market rental value

The purposes and bases are discussed in more detail below.

Valuations for acquisition/disposal

Open market value

If a valuation is required prior to acquisition or disposal of a property, the appropriate basis of valuation will normally be 'open market value'. This valuation basis is intended to represent the valuer's opinion of the best price at which the sale of a legal interest in the property would have been completed for cash consideration on the date of valuation (the full definition is set out in the red book).

As open market value supposes completion of a hypothetical sale on the date of valuation, the valuer has to assume that, prior to the date of valuation, there had been a reasonable period to allow for the proper marketing of the property, agreement of the price and terms, exchange of contracts and completion of the legal formalities.

When considering an open market valuation, specific factors to be aware of are as follows:

Special purchasers

Open market value excludes bids from purchasers with a special interest in the property. A special purchaser might comprise another party holding a legal interest in the same property, such as a tenant, or the owner of a neighbouring property, who might require the property for expansion or to create an access to a nearby development site. In such circumstances, the special purchaser may be justified in submitting a bid in excess of the open market value, although, of course, the amount the special purchaser chooses to offer in excess of the open market value will depend on how highly it values the property.

'Hope value'

Open market value assumes an unconditional sale. This is particularly important to note in the case of development land. In many instances, development land is sold on a conditional basis, subject to achieving an appropriate planning consent – for example, the disposal of a factory site for residential redevelopment. The open market value will reflect the circumstances of the property at the date of valuation. Therefore, if planning permission has not been obtained by that date, it will only reflect the so-called 'hope value' for an alternative use that exceeds the underlying value for the existing use.

The quantum of hope value will be determined by the probability, costs and timescale of obtaining planning permission. If a successful planning permission is unlikely, then the hope value will be limited. Alternatively, if achieving the required planning permission is a virtual certainty, the open market value without planning permission may show little, if any, discount relative to the open market value had planning permission already been obtained.

If a valuation is required of a property with the benefit of planning permission for an alternative use, before the planning consent has actually been obtained, then it will be necessary to request an "open market value of the property subject to the special assumption that planning permission has been granted". The details of the planning permission assumed to have been obtained should also be stipulated – for example, the density of development should be specified.

Further investigations

As open market value is intended to represent the transaction price, ideally it should take account of all the factors that would be considered as part of the transaction process. This might include a detailed consideration of such matters as:

- the condition of the property
- the possibility of land contamination
- any onerous restrictions in legal title

Often, for reasons of either cost or timescale, these further investigations are not undertaken when preparing a valuation and as a result assumptions or caveats are included in the valuation instruction letter and report. Thus, if a property is actually acquired or disposed of and full and detailed enquiries are made, it should be appreciated that the final price may differ from that included in an earlier valuation prepared without the benefit of such investigations (aside from any issues of market movement). In this context, it should be appreciated that it is difficult or impossible for a valuer to assess the impact of disrepair or land contamination on the value of a property without the costs of making good/remediation having been quantified. This would normally require additional expert advice from, for example, a building surveyor or an environmental consultant.

Net realisation proceeds

Facilities managers should be aware of the difference between open market value and net realisation proceeds. Whilst it would normally be the valuer's remit to provide the open market value figure, the responsibility for quantifying net realisation proceeds will often lie with the facilities manager. Net realisation proceeds will normally be lower than the open market value, reflecting deductions such as professional fees on disposal and holding costs, including rates, security and building insurance, as well as any factors that emerge during detailed enquiries when a sale takes place (see above). In a stable market, clearly the longer a property takes to sell, the greater the reduction in net realisation proceeds, reflecting holding costs over a longer period. When estimating net realisation proceeds, it is therefore useful to obtain details of the disposal period envisaged by the valuer.

Valuations for incorporation within company accounts

Key points to note include:

Existing use value

When valuing for accounts, non-specialised owner-occupied properties are valued on the basis of their 'existing use value', which closely follows the definition of open market value, except that it assumes the property can only be used for the existing use and that vacant possession is provided on completion of the sale of all parts of the property occupied by the business. It therefore excludes any hope value for more valuable alternative uses.

Depreciated replacement cost

'Specialised properties', such as an oil refinery, museum or power station, are those which are rarely, if ever, sold on the open market, other than as part of an ongoing business. The appropriate valuation basis for specialised properties is 'depreciated replacement cost', which by definition is not based on a market price.

In practice, the depreciated replacement cost is made up of the existing use value of the underlying land, together with the replacement cost of the buildings and building and site services, suitably depreciated to allow for age, condition, economic or functional obsolescence, environmental and other relevant factors. It is a prerequisite of depreciated replacement cost that every valuation assumes the adequate potential profitability of the business, taking into account the value of the total assets employed and the nature of the operation.

Properties for investment, development or disposal

Properties held as investments, for development or for disposal, are valued on the basis of open market value. Thus, owner-occupied properties normally valued on an existing use value or depreciated replacement cost basis, as set out above, will revert to an open market value basis if the properties are declared surplus and are held for disposal.

Financial Reporting Standard 15

The procedures to be followed when revaluing properties, other than investment properties, for company accounts are detailed in the Accounting Standard Board's Financial Reporting Standard 15 (FRS 15). Effectively this provides organisations with the choice of either revaluing their properties or holding them at historic cost. If the organisation decides to adopt a policy of revaluation, then it will be required thereafter to revalue the properties according to the specifications of FRS 15. The organisation will no longer be permitted to 'cherry pick' – that is, revalue chosen properties only – as either all properties or all properties within a specific category of asset (such as specialised properties) have to be revalued.

For accounting purposes, the value of owner-occupied properties needs to be allocated between the underlying land value and the value of the buildings, site works and site services. Whilst the value of the land is not depreciated, the portion of value attributable to the buildings, site works and site services is depreciated and reflected in a depreciation charge in the profit and loss account.

FRS15 does provide opportunities for depreciating individual elements of an asset over different periods – for example, building service installations might be depreciated over a shorter period than the structure of a building.

Valuation approach

Freehold interests

The approach to the valuation of freehold interests will depend upon whether a property is owner-occupied or let as an investment.

The majority of non-specialist owner-occupied properties can be valued by the 'sales comparison approach', which involves obtaining details of sale prices on comparable properties and then making adjustments to reflect physical differences and market circumstances.

Investment properties are normally valued using the 'income approach', which in the simplest case involves capitalising the passing rent to arrive at the capital value.

Long leasehold interests

Leasehold interests fall into two main categories. The first comprises long leasehold interests where the rent payable is normally only a small proportion of the full open market rental value and the lease term exceeds 50 years – for example, a 99-year lease at a nominal rent. Long leasehold interests will normally be categorised as assets, although these could be wasting assets as the unexpired lease term diminishes.

Short leasehold interests

The second category comprises short leasehold interests, such as a 10, 15 or 25-year lease, typically with five-yearly upward only rent reviews. In the late 1980s such leases were often treated as an asset; however, the cyclical nature of property values since then has altered perceptions dramatically. At present, short leasehold interests are often perceived as a liability in value terms, particularly if the supply of a category of property exceeds demand. Often incentives will have to be given to an incoming tenant to take over the leasehold interest. The existence of upward only rent reviews and a growing awareness that shorter, more flexible leases are available in other countries has resulted in the 25-year lease becoming far less common in the UK, so that today shorter leases and tenant's break clauses (see BUSINESS LEASES: TERM, P128) are more prevalent. Nonetheless, where a tenant has substantial capital costs, for example, in fitting out a property or installing plant and machinery, a longer lease may be required to ensure an adequate pay-back period on the investment.

The value of a leasehold interest

The value of a leasehold interest is dependent upon the relationship between the open market rental value and the rent passing under the lease. If the rent payable is less than the market rent, then a 'profit rent' is created and potentially a positive capital value might arise. This will often be the case with long leases where normally the rent passing is lower than the market rent. However, before reaching a conclusion as to the value of leases it is necessary to consider other factors, such as dilapidation liabilities and, in the case of short leases, what, if any, financial incentives might need to be granted to a new tenant to take on the lease. Such incentives could, for example, take the form of a rent-free period or payment of a reverse premium. With short leases, once these and other factors have been reflected, a positive value derived from a profit rent may in practice become a nil or negative value.

Negotiating lease terms

In the lease negotiation process, the facilities manager will often have a lead role in determining the heads of terms for the occupier (tenant). This will encompass defining the tenant's occupational requirements (such as the floorspace required, the length of lease needed and what level of rent is affordable). Once this has been done, the tenant will in effect have a shopping list of requirements. However, before entering the negotiating process, it is useful to also consider the landlord's motives. In most cases, a landlord will be seeking to maximise the income and capital return upon their investment. This return will be very much dependent upon the lease terms agreed.

The table opposite sets out some of the main terms of a lease, which will maximise or minimise the value of the landlord's interest. If the tenant has a particular wish to include a term or terms which reduce the capital value for the landlord (from the column on the right), it can in negotiating seek to

Enhances capital value for the landlord	Reduces capital value for the landlord
Maximum lease duration, eg. 25 years	Minimum lease duration, eg. five years
A higher rental value	A lower rental value
Maximum security of rental income – ie. tenant has strong financial covenant	Rental income at risk – ie. tenant has a weaker financial covenant
No incentives for the tenant at lease commencement	Extensive rent-free period and/or capital contribution from the landlord
More frequent rent reviews	Less frequent rent reviews
No tenant's break clauses	Frequent tenant's break clauses

counter the negative effect of this from the landlord's point of view by proposing the inclusion of a separate term or terms from the left hand column.

In a buoyant property market, when demand exceeds supply, the features in the left-hand column will come to the fore. However, in a bear market, such as existed during the recession of the 1990s, the issues in the right-hand column will prevail. This provides some insight into the cyclical nature of property investment values.

References

1. Section 57(1) of the *Town and Country Planning Act 1990*

2. Outside Greater London and the Metropolitan areas the development plan consist of the structure plan and the local plan; within Greater London and the Metropolitan area the development plan consist of the unitary development plan.

3. Internal works within listed buildings require listed buildings consent.

4. Part II(a) *Environmental Protection Act 1990*. See also *Contaminated Land (England) Regulations 2000* and DETR guidance on contaminated land, dated April 2000. The National Assembly is expected shortly to introduce similar regulations regarding contaminated land in Wales.

5. 'Harm' is defined as harm to health of living organisms or other interference with the ecological systems of which they form part and, in the case of man, includes harm to his property.

6. *Occupiers Liability Act 1957* section 1(2)

7. Duties are imposed on landlords who are under an obligation to repair by the *Defective Premises Act 1972*. The duty is wide and is even extended to trespassers. It is sufficient that the landlord merely has a right to enter to carry out repairs under the terms of the lease.

8. *Cooke v Midland Western Railway of Ireland* [1909] AC229, HL

Further reading

Appraisal and Valuation Manual, published by the Royal Institution of Chartered Surveyors (RICS)

Business Issues

4 Financial Management

Connel Bottom

Financial strategy and management are a core part of any business, supporting the achievement of the organisation's short, medium and long-term goals. For facilities managers, financial management refers specifically to the effective and efficient use of available finance through the use of planning and control mechanisms. This, ideally, is a proactive process which ensures that the right level of financial resource is available at the right times, enabling the required level of service quality to be delivered by a contractor, supplier or staff member.

Facilities management policy and strategy should be created, sponsored, monitored and reviewed by the intelligent client function (ICF) – the strategic management function of the facilities management department. The ICF's role will naturally extend to responsibility for financial management in so far as facilities management policy and strategy (subservient to business policy and strategy) is supported by available funds. Part of the facilities management policy will establish the financial planning and control mechanisms and the important link between cost of services and level of quality necessary to adequately support customer requirements.

Bernard Williams[1] establishes that financial policy and strategy objectives must be concerned with budgetary control, competitive procurement and value engineering (see FIGURE 1, P172). The illustration shows that these three facets are interrelated; the absence or misapplication of any one of them will jeopardise holistic and proactive financial management.

This chapter covers all of these issues, providing the facilities manager with practical skills for managing finance, and focusing on the theory and application of best practice management techniques associated with the strategic planning, analysis and/or control of facilities goods, services or projects.

Background economics

Financial management skills may be utilised and supported in different ways, according to the size, function, flexibility and complexity of an organisation. Before looking at the principles of issues such as cost control, benchmarking, procurement and value engineering, it is important to look at the economic structure of the organisation within which those principles will be applied.

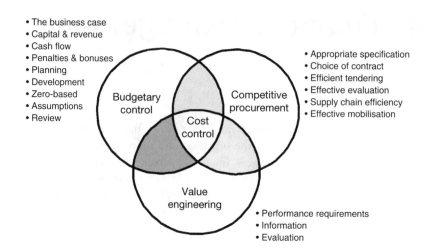

- The business case
- Capital & revenue
- Cash flow
- Penalties & bonuses
- Planning
- Development
- Zero-based
- Assumptions
- Review

Budgetary control

Competitive procurement

Cost control

Value engineering

- Appropriate specification
- Choice of contract
- Efficient tendering
- Effective evaluation
- Supply chain efficiency
- Effective mobilisation

- Performance requirements
- Information
- Evaluation

Figure 1: The three facets of facilities management cost control

Universal principles

Facilities management strategy, structure and scope within an organisation (public or private sector) may take many forms, for example:

- management of a direct labour team

- management through an ICF of both in-house and external service providers

- partial management through an ICF and assistance from an external managing agent or partnered provider, such as under the umbrella of TFM (total facilities management), PFI or PPP schemes

- management of facilities as a landlord/institutional investor or agent

However facilities management is organised, the principles outlined here give basic and practical building blocks which can be replicated by any facilities management function in pursuit of sound, proactive financial management.

The significance of facilities management costs

Typically, the facilities manager is concerned with a wide variety of costs associated with the provision of premises or buildings, business and staff support services. Figure 2 shows a typical classification of cost centres that might fall within the facilities manager's remit. It also illustrates audited annual costs for a UK portfolio (as an example) and their associated percentage significance to the facilities management team.

		£	
Property costs	Property: rent, rates, insurances, etc	4,028,692	33.12%
Premises costs	Building services maintenance	869,255	7.15%
	Building fabric maintenance	125,595	1.03%
	Grounds maintenance	80,180	0.66%
	Alterations and fitting out	672,835	5.53%
	Cleaning	922,083	7.58%
	Security	602,217	4.95%
	Utilities	1,189,355	9.78%
	Internal décor	55,371	0.46%
Business support	Archiving	18,990	0.16%
	Reprographics	670,450	5.51%
	Stationery	267,746	2.20%
	IT Communications	120,855	0.99%
	IT Computers	69,719	0.57%
	Mail room functions	174,521	1.43%
	Transport and fleet	92,744	0.76%
	Porterage	94,719	0.78%
	Travel management	8,569	0.07%
	Furniture	14,667	0.12%
	Business equipment	22,210	0.18%
Staff support	Catering	1,947,575	16.01%
	Gym	25,324	0.21%
	Occupational health service	49,430	0.41%
	Facilities management helpdesk	39,355	0.32%
		12,162,459	**100%**

Figure 2: Typical classification of facilities management cost centres

To put these costs into context, Figure 3 overleaf illustrates a typical facilities management budget compared with organisational turnover and profit.[1] While the facilities management budget may appear small in comparison, it is worth considering the impact of facilities services on an organisation. For example, failure of building services due to an inadequate maintenance strategy or the disruption caused by the absence of a disaster recovery plan following a terrorist bomb blast could have a significant effect on the core business financial statistics. Furthermore, staff resources are a significant cost in most organisations and the workplaces that support them, managed by the facilities manager, are known to influence productivity and organisational performance.

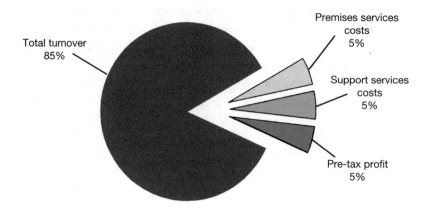

Figure 3: Typical facilities costs compared with organisational turnover

Systems technology and financial management

Organisations are increasingly investing in systems technology in order to gain competitive edge. Systems technology supports the organisation's infrastructure, including financial management and facilities management processes. Enterprise resource planning (ERP) systems have traditionally encompassed data and information associated with sales, accounting, manufacturing, inventory and supply chain management functions, but are, in general, inflexible. New developments, however, are providing more and more people, both internal and external to the organisation, with real-time connectivity through the medium of a web browser. For many organisations and systems providers, the goal is to build fully integrated supply chains that drive out waste and provide value to all participants (see E-PROCUREMENT, P190).

This holistic approach to e-business has far-reaching ramifications for the facilities management function. The facilities manager must be increasingly aware of how systems technology can support policy and strategy; the possibilities are immense.

All too often, an organisation's systems infrastructure is implemented without an understanding of the needs of the facilities management department. In some cases, this has the effect of encouraging individuals to set up or procure separate systems. It is quite common, for example, to see a facilities manager controlling and reporting budgetary performance using the organisation's ERP system and managing space-recharging or end-of-year benchmarking activities on separate spreadsheet files. However, infrastructure suppliers such as SAP, Oracle and Peregrine Systems now realise the significance and benefit of integrating facilities management information, and more and more facilities managers are turning to these. When setting such systems up, facilities managers should:

- ensure that there is no duplication of data input or storage
- ensure that the system uses meaningful budgetary codes and classifications
- ensure that the classification is sufficient for conducting external benchmarking
- where there are several buildings or clear functional boundaries, ensure that costs can be collated and managed flexibly and logically
- ensure that the system computes costs fairly for recharging purposes
- ensure that direct comparisons can be drawn with contract performance information – remember that financial management is important, but performance information is arguably more important to facilities management customers and their productivity
- ensure that costs can be logically combined with key benchmarking parameters – for example, floor areas and headcount
- ensure that there are adequate measurement definitions for other staff to follow – for example, what should be included within a net internal area (NIA) measurement, or the definition of full-time equivalent (FTE) staff numbers
- ensure that descriptive units in automated reports are correct and full – for example, never show costs as £/sq m, always define the units fully as £/sq m GIA/p.a.
- ensure that taxes are separately identified and described
- ensure that facilities management functions in other buildings or countries adopt the same principles

Best practice financial management

Budgetary control

Budgetary control is concerned with ensuring that the financial management plan that has been agreed with the board of management is achieved. Control is effected through monitoring expenditure before and after commitment to prevent under or over-expenditure. The principal considerations of budgetary control are:

- planning
- preparation
- coordination
- behavioral effects
- communication
- reporting and reconciliation
- change management
- evaluation

Planning

The budget-planning process is concerned with the following issues:

- forecasting
- facilities managers' skills
- information on required service levels
- information on the organisation's future business strategy

Budget planning is carried out in advance of the budget period; it is normal to plan for the next year's budget two to three months before the start of the new financial year. In some organisations budgets are prepared on a rolling basis and in these situations planning will be a recurrent activity carried out at pre-defined intervals – say quarterly or half-yearly.

The planning process relies partly on the facilities manager's skills of forecasting, and partly on the quality of information available on previous financial and service quality performance and future business objectives. The facilities manager will normally be able to control the quality of information on the former through an efficient facilities management information system (see SYSTEMS TECHNOLOGY AND FINANCIAL MANAGEMENT, P174), and the presence of an ICF or strategic management function with representation on (or at least good links with) the board of management would normally provide enough information on the latter. The absence of a strategic facilities management function in medium to large organisations can hinder the budget-planning phase. If financial planning is not informed and is consequently not proactive then the facilities manager will run the risk of having to react to problems as they arise – 'fire-fighting'. This scenario is clearly an inefficient use of resources in any organisation and is one that can be prevented through effective planning.

Preparation

Budget preparation is concerned with the following issues:

- the use of appropriate cost centres for management and benchmarking
- zero-based budgeting
- provision of data relating to service level quality and cost
- the declaration of all assumptions made
- capital and revenue planning
- treatment of depreciation
- tax planning

The first three of the above list are discussed below, and the latter four later in this chapter.

Cost centres

The facilities management department should have appropriate cost centres around which forecasts of expenditure and quality can be made. It is advisable to separate facilities services into functional groupings – for example, cleaning, services maintenance, furniture maintenance, security, catering, reprographics, and so on. These groupings can sometimes be sub-divided further – catering, for example, can be divided into staff dining, hospitality catering and vending. It is generally accepted that the more detailed the classification the better the forecast, although this depends to some extent on the amount and quality of data available at the preparation stage. The classification adopted by the facilities management department may be more detailed than that required by the organisation's finance department, which is typically more interested in the correct accounting for the needs of the business than in the efficiency and performance of the facilities services. To maximise efficiency and performance, the cost centres must be logical, both in the context of service functions and in terms of retrospective performance appraisal or benchmarking (see BENCHMARKING FACILITIES COSTS, P191). A suitable classification is effectively a benchmarking protocol, an example of which is given in APPENDIX 4.

Zero-based budgeting

The facilities manager normally forecasts the activities necessary, the quality required and the associated cost of each service. It is poor practice to use the previous year's budget figure and add on a percentage for market inflation, as this approach does not always reflect an accurate forecast of future change. Detailed forecasting using a clean sheet of paper is inherently much better practice – particularly where the facilities manager is not experienced or where it is expected that they will leave the organisation within the budget period. The construction of a new budget for each service from basic principles is referred to as zero-based budgeting. This approach has the effect of focusing attention on such issues as waste, unnecessary performance, leasing versus purchasing of equipment, and so on, prompting the facilities manager to ask such questions as 'Why do we do it this way?' and 'Why are we not getting better results?' – questions that are often asked by consultants after undertaking a benchmarking study.

Data

Effective forecasting depends on the availability of good quality data for such issues as:

- business strategy or changes being proposed that affect facilities services
- key dates associated with business change
- service level qualities and costs for supporting the business through any planned changes
- the facilities management market – for example, price increases in labour, equipment and materials
- facilities management staff costs – for example, recruitment, salary and benefit costs associated with new appointments
- stability of budgets/cost predictions on ongoing capital projects – for example, a new building
- the effect of new legislation being enforced – for example, the cost of providing disabled access
- currency or purchasing power parity, if applicable – for example, budgets for a European office portfolio
- flexibility associated with contracts – for example, supply and payment of personnel in disaster recovery circumstances
- travel costs

A zero-based budgeting approach will effectively accommodate all of these issues, assuming that the facilities manager has completed enough research into the potential for organisational or market change. The zero-based approach is in fact a step-by-step methodology that will ensure accurate forecasting, and the facilities manager should realise that it is important that all assumptions taken in relation to the above issues are well documented. Such information will be of use when reconciling the effect of change or if a new facilities manager is recruited during the budget period.

Whilst zero-based budgeting is considered to be a best practice approach to budget preparation, there are other sources of data that the facilities manager might wish to use. These encompass the following:

- contract prices from existing or recent agreements
- a schedule of rates for a certain element of the supply chain
- pricing books published within the industry/marketplace

In addition, contractors can often provide key budgeting information if requested and consultants usually record strategic and detailed cost information for many clients and buildings.

Typically there are three levels at which data may be used for forecasting a budget figure (Figure 4). The choice will normally depend both on the accuracy needed in the forecast and on the confidence and extent of the data available.

Coordination

Facilities management budgets need to be coordinated with other departmental forecasts in an organisation, such as marketing and human resources. Furthermore, if the facilities management department is sufficiently large, it is possible that there are individual facilities managers charged with budgeting for the services under their remit. Best practice is for the ICF to prepare an outline budget for the coming year which coordinates with the wider business strategy for the short (annual), medium (next five

High level	eg. Cleaning £11.00 per sq m of net internal area p.a.
Elemental	eg. Office areas £/sq m NIA p.a. 6.00 Toilets 2.00 Restaurant 1.00 Windows 1.50 Pest control 0.50 £11.00
Itemised	eg. Wash down partitions, 2,000 sq m @ £0.25 per sq m of partition surface area = £500

Figure 4: Illustration of pricing levels within budget preparation

years), and long term (over 10 years). Individual facilities managers should, within this framework, prepare more detailed budgets relating to their particular areas or 'bundles' (services that can be grouped and managed collectively).

Behavioral effects

The budget should provide tight financial constraints for managers to work within. The constraints must not be too tight or lax, however, as this can influence staff motivation to plan and control costs.

Responsibilities within the facilities management hierarchy must be clearly demarcated. For example, a recent benchmarking study found that a facilities manager could not control a particular budget because another department had management jurisdiction over the contractor. This frequently happens when there is a central procurement team letting contracts without full input from the facilities manager who will be responsible for managing service delivery.

Communication

The budget and its constituent components, including objectives in relation to service level qualities, need to be communicated to both facilities management staff and any core contract staff who need to appreciate the business requirements for the budgetary period. Effective communication will ensure that the facilities manager's plans are carried out as required.

Reporting and reconciliation

Reporting and reconciliation are mechanisms for control on a periodic basis – usually monthly. It is important that:

- the format used for reporting is clear, concise, meaningful and useful to the facilities management function
- the information is accurate
- the information is as close to real time as possible to promote proactive management
- the information is, ideally, conveyed in numerical and graphical formats (the latter will improve understanding and identification of potential problem areas)
- there is a written explanation of any numerical and graphical information
- the report is circulated to the staff responsible in advance of any control meetings – timely circulation will ensure that meetings are productive

The information presented in the report normally includes the following:

- the principal cost centres, and where possible any sub-divisions
- the monthly budget projection for each cost centre
- the actual cost incurred within each cost centre
- total projected and actual costs
- key resource-driver statistics, such as levels of staff resource and volumes associated with the actual costs incurred
- records of service level quality delivered in each main contract/cost centre

The vast majority of events or services envisaged in the budget preparation period are likely to go according to plan, as indicated by the example shown in Figure 5. With this in mind, the facilities manager can concentrate on controlling specific cost centres that are, by their nature, likely to vary. This concept is commonly called 'management by exception'.

Change management

Once authorisation has been granted for a budget, any changes should be resisted – correct preparation and treatment of uncertainty should have eliminated many of the potential areas likely to cause a variation. Particularly dynamic organisations, however, carry an increased degree of uncertainty,

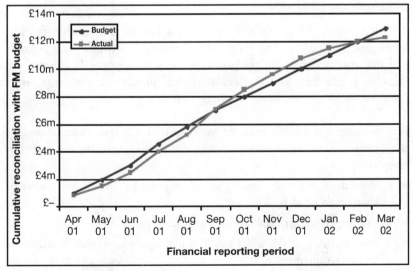

Figure 5: Typical budget/actual expenditure reconciliation chart for financial period

and change in planned facilities management services is possible. If this change is significant, and cannot be controlled within the normal reporting regime (see p 171), then specific reporting within the management hierarchy may be necessary, as well as extra managerial meetings to control the effects of change.

Significant change in facilities management is commonly associated with projects – for example, the relocation of staff in another building, or an office refurbishment. As such, projects are normally treated separately for management purposes.

Evaluation

The presence of detailed budgets within facilities management provides a means of evaluating the performance of individual facilities managers or demonstrating the value of having an ICF within the organisation. Such a process is considered best practice, particularly where the performance of individuals is linked to skill sets and the facilities management staff training strategy.

The evaluation process can also be considered a useful protocol for financial benchmarking, the procedures for which are discussed in BENCHMARKING FACILITIES COSTS, P191.

Procurement

Strategic considerations

The procurement of goods and services is a key function within facilities management, ensuring that goods and services are provided competitively and that they add value to the organisation's core business. In this respect, the choice, planning and implementation of procurement activities are a central tenet of efficient financial management.

Any procurement activity must be based around a sound understanding of the overriding strategic considerations. For most organisations these are essentially:

- the extent to which services are to be provided by contractors rather than in-house staff
- the scope/nature of the service that is to be provided
- the capability of the wider facilities management market to satisfy the service requirement

Contracted-out versus in-house service provision

In deciding whether service provision is to be delivered in-house or by a contractor, the facilities manager should focus on keeping what the organisation considers to be its core business activities in-house, and contracting out non-core business activities (see OUTSOURCING: WHAT TO OUTSOURCE, P238 for more on this topic).

There is a common presumption within British industry that contracted-out service provision is automatically more economical than its in-house equivalent. In fact, there are numerous examples in the facilities management industry where the opposite has been shown to be true. What is certain, however, is that in-house facilities management departments have traditionally been seen as being uncompetitive and inefficient. This perception arises for a number of reasons which include:

- **Poor communication** – facilities managers are notorious for not telling their customers how good they are (and for not having any performance statistics to prove it).

- **Over-provision** – it is easy for the in-house team to be sidetracked into providing more than is required under their service level agreement (SLA), if there is one, thus adding to operating costs.

- **Organic growth** – many facilities management departments have grown organically with the parent organisation. As a result, procedures that worked efficiently in a 100-person environment are struggling to cope when the headcount reaches 500.

Scope of services to be provided

Figure 6 (overleaf) illustrates the broad spectrum of services that the facilities manager might be expected to procure on behalf of the organisation.

Before initiating any procurement activity, firms should ensure they have a thorough understanding of the scope and nature of the service required (see OUTSOURCING: THE TENDER DOCUMENT, P242). This will enable an appropriate buying strategy to be put in place. The strategy adopted is likely to vary depending on whether the service required is:

- a single service (cleaning, catering, porterage, and so on)

- a group or 'bundle' of services (here the emphasis will be on the mutual compatibility of the services to be provided; thus it is common to find fabric, services and grounds maintenance bundled together)

- a 'total facilities management' package, whereby services across the three main facilities management sub-classifications are supplied by one provider under a single contract

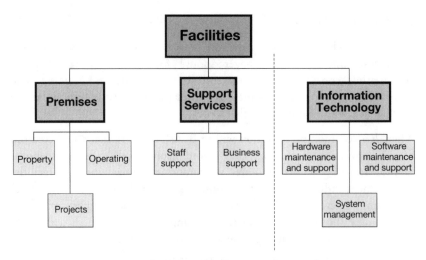

Figure 6: Scope of facilities management[1]

Facilities management market capability

Within the global marketplace there is a plethora of service providers all advertising themselves as 'facilities management contractors', but in reality offering widely varying types and levels of services to their customers. This can have a significant impact upon efficiency and quality of service provision, the level of support afforded to the core business units and thus the facilities cost/value model.

Any tender shortlist must therefore only be compiled after an exercise has been carried out to check that the core competencies of the prospective bidder companies are compatible with the scope and nature of the overall requirement. For example, there is little point in putting a facilities management contractor on a tender list for a catering contract if the company's core business revolves around the provision of maintenance services (for more on selecting contractors, see OUTSOURCING: CHOOSING CONTRACTORS, PP242–245).

It is possible to group facilities management contractors into broad categories which derive from the background of their parent organisation. These initial classifications can help to weed out weaker candidates from the selection process at an early stage. The categories are:

- **General contractors** – typically these organisations have moved into facilities management to take advantage of the improved profit margins (1–2% for contracting compared to 3–5% or greater for facilities management). Their core competencies tend to centre around the building-related disciplines.

- **Single service providers** – this group includes catering contractors, cleaning contractors and the like. In many instances such organisations have been encouraged to offer a broader range of services by their customers. Some have become facilities management contractors in the broadest sense, whilst others pay only lip service to the concept and may sub-contract these bolt-on services.

- **Management buy-outs** – over the years several of the larger property-owning/occupying corporates have outsourced their property departments. The majority of these ventures have proved extremely successful in a privatised environment; however, this was quickly recognised by the more predatorial elements of the marketplace and only a few of them retain their independence. Typically this type of organisation has strong managerial skills and operates at its best in a fee management/managing agent-type contractual arrangement.

- **Consultancy** – the recession of the late 1980s and early 1990s and the associated drop in the construction industry's workload forced professional consultancy organisations to seek alternative sources of income. Some of them moved into facilities management and again, on the whole, such ventures have proved successful. As is to be expected, such organisations also demonstrate strong managerial skills, but their preference is for the managing agent-type structure (this route is perceived as offering less business risk because the facilities managing agent does not have a direct contractual relationship with the service providers).

- **Consortia** – the advent of PFI and PPP has seen a growth of contracting organisations that have the capability of providing a total package of facilities and services to organisations in a long-term contractual arrangement.

Strategic management

In simplistic terms there are three elements to any facilities management operation:

- **the task itself** – the cleaning of carpets, for example
- **task management** – the day-to-day hands-on tactical management of the task – by the cleaning supervisor, for example
- **strategic management** – the management function that decides, to continue the analogy, what level of cleaning the organisation needs

The first two of these are relatively easy to outsource, and commonly are. However, outsourcing of the latter requires careful consideration, as there is a strong argument which states that only an 'insider' (in the form of an ICF) can ever hope to fully understand exactly what the business needs its facilities management regime to deliver. As discussed earlier, the ICF role is to create, sponsor, monitor and review facilities management policy and strategy – a remit that naturally encompasses tasks associated with value management, namely:

- identification of what services are needed and the options available to provide them, including option analysis (usually an evaluation will look at such issues as risk to the organisation, financial affordability criteria and value for money), resulting in a definition of the scope of the task(s)

- implementation of a related strategy (for instance, all procurement processes, including the setting of performance targets associated with specifications and service level agreements)

- monitoring (checking and reviewing the achievement of performance requirements)

Tendering process

The tendering process can be thought of as a chain of events that the facilities manager must undertake to result in the selection and mobilisation of a service provider. The important issue, in terms of financial management, is that each stage will normally have a set of associated tasks that will impact on efficiency, cost and value. Tendering processes in general are discussed in OUTSOURCING, PP242–250, but the more complex procurement processes specific to PPP projects are discussed below.

Private investment and partnership

Private investment and partnership is normally associated with the Private Finance Initiative (PFI), which was launched by the Government in 1992 and reviewed in 1997 (The Bates Review)[2] (now known as PPP). The central objective of the initiative is to involve private sector expertise directly in the procurement of new public sector buildings (or specific assets such as hospital equipment) and the operation of these facilities, including the provision of facilities management services, over a suitable life cycle period. The works and services are paid for over time by means of a single unitary charge. The methodology is equally applicable to the provision of buildings and services to another private sector organisation – sometimes referred to as a 'Private Sector PPP'.

The aims of PPP may be summarised as follows:

- to support the Government's aim of reducing the public sector borrowing requirement (PSBR)

- to obtain cost savings (in terms of initial capital and operating expenditure) and efficiency gains by using private sector experts to construct and service buildings
- to enable the transfer of appropriate risks from the public sector to the private sector
- to bring the benefit of using and paying for the asset over time (rather than significant initial expenditure), so that more funds are available for other projects and public services can generally be improved

The facilities manager should have a significant input throughout a PPP project, and therefore it is important to understand the generic stages involved in the PPP procurement process, which is more complex than that of traditional outsourcing. It normally follows the following steps:

1. **Establishing the business need for change**
    Issues such as poor building stock condition, lack of functionality and poor service levels are frequently key drivers for change.

2. **Appraisal of options**
    This will test how well different options would meet business requirements, particularly in terms of delivering value. Core facilities management skills at this stage will often relate to the preparation of strategic budgets (see BUDGETARY CONTROL, P175), the application of analysis techniques (see TECHNIQUES FOR FINANCIAL ANALYSIS, P199) and the ability to identify any restrictions relating to the capability of construction and facilities markets (see PROCUREMENT, P182).

3. **The preparation of a business case**
    This will establish whether an investment option exists that is affordable and sensible for the business. Normally output specifications (prescriptive outputs rather than descriptive inputs) are prepared at this stage which may additionally be used for the preparation of a reference project. Often the reference project becomes a public sector comparator which is used to model the investment/business case. The facilities manager has a significant role at this stage, essentially preparing detailed whole life budgets (see WHOLE LIFE ECONOMICS, P198) which include appropriate allowances for the risks to be borne by the private sector.

4. **Development of a procurement team**
    The correct level of resource is of paramount importance and there should be similar skills to those expected within the private sector bidder(s) or consortia.

5. **Developing tactics**
    Tactics relating to the number of selection/pre-qualification stages and the quantity of information to be released or requested must be

decided. These decisions normally relate to the complexity of the project.

6. **Invitations of 'expressions of interest'**
    These are issued and a notice is published in the *Official Journal of the European Community* (OJEC).

7. **Briefing day**
    A briefing day may be held with the aim of introducing the project to potential participants.

8. **Pre-qualification of bidders**
    This stage precedes shortlisting and is mainly concerned with identifying suitable or competent participants from a list of OJEC respondents using weighted quantitative criteria such as bid compliance, technical and financial capability. Under European law the processes involved in shortlisting should be open to scrutiny.

9. **The development of tender documents**
    This includes the output specification. The information contained within the output specification is normally revised and cross-checked with business case affordability/investment calculations in anticipation of stages 10, 11 and 12. The facilities manager's skills are important in the correct preparation of the documentation – particularly the wording of output/input specification items and the format proposed for scheduling construction and facilities costs. Construction (and life cycle replacement) costs should be requested in an elemental and sub-elemental format (such as the Royal Institution of Chartered Surveyors' (RICS) elemental form of cost analysis). Facilities costs should be scheduled against a set facilities management cost protocol (see BUDGETARY CONTROL: COST CENTRES, P177), illustrated in APPENDIX 4.

10. **Invitation to submit outline solutions (ISOP)**
    This effectively results in a long-list of bidders through the application of more detailed evaluative criteria, such as risk transfer, innovation, deliverability and long-term flexibility. The criteria may be applied to various subjects, such as proposals for planning, design, construction, decant, property disposals, facilities management/occupancy considerations, alternative revenue proposals and management structure.

11. **Invitation to tender (ITT)**
    This stage normally results in a shortlist based upon the bidders' proposals in relation to draft project documentation. Normally, three bidders go forward to the next stage. It is worth noting that the financial criteria used for evaluation are likely to be more heavily weighted from this stage onwards.

12. **Invitation to negotiate (ITN)**
    The ITN documentation will normally include the following:

    - a definition of the scope of work and/or services to be provided

    - a statement of requirements usually in terms of an output specification

    - proposed contractual terms covering such aspects as length of contract and payment mechanism (relating to the unitary charge); which operates like a service level agreement with financial penalties for unavailability of business space and/or under-performance

    - the evaluation or negotiation timetable including a description of the techniques or criteria that are intended for use

    - key dates, such as submission of the ITN response

    - policy in respect of submission of standard and variant bids where the bidders may identify better ways of constructing a facility or delivering services

    - the public sector comparator may be included for assisting the bidders in the preparation of their bids

13. **Receipt and evaluation of the ITN bids**
    Normally the evaluation is structured using weighted criteria which will include items of a contractual and financial nature, together with design and service provision issues. The facilities manager may be concerned with all of these items to some extent, but it is important to acknowledge the role of benchmarking within this process. The methodology outlined in the section on benchmarking (see PP191–198) can be used to great benefit at this stage, since design specification, service levels, method statements and financial information can all be evaluated by facilities management professionals (who will readily appreciate that all three are interrelated).

14. **Best and final offer (BAFO) and revise and confirm (R&C)**
    These stages may be employed to further reinforce the evaluations through requesting additional clarification and assurances. Financial evaluation criteria will normally carry their highest weightings at this stage.

15. **Contract award and financial close**
    These are associated with the final drafting of all contractual or legal documents and schedules, other than the material commercial terms of the transaction, which should have been agreed at preferred bidder stage.

16. **Contract management**
    Management of the contract will be of significance to facilities management throughout the life cycle or contract term – from the

point of view of both public and private sector organisations. It is common for the public sector client to develop a strategic ICF whose role will be the sponsoring of facilities management policy and the monitoring of performance and payment.

E-procurement

The global facilities management market offers great potential for the use of business-to-consumer and business-to-business e-commerce, not least in terms of the creation of procurement supply chains. Facilities managers in large organisations will undoubtedly be aware of the drive behind the introduction of enterprise management IT systems (See SYSTEMS TECHNOLOGY AND FINANCIAL MANAGEMENT, P174) for the effective control of all business information, financial or otherwise. Internet technology is making it possible to integrate office functions with key suppliers of all but the most complex facilities management services.

Growth of e-procurement

The growth of e-procurement within facilities management is being driven by the following factors:

- The pre-qualification process can happen much more quickly, as e-technology enables the rapid transfer of key information.

- The production, copying and distribution of tender documentation can be significantly reduced when e-technology is used for procurement.

- Economies of scale can be created where individual packages of services are procured through the medium of a 'club' e-commerce site. The packages are essentially components of a large contract negotiated on the terms of the buying power of the club as an entity. They create a closed supply chain, linking a defined customer base with selected suppliers. A site would be based on a front-end browser which allows clients access to a global catalogue of business supplies and equipment from approved suppliers, helping them to search for the best value for money in their chosen product category.

- E-technology can support online tendering of commodities such as utilities, where each bidder is allowed to make offers within a certain time frame and can view the result live in the form of a ranked league table.

Drawbacks

There are many problems associated with the movement towards e-commerce. Facilities managers should bear the following factors in mind:

- Portals can only create economies of scale if there are enough consumers and the volume of transactions is high. In other words, greater numbers of participants will bring greater economic benefits.

- Reliability of the technology and the supply chain information is of paramount importance if the system is to function efficiently. For example, service level performance capability information must be realistic and accurate if consumers are to remain confident in the e-procurement system.

- Many businesses or consumers need to streamline their existing purchasing and procurement processes if economies are to be expected. For example, poor business processes are often the cause when an organisation's travel department procures 'competitively' priced tickets that are in reality more costly than when individual staff purchase tickets directly from the airline. In such cases fundamental business processes may need to be re-engineered, and cultural changes must precede them.

- Many procurement departments will want to actually meet and study their potential service providers. In facilities management the 'people factor' is often an important issue when assessing the quality of proposals.

- Usability factors affect even the simplest of websites, not to mention large and complex procurement portals.

- Whilst experts claim that the security of e-commerce transactions is effective, many individuals still remain sceptical.

Benchmarking facilities costs

Rationale

Benchmarking is used by many organisations globally as a means of health-checking the deployment of resources. If used correctly, it will lead to the effective value management of facilities service provision. The fact that comparisons are made with an external peer group is what differentiates benchmarking from budgeting.

In facilities management, benchmarking has been defined as "a process of comparing a produce, service process – indeed, any activity or object – with other samples from a peer group, with a view to identifying 'best buy' or 'best practice' and targeting oneself to emulate it".[1] This definition effectively outlines one of the most important (but often misunderstood) aspects concerning facilities management benchmarking – that is, 'targeting' or taking action in order to release value to the organisation.

The paragraphs that follow provide a step-by-step guide, illustrated in Figure 7, for the facilities manager to implement benchmarking practice and techniques. The facilities policy normally dictates the frequency at which benchmarking activities are conducted. Most facilities services can be benchmarked on a recurrent annual basis – allowing performance improvements to be tracked and marketed to the board of management.

The facilities audit

The facilities audit represents a review of the costs of providing office space and services within an organisation. It is important to realise that the audit is not concerned with cost alone, but also includes analysis of the building and organisational characteristics that drive cost (resource drivers) and the associated levels of performance.

Resource drivers

A resource driver is a characteristic that influences the required levels and/or deployment of a resource. It is important for the facilities manager to understand that output performance (for example, how clean a building is) may remain at the same level even though the level of resource required (for example, the number of cleaners and frequency of cleaning operations) varies

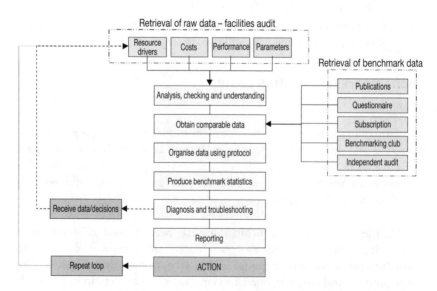

Figure 7: Methodology for benchmarking facilities management costs

in different buildings (an otherwise comparable building may, for example, be located beside an area of pollution which increases the amount of dirt accumulating on the glazing).

Resource drivers have been classified as:[1]

- **quantitative** – usually relating to characteristics of the building or organisation that can be readily measured – for example, floor area, window area, number of staff and contractors' staff, number of covers served in a restaurant

- **qualitative** – characteristics such as the location of the building or the specific preferences or aspirations of the organisation

- **economic** – for example, interest rates, market conditions

- **operating conditions** – for example, specific lease conditions, organisational aspirations

Performance data

Performance characteristics are important within benchmarking in order to identify the level of output associated with cost. Unfortunately, many organisations do not record sufficient performance-related information (although this is changing in the advent of developments in computer-aided facilities management (CAFM) and helpdesk software), and in any case it is difficult to make comparisons between organisations which measure performance metrics differently or not at all. In such cases the facilities manager has the difficult and subjective job of comparing and measuring performance. Customer satisfaction surveys can provide a quick means of procuring performance data.

Cost data

The retrieval of cost data will be a relatively simple process for the facilities manager who has developed and maintained facilities service budgets at a detailed level (see BUDGETARY CONTROL, P175). It is recommended that facilities costs are audited or collected at the greatest level of detail possible. This will ensure that the facilities manager understands what is included within an overall service cost. For example, from an accountancy point of view, a stationery budget may include reprographics supplies, whereas for the purpose of facilities management benchmarking it is often accounted for under the reprographics cost centre. It is often a lack of such understanding that leads to the failure of many commercial benchmarking groups or partnerships.

A spreadsheet is often the best way of assimilating cost information for analysis checking and ultimately for comparison with peer information. Figure 8 illustrates such a process for collecting and analysing the raw data.

Invoice description	Cost	Protocol categories	Services maintenance	Catering	Stationery	Mail/ distribution	Reprographics
Xy (lifts)	£7,612.00	Services maintenance	£7,612.00				
supplier → ABC (chillers)	£11,100.00	Services maintenance	£11,100.00				
Dp (sprinklers)	£1,010.00	Services maintenance	£1,010.00				
FG (CB cooler units)	£1,726.00	Services maintenance	£1,726.00				
HIJ (generator controls)	£46,000.00	Services maintenance	£46,000.00				
NOP (lighting controls)	£12,318.00	Services maintenance	£12,318.00				
EFG (kitchen equipment)	£6,840.00	Catering equip		£6,840.00			
P-touch tapes	£177.24	Stationery			£177.24		
stamps	£42.40	Distribution				£42.40	
April stationery	£3,028.25	Stationery			£3,028.25		
Xerox 3050 plan printer	£132.00	Printing & repro					£132.00
May stationery	£931.66	Stationery			£931.66		
July stationery	£782.49	Stationery			£782.49		
Staples for photocopiers (J23456Y)	£37.80	Printing & repro					£37.80
August stationery	£2,201.38	Stationery			£2,201.38		
Photos printed & framed for facilities	£151.00	Printing & repro					£151.00
		TOTALS	**£79,766.00**	**£6,840.00**	**£7,121.02**	**£42.40**	**£320.80**

etc.

Figure 8: Analysis of facilities service costs using a spreadsheet application

Parameters

Parameters are the metrics that are used to express the benchmark costs in a meaningful way. To give meaningful statistics, it is necessary to establish a direct relationship between the parameter and the cost of service. For example, it is unlikely that vending costs can be related to floor space, whereas there will under normal circumstances be a directly proportional relationship with the number of staff or occupants using the building in a 24-hour period. Similarly, it is common to express the costs associated with premises services on a cost per square metre of floor area, and support services such as catering, mail distribution and stationery are commonly expressed as costs per capita.

Parameters must be measured on a comparable basis between the organisation and its peer group. The RICS Code of Measurement Practice provides a standard protocol for floor space measurements that has been readily adopted within the industry. It should be noted that it is common for different countries to have slight deviations from this standard.

Comparing facilities costs using incorrect and incompatible parameters renders the benchmarking process ineffective. Services maintenance costs can be seen to vary significantly (in benchmarking terms) because of the use of gross internal area and net internal area; it is a common error for facilities managers to use the wrong parameter by mistake. All too often professional and managerial reports relating to premises and facilities are littered with incorrectly described floor area measurements. This is also a common reason for commercial benchmarking partnerships failing.

Obtaining comparable data

Obtaining good quality comparable data is probably the most difficult task that the facilities manager will experience during a benchmarking exercise. The primary sources of information are:

- **Publications** – frequently professional journals publish articles sharing information on facilities costs. However, usually this type of data has been desensitised and/or excludes knowledge concerning specific circumstances, performance characteristics, and so on.

- **Questionnaire** – from the very simplest to the most complex, questionnaires can provide good 'average' information. Individual respondents cannot necessarily be relied upon on to adhere to measurement rules, standards of accounting, and so on. For these reasons the data may represent a very wide variety of circumstances including resource drivers, performance characteristics and, therefore, costs.

- **Subscription services** – the industry has many subscription ventures, particularly on the internet. For a fee, facilities managers can obtain data relating to the costs and possibly performance characteristics of peer organisations. However, subscription companies must obtain the raw data in some manner – usually by way of questionnaires, so the quality of the data is constrained by the motivations of individual respondents and their accuracy of description and classification.

- **Benchmarking clubs** – a number of organisations can exchange best practice, cost and performance benchmarks and targets via a club. These are very worthwhile as long as each individual is fully committed and a facilitator is present – that is, someone who can make decisions about measurement standards, accounting methodologies, reporting standards and the implementation of best practice. The absence of a facilitator usually leads to failure.

- **Independent audit** – this is carried out by an independent expert who should understand all the problems and pitfalls associated with collecting and comparing data from different organisations. It is common for such experts to own a consistent database containing service costs, performance measures and resource driver characteristics. Such an approach allows an efficient and informed assembly of true peer-group data.

The facilities protocol

A facilities protocol or standard method of accounting is one of the facilities manager's most important tools. An industry standard is given in APPENDIX 4, and illustrates a classification of facilities management services using categories and more detailed sub-divisions of activity – called sections. For novice users, a good protocol also provides definitions or examples of the types of cost that a facilities manager must include, as well as indicating which items should be excluded from the analysis (and where these items should in fact be included).

When conducting benchmarking, the choice of protocol is not as important as ensuring that the rules of what must be included and excluded are standardised – that is, ensuring that what the protocol represents is clear to all those using it. The spreadsheet analysis of an organisation's costs shown in FIGURE 8, P194 illustrates how the facilities manager can label individual invoice costs with protocol category names. The methodology used is then clear to all parties participating in a club benchmarking arrangement.

The importance of clear protocol categories

The following example illustrates the importance of clear protocol categories. One benchmarking club was, on first comparison misled as to the cost of building services maintenance due to confusion over what should be included within this category. The original figures indicated that the total cost for maintenance was £50/sq m NIA/p.a. – although an expert benchmarker would have known that this was too much expenditure for the relatively new facility. Upon further analysis the club realised that this figure incorrectly included costs associated with alterations and churn – a distinct protocol category in its own right. The correct building services maintenance cost was in fact £25/sq m NIA/p.a.

Production of benchmark statistics and graphics

Before interpreting benchmarking results, the raw data from the analysis work must be turned into information ready for comparison. The choice of correct benchmarking parameters will result in meaningful statistics, such as cost/sq m GIA/p.a. However, the computation of statistics at this level is normally called 'first-strike benchmarking' – the most basic level – as opposed to a more detailed study using secondary indicators. These secondary indicators will help the facilities manager understand the occurrence of variance between benchmark statistics such as cost/capita/p.a.

The diagnostic indicators used by the analyst (generally in a more detailed study) usually include the following:
• resource driver characteristics – for example:

- space utilisation/occupancy density
- ratio of hard to soft landscaping
- window to floor ratio
- levels of resource – for example, cleaners' hours/sq m GIA/p.a.
- consumption of volume figures – for example:
  - kwh/p.a.
  - number of restaurant covers p.a.
  - number of black and white copies p.a.
  - number of mail items p.a.
- labour rates – for example, cleaning operative cost/hour
- output performance levels – for example:
  - percentage of planned maintenance tasks completed on time
  - user satisfaction statistics

Diagnosis and troubleshooting

Statistics are often meaningless when presented in tabular format. Graphical analysis is recommended for revealing the true relationships hidden in the data. An example of graphical analysis showing an organisation's costs compared to those of its peer group is shown in Figure 9.

A first-strike interpretation of Figure 9 reveals that cleaning expenditure is high in relation to the peer group.

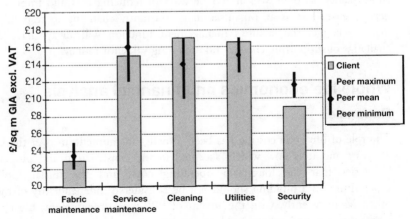

Figure 9: Facilities service cost benchmarking results

This should prompt the facilities manager to ask questions such as:

- Is there a mistake in the calculations/analysis?
- Has the peer group reflected all resource driver characteristics?
- Is the peer group comparable in terms of the business performance requirements?

The above three questions would indicate a discrepancy in the benchmarking process. Questions should then be asked relating to the function itself, for example:

- Is the level of resource too high?
- Is the hourly labour rate too high?

All these questions represent examples of the diagnostic process that must be conducted before reporting any benchmark information. At this stage the facilities manager should review all analysis decisions on a 'repeat loop' basis until all variations can be explained confidently without the possibility of error within the process.

Reporting and taking action

Benchmarking is all about learning and doing things better. Just as it is important to understand resource drivers and to use a standard analysis protocol, it is important to communicate the results of the exercise to all concerned. A benchmarking report must always look to the future – it is not good value for money to conduct a fine level of analysis only to report current levels of expenditure and performance. Broadly speaking, a well run facilities management function will show average levels of expenditure and performance. An 'average' performance, however, should not give rise to complacency, as there will always be ways of reducing cost and improving performance. Just as an organisation is constantly changing to respond to market change, the facilities management function will always have the challenge of supporting change and obtaining value for money.

Whole life economics and financial analysis

Rationale

The role of life cycle costing has been growing in momentum over the last 20 years and it is now widely accepted in the construction and property industries that the long-term operating costs and the initial capital expenditure on a building should not be considered independently of each other. More recently, with the advent of PPP-type procurement, life cycle costs and the techniques used to analyse them have dominated many boardroom discussions.

Increasingly the facilities manager is being recognised as an expert who understands the drivers behind life cycle costs – whether relating to premises, business or staff support costs. Decisions made at the start of a building project, during the design stages, will have most impact upon capital construction cost, but can also influence operating costs. Furthermore, there is an argument that if the design team proactively controls life cycle costs (with a correspondingly small increase in design cost) then unnecessary costs can be avoided over the life cycle of the building. Knowledge about facilities management markets, processes, business requirements and the interaction of organisations with buildings is of paramount importance when planning the whole life economics associated with a given project.

Life cycle costs comprise:

- **capital expenditure** – the cost of constructing an office building, for example
- **financing costs** – the cost of borrowing money to finance a particular project
- **occupancy costs** – subdivided into the following classification for ease of reference (note that these tie up with the protocol used for budgeting and benchmarking):
    - *Premises costs* – maintenance of building fabric and services, utilities, cleaning and replacement costs, for example
    - *Business support costs* – mail room, reprographics and archiving services, for example
    - *Staff support costs* – catering, crèche and fitness centre, for example
- **taxation** – capital allowances on certain costs associated with new construction, for example
- **residual values and disposal costs**

What are the techniques typically used in analysing these costs, and what situations are likely to require them?

Techniques for financial analysis

Financial analysis techniques are often considered difficult to apply and understand and are sometimes left to an accountant or financial analyst. They are, however, within the grasp of any facilities manager who can:

- accurately forecast expenditure (see BUDGETARY CONTROL, P175)
- decide which method of analysis is appropriate for the type of decision being made

- use spreadsheet software to conduct the analysis and interpret the results (although this is not a pre-requisite)

In practice, the techniques used often centre around the analysis of future cash flows. The techniques are:

- pay-back period
- discounted cash flow
- net present value
- internal rate of return
- cost/benefit analysis

Pay-back period

This technique is applicable if the underlying question for the facilities manager is how long it will take to pay back the full cost of an acquisition. Figure 10 illustrates the analysis in simple terms by showing that an initial expense of £10,000 is repaid at the end of year five.

However, the pay-back analysis shown in Figure 10 does not take into account the cost of borrowing the initial £10,000. Furthermore, the technique does not take account of time and income after the pay-back period – assuming that the equipment does not stop working at the end of year five.

Discounted cash flow

In this technique, the simple pay-back period analysis illustrated above is subjected to a discount rate which takes into account interest or the cost of borrowing the £10,000. It is important to understand what is commonly

Initial cost of new reprographics equipment £10,000		
Period	Income through recharge of occupants	Cumulative total
Year 1	£1,000	£1,000
Year 2	£1,500	£2,500
Year 3	£2,500	£5,000
Year 4	£3,500	£8,500
Year 5	£1,500	**£10,000**
Year 6	£3,000	£13,000

Figure 10: Pay-back analysis for new reprographics equipment

called the time value of money before using this technique. For example, if the facilities manager decides to buy another piece of equipment in year two, then what amount of money should be set aside or invested now (year zero) in order to match the anticipated expenditure? This can be illustrated as follows:

Year 2 expenditure (in 1 year's time)	£21,000
Real interest rate (net of tax and inflation)	5%
Amount of invest now (year 0)	£20,000
	(i.e. 20,000 × 1.05 = 21,000)

This example may be extended to allow for subsequent elements of cash flows, such as that created by a planned preventative maintenance contract for the new piece of equipment. The simplest way to deal with this scenario is to work out the discounting factor to be used when analysing each year's expenditure in the cash flow. To calculate the discounting factor, you can use a spreadsheet with the following formula:

$$= 1/((1+i)^\wedge y)$$

Where:
i = likely interest rate
y = the year in which a certain cash sum is spent, eg. 4 for year 4
(NB $^\wedge$ = to the power of)

A simple spreadsheet model using this equation to discount the income cash flows derived from the reprographics equipment example (above) is illustrated in Figure 11.

The further away a sum of money is planned to be spent, then the lower the present value of that future sum. This does not necessarily mean that expenditure in the future does not matter, rather the technique allows the facilities manager to compare between several options – for example, the technique could be used to good effect for evaluating options that differ in terms of specification quality and subsequent maintenance costs.

Discount rate	5%		
Year	1	2	3
Discounting factor	0.952	0.907	0.864
Net cash income	£ 1,000	£ 1,500	£ 2,500
Discounted income p.a.	£ 952	£ 1,361	£ 2,160

Figure 11: Example of discounted cash flow analysis

Net present value

The net present value (NPV) technique compares the sum of the discounted cash flows with the initial capital expenditure. Where the sum total of the discounted cash flows exceeds the initial capital expenditure then the NPV is said to be positive and the project can be viewed as economic. When the initial capital expenditure is greater than the total discounted cash flows then the NPV is negative and is deemed uneconomic. Using the reprographics equipment example used above, Figure 12 illustrates the use of the NPV technique.

Figure 12 uses a formula to calculate the discounting factor for each year and is used in this document purely for clarity, to illustrate all the stages necessary to calculate the NPV. However, most spreadsheet applications have built in functions that calculate the NPV using a single formula, for example:

=NPV(5%, -10000, 1000, 1500, 2500, 3500, 1500, 3000)

In this formula, 10,000 represents the initial capital sum and the following figures represent the yearly net cash income (these figures would normally be substituted by spreadsheet cell references). It is worth noting that each spreadsheet application will have rules regarding the nature of the values being incorporated in the formula – for example, that the net cash income should be at the end of a given period and that each period must be equal. In addition, because of slight differences in approach, the result given by a spreadsheet calculation can be slightly different from the more explicit methodology shown in Figure 12.

An important point to note is the fact that the pay-back period with discounting has increased to almost six years in this example. The higher the

Discount rate	5%						
Year	0	1	2	3	4	5	6
Discounting factor	1.000	0.952	0.907	0.864	0.823	0.784	0.746
Capital expenditure	£ 10,000						
Net cash income		£ 1,000	£ 1,500	£ 2,500	£ 3,500	£ 1,500	£ 3,000
Discounted income p.a.	£ –	£ 952	£ 1,361	£ 2,160	£ 2,879	£ 1,175	£ 2,239

£ 10,766   Present value of cash flows (sum of discounted income p.a.)
£ 10,000   Less capital expenditure
£ 766   Net present value

Figure 12: Example of net present value analysis

discount rate, the longer the (discounted) pay-back period. In terms of decision-making, the facilities manager is likely to be comparing several options. The key criteria would therefore be that:

- the NPV is positive (discounted income is greater than initial capital expenditure)

- the required rate of return (5%) is exceeded

- the project with the highest ratio of present value to capital expenditure is providing the greatest return (in the above example this profitability index equals 1.08)

- the discounted pay-back period should be the least possible

It would normally be considered best practice to present these statistics in tabular form, as they will vary with respect to one another according to the characteristics of the project. This will enable conclusions to be drawn easily and the best option for the particular company to be chosen.

Internal rate of return

The internal rate of return (IRR) determines the discount rate at which the present value of the cash flows equals the initial capital expenditure, that is where the NPV equals £0. The IRR percentage should be greater than the company's cost of capital if a project is to be considered as economic. In the spreadsheet example given in Figure 12, the facilities manager could use trial and error to find the discount percentage that results in an NPV of £0. However, most spreadsheet applications have an IRR function that automatically determines the correct percentage. The following equation is an example of how this can be set up:

$$=IRR(-10000, 1000, 1500, 2500, 3500, 1500, 3000)$$

Again, the individual cash values in this equation would normally be substituted by spreadsheet cell references.

Cost/benefit analysis

The techniques described above essentially compare initial costs, ongoing revenues and the timing of transactions. The techniques do not necessarily (in their basic application) take account of costs and qualitative benefits that affect the business, third parties or the wider environment. Often these benefits are considered intangible, soft or subjective and difficult to measure – for example, noise, smell, image or even productivity. Cost/benefit analysis is a widely used technique where costs are directly compared with the benefits – usually though the use of a simple two-column table.

Applying the techniques

Because decisions made during the design stages of a building impact on capital occupancy costs, the technique of discounting is particularly relevant for comparing different design options. For these reasons a facilities manager should insist upon the development of a life cycle cost model at the earliest stage of a project. As the design becomes more and more detailed the model will grow and should be capable of assisting with ongoing decision-making.

The methodology followed for the simple examples given above will assist in the development of practical financial analysis models. Indeed, the following are examples of some common uses of discounting future costs in relation to facilities management:

- **Maintenance** – a common example is the comparison of design options where specifications vary in quality, which impacts on the cost of maintenance and the life until replacement. The techniques are very important in this respect as there is a common misconception that high quality specifications will always lead to lower maintenance costs.

- **Energy** – the specification of lamp fittings frequently causes a significant difference in energy consumption and hence utilities costs.

- **Cleaning** – cleaning costs are largely associated with time, degree of mechanisation and type of consumables required. Specification of building finishes, therefore, commonly impacts on overall cleaning costs. The problem may be complicated further by the relationship between the cleaning method and the life cycle of components.

- **Component and material selection** – the above example establishes that material/component specification may impact on cleaning costs. However, the effects are not likely to be limited to cleaning alone and can affect other facilities services, such as utilities, security, churn costs, and so on.

- **Investment appraisal** – it is common for facilities managers to be involved in portfolio or estate management decisions where disposals, acquisitions (both lease and buy), refurbishment and new build options may need comparison. In such circumstances all of the techniques described above can be used.

Property costs

As occupancy in a building rises, premises and support services costs will also rise, whereas property costs will largely remain static (assuming a short time period for the increase in occupancy). For facilities economics, this means that the increase in facilities costs per capita (premises and support services) will be more than outweighed by the corresponding reduction (as staff numbers increase) in property costs per capita.

Facilities managers are, therefore, principally concerned with space (driving property costs) and occupancy (driving facilities costs). In addition, however, the facilities manager should have a working knowledge of costs associated with the provision of property.

Property expenditure is normally associated with payments for rent, rates, insurance and service charges. These costs normally form a significant proportion of the facilities management budget – for instance 33% in the example illustrated in FIGURE 2, P173.

Rent

Rent is an amount paid by a tenant in exchange for the use of a building and is usually regulated under the terms of a lease. Mortgage payments to a financial institution (commercial property loan) or 'internal rents' payable to a holding company may be encountered by the organisation if the property is freehold in title. Rent tends to be fixed for long periods of time which means that the facilities manager will only be able to exercise an influence on cost at the agreed rent review date (usually every five years).

Facilities managers are often faced with making the strategic decision of whether to rent/lease or own the freehold title of a particular building. Analysis of the options should be related to the organisation's internal rate of return (IRR) on capital employed (IRR is covered in FINANCIAL ANALYSIS: INTERNAL RATE OF RETURN, P203). The answer to the question relates to whether the organisation can earn more on the capital which is otherwise tied up in the freehold.

For more on the legal issues concerning rent, see PROPERTY LAW: BUSINESS LEASES: RENT, P130.

Rates

Within the UK, a uniform business rate (UBR) exists as a means of taxation based upon the value of the property. All commercial properties are assessed at prevailing market rent levels by the Inland Revenue Valuation Office, and a rateable value calculated and fixed for a certain period of time (reviewed every five years; values become effective after an additional two years). For occupied property the UBR is added to this value to calculate the total sum payable for rates. The facilities manager should be aware of these rules, together with the following opportunities for effective financial management:

- Unoccupied offices and retail property attract half the calculated total sum.

- Unoccupied industrial properties, warehouses and listed buildings attract the full sum.

- Appeals may be made against rating assessments, for which an expert surveyor's services should be sought.

- Where the property assets have changed materially – through part demolition, for example – then rate liability may be reduced.

- External factors, such as neighbouring road works or building works, can reduce the rateable value.

Service charges

Service charges are normally covered under the terms of the lease and serve as a means for the landlord to recoup the cost of facilities services (such as building maintenance, grounds maintenance, fire protection, cleaning, security, vending, fitness suite, and so on) provided to common parts of buildings or estates. From the landlord's point of view, the investment needs to be protected through maintenance and cleaning so that there is no adverse effect on its value over the lease term. Until recently, service charges were largely hidden in so far as tenants did not contest or renegotiate the levels of cost.

In addition to the principles of benchmarking outlined here, the facilities manager should:

- Study the wording of the lease with care, as this will influence the method of remedy as well as interaction with other payments due in connection with dilapidations or costs of reinstatement at the end of the lease term.

- Request copies of supporting documentation relating to the financial calculations for analysis.

- Remember that the landlord's procurement processes and service contracts may influence the competitiveness of the service costs. The facilities manager is likely to have a better understanding than the landlord of what the expected cost of a service should be, and should press for the renegotiation of any uncompetitive contracts.

- Determine if excessive or additional charges are being levied by managing agents.

- Determine if excessive monies are being diverted to sinking funds for large life cycle replacement costs, such as lifts, air conditioning plant, and so forth.

- Check the measurement of parameters used in the calculation and apportionment of service charges.

- Remember that the common approach for large service charges is for the landlord or agent to budget for the year ahead, recover actual sums periodically and reconcile the balance at the end of the year. In this respect the facilities manager has to rely on the other party's skills of budgeting for facilities management services.

The legal issues relating to service charges are covered in PROPERTY LAW: SERVICE CHARGES, P134.

Insurance

Like service charges, insurances payable under the terms of a lease have also tended to be 'lost' amongst other charges levied by the landlord and therefore not generally contested or analysed until recently. Consider the following:

- Determine the exact scope (or comprehensiveness) of the policy and whether it is suitable for the business.

- Insurance policies may cover loss arising in connection with buildings (and foundations but not the site), contents, rent abatement/loss of rent, contracts and loss of profits.

- The insured party should know the exact period of the insurance so that it is not allowed to lapse.

- In cases of indemnification (where the insured party is to be left in the same position after the occurrence as before), the insurance payment will be the cost of works less both depreciation and betterment allowances.

- In cases of reinstatement (where the insured party to be covered for the cost of reconstruction or repairs to restore the property to its original condition), no adjustments are made for depreciation or wear and tear, although a deduction for betterment may be made.

- The effects of inflation may be covered in the insurance policy by way of index-linking. This can have a significant effect if inflation has risen and a claim is made within the insurance period.

- Where statutory requirements have changed, the insured party may not be covered for the additional cost of complying with new standards.

- Insurers of commercial and industrial property are normally protected against under-insurance by an 'average clause' which works by adjusting a claim amount by the same proportion as the difference between the full reinstatement value and the sum insured. The remaining balance is normally paid by the insured.

- Remember that the insurance premium is affected by such issues as specification of materials and fire protection measures, which may be under the control of the facilities manager, therefore compliance with the insurance contract and/or legislation is important.

The legal issues relating to insurance are covered in PROPERTY LAW: BUSINESS LEASES: INSURANCE, P133.

Principles of facilities finance

The facilities manager should have a clear understanding of the background principles of business finance before embarking on any matters relating to the preparation and planning of budgets, the procurement of goods and services, benchmarking facilities costs and the study of occupancy costs and whole life economics.

Taxation

The facilities manager can contribute significantly to reducing an organisation's overall tax burden. In many organisations, however, there are no processes encouraging the facilities manager to consider the effects of taxation on any particular service or product. Significant investments in facilities should be evaluated carefully through the identification of the correct tax burdens throughout the life cycle and using financial analysis techniques (see TECHNIQUES FOR FINANCIAL ANALYSIS, P199). The effect of input and output VAT payments and recovery on cash flow is particularly significant in financial models. The facilities manager should always consult the services of a tax specialist, as rules and regulations are complex and constantly changing. As a general rule, however, the following issues normally affect the availability of tax exemptions, reliefs and concessions.

* the nature of the company or legal entity performing business

* transactions or works being carried out

* location – different countries have different tax/allowance regulations

* the nature of any funding arrangements

* the nature of the industry or business – some organisations may attract significant tax benefits

The principal types of taxation that the facilities manager should consider when budgeting are discussed below, together with indicative (non-exhaustive) taxation rules.

Corporation tax

Corporation tax is tax payable as a result of income calculated on a trading account. Rates may vary between countries, but additional charges such as social security contributions should be taken into account in financial planning. For the 2001/02 UK accounting period the principal corporation tax rates are:

- 20% for small companies
- 30% main rate

Income tax

Income tax is payable on the portion of staff wages that are taxable – that is, the salary, adjusted for allowances and benefits. For the 2001/02 UK accounting period income tax rates are:

- 10% starting rate for income between £0 and £1,880
- 22% basic rate for remaining income between £1,881 and £29,400
- 40% higher rate for remaining income over £29,400

Note that some European Union member states also impose a tax linked to various measures of wealth.

Capital gains tax

Capital gains tax (CGT) is payable upon disposal (sales and/or gifts) of a capital asset (where there is a gain in value), subject to exemptions, allowances and other reliefs. For the 2001/02 UK accounting period CGT rates are:

- 10% for income below the income tax starting rate limit
- 20% for the portion of income falling within the basic rate bracket
- 40% for the portion of income exceeding the higher rate income tax threshold

Inheritance and gift taxes are applied to the value of the inheritance or gift. For the 2001/02 UK accounting period the rate is 40% of the value above £242,000.

Value added tax

Value added tax (VAT) is chargeable on the supply or purchase of goods and services. When organisations supply goods or services they will normally be liable to VAT as an output tax. For example, facilities managers should recognise that sales to staff by way of restaurant facilities or vending machines are liable for (output) VAT.

Many goods and services that are bought by an organisation will bear VAT as an input tax. Businesses who make taxable supplies in excess of £54,000 (usually over a 12-month period) must be VAT-registered, which normally means that input taxes can be reclaimed, though not for such items as cars available for private motoring or supplies for business entertainment.

Generally, in the case of public sector organisations, VAT treatment depends first and foremost on whether goods or services are supplied in the course or furtherance of business. If this is not the case (as in the majority of cases), the activities are deemed outside the scope of VAT and there is no tax liability. There are nevertheless grey areas in the application of this rule and HM Customs and Excise provide guidance for public sector organisations.

There are currently three rates of VAT:

- 17.5% (standard rate)

- 5% (reduced rate for domestic fuel and power and the installation of energy-saving materials)

- nil or zero rate (where no tax is payable)

The following are examples of the goods and services liable for VAT:

Standard-rated supplies:

- new construction work (other than for houses, flats and buildings for charities)

- repairs and improvements to buildings (except protected buildings)

- professional fees in connection with construction works

- the sale of freehold interests in new buildings (less than three years old since completion) that are neither houses or flats, nor of charitable status

- the sale of freehold interests, lease, tenancy or licences of 'new' holiday accommodation

- where an election to waive exemption (otherwise known as an option to tax) has been made to allow the recovery of some or all of the input tax incurred in supplying the property (for example, where a landlord has waived exemption, VAT will normally be chargeable on the rent and service charge costs – indeed any cost that is consideration for the supply of the property, such as charges for insurance, rates, telephones, reception/switchboard services, recreation facilities, unmetered utilities and management, where clearly supplied by the landlord) (see also PROPERTY LAW: VALUE ADDED TAX, p124)

- the provision of car parking facilities and sales of land to be used for car parking, except where related to an exempt supply of a building

- building demolition works

- inducements paid by a landlord to a tenant or by a tenant to a sub-tenant

Zero-rated supplies

- the sales of new houses or flats by builders and developers (less than three years since completion)
- the granting of long leases (21 years or more) for new houses or flats
- construction of new residential homes, student hostels, and so on
- construction of new buildings for charitable organisations
- significant repairs and improvements to protected buildings (listed as Grade I or II or ancient monuments) where use is residential or charitable
- most food (but not meals in restaurants and cafes and hot takeaway food and drink)
- books and newspapers
- young children's clothing and shoes
- prescriptions and many aids for disabled people

Exempt supplies

(exempt unless the option to tax has been exercised)

- selling, leasing and letting land and buildings (but not lettings of garages, parking spaces or hotel and holiday accommodation)
- sales of freehold buildings over three years of age
- rent and service charges (unless exemption is waived by a landlord)
- betting, gambling and lotteries (but not the takings from gambling machines)
- insurance sales or supplies relating to credit provision
- certain education and training supplies

Other points of interest to the facilities manager are:

- Where property forms part of the transfer of a business as part of a going concern and the purchaser (who is registered for VAT) intends to carry on the same business, then the supply is outside the scope of VAT. This rule also applies to a landlord who sells a let building to another who has the intention of carrying on the same business.
- Rent-free periods are not seen as a supply for VAT purposes and no tax is payable. However, if the rent-free period is given by the landlord in exchange for something which the tenant agrees to do (such as carrying out refurbishment works that benefit the landlord), then VAT is payable on the amount of rent that the landlord agrees to forego.

- Dilapidation payments are deemed to represent claims for damages by a landlord against a tenant and are considered outside the scope of VAT.

Stamp duty

Stamp duty is usually related to legal documents associated with property transactions or company shares. Current UK rates for stamp duty related to conveyances or land transfers are:

- nil (certified value up to and including £60,000)
- 1% (certified value over £60,000 and not exceeding £250,000)
- 3% (certified value over £250,000 and not exceeding £500,000)
- 4% (certified value over £500,000)

Current UK stamp duty rates payable on average rent associated with a lease term are:

- 1% (where the term does not exceed seven years; only applicable if rent exceeds £5,000 p.a.)
- 2% (more then seven years but less than 35 years)
- 12% (more then 35 years and less then 100 years)
- 24% (over 100 years)

Current UK stamp duty rates payable on the premium are:

- nil (up to and including £60,000 with an annual rent of £600 or less)
- 1% (over £60,000 and less than £250,000)
- 3% (over £250,000 and less than £500,000)
- 4% (over £500,000)

Social security tax

Social security taxes or national insurance contributions (NICs) are payable on all wages, salaries, commission, profit-related pay and overtime, in addition to sick pay and maternity pay from an employer (essentially payable on gross earnings before pension and income tax deductions). The percentage is payable by employees between a primary threshold (£87 per week) and upper earnings limit (£575 per week). Where an employer's pension scheme is contracted out of state earnings related pension, the employees' NICs are reduced from 10% to 8.4%. Employers must pay NICs at 11.9% of all their employees' earnings over the primary threshold. Note that there are additional rules for self-employed and voluntary workers.

Climate Change Levy

Environmental taxation may be broadly classified into taxes associated with energy consumption, pollution of the environment and health. All UK organisations, businesses and public sector facilities are liable for taxes associated with the Climate Change Levy (CCL). The levy is designed to be calculated prior to any VAT calculation which is then applied on top. The tax will be applied where energy consumption is in excess of 33kWh electricity per day, 145kWh gas per day, 1 tonne of coal or 50kg cylinders of liquefied petroleum gas (LPG). These thresholds effectively exclude liability of small businesses. Other fuels are taxed on the basis of excise duty. The levy rates are:

- 0.43p/kWh for electricity
- 0.15p/kWh for gas
- 0.15p/kWh for coal (£1.17/kg)
- 0.07p/kWh for LPG (0.96p/kg)

Apart from the fact that the levy creates an incentive for the facilities manager to reduce consumption and/or negotiate good tariffs, it should be noted that there are various discounts and exemptions that apply, for example:

- Green energy sources such as photovoltaics or wind turbines are not included in the levy rules.

- The energy used for combined heat and power (CHP) plants is currently exempted if the system meets efficiency regulations.

- Energy-intensive organisations may qualify for exemptions if they can agree targets for future reduction.

- Enhanced capital allowances (ECAs) are available to private sector organisations so that particular pieces of energy-saving technology or equipment (such as insulation, lighting, boilers and refrigeration) may attract 100% allowances against their write-off value in an accounting year (thus reducing the annual corporation tax burden). Normally businesses are only allowed to write off 25% of the equipment value to tax.

For best practice advice relating to the CCL, see WORKPLACE FACILITIES: CLIMATE CHANGE LEVY, P299, and for the legal issues and full details of exemptions, see HEALTH AND SAFETY LAW: CLIMATE CHANGE LEVY, P66.

Landfill tax

Landfill tax applies to waste disposed of at landfill sites in the UK licensed under environmental law. Liability rests with the landfill site operators who in turn pass on the cost to their customers by way of commercial disposal rates. The current UK tax rates are:

- £2/tonne where the waste is certified as inactive or inert (rock, clay, sand, soil, concrete waste, non-contaminated water, brine, and so on)

- £12/tonne for all other taxable waste. The Government intends to increase this rate by £1 p.a. until 2004.

Capital and revenue expenditure

A business commonly has two types of expenditure – capital and revenue expenditure. The traditional (basic) accounting definitions of these are as follows:

- **Revenue expenditure** is associated with purchasing goods and services in the short term, including any associated business input costs – materials, labour, rent, rates, insurance, utilities, maintenance, and so on (common facilities management cost centres).

- **Capital expenditure** is the cost associated with acquiring fixed assets which cost a significant amount and usually provide economic benefits in the long term.

It is normal for a finance department to require capital and revenue expenditure to be budgeted and managed on a monthly basis so that the company will understand any peaks and troughs in cash flow. Such forecasting is intended to help financial managers ascertain the impact of capital and revenue expenditure on the working capital of the organisation and on company borrowing.

Revenue expenditure (for example, that associated with maintenance and repair work) is allowable as a deduction from the gross profits of an organisation. In this respect, a full rate taxpayer who pays 30% corporation tax on taxable income effectively avoids any tax liability for facilities services associated with revenue expenditure (the equivalent of a refund of 30% of the cost of qualifying works).

Depreciation

Fixed assets are normally discounted in the accountancy process in order to show the true (reducing) economic benefit of a capital investment over a period of years (the assets lose value due to use, the passage of time and obsolescence). Another way of looking at the issue is that it would be 'unfair' if expenditure relating to assets purchased in a particular year were included as an expense in the profit and loss account for that year – thus significantly reducing profit levels. In facilities management terms, an effective building services maintenance strategy will normally extend the economic life of assets, which in turn reduces depreciation (thus profits will be higher). Furthermore, capital expenditure associated with improving an asset (for example, life cycle replacement works) should never be charged as an expense on the profit and loss account. Using alternative accountancy terms, such expenditure should be 'capitalised' and not 'expensed'.

There are two common methodologies for calculating depreciation:

- **The 'straight line' method** – this divides the capital sum (less final salvage value if applicable) by the useful economic life of the asset. The resultant figure is the annual amount of depreciation that reduces the company's profit measurement.

- **The 'reducing installment' method** – this is considered closer to reality in that the asset is treated as if it loses its value more quickly in the early years compared with later years. A fixed percentage is applied to the reducing balance year on year.

Capital allowances

The law and regulations surrounding capital allowances are particularly complex, with the primary difficulty being how to determine 'qualifying expenditure' – that is, capital and revenue expenditure, described above in basic terms.

In most cases an organisation will prefer expenditure to be classified as revenue so that it is deducted in the calculation of profits, and thereby 100% tax relief is obtained (equivalent to a 100% refund of the 30% main rate corporation tax on taxable income). In contrast, there are only a few capital allowances that deliver 100% tax relief (the full refund of 20% or 30% corporation tax). The current rates for applying capital allowances are as follows:

Plant and machinery allowances for the first year:

- 100% on expenditure on energy-saving technology (applies to all firms)
- 100% on expenditure on information technology between 1 April 2000 and 31 March 2003 (applies to small firms only)
- 40% on expenditure on most assets (applies to small or medium-sized firms only)
- 25% on expenditure on most assets (applies to large firms only)
- 6% on expenditure on long-life assets (where economic life is deemed greater than or equal to 25 years) (applies to large firms only)

Plant and machinery allowances for subsequent years:

- 25% on the reducing balance for most assets
- 6% on the reducing balance for long-life assets

Buildings

- 4% annually (straight line method) on the cost of agricultural and forestry land
- 4% annually on the cost of new agricultural and industrial buildings or structures excluding land costs – for example, mills, factories, bridges, telecommunications buildings
- 4% annually on the cost of hotels that are permanent, have more than 10 lettable rooms, are open for business for at least four months (between April and October) and support hotel services such as cleaning, laundry and a restaurant
- 100% on qualifying enterprise zone buildings and fixtures expenditure (excludes land costs) in the year in which it is incurred (furthermore, the taxpayer may wish to accept a reduced initial allowance and claim the balance of expenditure over four years)
- 100% on expenditure on buildings and assets that are used primarily for research activities; in addition, enhanced rates (exceeding 100%) are also available for some businesses carrying on research activities as a means of incentivising economic growth

Facilities managers will normally be interested in plant and machinery assets within buildings which qualify for capital allowances. Typically, qualifying expenditure can range from 15–75% of the overall construction budget for a new building (depending upon specification). Whilst the rules relating to qualification are particularly complex and depend on the precise nature of the business, the following list provides some primary examples:

- air conditioning installations – in some circumstances floors and ceilings used as plenums for air conditioning can also qualify
- heating and hot water systems (also CHP, see above under CLIMATE CHANGE LEVY, p213)
- lifts
- security and fire protection/safety systems
- furniture
- demountable partitions (providing you can prove that they are moveable, by showing space plan changes over a number of years, for example)

- carpet tiles
- incidental expenditure relating to the installation of plant and machinery in existing buildings

Given that significant benefits can be accrued through careful tax planning, the facilities manager should:

- identify allowances as early as possible for new buildings – even at concept design stage
- consider optimal design solutions, such as demountable versus fixed partitions
- identify allowances in connection with potential new acquisitions
- identify allowances associated with beneficial locations, such as enterprise zones
- if applicable, optimise the structuring of tenancy agreements for benefits accruing from fitting-out works
- maintain sufficient information in an asset register for supporting claim calculations

References

1. Williams, B (2001), *Facilities Economics in the European Union*, Building Economics Bureau Ltd, London

2. Sir Malcolm Bates, *The first report on the Private Finance Initiative*, for HM Government, June 1997

Further reading

Kelly, J and Male, S (1993), *Value Management In Design and Construction, The Economic Management of Projects*, first edition, E & FN Spon, London, p17

Lucey, T (1996), *Costing*, DP Publications, first edition, London, p387

Robson, W (1997), *Strategic Management and Information Systems*, second edition, Pitman Publishing, London, p226

5 Business Continuity

Frank Booty

Disaster can strike at any time, and often from the least expected source in the least expected area. Disaster can encompass fire, flood, theft, a crash, a bomb, or any event occurring against the odds which stops a company operating at its expected level. There are over 30,000 commercial building fires each year. IT and telecom – particularly mobile phone – theft increases continually; the Association of British Insurers reckons over £600 million worth of IT equipment is stolen each year in England alone. Natural disasters such as floods are difficult to prepare for and predict. Terrorist activity continues to pose real threats and, as any company dealing with commercially sensitive information knows, it need not come from any particular or well known terrorist organisation. So how does a business continue in the face of such an event? Business continuity is about the business of survival.

The Turnbull Report

The Institute of Chartered Accountants of England and Wales published the *Turnbull Report* in October 1999, to the Stock Exchange, recommending all quoted companies should have a risk management strategy in place by 23 December 2000. Public companies should certainly have all complied with the deadline. They didn't. Further, some 80% of UK plcs also failed to comply.

Companies not planning for interruption stand to lose more than just cash flow, customers and confidence – eight out of 10 companies cease trading after a major incident. Partly because of that, many organisations stipulate that their suppliers must have business continuity plans in place to minimise the knock-on effects any catastrophe would have. In the seven years after 1994, business interruptions affected some 7.5% of businesses, costing the UK some £3 billion each year.

Under 50% of companies who depend on computer systems and other technology have formal business continuity plans, and only 12% of those plans are considered to be effective outside the IT department and across the business. One of the most valuable contributions Turnbull has made is to help companies see risk management not just as a means of staying afloat, but as a way of embracing business continuity in order to thrive in the future.

Research has shown that 82% of listed companies and 78% of non-listed companies state Turnbull will have an impact on the perception of business continuity planning. But 58% have not reviewed their policies since the advent of Turnbull.

Business continuity demands total commitment at board level, the dedication of key individuals in a company, assistance from business continuity specialists and an enthusiastic and informed staff to carry out all the necessary processes. Minimising risk plays a vitally important role in the overall scheme, and must be addressed at the outset and allowed to influence all future planning.

Developing a strategy

Business continuity management can best be defined as:

"The ongoing process of ensuring the continual operation of critical business processes through the evaluation of risk and resilience, and the implementation of mitigation measures."

Business continuity management had its roots in disaster recovery planning, but as the market and the players within have matured, so too has the belief that risks to business can be mitigated as well as recovered. Disaster recovery set out with the intention of providing business with protection further to that originally provided by standard maintenance and insurance contracts. Companies have accepted that whilst an investment in business continuity directly affects the bottom line, and often with no immediate tangible benefits, it is the most important investment they will make. Crucially, companies have woken up to the difference between business continuity and simple insurance, which will at best replenish the value of the equipment lost, and that at a time when it could already be too late.

To put it plainly, business continuity planning is about planning for interruption and having the appropriate mechanisms installed to respond to disaster. Whilst it encompasses much more than simple insurance cover, like insurance it places risk firmly at the centre of all its processes.

Risk management

A company's exposure to operational risks depends on the likelihood of that risk occurring and the impact it would have on the organisation if it were to do so. Impact is measured financially and an impact profile produced on current loss and future effects on the organisation. If likelihood and/or impact is zero, then the business continuity manager does not need to plan for that particular interruption to business.

To establish a threat profile, it is necessary to examine the likelihood of the threat occurring, the potential effects of the threats, and how fast and effective disaster recovery measures are.

- **Likelihood** – the likelihood of threats occurring can be reduced by introducing preventative measures into the organisation, such as a no smoking policy or security system.

- **Effects** – the potential effects of the threats are few and, to contain them, organisations must understand how their vulnerabilities affect the business, both within and between different layers in the company. These layers can be typically categorised as financial, operational, IT and communications, staff, the marketplace and even the company's upstream and downstream supply chain.

- **Disaster recovery** – after the risk has manifested itself as a disaster, and preventative measures cannot be implemented, disaster recovery measures are employed. The direct financial impact on the organisation of suffering that disaster is now wholly dependent on the speed at which the organisation can recover.

Assessing the company's exposure to operational risk depends on the company's ability to quantify impact and measure likelihood, to produce an analysis that takes account of time frames and priorities, simulates scenarios, identifies gaps and threats and makes recommendations for further action.

Conducting a business impact analysis

A business impact analysis (BIA) can be defined as "a management-level analysis which identifies the impacts of losing company resources"; it "measures the effect of resource loss and escalating losses over time to provide senior management with reliable data on which to base decisions on risk mitigation and continuity planning".[1]

If conducted correctly, business continuity planning should be a modular exercise, where every phase adds value to the overall effectiveness of the plan. The first step is to look at the risks faced by a company. The following questions should be addressed:

- Where is the company located?

- Who are the neighbours?

- Which of the staff are mission critical?

- What technology could the company not do without?
- Where is the company most vulnerable?

Answers to these questions, the last of which is the most significant, will determine where the possible risks lie. This information can then be used in a BIA of the company, where it is necessary to quantify the risk predicament, both to clarify what needs to be done, and to gain that all-important board approval (which typically proves to be the biggest stumbling block). The BIA looks at all the risks faced by all aspects of the company, the chances of them happening and the predicted outage should they be encountered. This is all carried out from the perspective of the company's key business priorities – reputation, image and profits – which directly influence the nature of the plan.

Drawing up a plan

Planning is the next logical step and procedures need to be in place for staff, recovery of IT and buildings, evacuation procedures, media management and dealing with trauma, as well as any other issue pertinent to the company's operations. A business continuity plan need not be a sprawling document, and if there is confidence in the staff's capabilities, the smaller it is the better. This, together with ongoing training, will also encourage staff at all levels to back the project; any plan is useless unless the people operating it both support it and are capable of implementing it. The plan must be amended with the emergence of new staff, buildings, procedures and any technological upgrades, in conjunction with any third-party disaster recovery supplier.

Rehearsing the plan

But the work does not end once the plan has been drawn up. The final and critical step is to carry out rehearsals and maintenance. The Business Continuity Institute reckons only 18% of companies rehearse their plans; but non-rehearsal is the biggest weakness in a business continuity plan. Rehearsal identifies weaknesses in both the plan and the people in the designated crisis management team. The plan has to be kept relevant and up-to-date, and rehearsals should be carried out at least biannually. Testing the plan until it runs smoothly and everyone knows exactly what to do is the only way to stay prepared.

Business vulnerability

Each business has a different threat portfolio, as no two businesses are exactly alike. In the event of a disaster, at best an organisation can expect to suffer damage to its principal reason for operating. This will mainly be financial, but may also mean damage to reputation, share price, image and customer support. At worst it will result in the damages being irreversible, and the total failure of the business.

There are many statistics published about UK business interruption:

- Power failure accounts for over 10% of all business interruptions.
- 57% of disasters are IT-related.
- 61% of companies don't publish their business continuity plans throughout their organisation.
- 84% of companies do not identify risks in the supply chain.

Average outage times of business interruption in the UK are:

- fire – 28 days
- IT failure – 10 days
- lightning – 22 days
- flood – 10 days
- theft – 26 days
- power failure – 1 day

Another non-quantifiable aspect is job loss.

Arguments in the business continuity industry suggest that, rather than being the forum for doom-and-gloom merchants to excel, business continuity can be rightly seen as an investment which, rather than just reducing the impact of disaster on business, can also increase employee, investor and shareholder confidence in the company. Note, a good business continuity services provider can be measured by how regularly it is asked to speak to executive boards about the corporate requirement for continuity planning.

An effective strategy

A business continuity strategy has to meet several criteria to be effective:

- It is crucial that the board lead, and are seen to lead; the strategy must be constructed and implemented as an integral part of the company's structure.
- There can be no parts of the organisation that the strategy does not touch. As well as becoming a key and integral part of each department, the strategy has to cross all departmental and functional boundaries.
- The strategy must reflect the way the company interacts with its environment, and it must equally anticipate future demands from that environment and from within the company.

- All necessary resources (vital information such as contact names and numbers) must be available, appropriate to the nature of the company's business.

- Through a greater awareness and better management of risks, the strategy should seek to add value to the company. The reduced uncertainty in the implementation of business strategy will aid this process.

The ultimate aim is for a cost-effective and focused business continuity infrastructure.

An organisation's exposure to operational risk is a measure of its susceptibility to unwanted, unplanned events. The implication is that if the two dimensions of 'unwanted' and 'unplanned' can be managed effectively, the organisation's exposure to risk is *de facto* under control.

At the core of continuity planning is an understanding of the organisation's unique threat profile and subsequent exposure to operational risk. Central to this is the BIA. Note, neither management nor the board will ever truly buy into the concept of business continuity until they can see the *quantified* risks of failure associated with serious business interruptions. Unless the board can see risks broken down into £s and $s they are unlikely to appreciate the issues.

Analysis of potential risk

The first step is to look around you:

- **Study historical data** – what types of emergencies have occurred in the community, at the company's premises and others in the area?

- **Look at the local environment** – is the site near major transportation routes, airports, flood plains, dams or power plants? Is the company close to other companies which produce, store or transport hazardous materials (which may be a terrorist target)?

- **Analyse the technological risks** – what could result from a process or system failure? What emergencies can be caused by an employee error? Human error is the single biggest cause of workplace emergencies and can result from poor training, poor equipment maintenance, carelessness, misconduct and fatigue.

Analyse each potential emergency from beginning to end. Consider what could happen as a result of:

- prohibited access to the facility
- loss of electrical power

- communication lines going down
- ruptured gas mains, water damage
- smoke damage
- structural damage
- air or water contamination
- explosion
- building collapse
- chemical release

Once all the risks have been considered, estimate probability and plot the results on a graph. The x-axis should indicate probability and the y-axis should show the amount of probable downtime (the outage) in terms of days. So, for example, while a power failure is highly probable, it causes minimal downtime, while flood is unlikely but will have a serious long-term effect (see Figure 1).

To assess the potential business impact, consider the loss of market share. Assess the potential impact of:

- employees unable to work
- customers unable to reach the facility

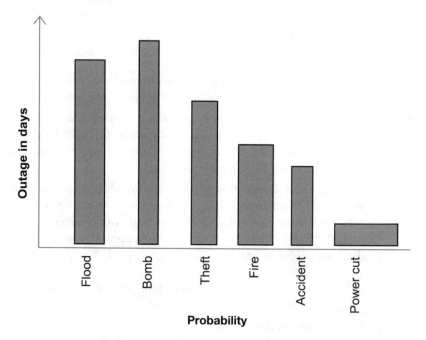

Figure 1: Effect and probability of risk

- company violation of contractual agreements
- imposition of fines and penalties or legal costs
- cash flow slowdown
- damaged reputation and image
- job losses
- lack of delivery of critical supplies
- slowed or halted product distribution
- damage to the environment
- drop in shareholder and stakeholder confidence
- compliance with statutory obligations

Once a company appreciates the impact an interruption could have on its business, it will be in a position to minimise the risks on a priority basis. If it decides reputation is more important than profits, it should first minimise those risks that could affect its reputation.

If the BIA is done objectively, it will have a stimulating effect on the business. Employees will understand how seriously the whole continuity issue is taken. Suppliers – who have to be approached as part of the analysis – will realise they should conduct a similar exercise which in itself will help to protect the company's business. Also, the board will start to take the matter of business continuity seriously.

Strategic management of business continuity can be looked at as an operational framework with three key phases of analysis, decision and implementation. Once the risks have been assessed and the priorities decided, there can often be a discrepancy between the company's business continuity needs and what the market has to offer. The next step, therefore, is to decide on an appropriate level of business continuity provision that is built on solid cost/benefit evaluations.

Implementing the strategy

Emergency planning

Emergency planning ensures the ability to respond to extraordinary service demand. It involves setting a procedure in case something goes wrong which is outside local capability to control or fix – for example, the definition of roles and responsibilities in the case of a major incident. Often an organisation will have failed to address all the emergency plans needed, such as a hospital which often looks to external risks and so may be 'blind' to incidents that could occur on site. Plans – operationally oriented – should address or include:

- up-to-date record drawings
- asset registers (addressing those critical to the business)
- how staff or visitors on site will be identified and accounted for
- safety procedures
- mirroring of facilities if these are critical to operations (such as duplicate dealing rooms in the City)
- fall-back communication systems
- essential utility supplies in case of mains failures
- triggers that will initiate the plan or component parts
- prioritisation of action
- any necessary training requirements
- recovery process
- stockpiling of critical supplies – do not forget dependence on single small items which are used 'once in a blue moon' but without which a service folds
- regular updates – remember, staff change, buildings develop, and so on

Plans can be developed by considering exactly what aspects of your operation the business is dependent on. It is important to create a vision of what the business capability will be in the event of an incident – will it be business as usual or will output be reduced?

Roles and responsibilities

Most companies will have a management team to continue running unaffected or undamaged sections of the business, consisting of existing personnel carrying out their normal duties. A second team – the emergency management team – has the task of accomplishing the recovery or continuance of the damaged sections of the business. Such a team is supported by the business continuity manager, business continuity teams and other teams involved in the recovery effort. Mobilisation only occurs in the event of an incident.

The constitution of these teams will have to cover many key areas:

- damage assessment and salvage
- IT recovery
- telecom and data communications recovery and call centre operations

- premises restoration
- procurement of disaster recovery resources (such as sandbags)
- media management (covering corporate communications, public relations and marketing)
- operational/production recovery
- business unit/departmental recovery
- support and coordination for such areas as personnel, transport, administration
- welfare support for staff affected by the disaster
- dealing with insurers

There needs to be a team leader and a deputy for each business continuity team. All staff must be trained. In the event of a disaster, staff need clear communication informing them of what to do. One way of effecting this is to issue everyone with a telephone number and/or website where up-to-date details of the status of the business can be communicated (if there is a disaster). This system should be tested regularly.

Roles and responsibilities must be assigned and understood. Details must be rolled out to all sites for multi-site operations (an obvious but often overlooked fact). Back-up sites and locations have to be planned. The location of all staff members at work must be known, and full details on home addresses and phone contacts available.

Outsourcing disaster recovery

Disaster recovery is fast becoming a mission-critical service. Customers need the best the industry has to offer to keep their businesses operational whatever the circumstances. As part of their business-wide disaster recovery policy, businesses almost without exception have chosen to invest in one or a series of third-party disaster recovery agreements. Disaster recovery companies can now help protect almost any vital asset a company may own. This may be a critical server or PC, or may also include standby facilities, buildings or even people.

Disaster recovery companies work by responding to a company's invocation, in a pre-contracted time frame. This is achieved through taking the actual technology and engineering support into the client or recovery site.

Risk management should be central to disaster recovery provision. Companies must first understand what they stand to lose (in real terms) in the event of an interruption to business. This will hopefully have been calculated at the BIA stage of the planning cycle. The investment in the disaster recovery project will only be a valuable one if it is outweighed by the potential loss in the event of an interruption. It is because of this that the industry has only recently seen the small and medium enterprise and public sector markets invest in disaster recovery planning.

Organisations need to make sure their disaster recovery contracts minimise their risk exposure by catering for any eventuality. A thorough understanding of IT and information systems is essential for a disaster recovery company, but business continuity and disaster recovery are primarily risk management tools.

Selecting a disaster recovery supplier

Although a disaster recovery contract is much more sophisticated than an ordinary insurance policy, it is nevertheless based on a similar principle – risk assessment. A dedicated disaster recovery company should have a comprehensive system of risk analysis that considers every type of risk with probable occurrence rates. This system should include site inspectors and a detailed evaluation of the customer's own risk management plans.

Ideally, customers should be grouped in small syndicates based on contrasting risk levels, including geographical location and industrial sector. The risk assessment should also consider factors such as:

- proximity to transport infrastructure
- electricity supplies
- telecom networks

Each grouping should minimise the risk to individual members and ensure there are adequate resources to cope with multiple invocations.

The supplier of disaster recovery services should sell contracts on a risk, rather than unit numbers, basis. There is no point in buying a contract that covers 200 PCs only to find that when the contract is invoked, the service provider cannot supply 200 computers because it underestimated or miscalculated the risk exposure. The likelihood of invocation, rather than the number of machines covered, should be the key consideration in a disaster recovery contract.

Invest wisely

As more organisations turn their attention to disaster recovery and start investigating the market, it is only natural that some choose to select their supplier on the basis of cost. But disaster recovery, like insurance, is one area where buying on price could prove to be a mistake. Cheap insurance or disaster recovery cover can soon turn out to be expensive if the provider cannot honour its policies.

If a disaster recovery contract is very cheap, there is usually a good reason. The supplier may:

- have failed to make an adequate risk assessment
- have deliberately underestimated risk exposure to keep prices down
- be overselling its PC recovery stock to make a profit

Whatever the reason, underpricing is a risky strategy with single, disparate invocations. With the simultaneous multiple invocations becoming increasingly commonplace, it can be fatal.

If a disaster recovery provider fails to honour a contract, a company can seek redress through the courts, but this may be difficult or impossible if that company has already gone out of business. A company selling cheap disaster recovery contracts may well go out of business during the term of the contract or, worse still, as a result of invocation.

Demand the best

Today's competitive economic environment dictates that companies must move towards best practices and procedures. They should demand the very best the disaster recovery industry has to offer, including complete risk assessment to highlight areas of vulnerability, dedicated disaster recovery stock in secure storage facilities, and reliable up-to-date equipment. Above all, customers should insist on a disaster recovery company with a successful track record of providing total business continuity solutions for companies of all sizes.

Specifically, a good disaster recovery firm should:

- **Assess and respond to change** – it is important to remember that risk, like all business continuity issues, is not static. It changes as political, economic and social trends develop. Disaster recovery firms must understand these changes and appreciate their impact on risk calculations. This fact makes it essential for a disaster recovery company to review each customer's circumstances regularly and to advise on appropriate changes where necessary. Active response to risk assessment should ensure there are no nasty surprises if a company's disaster recovery cover has to be used in a real emergency.

- **Keep abreast of changes in technology** – not just in terms of staff training but also in their hardware profiles. Dedicated disaster recovery stock should be continually updated to keep pace with technology. As customers regularly update their IT infrastructure with more powerful and efficient equipment, they should expect their disaster recovery provider to do the same.

- **Provide regular testing for recovery plans** – a company should not have to ask for this, the disaster recovery firm should insist on it itself.

Finally, the term 'disaster' should be applied to any incident that prevents businesses operating as usual, from micro-chip theft to computer virus outbreaks, not just to large-scale incidents such as fires, floods or terrorist bombings. Ideally, it should be defined by the client.

The human factor

Care of staff is the final piece of the business continuity jigsaw. A company's people constitute its best (and potentially worst) asset. It is not enough simply to include them in a business continuity plan – they must be at its core. Key to this must be dedicated training of staff, where politics is discarded, and everyone is suitably prepared for the shock factor an interruption can bring. Communication is also vital and must be regular and company-wide – before, during and after an interruption. People will take note and follow procedures if they feel they are part of them.

If research figures are to be believed, just 7% of companies have a tried and tested business continuity plan that is not simply IT-specific. Less than 50% of these plans make direct reference to people. Taken at face value, these figures would suggest that the focus of disaster recovery provision should be IT infrastructure and similar technical requirements. However, it is human error that is the single largest cause of workplace emergencies: 95% of all commercial building fires are started by employees. If a PC is stolen from an office, there is a 60–70% chance that an employee has taken it. People also cause disasters without malicious intent if:

- they have not been trained properly
- they have not been adequately communicated with
- they are tired or unhappy
- they are put under extreme pressure

A company's staff is central to its success. If a whole department were to win the National Lottery as a syndicate and decide to leave, business would undoubtedly be severely disrupted. Whilst IT would still be operational, there would be no one there to use it. Some insurance companies are offering advice and premiums against the possibility of this happening, although this will obviously not cover the potential loss to credibility and image that such an interruption would bring. Planning for such interruptions should be as central to business continuity management as the potential loss of IT.

Equally important should be an effective channel of communication to ensure staff know how best to avoid causing a potential disaster. This needs to be implemented as early as induction, and continue to be regularly updated and communicated. Failing to communicate clearly and regularly not only threatens recovery should a disaster occur, it also demotivates individuals who interpret a lack of board-level endorsement of business continuity issues as an evaluation of their own personal function at the company as not 'mission-critical'.

All too often, the human aspect is overlooked for PCs, servers and work areas in disaster recovery planning. Business continuity professionals working within organisations will tell you that their plan mitigates against every possible interruption and the effects of that interruption. But whether they have given sufficient, or indeed any, thought to their staff will remain unclear until they are faced with a departmental resignation, an evacuation procedure or a traumatised member of staff.

Immediate disaster response procedures

After any full-scale interruption, such as fire or flood, management must be confident its staff are suitably prepared to act in a controlled manner and will know exactly what procedures they need to follow. If the media are present, they too will want immediate responses (see DEALING WITH THE MEDIA, P233), with many of them telling the story through the eyes of an employee to lend the coverage credibility and to provide an emotive angle.

Business continuity is all about protecting image, and this will be severely tarnished if companies are not seen to respect and look after their staff. Depending on the nature of the interruption, it may be safer to stay in the building rather than evacuating immediately. Yet in the middle of what is likely to be a disruptive environment, people's actions will change as their thoughts turn to their welfare and that of any family and friends who may be situated in buildings not far from the disruption. For one principal business continuity manager, this was precisely what happened during London's Canary Wharf bombing incident in 1996.

If a business evacuates its building, it must be to a location that is safe for its staff to group and far enough from any neighbouring businesses that may have been forced to do the same. Typically, businesses should avoid underground car parks, or areas too close to offices. It is important that the situation is controlled efficiently. Many people may leave personal belongings in the building and need transportation to return home, for which money should be readily available. There should be a plentiful supply of mobile phones for staff to check that others are safe and to reassure them of their own welfare.

Staff welfare

Human beings are emotional creatures, capable of responding in a number of ways to a disaster, which do not necessarily depend on its severity. Intense emotions, numbness, flashbacks and severe reactions can be triggered by seemingly unrelated events. Professional trauma counsellors for post traumatic stress disorder (PTSD) argue that an ideal PTSD system should include both an external consultant and system facilitators within the organisation, as well as a debriefing team and occupational health staff, all tailored to the structure and specific nature of the business. A company should immediately issue all personnel with a generic statement in the aftermath of a disaster to let them know the company respects their feelings and actions, and continue to support them long after the event by including trauma counselling as an integral part of its disaster recovery plan.

Businesses cannot cope with this on their own, but must make provision for it in a contingency plan. This is where dedicated business continuity groups are able to offer advice and help, through training, seminars and other similar media. Again, dealing with trauma should not be restricted to company-specific incidents, but should encompass any severe change in mood in an employee. Research has shown that 71% of men and 57% of women became sleepless as a direct result of stress arising from a previously unrecognised work-related issue.

Training

Business continuity training is often overlooked in an organisation, but in a real-life disaster it is the experience, or at least belief and confidence, in successful crisis management that will keep a company alive. Training will:

- raise the awareness of business continuity and its importance within the organisation
- lend ownership of the business continuity plan to employees of the organisation
- ensure the business continuity plan will be effective (even the best-laid plans won't work unless people are aware of their role and how to carry out that role)
- motivate – individuals will feel that the organisation is investing to meet their needs

- help streamline the business continuity plan (in time) as key employees become business continuity experts

Awareness raising for senior management is often most effective when carried out by an outside agency. Outsiders will not be seen to have any ulterior motive for promoting business continuity, whereas an in-house presentation may be seen as 'empire building'. Outsiders may also be seen to be more credible. They should have had first-hand experience of crisis situations and their repercussions and be able to convince senior managers of the real risks the company faces if it doesn't fully commit to a business continuity plan.

Training the business continuity planner

Practical training for the business continuity planner should also be outsourced from a reputable training supplier. Often, the most effective training course is a bespoke course held on the organisation's own premises. The trainer would normally meet with the business continuity planner, look at existing business continuity plans and procedures, and from there design a course around individual training needs, addressing any information gaps identified. Standard training courses and seminars are also useful, but by their nature will address generalities rather than the specific needs of an organisation.

One of the roles of the planner is general staff training, typically working with the human resources department. Methods used to raise awareness include information packages, presentations, newsletters, line manager briefings and simulations.

Dealing with the media

In the event of a disaster, the media will want immediate responses. The crisis management function needs to focus on the media interface: one individual must be appointed through whom all communications will be made or managed, who will report directly to the business continuity management team. No individual member of the company should talk to the media – instead a unified agreed message must be given out. The crux of this vitally important area should be viewed as turning a negative scenario into a positive situation.

Media management does, of course, vary according to the type of business affected. The financial sector, for example, is very coy about releasing information, whereas companies in the retail and distribution sector generally address the situation openly.

> ## A unified agreed message
>
> A good example of the success of this strategy is a situation where a fire started at a company in part of its manufacturing facility and administrative complex. The business continuity plan was invoked and the fire was brought under control. The crisis management team agreed a message which was broadcast through a glossy in-house publication with pictures of the fire, key messages and pictures of the facility after the event. The company survived. The publication was then sent to suppliers and customers – not one of them had been aware that there had been a disaster at the company. The continuity plan had ensured it was business as usual.

It is widely regarded that media relations is bottom of the list where the small to medium-sized enterprise market is concerned. This is indeed their Achilles heel. Large companies are typically much better prepared.

Actions, inventory and restoration

Business continuity is not a complicated science but to carry it through successfully, it does require:

- dedication from a number of key people in an organisation
- total commitment at board level
- assistance where appropriate of dedicated business continuity specialists
- enthusiasm and understanding of staff
- inventory control

Inventory control

Inventory control is a key but difficult area. The biggest problem by far is management – and management of assets in particular. Strategy-planning software is recommended to cover suppliers and inventory. Everything is relevant – all IT for example – and the complete asset list must be incorporated into the contingency plan. The software allows companies to run different scenarios of disasters to see what would be lost, what the company would still have, and where the company stands. In a disaster situation, a company might lose 100 PCs but still have 300 or so elsewhere within the company. The plan would be to allow the reallocation of existing resources, as well as having another company ready to be able to supply 100 PCs at short notice. It will all depend on what applications are being run and how critical they are to the business.

Restoration of the business

Many business continuity specialists will have relationships with restoration specialist companies. This will cover such reactive services as cleaning and drying, providing advice and counselling services, all the way through to loss adjuster specialists. Many environmental issues, which are not obvious to most people, will prove crucial in the event of a disaster. Not many people are aware that in the event of a fire, mixing water with PVC results in the production of hydrochloric acid – as happened once with a chemicals and plastics supplier. The smoke was bad enough, but acid contamination caused widespread environmental damage. Specialist decontamination companies are required to deal with acid spills and damage.

Restoration is not generally the province of disaster recovery providers. It is a specialist service, which is typically outsourced. Disaster recovery providers would usually carry out an environmental survey prior to any incidents to provide a breakdown of what can be covered. Health and safety and environmental issues are key, and are core responsibilities of the facilities department.

Technology

The challenges now facing facilities managers relate to the integration of technology. The following are all vulnerable:

- voice over IP (VoIP)
- computer telephony integration (CTI)
- 'smart' telephone switches
- call centres

Re-establishing matrices across such networks is automated, and in so doing poses problems for the business continuity industry. With data transmitted over voice cables, wide area networks and flexible bandwidth networks spread across Europe, single points of failure are difficult to track.

Call centres are seen as being particularly vulnerable due to the need for re-scripting the complex computerised switches deployed across the IT and communications infrastructures of these sites, should a disaster occur. Companies with one or more centres would usually need to implement a plan involving fall-back or mirroring policies. It is a specialist area and one that is only now emerging.

Best practice procedures

Business continuity issues are present every day in the working environment. There are a number of procedures that companies can be implementing now to improve their plans and help create a business continuity ethic across their organisations:

- Ensure visitor parking is as far from the reception area as possible, reducing the risk of suspect cars containing dangerous devices being left close to the building.

- In a multi-tenancy building, check the evacuation procedures of the other companies – where do they go, if indeed they evacuate at all?

- Cover all windows in protective film to minimise damage caused by exploding glass.

- Back up all data regularly and store off site in a secure environment.

- Use a password-protected screen saver so that no one can use a PC if the building has to be evacuated in a hurry.

- Perform a weekly restore test to check back-ups – restore failure is the most common reason for total data loss.

- Agree with the company's insurers now what the policy is on paying out for bomb and explosion-damaged PCs and servers, as loss assessment here is a lengthy and often unrewarding process.

- Make sure that safe areas are away from windows, stairwells, lift shafts and rooms with suspended ceilings.

- Keep hard hats, goggles, and so on in every office.

- Ask insurers now for the policy on injury claims, especially if the police advise on evacuation of a building in a disaster and there is a decision not to do so.

- Do not let the marketing department list the company's IT equipment, software and details about the IT infrastructure in the *Computer users' year book* or similar publications – such books are an ideal source of information for thieves, fraudsters and terrorists.

- Make a video of the property to help with insurance claims, finding things in a hurry, loss adjusters.

- If answering machines are relied on to take messages during a building evacuation, check how many minutes of recording time there are – it's no good evacuating for four hours if there is not sufficient storage capacity to cover the period.

- When off-site data storage tape is delivered back to the office premises, ensure there is a procedure for accepting delivery – under no circumstances should it be left in reception awaiting collection.

> ### Simple steps to effective business continuity
>
> - Train all key staff to the criteria already outlined.
> - Identify all mission-critical processes, people and applications.
> - Perform a risk and business impact analysis (BIA).
> - Write the plan, preferably using an experienced third-party consultancy and a recognised software package.
> - Take out any necessary additional disaster recovery cover on any mission-critical equipment.
> - Ensure the plan is kept current and up to date, in accordance with changes in technology, staff and company direction.

The future

Sadly, the attitude most often adopted is 'It won't happen to us'. Companies will have to adapt to a changing world much faster than they have had to in the past. Technology today is both a tool and a major defining feature of the business environment. IT is no longer just a function making a definable contribution to a business. A failure to protect technology is a failure to protect the business. Companies will have to learn that it is not enough just to embrace change in the future, they will have to live that change, indeed be it. There isn't a company around that can foresee every event and action that could adversely affect its development. But just think of those companies in business 50 or 60 years ago. They tend to be the ones that were (and still are) aware of risk; they did not and do not fear it. They are aware risks can pose threats, but they can equally take the measures that can secure their future.

Reference

1. Business Continuity Institute

Information

British Standard 7799 – UK standard for information security management, section 9 of which deals with business continuity management

Business Continuity Institute, tel: 0870 603 8783, *www.thebci.org*

Centre for Crisis Psychology, tel: 01756 796383, *www.ccpdirect.co.uk*

Cranfield School of Management, tel: 01234 751122, *www.som.cranfield.ac.uk/som/*

Institute of Business Management (IBM) (for advice on business continuity risk), *www.ibm.com*

Survive, international industry association, tel: 01483 710600, *www.survive.com*

Outsourcing

Chris Taylor

Outsourcing today is an increasingly common way of doing business. There are sound financial reasons for not employing permanent staff – who must be fully paid regardless of work flows – when you can buy in outside expertise which may be able to do the job better, cheaper and more quickly.

Facilities managers' time is, therefore, increasingly dominated by managing contracts with external suppliers. This has required facilities managers to develop new skills. Whereas before, facilities professionals had to be multi-skilled, multi-functional and good managers of people from a variety of backgrounds, now – on top of all that – comes the responsibility for continuing to motivate those over whom they have no immediate line management authority, whilst managing outcomes through a third-party employer with their hands tied by legal contracts.

Successfully working with contractors on a strategic level is another challenge facing the facilities manager. Today's outsourced contractors are 'partners' who 'add value' to a company's operations. Command and control, as a management style, would be as self-defeating here as anywhere else. Partners are looking for long-term relationships, where trust means more than mere on-time delivery. It means sharing cost bases, profit ratios and business objectives. To a degree, it means sharing information you might prefer to keep in-house.

This chapter aims to explain the nuts and bolts of outsourcing, with guidance on the whole process from choosing what to outsource, to writing and managing the contract, to maintaining a dynamic working relationship.

What to outsource

When outsourcing first entered the management arena in the 1980s, it was all about saving money on essentially manual tasks; premises cleaning was a typical and early example. This has now changed towards a key focus on access to skills, with outsourcing expanding to include areas closer and closer to the centre of business; companies are now looking to buy in outside expertise so that they can concentrate on their own core activities, and contract with external suppliers to provide many or most of the tactical elements.

Expertise

The shift from those early manual tasks has seen us move through other administrative and infrastructure areas, towards innovation: how can the company move further ahead faster than the competition? Outsourcing today, and the expertise that comes with the specialist contractors, has now embraced R&D, design, product management, marketing, communications, even personnel supply and management.

Outsourcing should no longer be seen as just a money-saving management device, but considered in terms of the potential value it can bring to a business. It may cost more to outsource, but the job may be better performed, the company image may be enhanced, and it may release expensive management time for core activities.

Core and non-core activities

So what, in your specific business, should you outsource and what retain in-house?

A vital first assessment in considering whether or not to outsource is defining what you consider to be your core business activities – you must retain full control over those activities. It is non-core elements that are candidates for outsourcing.

The thinking behind this is that organisations should be left to concentrate on their core business activities without the distraction of providing and managing non-core activities, which are better provided via an outsourced commercial situation whereby the personnel involved can be better motivated and rewarded in an environment that recognises their special training and skills.

Of course, what is defined as 'core' will vary significantly from organisation to organisation. A good example here would be the law firm that outsources its conveyancing work on the basis that its core skill is commercial litigation and it is from the latter that it earns the majority of its income.

Consider next the degree to which any selected function is routine and well defined. If it can be easily defined, then it can be more easily measured, and managed at arm's length – and remember, you are not devolving responsibility, just functionality. So, if a non-core function can be defined and measured, it may be worth considering for outsourcing.

Anticipating pitfalls

Before embarking on any outsourcing initiative, there are a number of potential problems which should be anticipated and evaluated. Many of these are concerned with the people affected by the change in operation, others are to do with changes in the business itself and the manner in which the business is undertaken.

People issues

It is unfortunate that outsourcing is rarely welcomed by a workforce, especially that section responsible for the function being outsourced. Very often it is perceived as downsizing by other means, and strenuous efforts are made to oppose it – diverting business time and energy from development to fire-fighting. Most of the problems that can arise can be pre-empted through intensive discussions and planning. Talk continuously with staff; be certain they understand what is happening, why, how and when – and understand that simply telling them is not the same as being certain they understand.

Before proceeding, ask the following questions:

- Is there a convincing case for outsourcing? People – and unions – will generally accept an argument in which the logic is unassailable, in which all the numbers, from every source, have been reviewed and checked, and where every aspect has been openly examined. Secrecy is not a good strategy here.

- What are the legal requirements? Does TUPE apply? (See EMPLOYMENT LAW, P90.) How much will it cost to be generous, rather than just to stick to the letter of the law? Is the cost worth it?

- How have the levels of knowledge and skill which exist within the organisation been established, especially within the area to be outsourced? Is the loss of some of these skills acceptable – most probably as a gift to the contractor – or should some or all of these be kept in-house as a supervisory or management resource?

- Is everything possible being done to involve and inform all staff – not just in the affected areas – of the progress towards outsourcing? Be aware, however, that different circumstances apply when an internal bid is on the table alongside external competitive bids; managing information in these circumstances is especially challenging. The function must continue, but one bidder has an effective stranglehold; tell them too much, and external bidders will claim favouritism; too little, and the existing team claim secrecy. The only option here is honesty and openness, supported by a policy, clearly stated, of what is acceptable and what is not, and what information is to be shared and what is not.

Business change

All businesses change. Before entering into an outsourcing contract, you need to consider the following questions so that you are not hampered by a restrictive contract as you pursue your development goals:

- What happens if you are bought out, or buy out another company? They may have a state-of-the-art in-house provision for what you have outsourced – or they may have none, and you need to look at rapid expansion of the service.

- What happens if you have a fundamental shift in business focus – if you decide, for example, to close plant, move headquarters of strategically important offices, or pursue a new but promising business direction which affects the need for the outsourced service?

- What happens in cases of force majeure – in the case, for example, of a significant market downturn which leaves expensive equipment and facilities underused? What provision has been made to allow for a ratcheting down of the service, and the associated costs?

Process change

The way business is done changes continuously. Think how long you have been using e-mail as a key communications channel. How many standalone fax machines are still used regularly in your business? Do your younger staff even know what a telex machine looks like? Such technological changes can significantly alter the manner in which an outsourcing contract will work over time. For example, if outsourcing had been a significant factor a generation ago, the typing pool would almost certainly have been a prime candidate for it – now typing pools simply don't exist. And it's not just the technology; working and management styles can alter considerably over the duration of a contract.

Consider the following:

- What structural changes could affect the outsourcing agreement? Consider, for example, the effect on the catering service of introducing flexible working; or how devolving autonomy from head office to regional offices could impact on supplier strategies, from transport to telephony or utilities.

- Bearing in mind the growth in power of computing (remember the old axiom which still holds good: every two years double the power/speed and halve the price), what could you be doing for free which used to require specialist input? Think of display media, and how that function has been usurped with presentation software packaged into most laptops, or of the production of newsletters, posters, or other promotional material.

Choosing contractors

The tender document

Time spent preparing the tender document is a requirement, not an option. Although you may feel there is only one logical choice for contractor, it is essential that you approach the tender process with an open mind, and ensure that the process is competitive. Do not rule out the possibility of bids from angles you may not have considered, not least the existing function team, and do not assume you know all the potential bidders.

The process involves three stages:

- detailed specification of requirements
- invitation to tender
- preferred contractor selection

The first stage, the detailed specification of requirements, is the most time consuming. It involves a microscopically close examination of the function concerned, and a thorough definition of that function. This is necessary because few if any functions of a business can be said to be completely self-contained; all have areas of overlap with other functions, and these must be resolved before you can spell out unequivocally exactly what you are asking a contractor to take on. It may be as simple as defining reporting procedures from company to contractor, or it may involve changing internal processes – between, say, the area being outsourced and the accounts department – to enable an unambiguous command line.

The outcome of this stage should be a document which will inevitably be lengthy. It will describe the function in detail, in terms of actions as well as outcomes, and how it dovetails into the organisation. If changes are planned or being considered that will affect the function, they should be spelt out here – but not to a degree that compromises company confidentiality. While the document should state that the contents should be treated as commercially confidential, it is essentially a public document over whose circulation you have less than perfect control.

Invitation to tender

So, to whom should the document be sent? The second stage, the invitation to tender, can be as broad or as narrow as you choose. One option is to advertise in an appropriate trade journal or newspaper, send out multiple copies of the tender document, and accept bids from all and sundry; more than one company has discovered the perfect outsourcing partner in just this manner, from businesses they would not have heard of otherwise. Alternatively, you may prefer to limit the number of bids at the outset through a preselection process, either through advertisements asking for 'expressions of interest', or through a strict invitation-only process where you involve only a shortlist of contractors already known to you, or discovered through advertising or word of mouth recommendation. The 'expressions of interest' route ultimately comes down to a similar selection – all manner of relevant information can be asked of prospective bidders to enable an informed choice of candidates to invite to tender.

Final selection

The next challenge is to draw closer to a final selection. You will have received a wealth of information, and almost certainly business references, from several companies, and three or four will stand out as meriting deeper investigation. A systematic comparison is important, as is involving people close to the function to be outsourced – but clearly, this can be sensitive if the in-house team are amongst the bidders, whether they have made it past the first 'cut' or not. Be sure to establish what each candidate has to offer. You are not just buying another pair of hands, but a functional expert with a brain. If this is to be the partnership you want and expect, it is reasonable to expect them to bring ideas as well as skills with them, and you should listen carefully to their suggestions as to how the function can be tailored more closely to the objectives spelt out in the tender document.

After discussions, and perhaps more formal interviews, it is likely you will be able to reach 'preferred contractor' status with one candidate. This is the goal of the exercise so far, and, arguably, where the real work begins!

Final negotiations

Next in the process is the interval between the selection of a preferred bidder and the contract signing. This is when 'proceed with caution' is wise advice; this stage can be compared with the period between choosing a new home and exchanging contracts. Both parties have reached an understanding and have a period of time – which their enthusiasm may seek to shorten – to make certain that the decision is the right one; mistakes can be costly.

Sometimes a bidder will fall at this final hurdle. Through a detailed examination of needs and abilities on either side, your goal is to agree a service level agreement which will be your working blueprint for the day-today operation of the contract. These final negotiations may reveal incompatibilities, and it is better to discover this before signing contracts than afterwards. Remember that the selection of a contractor is not necessarily a one-off process; you may almost get to the 'altar' and then have to start all over again with a different partner.

Creating a synergy

So what are the areas you should be discussing? It is important for any company to start with questions of its preferred bidder:

- What skills and abilities do both parties have that will provide a synergy, creating added value?
- How will the intellectual property and expertise be managed to the benefit of each?
- What cultural factors will make working together easier or more difficult?

Good channels of communication and working towards shared goals are critical from day one, and objectives must be clearly defined. Ensure you discuss:

- the establishment of unequivocal and open lines of communication between named individuals at all levels of operation
- the level of priority that customer satisfaction should hold – the final consumer of your goods or services will notice, and be confused by, conflicting priorities

Flexibility

Look, above all, for flexibility to adapt to the changes that will come. Think of the future, and look for special skills a partner can bring to the table:

- Can the outsourcing contractor come to the management team with a strategic plan?
- Is the prospective partner able to offer potential value-adding concepts?
- Can the partner demonstrate commitment to a long-term relationship?

A two-way process

Remember that to turn the supplier into an asset, they need to be part of the organisation, and this means flexibility on both sides. The choice of supplier may come down to how much risk a company is prepared to take. Things will change, and companies should be willing to adapt:

- be willing to change your corporate culture if necessary

- focus on business objectives

- consider making your outsourcing partner a risk-sharing partner – a recent trend is to offer the supplier shares within the client company so they have a direct interest in profits

- establish and agree metrics to reward risk sharing

And, of course, accept that all parties need to feel that what is offered and received represents value for money.

The specific procurement process particular to PPP projects is outlined in FINANCIAL MANAGEMENT, PP186-190.

Service level agreements

A service level agreement (SLA) is not a summary document, nor is it an outsourcing contract. It is, quite simply, a detailed memorandum specifying the outcomes from many elements of the outsourced function. SLAs need to be defined in detail, as they are an important way of measuring an outsourcing supplier's performance. The most common metrics of quality, speed and accuracy clearly enable each partner to assess the current level of service the buyer is receiving. If performance slides, the SLA may trigger penalties. Putting these metrics in writing provides a legal basis (in the worst case) for contract termination – and gives the client the ability to influence the supplier's performance.

Negotiating an effective SLA that will provide value in the outsourcing relationship need not be – should not be – a one-sided process. The willingness of a preferred bidder to enter into the negotiation of the SLA design speaks volumes for their future acceptance of it, and indeed, they may have as much or more experience in the task as the client. Furthermore, whilst it is important to specify the desired outcomes in detail, the SLA must not be so prescriptive in the inputs side that it prevents the contractor from seeking ways to do a better job.

An effective SLA:

- identifies certain service levels or performance standards that the outsourcing contractor must meet or exceed

- specifies the consequences for failure to achieve one or more service levels

- includes credits or bonus incentives for performance that exceeds targets

- establishes the level of importance of key service areas by a weighting system

SLAs are not easy to design or negotiate. But a comprehensive, fair and effective SLA is critical for a successful outsourcing relationship. In the course of negotiation, outsourcing clients and suppliers have the opportunity to learn a lot about how their future partner will approach important issues in the outsourcing relationship, which can only help in the smooth running of a contract.

Penalties and incentives

The most important factor at this stage is for the outsourcing supplier and client to agree on credible measurements, and establish what would be classed as above and below acceptable levels of service. By weighting the impact on key areas of exceeding or falling short of these measurements, to total 100%, then penalties or payouts can be tailored to fit. If the outsourcing supplier then fails to achieve some of the key service levels, the percentage missed for the month can be applied as a service level credit against a proportion of the invoice.

Often the parties identify a subset of the key service levels as critical. For these elements, the parties will agree that more extreme penalties will apply, even that the outsourcing contract may be terminated if the levels are not reached to the frequency specified. Contract law generally entitles one party to terminate a contract if the other party 'materially breaches' the contract; defining critical service levels and providing specific conditions for termination eliminates ambiguity by determining what is, and what is not, 'material'.

Reasonable clients will avoid over-measuring and trying to include every imaginable service level. They should agree to fair credits for failures in meeting service levels. Suppliers should be willing to understand that the client requires significant protection in the SLA and to acknowledge that there are certain levels of performance that would justify termination of the contract.

Similarly, exceeding the levels may be seen as a potential trigger for bonus payments or other incentives, payable when a quantifiable benefit to the client can be seen, far beyond any expected performance as laid down in the SLA. It is important for the contractor to know they will be properly rewarded for success. If the supplier can add real value to the client's business, clients should be willing to share the value gained as a result of superior performance. In this way, service level objectives become highlighted as a critical parameter for both parties.

Force majeure clauses

Force majeure clauses excuse a party's failure to perform if the failure resulted from a natural disaster. In outsourcing contracts, negotiating the provisions of excused performance in the context of the outsourcing contractor's responsibilities and liabilities can be challenging and time consuming. Examples include:

- failures resulting from the client's non-performance
- failures of third parties
- failures in hardware and software

Outsourcing suppliers tend to seek a broad definition of force majeure, while clients seek a narrow, tightly defined provision. Most organisations accept that a fair agreement lies somewhere in the middle, without absolving entirely the supplier from the responsibility of correcting and mitigating the effects of an excused performance failure.

What to include

Every SLA will be different, tailored to the specifics of the contract and its application, but they will usually have several sections in common, including:

- introduction
- definition, boundaries and parameters of the service being outsourced
- minimum acceptable service levels for all aspects of the job
- detailing of improvements from the status quo (if sought)
- agreed cultural norms of (for example) appearance (if contractors are to be perceived as company employees)
- quality criteria (where contractors have to supply materials)
- who reports to whom, how, when, and why
- how service levels are to be monitored, when and by whom
- measures for rewarding exceptional performance, if appropriate
- measures for penalising under-performance, if appropriate
- general payment terms and conditions
- conflict resolution procedures

Contractual arrangements

Having established an agreement with a single supplier, the next step is to finalise the contract. Only when all the details are agreed is it time to sign. It can take well over a year to reach this stage, and should not be rushed: it is a contract you never want to terminate, so it is important to get it right first time.

The function of the contract

The contract should define both the work itself and the manner in which it is to be undertaken. If the task to be undertaken is ambiguously defined, both in terms of scope (the work to be done) and style (when and to what standard), then there is room for individual interpretation – and one interpretation will almost certainly differ from the next. The contract process is the best system to define unambiguously what is needed and at the same to lay down performance criteria so the execution of the contract can be monitored.

The SLA is arguably the most important document in the tactical day-to-day management of the contract. It provides the key performance criteria by which success or failure will be assessed. Whilst in industry practice the SLA is a separate addendum to the outsourcing contract, in law it is not a separate agreement, but merely a set of terms and conditions of the substantive contract itself. In other words, the function of the SLA is to specify the goals of the outsourcing relationship, whilst the contract is the administrative document which outlines all the practical arrangements necessary to ensure these goals are met.

What should the contract include?

As well as terms and conditions, renewal dates and criteria, payment terms, and arrangements for rewards or penalties in the case of over or underperformance (with definitions of these being spelt out), a contract should build in the following considerations:

Flexibility

If you know what's going to happen, you make plans. If you don't know, you make contingency plans. It is inevitable that circumstances – markets, technology, supply chain, and so forth – will change, and that some of those changes are likely to be radical. A contract which allows no flexibility, therefore, is a bad contract.

Unless the contract allows for change, the client may find himself tied down to the letter of the contract by the supplier, even though it may be obvious that a failure to change will be detrimental to the business. That will clearly lead to distress, or worse, dispute.

Disputes and exit strategy

Be aware that there are likely to be disagreements – every relationship has them – and there needs to be an agreed methodology for dealing with them, configured in such a way that the work continues while the disagreement is resolved. This methodology should be written into the contract.

In the worst possible case, disagreement may lead to a complete breakdown of the relationship, so an exit strategy should also be agreed. In many cases contracts are expensive and difficult to terminate prematurely, and without careful management – and the right contract in the first place – the outsourcing contractor can easily gain the upper hand, which can be disastrous for the prospects of a long-term relationship. No client should be obliged to continue with an unsatisfactory contract, simply because the implications of breakdown are worse than continuing with the status quo.

The client should ensure the existence of a reasonable exit route in case the relationship becomes unmanageable. Terminating a contract is the worst case scenario in the relationship: ideally, the contract should define less final consequences for any lack of service or failure to provide to agreed service levels.

Decision-making

Outsourcing relationships should be true partnerships, but one party must take the lead. There are decisions where there may be no right or wrong in qualitative terms, but where someone has to call the shots. It should be made explicit in the contract that while the partnership recognises the expertise brought to the relationship by the supplier, the ultimate call comes from the client.

Contract 'management'

Anyone can sign a contract, but unless it is adhered to, monitored and driven to its optimum, it is simply paperwork. Managing the contract is indisputably the clever bit. It is not the same as managing the same process when handled in-house. Once contracts have been signed and the supplier is providing the service, you have less direct influence on how the job is undertaken, as you have delegated away the tactical element of execution – except in so far as the contract allows. You can no longer hire and fire, or change emphasis or priority; you have a set of rules set down that must be adhered to, no less by you than by the contractor.

Yet at the same time you have a team to inspire and motivate – but this team does not report to you. You have to be seen to be interested and involved, to be monitoring and checking; it is important that the supplier shares your enthusiasm for continuous improvement. Unless you are seen to be involved in the contract – without treading on the toes of the supplier – demotivation will follow, leading to declining standards and ultimate contract failure. These issues are covered in more detail in the section on BUILDING THE RELATIONSHIP, PP252–256.

Consequences, positive or negative, can take the form of financial penalties or additional payments for high levels of performance by the supplier (see PENALTIES AND INCENTIVES, P246).

Key performance indicators

A balanced scorecard

If an outsourcing relationship is to be successful, clear measurements are needed to manage achievements and expectations on both sides. One of the best ways to establish this is through the balanced scorecard approach.

A balanced scorecard involves goal setting, target setting and an information collection process. It includes a number of categories that represent the most general level of expectations – usually around cost, service and quality. Categories are divided into a number of subsets, known as attributes, defined through a joint buyer-provider process, with the exact composition and number depending on the goals of the relationship and the service in question. Choices are made about an appropriate measure for each attribute.

When establishing the scorecard, some of the key areas to consider are:

- Does the overall scorecard balance long-term and short-term goals, and financial and non-financial goals?

- Do the metrics and measures compensate for each other's blind spots? Consider balancing subjective and objective measures, and qualitative and quantitative measures.

- Are multiple perspectives taken into consideration? Does the scorecard balance the perspectives of the strategic and operation managers, the buyer and the provider, and so forth?

What will a balanced scorecard achieve?

Having balanced scorecards in place during an outsourcing relationship accomplishes at least three things, namely:

- a client-defined, mutually agreed performance management system to reward exemplary service and to discourage sub-par performance
- an established set of metrics by which performance is measured with the opportunity to make ongoing changes in service levels and expectations
- the provision of historical information to help decide the future of the relationship when it comes to contract renewal

Client satisfaction

Signing an outsourcing arrangement should not mean the abdication of responsibility for a business activity to an outside provider. Whilst one of the true benefits of outsourcing is the transfer of responsibility to an outside expert who is well equipped to handle the task, clients must put systems in place to ensure their own satisfaction with the service. Below are some guidelines for measurement and evaluation.

- **Measure what you want to manage** – you can only manage what you can measure and you can only measure what you can see. However, it is possible to come up with creative and useful solutions to measuring and managing activities that were previously beyond reach – cost savings and customer satisfaction to name but two.
- **Change what you can control** – not measuring and, in turn, holding providers accountable for things beyond their control is counterproductive and frustrating for all. The activities and measures must be within the service provider's control and having them at the table defining the scorecard is the best way to understand that.
- **Recycle and reuse, don't repeat** – the last thing anybody wants is competing measurement systems; a single 'good enough' system will do – defined as providing the information you need to manage with. The balanced scorecard can absorb earlier measurement systems; don't reinvent the wheel – use the best measures that already exist.
- **Set the systems early** – construct a balanced scorecard as early as possible, customise it once the provider is chosen and then jointly set target levels. A provider's ability and willingness to live up to the criteria set in a balanced scorecard can be a consideration in the selection process.
- **Timely and efficient measurement** – the measurement system to support a balanced scorecard should collect only what is useful and not

duplicate material. Unnecessary and overlapping measurement processes are wasteful. Collecting information to support balanced scorecards should also happen as soon after the fact as possible.

- **Measure realistically** – be realistic in what can be inexpensively, quickly, and easily measured. Certain things should not be scorecarded. For example, don't measure the number of failed state inspections – such events do not provide for ongoing management of the relationship, they represent significant and immediate problems.

- **Use all the measurement tools and data sources at your disposal** – there are at least three tools buyers and providers have at their disposal:

  - **Surveys** – these can be used with external customers, internal customers, and employees of both provider and buyer. Surveys are effective at collecting behavioural information or opinions but the measures tend to be subjective. Relying on this method leaves the process open to serious questions and undercuts the ideal of balance. When they take the form of checklists, surveys provide for more objectivity.

  - **Management information systems** – these can provide valuable information on costs, inventories and other accounting-related data. It has the limitation of being predominantly financial.

  - **Audits** – These avoid the subjectivity of surveys, while collecting non-financial and other specific information not present in management information systems designed for other purposes.

Building the relationship

Surveys have consistently shown that companies are, in general, dissatisfied with the overall results of their outsourcing agreements. So how can you make the outsourcing relationship one of value, providing ongoing benefit to your business?

Continuous improvement model

To have an outsourcing relationship that works it is important to consider the supplier as a source of value that needs to be constantly realigned if the contract is to succeed. Levels of service need to be continuously improved if they are to result in long-term relationships. This calls for flexibility, which starts in the planning stage and should be the result of candid communication, frankness and a willing approach to working with the aim of creating a 'win-win' situation. With a good plan, there should be flexibility to meet new opportunities and redefine the relationship on an ongoing basis. That means measuring the value and rewarding the supplier on their ability to deliver that value. Then the bar can be raised on a continual basis and the relationships can be moved and aligned with business objectives.

Defining added value

Decide early on how to define added value. Look for one or more of the following:

- the ability of the supplier to come up with the initiatives that reshape the relationship to meet ongoing objectives
- the ability and willingness of the supplier to set and meet concrete and measurable service levels
- the ability of the supplier to commit to and meet specific financial targets

Clear channels of communication need to be mapped out which encourage the supplier to be proactive and bring ideas to the strategy of your business. The supplier should also be rewarded for ideas and revenue opportunities, with rewards reflecting the benefits brought by the implementation of ideas.

Good communication

Ideally the relationship should start with each organisation appointing an informed and empowered point of contact, to act as contract administrator. These two individuals are responsible for making the relationship work – as opposed to the site managers who will oversee the day-to-day running of the function on site. This is an important first step in implementing a successful outsourcing relationship. Other factors which help to build and sustain the partnership include:

- a strong management team
- a dedicated account manager
- a good working relationship between management on both sides
- a consistent communication chain
- a single point of contact – possibly the administrator (see above) – to resolve queries and remove duplication
- a database of written communication between parties to track commitments

Trust is essential in developing a successful outsourcing relationship, and communications need to be based on this. An outsourcing contractor should be instrumental in the client's success, therefore they need to have access to the information they need. It is necessary to:

- drive home what the business is all about
- highlight objectives
- be frank in disclosing issues facing the company or its industry – both short and long-term
- give the supplier the tools they need to achieve or maintain status as an industry leader
- be clear about the roles in the relationship

Coordinating standards and budgets

Relationships need to be developed at multiple levels throughout the organisations involved, to create trust and develop the understanding required for long-term success. Companies need to speak the same language and both parties need to coordinate standards, such as protocols and business processes. Also, both parties need to perform joint budgeting exercises to understand the key cost driver information inherent in the other's infrastructure. In addition, there needs to be qualitative information associated with the reliability and performance of the outsourced services.

Anticipating problems

The problems that come up consistently tend to be because the client underestimates the future work they will require the supplier to undertake. Also, there is a failure to say up front what work is in the scope of the contract and what work is additional. This can lead to a misunderstanding of responsibilities. For example, a manager of the client's data centre is frequently retained in-house to help manage the supplier. That manager is familiar with the way the centre used to be operated in the past. Just because a company used to do it one way does not necessarily mean that is the way the supplier is going to do it. This may cause problems for the manager who has been controlling an area for a long period of time.

As this example shows, most management problems are not actually 'people' problems. It is more a case of a lack of clarity over how key objectives are to be implemented. This highlights the importance of the contract. Without a suitable contract the two parties enter their 'marriage' and go into the honeymoon stage, where everyone is enthusiastic and focused on the objectives of the agreement and can see the potential benefits that are to follow.

At this stage everyone:

- talks frequently
- gets involved with fine-tuning objectives
- works enthusiastically towards service levels
- has great expectations

Time, too often, erodes this initial flurry of excitement and soon there is an anti-climatic effect which can lead to exasperation. An outsourcing relationship, like every other business relationship, runs the same risk.

At this point:

- communication breaks down
- key people leave
- the original mission is lost
- the client and supplier forget original objectives
- frustrations grow

Ensuring that the contract is clearly defined, that flexibility is built into it and that there is constant scope for communication and assessment and reassessment of the tasks and responsibilities in hand will help prevent misunderstandings and frustrations.

Team dynamics

Most outsourcing agreements represent long-term, dynamic relationships in which unforeseen opportunities and conditions will appear and will have to be addressed. This means there is a need for flexibility, which should be built in to the first stages of the relationship. However, keeping on an even keel can be fraught with difficulties. Day-to-day decisions have strategic impact while lack of planning and misunderstanding can create difficulties in moving forward. Personality clashes can also cause rifts – managers on both sides need to have good people skills.

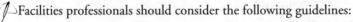Facilities professionals should consider the following guidelines:

- the client should ensure that the supplier's best people are working in the relationship
- there should be contractual terms and conditions spelling out certain processes and disciplines
- the client should have the first right of refusal for members of the supplier's team

Regular reviews

Many problems can be avoided if the dangers are anticipated and dealt with in the planning process. Communication and incentives for success are key to nurturing long-term relationships, with the company's outsourcing team focusing daily on the mission in hand. Outsourcing specialists often suggest that companies should communicate clearly on a month-to-month basis, discussing performance and anticipating any changes for the next month. These discussions can provide short-term measurement to monitor ongoing behaviour, and benefits expected to be achieved over the length of the contract can be reaffirmed.

Successful contract management

The key messages are:

- avoid relationship deterioration by planning for the pitfalls
- schedule monthly meetings to reaffirm objectives and measure performance
- give the supplier financial incentives to succeed

Managing the end of the contract

A key area, often overlooked at the outset of any contractual relationship, is what happens when the contract comes to an end – it will, eventually. And here we are not necessarily talking about a contract ending in dispute, rather what happens to a contract when its agreed term has run. Few companies can afford to go 'on hold' while they sort themselves out; competitors are waiting to swoop in and take advantage of the gap in the market.

So what then are the alternatives on contract termination? Assuming the function remains necessary, they are limited. You can:

- continue with the same contractor
- find a different contractor
- bring the function back in-house

Many companies stay with existing providers through inertia – and fear of change. They may be unsatisfied with the existing arrangement, but they suspect that it would be easier to get improved contract terms, and tighter SLAs, from a new contractor, than by renegotiating the existing arrangement. This has dubious logic! The possibility – necessity, even – for change and continuous improvement should have been built in from the start.

Changing contractors can take a year or more to organise, and is fraught with hazards, including the possibility of delaying tactics from the outgoing contractor, removal of key staff and run-down of efficiency, and possible confusion over ownership issues of dedicated equipment. Many of the same reservations apply if attempts are made to bring operations back in-house – key assets, in terms of people, knowledge and equipment, have been relinquished – and you should also ask why you chose to outsource in the first place.

Key lessons

First, too few contracts have adequate provision concerning termination or expiry, and fail to take account of the way business needs will change over the relationship term. Second, usually, it's 'better the devil you know' – that is, it's preferable to stay with the existing provider, who knows your business. If you want new SLAs, renegotiate. Asking them, with others, to re-tender can focus everyone's attention on the key aspects of the task, as well as pinpointing whether there really is a better option out there.

7 Transport Policies

Frank Booty

Transport costs remain one of the biggest factors impacting on the bottom line. For many businesses, it is the second largest cost after personnel. With the Government's tax changes now impacting on companies' transport budgets, this situation is unlikely to change. However, with businesses constantly evolving towards a more global working culture, the need for transport is greater than ever before. How can facilities managers seek to resolve this conflict of interests?

Careful travel planning can bring huge benefits to a company. The environmental imperatives remain: transport-derived air pollution, carbon dioxide emissions and traffic congestion still need to be reduced. But the reasons for developing travel plans go beyond environmentalism. Other benefits include time and cost savings, greater flexibility and accessibility for the workforce.

It is easy to overlook the parking issue. The car park represents the largest untapped asset in the property portfolio, with brand names waking up to the potential they offer for floor graphic advertising. But the car park is also becoming the target of both government regulators and taxmen. How can facilities managers ensure they get the most out of their car parks, while taking new government guidance into account?

Travel plans

Legislation

A travel plan is an effective site management tool that also meets the need for continuous improvement in environmental management. When the white paper *New Deal for Transport: Better for Everyone* was published in July 1998, 'green' transport plans became an explicit component in the new approach to transport. The DTLR (Department for Transport, Local Government and the Regions) now uses a more generic term, 'travel plans', which reflects the department's increasing recognition of the function as a mainstream management tool, rather than a fringe activity.

Facilities managers must familiarise themselves with the final version of the Government's *Planning Policy Guidance Note 13: Transport* (PPG13), issued in April 2001.[1] The guidance pushes environmental points by encouraging all businesses to try their utmost to encourage their staff to take up car sharing, use public transport and work from home wherever practicable. Local councils are expected to consider setting targets for the adoption of travel plans by local businesses. There is even the point that green travel plans should be submitted alongside planning applications. One interesting point to note is that the guidance does not preclude park-and-ride schemes being adopted inside the green belt, where hitherto rigorous planning rules have operated.

Planning authorities will have to advise local businesses on the impact of this legislation. The squeeze on using the car to get employees to and from the workplace is starting to be felt. Companies contemplating expansion of their sites, relocation, increasing the workforce, or those involved with out-of-town business parks or retail sites will have to draw up different strategies. From now on, travel plans, building databases of potential car sharers, offering company bus/coach travel facilities and/or concessions, bicycle parks, and so on, will all have increasingly important parts to play.

Objectives

Travel plans are designed to reduce the adverse environmental impacts of transport to and from a specific site or building. Travel plans seek to reduce over-dependence on cars, especially when the driver is alone, through encouraging changes in travel behaviour in favour of more environmentally benign modes, such as public transport, walking and cycling. To complement this, particularly where it is more difficult to provide alternatives to the car, travel plans incorporate measures to reduce the impact of vehicles (for example, through greener fleet management).

Travel plans also seek to reduce the need to travel – both travel undertaken by employees when carrying out their duties – for example, when

---

Travel plans: a management tool

For facilities managers, the travel plan is a powerful management tool that offers considerable benefits to the company or organisation. Travel plans can help a business to:

- stay operational at a time of expansion
- reduce the costs of car parking provision and/or business travel costs
- improve, or at least maintain, staff journey times to and from work
- contribute to a healthier environment
- enjoy the additional bonus of a healthier workforce

---

attending meetings, exhibitions, training courses or visiting clients – and travel to and from the workplace. Alternative methods of communication, such as telephone conference calls, are encouraged, as well as vehicle sharing.

Guide to effective travel planning

Convincing the CEO

The first step is always to convince the CEO and other senior managers that the travel plan combines resource, facility and site management in one package and that it is essential for the future of the organisation and its site. In other words, the adoption of a travel plan is a strategic issue which needs director-level support.

Establishing the baseline

A survey of staff travel habits needs to be conducted. The questions should be designed to ensure a comprehensive understanding can be gained of how people are currently travelling and what charges they may be willing to make in the future. This should be complemented by a series of audits to obtain a clear picture of current arrangements regarding the following:

- personal security for cyclists and pedestrians on site and along key routes to the site
- business travel – staff travel expenses budget, mileage undertaken and by what method
- car parking arrangements and charges
- traffic counts by vehicle type, time of day and day of week
- access to site by bus, train, on two wheels and on foot
- shift patterns and their impact on staff travel to work

A package of complementary measures

Possible measures to take include:

- car sharing
- charges for car parking
- encouraging public transport use
- enhanced bus services
- improving cycling facilities
- improving the pedestrian environment (on and off site)
- reduction in the need to travel

The emphasis placed on different measures varies enormously, according to local circumstances. If, as is the case at a major Liverpool hospital, over two-thirds of staff already travel to work by public transport, then the emphasis will be on helping them to avoid switching to the car. On the other hand, if the site is never going to be well served by public transport and your staff live in rural areas some distance from it, sharing car journeys to work is likely to be a more important measure. The priorities for action will be determined in part by the baseline assessment and in part by what is judged politically and economically feasible.

Consultation about the plan

A transport working group should be established, which should act as a reference point throughout the development of the travel plan and then assist with its implementation. Membership should comprise:

- facilities manager
- human resources manager
- environmental manager
- staff representatives
- staff willing to champion change
- council officers (on planning, transport, car parking, cycling, local agenda 21)

Because a travel plan involves everyone, it is vital that everyone is on board, so the next stage is to consult all staff about the plan and the changes it envisages. Interest groups can be established (for example, a cycle opportunity group or bus-user group). Employ also the usual methods of raising awareness – an in-house newsletter, team briefings, leaflets accompanying salary slips, or noticeboards.

Adoption of the travel plan

With the results of the consultation process collated and analysed, the plan now needs to be finalised, costed and approved at the appropriate level. A travel plan cuts across traditional disciplinary boundaries and is of strategic importance. So, in most organisations, it is presented formally to the board for endorsement.

Resources for implementation

It is accepted that someone has to drive the travel plan forward. For organisations with many staff on one site, or where there are many employers in an identifiable geographical area, a travel coordinator should be appointed. The coordinator should be:

- a good communicator at all levels
- able to use information and communications technologies
- able to motivate people
- a pragmatic organiser

This person will need to be fully resourced and supported and will need access to the decision-making process. All of these costs will form part of the business case for the travel plan and are usually offset against savings in staff travel expenses budgets and the reduced need for more car parking, for example.

Project management

As with any strategic plan, the facilities manager's project management skills will be important. By now, the priorities, costings and a timetable have been established and the transport working group should be ensuring coordination across departments and with external bodies. There will be actions that can be taken immediately – for example:

- provision of cycle lockers and better cycle security
- promotion of existing bus services
- telephone conference calls
- improvements to pedestrian routes
- priority parking for car sharers

Other measures take more time to plan and introduce, such as revising car parking and staff travel policies (severing the link between the pay packet and travel by car), flexible working schemes and improvements to the public transport infrastructure.

Marketing the travel plan

Facilities managers are familiar with energy conservation campaigns. Successful ones have involved all staff in the process and in many instances have produced dramatic efficiency gains. Travel plans also require a constant marketing effort to be made in order to reach every nook and cranny of the organisation and to keep people informed of developments, new incentives for car sharing, walking and cycling, support for public transport users and so on.

Setting targets

Starting with the figures derived from the staff survey, it will be practical to establish desired targets for changes in the way people travel to your site. In the worked example shown in Table 1, the emphasis happens to be on more car sharing and public transport.

Table 1: Staff travel targets

Mode of transport to work	Actual 2001 (%)	Targets 2003 (%)	2005 (%)
Car, as driver alone	65	60	55
Car, as passenger	15	17	18
Car, dropped off	9	9	8
Bus	8	9	11
Train	1	1.5	2
Bicycle	0.5	1	2
Motorcycle	0.5	1	1.5
Walk	1	1	2.5

Assuming there are 3,000 staff in the work premises on any one working day, the 2003 targets outlined in the table represent:

- 90 fewer staff coming by car
- 30 more staff coming by bus
- 15 more coming by train
- 15 more cycling
- 15 more coming by motorbike
- 15 more walking

Monitoring and evaluating results

Measurable targets need to be established for each element of the travel plan. For example, take-up monitoring will show the number of annual bus passes sold, the number of cycle lockers in use and so forth. Frequent staff surveys will be expensive and are likely to produce diminishing returns. However, conducting a repeat of your survey of staff travel habits every two years will be essential to check whether you are achieving the desired modal shift. Other monitoring methods include checks on key budgets, periodic comparisons of service levels and recording anecdotal and intuitive evidence.

Encouraging behavioural change

Facilities managers will need to employ a range of skills in implementing travel plans. Those more used to building roads and maintaining buildings will find their traditional working methods are needed when it comes to site infrastructure changes, but new skills are required when it comes to encouraging behavioural change. Travel plans have to be handled with sensitivity and care, as reducing over-dependence on the car calls for lifestyle changes – which is distinctly intimate and personal territory. For this reason, words such as 'consultation' and 'partnership' must not just be part of a new facilities management vocabulary, but must also be translated into meaningful actions, capable of being verified and evaluated.

The Energy Efficiency Best Practice Programme

The Energy Efficiency Best Practice Programme provided a service to the road freight transport industry for many years. Covering such topics as energy-efficient fleet management, its impartial and authoritative advice on energy-efficiency techniques and technologies in industry, transport and buildings is widely respected. It now offers an expanded service covering travel plans, which includes free publications on travel planning and access to free expert advice and assistance.

Car park management

Parking restrictions

Overly draconian parking measures were feared at one point in the progress of the Government's PPG13 (see LEGISLATION, P258), namely that car parking spaces at hospital developments were to be linked to bed numbers. Now, new hospitals plus school developments are all to be planned to maximise accessibility by non-car modes of transport while simultaneously allowing good access for emergency vehicles and those who need to use cars. Office developments should have one car parking space per 30 sq m – originally it had been 35 sq m – for all developments above 2,500 sq m. Any threats to new office developments are thus eased.

Parking is, however, going to get tougher. Consider, for example, government plans to raise £2.7 billion a year "for better transport schemes" by allowing local authorities to charge people who work in towns and cities between £150 and £500 a year to park at their own place of work. These plans will hit the low paid, as employers are likely to pass on charges to the workforce. The answer is to give massive re-location incentives and tax breaks to work-intensive business operations to encourage them to move to accessible locations where people can get to work cheaply and easily or park for free.

Planning a car park

The first questions to ask when planning a car park are:

- Why do you want a car park?
- How does it fit in with your transport strategy?
- How big does it need to be?
- What other facilities are involved?
- What material will it be built from?
- What buildings will the car park relate to?

The car park may be designed to serve office blocks, in which case it will be predominantly busy for 30 minutes at the start and end of the day, and quiet in between. A shopping centre car park will have more regular patterns of usage, except demand will double or triple in the weeks before Christmas. A multiplex cinema will be busiest at the end of the evening, as all films are timed to finish within a 30-minute window so staff can go home.

When developing a new car parking facility, it is important to:

- identify both the users and the demand
- perform a traffic impact study
- determine the land availability
- aim to provide the maximum number of spaces whilst maintaining high standards of circulation
- draw up conceptual layouts

Facilities managers may buy an all-inclusive site package – office blocks, retail outlets and car park. The car parks here will feature less optimisation in design. They will be add-on extras, purely functional. In large structures like shopping centres, the car parks can be underground or multi-storey.

Design

The car park is (or should be) the gateway to the business, town, office, retail centre or facility – it is the first thing a visitor will see. If it is dirty, scruffy, ill lit and smelly, that is the impression the visitor will have of the facility. If it is clean, well maintained, well lit and of pleasant design, the visitor will take that memory away. Given that 2.4m is needed for a car space, the concrete supports need to be spaced at least at 2.4m or multiples of 2.4m intervals. It is no good spacing at, say, 7m and then expecting that gap to accommodate three cars. People will try and squeeze in, damage their vehicles and never come back.

Outsourcing car park maintenance

Aside from an architectural overhaul and/or repainting and cleaning, ensuring car parks are well maintained can be achieved through outsourcing. The Waitrose retail group of the John Lewis Partnership, for example, has outsourced the running of the car parks attached to its stores to Euro Car Parks. Airports have many companies competing for business. Ford Motor Company extended its existing facilities management contracts with Sodhexho to cover services in car parks at its Dunton site – that included resurfacing works, entry/exit barriers and general maintenance.

Floor graphic advertising

In the US, outdoor floor advertising is worth £140 million a year, and growing (indeed it is one of the fastest growing media sectors). Now it is over here. The Parkvertising concept allows owners or operators of car parks to tap into a large source of revenue that grows and is replenished year-on-year. By forming a partnership with Parkvertising, the owner opens up huge potential from what has previously been a cost centre. Neither the property manager nor Parkvertising are important in the digital imaging process equation – the key player there is the advertiser.

Outdoor media houses are used to promote the national campaigns and products, coupled with specialist regional media groups who concentrate on picking up the local advertiser and business promoter. The concept works for local authority and private car park operators. For example, National Car Parks (NCP) signed up with a company who will sell advertising on the floors of its nationwide network of car parks.

Arrangements are being discussed and agreed with other car park owners and operators, as well as organisations such as supermarkets and NHS trusts, which are seen as ideal locations to capture the attentions of high-spending car drivers and users. There are many other potential locations too – airports, railway stations, universities, commercial and business estates, ports – indeed, anywhere which offers a parking facility for consumers or office workers. Income derived from the advertising can be applied to finance refurbishment costs, or to generate significant incremental revenue, for example.

Advertisements of up to 4 × 4m can be produced (subject to local space availability) using a combination of flat line colours. Designed to withstand up to three years' constant use, these advertisements are produced using materials that comply with all current health and safety legislation. The materials used have a luminescence some five times greater than highway cats' eyes, making the messages highly visible at night. As well as on the floor (in the parking bays or on the way to ticket machines or pay points), the advertisements can also be located on the entry/exit barriers.

Lighting and security

Staff working late or hospital visitors, for example, walking to or from their cars in the dark will need good lighting. Under the Chief Police Officers' secure car park scheme, the advice for the design of car parks is to avoid dark corners and corridors. Much emphasis is put on the design and management of the facilities. Now, there are more staff involved in continuous on-site surveillance, as well as CCTV (closed circuit television) facilities being deployed (security issues are covered in detail in ACCESS AND SECURITY, P374–390.)

In the UK today there are some 15,000 underground and multi-storey car parks, many hailing from the 1960s. Quick visual improvements can be achieved through improving the lighting and painting using bright colours, but structural difficulties are more awkward to rectify.

Fleet management

It is important that a fleet is not seen as a secondary consideration for a business. It is a vital part of the company's operational effectiveness, whether that means salespeople arriving punctually for meetings or equipment arriving on site in plenty of time and in suitable condition. Facilities managers with fleet responsibility should realise that proactive cost management and policy advice from fleet management companies is vital to business today in the UK.

The company car

There is a lot of talk that the company car is no longer seen as a 'perk'. As part of this alleged move away from this most British of benefits, the Government has long been pursuing a policy of 'greener' motoring. The overall aim is to get drivers out of big, petrol-thirsty saloons and into more environmentally friendly vehicles.

However, what this ignores is the vital commercial need that company vehicles, whether cars, vans or trucks, continue to fulfil. With rail transport unreliable and air travel still both expensive and highly regionalised, the need for the company car remains just as strong, if not stronger than ever.

Companies need expert guidance on every aspect of their fleet, from vehicle acquisition and disposal to maintenance and accident management – not to mention fuel costs, which in the existing UK climate increasingly form a heavy burden on any business. However, where a fleet management company can be at its most valuable is in providing expertise on the financial, tax-related and environmental issues faced by any firm with a fleet.

Tax increases

The biggest issue as far as most fleets are concerned is the change in the way company cars are taxed. As from April 2002, the existing benefit-in-kind (BIK) tax, paid by all employees who have a company car, will change. Whereas it has been based on the amount of business mileage driven, with high mileage drivers paying less tax, it will change to reflect the carbon dioxide emissions of the car. This means that vehicles emitting lower levels of carbon dioxide will attract less BIK tax. To qualify for the lowest category, a vehicle must emit 165g/km of carbon dioxide – for which few actually qualify.

Fleet drivers can avoid a potential tax hike by moving into smaller cars, and there is also much to be said for choosing a diesel car. Diesel cars generally produce less carbon dioxide than their petrol counterparts, and modern engines mean the performance gap between the two has narrowed considerably, if not vanished altogether.

Research has suggested that awareness of these tax changes, both among companies and the drivers who will end up paying for them, remains low. As most cars are taken on three or four-year leases, and the tax changes will take effect from April 2002, drivers could find themselves paying a year or two of higher tax on a large car taken on lease since 1999 or 2000, for example. If the time for renewal is approaching, companies need to examine these changes immediately. No action could result in irate employees besieging the company's administrative offices from 2002 onward.

Fuel tracking

A further key concern is fuel management, given the continued high cost of petrol in the UK. This is where fuel cards, such as AllStar from ARVAL PHH or TOTAL*Card* from Total, are at their most useful, providing detailed management information that allows high cost areas to be identified and dealt with efficiently. A driver who is filling up their tank more often than seems necessary or filling up on super unleaded instead of premium will show up on the management reports.

There is, then, a second potential tax burden faced by fleet drivers. Nearly one million of them receive free private fuel as a 'perk' from their employers, but recent increases in the BIK tax payable on this particular 'benefit' means any advantages for many drivers have long since disappeared. Thousands of drivers could be in the situation where they are paying more in tax for getting free fuel than the actual cost of the fuel they're using – in other words, they would be better off paying for the petrol themselves. This is another area where fuel cards, which allow for easy separation of private and business mileage, are useful, as the full amount of BIK tax is payable if the company pays for even 1p worth of private fuel.

Commercial assets

Aside from cars, the operation of commercial vehicles is another area where it pays to use a specialist provider. That way, costs such as downtime and maintenance can be managed most effectively, using the economies of scale obtained through a large fleet service provider. It is also critical for any firm using commercial vehicles that they have the right vehicle for the job – refrigerated goods, electronic components and construction equipment, for example, all have different and case-specific transportation requirements.

Fleet management and tracking

Insurance premiums seem set to rise for the foreseeable future. Vehicle insurance claims continued to rise at the end of the 1990s and were expected to rise 25% over 2001/2. The company Global Telematics produced a programme to help service organisations drive down insurance premiums by up to 50%, using 'next generation' telematics technology. Its Orchid vehicle tracking solution is intended to reduce the threat of vehicle theft, improve driver safety and reduce accident frequency and cost for field service companies.

Global Telematics will work with insurance to deliver the reductions. One insurance company uses the Orchid telematics solution to track and assess fleet behaviour to produce a risk management report, whilst another offers exclusive premiums in exchange for a commitment to proactive risk management based on this report. Orchid also enables service companies to pinpoint any of their vehicles in real time to improve operating efficiency and cut overall running costs.

Orchid can also help reduce petrol usage, maximise staff deployment, and so on. Fleet running cost reductions of 30% a year are claimed – so a company running 20 vehicles with annual expenditures of £250,000 could save up to £75,000 a year.

Meanwhile, systems are being introduced to improve the efficiency and effectiveness of vehicle fleets through closer control and a greater knowledge of actual vehicle movements. Tracker systems are based on a combination of satellite location and mobile communications (GSM – global system for mobiles) technologies. Vehicles are equipped with function-rich 'black boxes' which provide such functions as speed, distance travelled and idling time – all accessible via an internet browser.

Reference

1. See *www.planning.detr.gov.uk/ppg/ppg13/index.htm*

Information

Energy Efficiency Best Practice Programme (EEBPP) Environment and Energy helpline, tel: 0800 585794

8 Communications

Frank Booty

The past few years have brought accelerating growth in mobile telephony and an equally rapid expansion of internet use. By 2003 the number of mobile subscribers is expected to top one billion. Yet commentators speculate even that huge number will be insignificant compared to the expected growth in internet traffic – some five times greater than in 2001. The e-business market is expected to be massive by 2005, with analysts talking of global revenues of $5 trillion. The facilities manager needs to stay on top of this ever-changing market.

The convergence of data and telecom

Facilities managers will need to be prepared for the coming convergence of the data and telecom markets, embracing the fields of IT, telecom, the internet and mobile communications. Globally, many carriers are constructing a web of broadband (high capacity) networks to offer companies raw capacity and increasingly sophisticated added-value services. What are the factors driving this market?

Mobile growth

Pre-paid calls, widespread availability, reduced charges for normal mobile calls, free offers and marked increases in wireless data communications are all factors behind the growth in the mobile phone networks.

However, the technologies driving this growth, GPRS and UMTS (general packet radio service and universal mobile telecom system, the name of the third-generation or 3G mobile phone standard) hit the headlines in early 2001 for the wrong reasons. The WAP (wireless application protocol) standard had a notoriously rocky start and whilst it enables access to the internet from a mobile phone and the creation of advanced telecom services, its reception, performance and subsequent developments are lacklustre.

Fixed network need

The growth curve for voice telephony has levelled, while the already strong growth of data traffic in fixed networks is accelerating, especially in packet-switched networks, which are increasingly based on IP (internet protocol).

Most telecom operator revenues still derive from voice traffic, although already moves to lower call charges are noticeable.

The number of internet users continues to rise. At present, the figure is about half the 740 million global fixed telephone connections. Average connect times are increasing, but the unbundling of the local loop is still a key concern.

What will convergence mean?

For facilities managers, convergence will mean:

- the ability to run voice traffic over existing data infrastructure, resulting in reduced support overheads and enabling low-cost add-ons, moves and changes
- the delivery of voice, data, video, and so on, through one service, leading to reduced billing costs
- a growth in specialist data centre providers, tele-hotel companies and communications-related outsourcing in general
- increasingly flexible, wireless communication infrastructures, enabling seamless integration between mobile and fixed work, with implications for office space needs

---

Bluetooth

Much of future communication is expected to be handled between computers. One way for computers to connect to other systems is through a wireless connection. The glue to provide that connection is Bluetooth, an open standard for short-range digital radio – it is not a competing technology for the equally new third-generation mobile phone systems, but a supporting one. It operates in the industrial, scientific and medical (ISM) applications band, which is available almost everywhere globally. It is cheaper than competing technologies and provides up to three voice channels for speech applications. While it is not a replacement for a local area network (LAN), it can provide the final connection to the network through its ports, enabling wireless access from anywhere within the ports' coverage area.

Voice becomes data

The big swing in the future will be the move in the content of traffic carried over networks from voice to data. At present, more voice than data is carried, but by 2005 that situation is expected to change. Note that in digitising voice, the voice patterns become represented as '1's and '0's, which is exactly how data is represented. Networks will be carrying only data – everything (voice, text, video, TV, multimedia, tele and video-conferences, e-mails, messages, and so on) will be delivered through one service. The billing will prove a fascinating exercise.

A prospect for the future

Imagine being always online in a wired and wireless world. A manager in their office receives e-mail via the office local area network (LAN). They leave the office for a meeting in the conference room. E-mail carries on coming via wireless LAN technology, such as Bluetooth. At lunchtime they switch off the PC and leave the office. E-mail continues to be delivered, this time to their mobile phone or personal digital assistant (PDA) or a hybrid of the two. Back in the office, when the system is next switched on, Bluetooth updates the company server with the PDA/phone's latest information. While this is going on, a phone call comes in from the manager's superior who is travelling over the Atlantic. Access to a video graphic is required during the call, as well as conferencing with colleagues in Australia and Singapore.

- Synchronisation is handled automatically.
- The capability exists of moving seamlessly between data and telecom bearers, no matter how many devices are being used or where they are located.
- Mobile and fixed devices work seamlessly together.

Mobile IT and flexible working

With mobile and remote staff placing increasing demands on communications equipment, mobility is central to future work patterns. Flexible working will take on a fresh dimension – 'out of the office' will no longer mean 'out of touch'. Companies will be able to extend business processes directly to personnel in the field. Mobile IT will greatly assist the role of flexible working, as the nature of 'anytime, anywhere' wireless internet access opens up boundless possibilities – mobile data and computer networks, internet access, commerce and billing.

The cordless office

The technology needed to create the cordless office, a dream for many facilities managers, is either already here, or fast approaching. Soon, carriers and providers are expected to upgrade their cellular networks to offer mobile wireless internet protocol (IP) at speeds that will rival terrestrial telecom. The slimmed down version of IP for mobile applications, WAP, has received lukewarm response (see MOBILE GROWTH, P271) and is soon to be superseded. Short messaging services (SMS) are proving popular to transmit basic data to workers on the move. High-speed access is possible through GPRS (general packet radio service), while Bluetooth is being touted around with its personal wireless connectivity through a radio version of infra-red. PDAs are gaining popularity for accessing information and resources using cordless links.

Technologies such as GSM (global system for mobiles), CDPD (cellular digital packet data), CDMA (call division multiple access) and HSCSD (high-speed circuit-switched data) can be rolled out via software. Others such as GPRS and Edge (enhanced data rates for global evolution) and wireless LANs will need substantial investment in hardware infrastructure and software.

Benefits

Cordless technology does not just make workers more flexible and contactable but offers benefits including increased customer satisfaction, employee interaction and cost savings. New protocols also enable cross-compatibility, eliminating the need to purchase new equipment.

IT infrastructure management

Future-proofing

The cost of installing an inadequate IT infrastructure that does not support the company's future requirements is considerable. Whether facilities managers are responsible for IT or whether they work with an IT department, ultimately facilities and IT management converge. If your business is moving or building a new set of premises, make sure you are involved in planning right from the start.

It would have been nearly impossible to future-proof a business 10 years ago against today's IT demands, and it is still difficult for facilities managers to predict what demand will be in the next few years. But continual changes in the way organisations work are generating demand for bandwidth-hungry applications, more efficient data flows and, all-importantly, flexibility.

Any changes to existing systems, or replacement of those systems, should be done with the maximum of forethought. A well-structured infrastructure should build in the flexibility necessary for facilities and IT managers to handle future moves and technological changes.

Resource planning

Infrastructure management or infrastructure resource planning may be a recent concept in facilities management, but taking the principles behind it into account is common sense. It is good practice to assess what you have and how well it is working before moving on to the next step. Consider the following:

- What are your current IT assets – computers, cabling and telephone systems? How old are they – are they nearing the end of their lifetime? Where are they and who is using them?

- What is the gap between their existing value to the company and what company directors and/or employees would like them to deliver?

- Are there ways of maximising the use of existing assets rather than buying new ones?

- Are there ways that your existing system can work 'smarter, not harder' – through better network set-ups which minimise network congestion, for example?

Assessing the market

The facilities management world is full of companies making claims about what their technology can do for you. Each option has its own advantages and disadvantages, and it can be all too easy to be persuaded down a given route without exploring all the options. Assess the products on offer and look carefully at the experience of the companies offering them. When considering a new IT infrastructure, ask the following:

- Is the system easy to deploy and reliable? Is it likely to be overtaken by future developments?
- Will it fit with existing systems?
- Is it based on open standards, allowing flexibility in future?
- What are the cost implications?

As each technology possesses its own particular strength, businesses should always begin by understanding how they differ and what works best for their own networking needs. Before opting for the latest technology, question what value you are looking for over what you already have. Upgrade networks only when it is necessary to incorporate newer technologies, rather than changing investment unnecessarily simply because an older technology is no longer fashionable.

Structured cabling

Structured cabling is a single, integrated wiring infrastructure ensuring interoperability of communications functions such as voice, data, video and security. Structured cabling systems comprise two basic components:

- **Backbone cabling** – this begins where transmissions enter the building from outside and are routed to a series of telecom rooms serving an individual floor or discrete area of the building.

- **Horizontal cabling** – this is pulled from each room to the individual workstations or outlets on that floor.

The choice of cable – fibre optic, copper or wireless – is crucial and will have an impact on the design, installation and performance of the system.

Structured cabling must be considered as early as possible in the process of planning changes to a building's systems or planning a new building. Combining structured cable planning with heating, ventilation, air conditioning, plumbing and electrical systems can prevent problems of cables interfering with ductwork, electrical wires, or ceiling and flooring grids. When cabling projects are completed, all details of cable routes, types, connections and associated hardware and software, along with documentation of standards and testing procedures, must at least be filed with easy access, and at best incorporated into the company's computer-aided facilities management (CAFM) system (see SPACE DESIGN AND PLANNING, PP365–373, for more on CAFM systems).

Cabling category required

To a great extent, category 5 twisted pair cabling has replaced coaxial cable in local area network cabling for horizontal distribution, while multi-mode optical fibre has become the main media type for intra-building backbones. Standards are constantly evolving towards new cabling categories with better performance. Such improvements are vital to satisfy the growing demand for more bandwidth and for flexible solutions to changing working environments.

The key factor in choosing the right cabling option is the anticipated demand on network capacity. For office IT, such as word processing and accounts, category 5 offers 100Mbps, which is commonly regarded as more than enough. However, for data-intensive applications, enhanced category 5 (5e) or category 6 may be required, offering up to 1Gbps.

Category 5e is an improvement over category 5, but category 6 is already around. The Telecommunications Industry Association (TIA) and the International Standards Organisation (ISO) have collaborated on the technical work associated with the category 6 standard. The aim of the standard is to have a power sum bandwidth of 200MHz, twice that of category 5.

Meanwhile, category 7 has the aim of providing a power sum bandwidth of at least 500MHz. TIA is planning to develop specifications of connecting hardware to ensure backward compatibility and interoperability with category 5 and 5e cabling.

Voice over IP

Facilities managers need to consider the advantages and disadvantages of voice over internet protocol (VoIP), sometimes referred to as IP telephony. Unlike the conventional phone system, which is a circuit-switched network, VoIP sends calls over the internet, a packet-switched network. It first converts the voice traffic into data packets. These packets are then routed over the internet in the same way as other data, reassembled at the point of arrival and then converted back into voice.

While some internet phone traffic may travel from computer to computer, most VoIP traffic uses the current phone and fax systems. At the network level, this traffic is managed by a VoIP gateway, which converts the call between the internet and the public telephone service. This gateway may be located at the company's premises, or at the office of a service provider such as an ISP (internet service provider).

VoIP can offer new applications which can boost productivity. These include:

- integrated voice, e-mail and fax messaging
- computer-telephone integration for call centre representatives
- enhanced network collaboration

Features of VoIP

- **Unified messaging** – with a conventional system, business employees may phone, fax, e-mail or share files over the company network or the internet. VoIP combines these into one channel. For example, technology called 'unified messaging' can be used to funnel each employee's voicemail, e-mail, and faxes to a single mailbox, to be retrieved from a single end-station (PC or phone). Calls between offices travel over the existing data network through VoIP. By staying on the company network, these inter-office calls travel free of toll charges.

- **Toll-free telephony features** – IP phones deliver a complete suite of business telephony features, including call-waiting, caller ID, transfer, conference calling, and so on. These features can be deployed across any number of sites that are connected by a company's data network, without incurring toll charges.

- **Remote access via single interface** – VoIP makes it possible to make voicemail, e-mail, fax and video messages remotely accessible through a single interface – PC or phone – at each user's office desktop. This set-up increases productivity for mobile sales and service people and eliminates the cost and hassle of managing separate voicemail, e-mail and fax systems. Employees will have faster access to customer requests from any location.

- **Customer service** – integrated call systems can tie phone and e-mail systems to back-office applications where customer account information is stored. When customers call, call centre agents have instant access to their account history and can deliver a more personalised and timely service. In addition, customers visiting a company's website can use internet tools to request assistance from a live agent. VoIP enables the agent to deliver voice assistance over the phone while assisting the customer online in real time.

- **Information sharing** – employees can collaborate more easily, sharing documents online in real time, during conversations or during conference calls. VoIP also supports video transmissions over the network, enabling employees to view video-based training modules, product announcements and presentations from their desktops, enhancing productivity, saving time and lowering travel costs.

Infrastructure

Using VoIP means connecting your voice equipment – phones, fax, machines and private branch exchange (PBX) or key system – to your data network. Users can then be equipped with individual IP handsets which work like traditional phones but plug directly into network LAN switches and deliver enhanced integration with the data network.

Quality

Two main issues affect internet voice traffic: latency or sound delays and voice quality. Both of these issues are being addressed.

Voice quality is affected by many issues, including how it is compressed and decompressed for delivery over the internet, and how packets are processed. Often, voice calls sound shaky or robotic – obviously unacceptable for many typical business applications.

Voice quality is often driven by packet loss (data packets failing to arrive, not arriving on time or arriving with errors). To ensure steady quality, experts recommend a packet loss of less than 5%. At 10% voices start to quiver; at 20% they start to sound like robots. In terms of sound delay, a one-way latency of less than 100 milliseconds is acceptable.

The latest round of VoIP products do provide much improved call quality. Increased use of broadband technologies such as DSL (digital subscriber line) and cable modems will also help make VoIP more accessible.

Standards

VoIP standards are not fully established. There is a standard – *H.323* – from the International Telecommunications Union (ITU) for carrying multimedia traffic over IP networks. This defines how delay-sensitive traffic, such as voice and video, is prioritised on LANs and WANs. But many products are not interoperable with competitors' offerings because of the leeway in implementing *H.323*. The answer is to install gateways from a single vendor.

Security

Businesses need to take security measures when implementing VoIP. Traffic must be encrypted as eavesdroppers can listen in on conversations wherever packets pass. The issue is being addressed through the *H.235* standard, which covers authentication, encryption and other security measures.

Developments

IP traffic is increasing exponentially at a time when overall growth in international traffic is slowing. One major carrier estimates it will increase its capacity to carry voice traffic over IP-based networks by 1,300% up to 2006, at a quarter of the cost of doing so over a conventional circuit-switched network.

IP telephony can generally be offered to customers at prices very much below those offered over conventional circuit-switched networks, particularly on long-distance and international calls, because traffic pricing on IP-based networks is largely distance-independent. Comments aired in the US, however, state that VoIP is more about making money than saving money – users should look beyond a chance to cut long-distance costs. Rather, they should think about a new generation of VoIP-based computer telephony integration (CTI) applications which can produce increased turnover and boost a company's productivity.

It is difficult to predict a size for such a market, but London-based market analyst Ovum estimates IP services will grow from $25 million in 2000 to $6.6 billion in 2006.

Conferencing and presentation technology

Technology has made and continues to make enormous strides, but the art of conducting meetings and sharing information has mostly failed to catch up. Now possible are audio-conferences (also known as conference calls or tele-conferences), video-conferencing, data-conferencing and e-mail:

- **Audio-conferencing** – this extends the two-way telephone call, allowing multiple parties to interact on a single call.

- **Video-conferencing** – this is a fully interactive two-way video and audio communication using specialist equipment, most of which has data-conferencing facilities included.

- **Data-conferencing** – this can be used with either a conference call or video-conferencing to allow people to share data files and applications between computers during their meeting. E-mail is useful for pre-meeting exchange of information.

Business can use portable, desktop or installed projectors – there are some 300 projectors from over 40 manufacturers (see PROJECTORS, P282). Room control systems coordinate lighting, curtains/blinds and audio-visual equipment to create different environments, and to integrate different types of audio-visual equipment to make them work as one. Gas plasma display screens of up to 50 inches diagonally, 130mm in depth and with a 160° viewing angle are available, as are wireless handset controls and TV displays with widescreen and HDTV (high definition television) standards.

Conference technology vs meetings

Today's managers typically spend up to one-third of each business day in meetings. UK executives on average attend six meetings a week, spending 11 hours travelling between them. While new technologies will not replace all face-to-face meetings, they provide less costly, quicker and more productive ways of communicating. Costs of meetings are not only confined to travel. There are also hidden costs, such as administrative time used for meeting preparations, travel cancellations and the cost of time in transit.

Some meetings are particularly suitable for conferencing, for example:

- meetings that need to take place quickly
- meetings involving lots of people

- international meetings
- briefings to a large number of people

However, many sales meetings, relationship-building meetings with customers or colleagues and introductory meetings where social interaction can be more important than the task all necessitate the personal contact of a face-to-face meeting.

Audio-conferencing

Audio-conferencing is an under-used business tool in Europe. Businesses in Europe spend millions on IT every year to reduce costs and become more productive and competitive. Audio-conferencing is a relatively inexpensive solution to help address such business issues, enabling its users to communicate across large distances quickly and keep in touch with suppliers, customers, partners and colleagues, thus improving productivity whilst keeping costs low.

New technologies have improved the quality of conference calls and provided a range of call services and facilities that businesses can use to benefit communications. Different features available for audio-conferencing include security – ensuring that no one else can listen in on the call – and the ability to involve other parties in the call as and when required.

In-person meetings have been found to be nine times more expensive than audio-conferencing. Intriguingly, audio-conferencing can improve the quality and effectiveness of face-to-face meetings by adding focus to those meetings.

Applications

Typical uses for audio-conferencing include:
- business meetings
- focus groups
- seminars
- press conferences
- rapid dissemination of financial or business news
- monitoring commodities pricing
- crisis management

Crisis management

Effective conference management makes it easy to contact large groups of participants. An operator from the audio-conferencing service provider is able to dial up all participants simultaneously. The operator can then connect the host. Interaction is possible, but the host can maintain control of the conference by asking participants to press a particular key on their phone if they wish to ask a question.

Information dissemination

Audio-conferencing makes it possible to release information instantaneously to suppliers, customers and partners. For example, human resources and marketing departments could schedule a news broadcast for three to 1,000 people. Without audio-conferencing, these people would have to travel to a company site and the news dissemination would be delayed. Faster access to news keeps employees informed and motivated.

Booking

Generally, audio-conference calls are scheduled through a service provider or telecom operator. This can be done over the phone or by faxing over a booking form. Developments also enable users to book audio-conferences over the web or by e-mail.

Audio-conferencing with the internet

When a traditional conference call is combined with the internet, people can share and work collaboratively on documents. Participants can see a group of up to 30 people via a virtual meeting room on the internet with computer-generated images of each participant seated around a table. Those taking part need a telephone and PC with internet access. Such a facility – the Forum Meeting Space – is offered through BT Conferencing. There are two features to note:

- an animated 3D interface
- symbolic acting

Instead of static icons, users are represented by 3D avatars (digital representations of people) which perform animations prompted by user actions. The symbolic acting allows participants to see what others are doing (entering, leaving or using the whiteboard).

Projectors

Reliability, projection quality, size and portability are all factors that facilities managers should consider when choosing projectors. Ultimately, choosing the right model comes down to deciding on what best satisfies all personal or corporate criteria:

- **Fixed projectors** – any company carrying out regular presentations at a central base where quality of presentation is a critical factor will need a fixed solution – with maximum flexibility of input options (PC, VCR and DVD). Typical users will be trainers, directors and other senior members of staff, with applications ranging from internal training and demonstrations to product launches and sales pitches. Room costs will range from £4,000 for a basic ceiling-mounted projector to £100,000 for a boardroom incorporating the highest specification products. Features that should be considered are angle, brightness, resolution and maintenance.

- **Desktop projectors** – these are designed for organisations in which different people need access to the system within different areas of the business, in different rooms and even externally, such as conferences and exhibitions. Users could be anyone in the organisation, and ease of set-up and reliability are therefore important. Costs can vary from £2,000 to £8,000 with weight being a major issue (under 7kg is ideal, plus a hard carry case).

- **Fully portable projectors** – models cost between £2,500 and £5,000. Weight needs to be under 4.5kg. These units are typically aimed at those launching products to potential customers, or visiting colleagues in satellite offices.

Doing business over the web

Customer service concerns are seen as the main driver of e-mail for business document distribution, while elsewhere moves to an e-business culture are set to embrace the use of internet technology, providing there is total buy-in at board level. Without the right e-business approach, companies risk losing a significant portion of sales volume and profit margin to companies that have more effectively aligned themselves with their customers' supply chains.

By 2004, it is expected that businesses on both sides of the Atlantic will have migrated most of their document distribution to e-mail. A key factor behind increased e-mail deployment is the desire for a more responsive customer service. E-mail is seen as the key to cutting response times and increasing the quality of customer communications.

Furthermore, e-business enables interactive one-to-one marketing and sales but at practically zero incremental cost, whether the company is trying to reach one customer or thousands.

Top-down approach

The approach to e-business must be sold from the very top of the company down, and the facilities manager will have a major role to play as the enabler for the organisation. The emerging electronic marketplace is one which demands anytime, anywhere access (the so-called 24×7×360 model) over a number of devices and converging fixed and mobile networks.

Major stumbling blocks affecting take-up of e-business in earnest are security and trust. The former can be a problem of perception while the latter is a tactical issue that can be resolved by discussion and agreement.

E-procurement

An inevitable consequence of e-business business-to-business trading is the closer integration of companies' IT systems with the web to allow linking of accounting applications for orders, invoices and payments. It is not a new idea. Electronic data interchange (EDI) systems have been around for over 20 years but have failed to achieved the expected level of take-up because they require extensive customisation to create common information standards between organisations.

More recently, enterprise management systems have been promoted as a more effective means of controlling business finances, offering improved reporting and management information (see FINANCIAL MANAGEMENT, E-PROCUREMENT, P190). But these again rely on consistent information coding using agreed cost centres which often vary significantly between clients and suppliers.

The problem is that many of the new systems and processes cannot make use of legacy data, and then perpetuate the problem by creating a new set of bespoke information. In general, suppliers are not yet well geared up for web-based trading.

There is much potential in the technology, not only to assist in bypassing cumbersome manual processes, but also, if handled correctly, to generate valuable management and benchmarking information. Much expectation surrounds universal communications standards such as XML, a preferred choice by many for future e-business applications. Without common ground on information exchange, internet trading many never achieve its potential.

For more information relating to the growth and drawbacks of e-procurement, including 'club' e-commerce sites for procurement, see FINANCIAL MANAGEMENT, E-PROCUREMENT, P190.

Negotiating by e-mail

It has been estimated that some 610 billion e-mails are sent each year in the US, with the UK not far behind. Many routine communications between facilities managers and their user group or supply chain are now based on e-mail exchange. However, recent research at the Harvard Business School has shown that people are less inclined to share information when communicating via e-mail than through a face-to-face meeting or voice-to-voice communication. To minimise the negative features of e-mail communication, it is important to create a rapport with the other party, by meeting beforehand, engaging in 'virtual small talk', and avoiding terse statements or shorthand which could create tension or misunderstanding. If the negotiation seems to be getting angry or personal then stop e-mailing and make a phone call or arrange a meeting.

The role of the intranet site

Many facilities managers are now supporting their operations through a web-based interface with their internal customers. A well-designed interface can make a positive contribution to the climate for virtual negotiation. According to research by Cisco Systems, a successful site has three main features:

- quality of the information architecture
- quality of the graphic design
- readability

Action points

When designing a site, consider the following:

- Base the content of the site on a survey of user/customer feedback.
- Make sure information content is regularly updated.
- Make sure navigation through the site is consistent.
- Field test the usability of the site with a focus group.
- Minimise the graphic content to speed downloading.
- Present the material in a format that the reader can glance through and easily retain the main points of information.

In addition, facilities managers should identify the key stakeholder groups and design specific information resources for their individual needs. Most facilities managers will have three key stakeholder groups:

- interactive customers wanting to access services

- senior management who want to understand the organisation and performance of service delivery
- interactive suppliers who want to access the operation of the supply chain

Digital print

Those who prepare business budgets are aware that one of the biggest overheads involved in running any concern is the print, paper, stationery and communications budget. Forms continue to constitute some 83% of all company documentation and most are in paper, as opposed to electronic form.

Distributed printing

It is fair to say the consensus is there will never be a paperless office. However, it is true that print volumes are moving to the network, and customer requirements and expectations are changing, with emphasis on the need for scalability and flexibility. Further, the emergence of multifunction products is expected – hybrid printer breeds with the added functionality of scanning, faxing and copying.

Distributed printing presenting the opportunity to standardise processes and consolidate the range of office equipment is the expected scenario. In the office of the future it is expected there will be print on demand close to the user of the document – and payment on demand per page as it is used. Three things are needed: a means of moving from paper to electronic forms, use of colour output devices and printing from wireless devices, such as Bluetooth (for more on Bluetooth see P272).

Solutions for business

Companies spend up to 3% of their revenue on output management (printed documents, e-mails, faxes). Analysts at Merrill Lynch surveyed 70 chief information officers and discovered the average spend on copying and printing is 1.8% of revenue. The output management space is unmanaged. The compound annual growth rate worldwide in office page printers is 8%. There is a decrease in the numbers of standalone copiers and fax machines.

In the 'old' world of the late 1990s, the change was serial. In the 'new' world, there is concurrent change – the rate of technological change is quicker than many organisations can learn. One answer to controlling the cost of print is to outsource. The example is touted of a well known airline presenting a facilities manager's nightmare – 217 different types of printer across the estate, because of a fragmented purchase decision process early on. The answer is to measure what you can manage:

- understand the drivers
- focus on the benefits
- wake up senior management
- create and resource a project – or outsource

Analysis shows that such an approach, including asset management and helpdesks, can lower costs by 20%. Experience has shown that 40–50% of helpdesk usage concerns print(er) problems.

Electronic statement presentment

Paper use is declining in business in general, and undoubtedly the emerging sector of electronic statement presentment (ESP) is a major factor contributing to this. Enterprises spend over $200 billion printing and delivering financial and other statements to customers and employees. Recent research exploring how airlines, financial institutions, hotels and other businesses can apply ESP approaches to substantially reduce the use of paper showed the benefits to be improved communications and customer service, and reduced costs.

The Built Environment

9 Workplace Facilities

Frank Booty

The day-to-day running of the building is fundamental to facilities professionals. From procuring the most competitive electricity contract, to selecting the most appropriate air conditioning system, the facilities manager needs to be aware of the market, costs and benefits of all aspects of workplace facilities and equipment.

The increasing impetus on energy efficiency in business operations, health and safety issues and maximum productivity are now among the business objectives that facilities professionals must address. Ensuring that the appropriate services and facilities meet the needs of their users and are functioning efficiently and cost effectively will bring benefits to all aspects of an organisation's operations.

Buying gas, electricity and water

It is becoming an accepted view that facilities managers are being kept in the dark over energy costs. Lack of transparency in the existing deregulated gas and electricity markets is costing UK businesses valuable time and money. The sheer number of companies selling gas and electricity in the UK is in itself a headache for facilities managers trying to locate the best deal for their business. There are, for example, some 60 companies in the UK selling natural gas.

Some facilities managers also feel they are taking a gamble when choosing between an established, but potentially more expensive, supplier versus one of the many new but equally viable entrants to the marketplace. The popular view is that the deregulation of energy industries across Europe is likely to intensify the problem further, as foreign suppliers join the market.

How to get the best deal

The solutions to the energy-buying conundrum for facilities managers comprise a much simplified procurement process and more transparency in the market. Some facilities managers utilise the (free) services of reverse auction agencies. Any organisation seeking to obtain the best quote on energy enters a few details about its current set-up on an agency website. All Ofgem-registered gas companies in the UK then 'blind bid' for the organisation's business in a reverse auction to offer the most competitive price. Ofgem (the office for gas and electricity markets) is the official regulator. Similar arrangements exist for buying electricity. The view promulgated is that only with a truly open market can those in charge of buying commercial and industrial energy be sure they are getting the best deal.

NETA

The new electricity trading arrangements (NETA) went live in late March 2001. Government ministers and officials who visited St Thomas' Hospital in London, one of the major users of electricity, have already witnessed benefits from these reforms: the hospital saw its electricity bills fall by 13%. Larger reductions were experienced at other hospital trusts.

The previous pool arrangement was regarded as deeply flawed and seen as "effectively a means for generators to set a wholesale price which suppliers and large consumers had little choice but to accept". It was considered to be "no better than a generators' club". In contrast, NETA is a genuine market in which, for the first time, generators seek out customers (they have to), giving electricity suppliers and large organisations real choice. Indeed, forward contracts were seen soon after NETA's debut of 30% cuts in real terms compared with wholesale prices in 1998, when the Government started the reform process.

Large energy users

Suppliers are expected to focus heavily on the small to medium enterprises market, where better margins and profits can be made compared to the high volume business. What then can larger users do to improve their position?

When looking at contracts:

- be prepared to be innovative
- look to load-manage
- talk to suppliers about the usage profile
- communicate regularly regarding any changes in consumption habits
- watch the markets and supplier activity and know which suppliers are best suited to match a company's needs
- set budgets in line with an educated view as to where prices might be heading

Ofgem's advice is to "shop around to get the best deal". The role of this government watchdog is to make sure that markets are operating as competitively as possible. What Ofgem has no control over, and nor does it administer, is the Climate Change Levy (CCL) (see P**299**). This presents a conundrum. On the one hand electricity prices are lower than they would be otherwise thanks to NETA, while on the other hand the CCL has the effect of raising prices.

Combined heat and power

Combined heat and power (CHP) is a very efficient technology for generating electricity and heat together. A CHP plant is an installation where there is simultaneous generation of usable heat and power (usually electricity) in a single process. The term CHP is synonymous with 'co-generation' and 'total energy', which are terms often used in other European Community member states or in the US. The basic elements of CHP plant consist of one or more prime movers usually driving electrical generators, where the heat generated in the process is utilised via suitable heat recovery equipment for a variety of purposes, including industrial processes, community heating and space heating.

Efficiency

CHP can provide a secure and efficient method of generating electricity and heat at the point of use. Typically, CHP achieves a 35% reduction in primary energy usage when compared with power stations and heat-only boilers, as it uses heat from electricity generation and does not suffer any transmission losses, since the electricity is produced on site. So, when there is an optimum balance between heat and power loads, the host company should be able to make economic savings. Today, the existing CHP installed base achieves over 30% reductions in carbon dioxide emissions when compared with coal-fired power station equivalents, and over 10% compared with gas-fired combined cycle gas turbines. Further, the latest CHP installations produce over 50% reductions when compared with power generated by coal-fired complexes.

The total number of CHP schemes in buildings in the UK was approximately 1,500 in mid-2001 (the number of sites increased steadily from 1,220 in 1995 to 1,313 in 1999, with a net increase in electricity capacity of 354MWe). In 1999, the latest available statistics showed 93% of capacity (361 sites) is in the industrial sector and 7% of capacity (952 sites) is in the commercial, public and residential sectors.

The CHP Club

The Government is eager to achieve its target of 10GW of CHP capacity by 2010, and has set up the CHP Club to help achieve this. Established under the EEBPP (see P**301**), the Club will build on and refocus the help which is already available. It is particularly targeted at new and potential CHP users, and also aims to help existing users to extend their schemes. It intends to provide members with a one-stop shop – a combination of information, exchange of experience and advice facilities on CHP and related topics, all for free.

The CHP Quality Assurance (CHPQA) programme will enable good quality CHP to earn exemption from the CCL; potential members can visit and register with the CHP Club website. The Government issued a consultation paper *CHPQA – A Quality Assurance Programme for Combined Heat and Power* in 2000. The operation of CHPQA is to be reviewed in the light of experience. However, any changes made will apply to subsequent CHP developments and will not be applied retrospectively to existing CHP schemes. What is wanted is a simple, fair and robust system that benefits all possible types and sizes of CHP, including small-scale packaged systems, alternative fuels and community heating systems.

Totally integrated power

A lack of a uniform approach to energy monitoring, control and delivery has meant that occupants of industrial and commercial buildings have found it practically impossible to integrate energy supply to the same extent as other critical building services, such as HVAC and security. Heating, lighting, access control and fire and security systems all need to be controlled, along with a building's energy requirements.

Totally integrated power, a concept developed by Siemens, offers integrated power distribution from medium voltage switchgear all the way through to socket outlets on an office wall. The concept covers every aspect of power distribution and electricity management required in an industrial environment. It has been estimated that totally integrated power can bring power use savings of 25%, because it enables electricity users to reduce their total power costs, as well as increasing the efficiency of operation of plant equipment. The market size for totally integrated power has been estimated at €10 billion, and is expected to grow by some 2% per annum. Operators of public buildings, including museums, hospitals and airports, are said to benefit from totally integrated power just as much as industrial and office markets. The theory is that by expanding the capability of data control and management through an entire building, all aspects of energy delivery and consumption can be integrated.

Open systems in building control

The International Alliance for Interoperability (IAI) has the mission "to provide a universal basis for process improvement and information sharing in the construction and facilities management industries, using industry foundation classes (IFCs)". IFCs are a practical tool for information sharing, using object technology; they are information-rich, swiftly transmitted and not limited to any one software vendor or system. The IAI's first chapter was set up in the US in 1995 and the second in the UK in 1996. Other chapters now cover German-speaking, French-speaking and Nordic countries, Japan, Singapore, Korea and Australasia.

The IAI has chapters covering facilities management areas such as reactive and preventative maintenance, asset management, move management, change management, helpdesk, energy consumption profiles and performance data, but nothing currently in the signals area. This is the domain of open systems protocols and interoperability, principally involving the use of LONworks, BACnet and EIB. With these systems, the situation is one where central systems increasingly feature distributed intelligence at all outstations.

The LONmark Interoperability Association is a key driving force in the establishment of interoperable guidelines for building, industrial, transportation and residential/utility automation. LONmark membership is open to any manufacturer, end-user and system integrator committed to the development and use of open, interoperable products using multi-vendor LONworks control networks.

BACnet is a data communications protocol for building automation and control networks. Developed by ASHRAE (American Society of Heating, Refrigerating and Air-conditioning Engineers), BACnet is a US standard, a European 'pre-standard' and a potential global standard.

The EIB bus – EIB stands for European Integration Bus but is always referred to as EIB – serves the same function as LONworks and BACnet, offering the sensor-to-sensor and unit-to-unit links of LONworks and the controller-to-controller-level protocol of BACnet.

As of yet there is no 100% open communication. The Building Research Establishment runs an EIB and BACnet training centre. The Energy Systems Trade Association's Building Controls Group is one possible source of information.

Avoiding power failures

Organisations reliant on sensitive electronic and computer-based equipment are vulnerable to even momentary cuts in the electricity supply. Mains failure could bring most workplaces to a standstill. PCs, workstations, network servers, retail point-of-sale systems, medical equipment and telecom systems all depend on a high quality uninterrupted power supply. A distortion of only a few milliseconds can destroy data, disconnect communication links and damage delicate instrumentation.

The best way to limit or prevent potential damage caused by power irregularities is with battery back-ups known as uninterruptible power supplies (UPS) and standby generators. The cost of UPS systems ranges from under £100 to some £150,000 and generators start at £25,000 and can cost hundreds of thousands of pounds. When selecting a UPS, there are several important issues to consider:

- What are the potential consequences of power loss in both the short and long term?

- How much load requires protecting and which pieces of equipment are most critical?

- What is the length of time power needs to be sustained?

- What are the power requirements of critical equipment?

- What is the likelihood and possible duration of power losses or fluctuations?

The use and application of UPS systems needs to be part of a company's disaster recovery policy (see BUSINESS CONTINUITY, P218). For maintenance of UPS systems see MAINTENANCE AND REPAIR, PP400–402.

Water competition

The Government is to further boost the opportunities for competition in the water industry in England and Wales. Proposals should bring customers more choice, keener prices and better services. The Government intends to license new entrants in production (extraction) of water and for retail of water to customers. Companies are to be given clearer rights to enter the water market and the incumbent companies would remain vertically integrated statutory undertakers, retaining their key strategic water resource and environmental duties, whilst the Government will continue to ensure that public health, the environment and the quality of drinking water are safeguarded.

Ofwat (the office of water services) is to review its regulatory regime to consider what changes, such as further transparency in incumbents' costing information, are needed to promote competition. Parliamentary information can be found on the DEFRA or Ofwat websites.

Checking utility invoices

It pays to check all utility bills thoroughly – costly mistakes in the supplier's favour can and do occur. Anecdotal evidence suggests major users can expect average refunds of 2–4% from rigorous attention to bill validation. Smaller users are not immune; although errors may affect them less regularly, their effect can be quite disproportionate.

Companies may already have some form of bill-checking procedures in place, supported by specialised software. But it is worthwhile reviewing how effective and efficient the systems are by questioning if the checking process can validate the following items:

- Is it the correct supplier? Ensure, for example, there is no double billing by a previous incumbent overlapping with a new contract.
- Are the prices correct – including transportation of use-of-system charges if separately itemised?
- Is there continuity – for example, no mismatch of 'previous' meter readings, no double-counted or phantom bulk deliveries?
- Is the arithmetic correct?
- Is there proof of delivery – that is, independent verification of meter readings and bulk fuel drops?
- Is there consistency with earlier billing patterns?

The complexity of some utility invoices can make it a daunting task to apply thorough vetting. Bills for contract electricity supplies and effluent charges, for example, can be quite complex. Worse still, much of the proprietary software sold for the purpose is not up to the job and becomes less relevant as non-tariff contract deals proliferate in the deregulated utility marketplace.

One practical approach is to model the invoice for each account with a spreadsheet. The current supplier's details and contract price structure can be built in as constants. When the variable data from a new bill is entered into the appropriate boxes, the grand total should match that shown on the real bill. Changes of supplier, changes of price and even changes of tariff structure can be accommodated by creating a modified version of the model bill.

Meter-reading errors

Experience shows that arithmetic errors are rare. Meter-reading discrepancies, however, do occur. Agreed, an incorrect or estimated reading will usually be corrected on the subsequent read and any resulting overcharging will be balanced by a compensating undercharge, but there are important exceptions to this general rule. One is when the estimated reading occurs on the date of a change of supplier or end of contract year, when the price changes. Too much consumption may then be charged at the higher price and too little at the lower price.

More significant is the situation where the meter is changed and the final reading on the outgoing meter is estimated or wrong. Take the case where a refund for 500 cubic metres of water was obtained by successfully arguing that a final reading of 13,700 was inconsistent with earlier consumption and appeared to be a misreading for 13,200, which gave a more reasonable result.

Cases of inaccurate billing

- A department store, buying electricity on a maximum demand tariff, had an agreed supply capacity (ASC) of 211kVA, much more than was required to cope with a consistent monthly peak of 110–130kVA. When a year's bills were examined, it was found that the reason for this was one isolated month when demand had apparently peaked at 211kVA. Before that, the ASC had been 160kVA and the increase to 211kVA (a permanent extra monthly charge) had been triggered by that single freak maximum demand. On reviewing the situation, the figure of 211kVA was seen as a clerical error. It was more likely to have been 121kVA. The supplier agreed, repaid the excess, and reduced the ASC to 130kVA to give further long-term savings.

  The case was easily dealt with because it concerned a user supplied by the local electricity company.

- In a similar case, a NORWEB customer in the Southern Electric franchise area, with London Electricity as the meter reader, was concerned about a £2,400 exceptional charge which appeared on a bill, ostensibly to recover unpaid ASC charges arising from the fact that Southern Electric had 'discovered' a previously unregistered peak demand of 415kVA some months earlier. Normal peak demand was 50–90kVA. The 415kVA peak was fiction and fortunately there was half-hourly data for the period concerned to prove it. After some further work, the buck stopped where it belonged – with the electricity supplier – and the spurious charge was cancelled.

- More worrying still is the case of the client whose ASC doubled from 7MW to 14MW when the meter operator changed the half-hourly meters and carelessly added the two meters' records together without allowing for the fact that both were registering simultaneously on the same date.

These are dramatic examples of what has happened in specific cases. Maybe similar things have happened to managers without errors coming to light – yet. It pays to check.

Climate Change Levy

Energy consumption contributes significantly to the UK's carbon dioxide emissions. Business accounts for nearly 70% of these emissions – industry and commerce alone are responsible for nearly 42%. The UK Government has set an ambitious target for a 20% cut in the country's carbon dioxide emissions by 2010 (the UK had agreed with the EU to a 12.5% cut on 1990 levels). Initiatives have been launched by the Government to assist companies in reducing their energy consumption. However, it is the Climate Change Levy which is expected to provide the push behind getting businesses to think about how they can cut their energy consumption and costs.

The levy is basically a tax on coal, gas and electricity affecting both private and public sectors. Its existence has increased the viability of renewable energy options and combined heat and power (CHP), as these supplies will be exempt. British Gas estimates that the levy will add 10% to electricity bills and 15% to gas bills. Most utilities will, like British Gas, display the levy as a separate subtotal at the bottom of the bill so that you can tell how much you are paying for it and whether you are exempted in that billing period. See HEALTH AND SAFETY LAW: CLIMATE CHANGE LEVY, PP66–68 for details of levy rates and exemptions.

Objectives

The aim of the levy – which was introduced in April 2001 – is to encourage greater energy efficiency and use of greener power supplies. Reduced levy rates will be accorded to those who demonstrate they have invested in energy efficiency. The levy is expected to hit most UK companies unless action is taken to minimise energy consumption and emissions. Any company pursuing an efficiency path will benefit from the levy; the Government estimates that most businesses could save 10% of their energy at little cost. Such a reduction would amount to more than just a 10% reduction on the levy – it would also cut the overall fuel bill by a significant sum.

The levy is not aimed at the small to medium business sector directly, but this group does have a key role to play. According to the Institute of Directors, if every small business in the UK were to cut its energy requirements by 20%, the nation's energy bill would be reduced by £1 billion, and three million tonnes of carbon dioxide emissions would be eliminated. Whatever the size of the organisation, every company needs to have an energy management policy. The backing, understanding and support of everyone – from directors to staff – is mandatory.

Reducing emissions and costs

The Government has made it clear that the CCL is not a one-off but part of a trend to shift business taxes away from positive activities like job creation and investment to environmental performance. Clearly the levy is not going to go away. An estimated saving of 1.5 million tonnes of carbon a year by 2010 is expected as a result but, in so doing, industry will be paying a bill of £1.75 billion in the first year alone. Most organisations will be looking to the facilities manager to reduce that bill.

Four key factors have been proposed that will reduce emissions and reduce costs:

- **Data logging** – an inexpensive and investigative method for analysing energy usage which can be applied to specific processes – it is a powerful tool in the hands of those who know what they are looking for.

- **CHP** – viable even at less than 80kW. The excess heat from engines and turbines can be used for process plant, heating and chilling (see COMBINED HEAT AND POWER, P293).

- **Boiler plant** – investigate operating costs and consider the use of the latest energy-saving techniques.

- **Enhanced capital allowance (ECA) scheme** – a first year tax relief of 100% is available for eight categories of energy-saving equipment:
  - variable speed drives
  - high-efficiency motors
  - boiler systems
  - refrigeration systems
  - CHP systems
  - lighting systems
  - thermal systems
  - pipework insulation

One of the most important factors for companies is the need to address the complete plant, rather than particular divisions. By focusing on the process as a whole it is possible to achieve the lowest overall running costs.

Practical measures to reduce consumption

Even if long-term levy revenues do get pumped back into business, how is the facilities manager, concerned about short-term rising costs, to ensure that the levy is as small a burden as possible? The short answer is to measure your energy consumption, compare it with industry norms and then manage it down. New ways of doing this are constantly being explored, and nine local or industry-specific pilot initiatives across the country have received funding of £460,000 from the Energy Savings Trust to uncover and set up new ways of improving energy efficiency, and to act as role models. Each project has a target of a 10% reduction in energy usage. The Energy Efficiency Best Practice Programme (EEBPP) publishes a number of helpful leaflets, while free visits to discuss energy efficiency are offered through Energy Efficiency Advice Centres. An Environment and Energy helpline is also available. The EEBPP has now been restructured, with the Government passing management of the programme from the DETR to Quantum Partnership, wholly owned by the Foundation for the Built Environment, who will run the programme on behalf of the Carbon Trust.

Meanwhile, the utility firm Scottish Power has issued some practical advice:

- Include energy efficiency in buying specifications and for all equipment.
- Get office equipment switched onto standby mode – this can help make energy savings from 25% to over 50%.
- Make staff aware which equipment can be switched off when not in use.
- Inspect and replace worn or damaged refrigeration seals.
- Install motor controllers to reduce fuel consumption of refrigerators and freezers.
- Reduce building heat losses by up to 90% by insulation (while maintaining adequate ventilation).
- Make thorough checks on the building fabric for damp, which reduces insulating qualities.
- Consider reducing the volume of air to be heated by installing suspended ceilings.
- Fit temperature controls, check thermostat settings, draught-proof windows and doors and raise staff awareness – the maximum recommended office heating level is 19°C and for each one degree of overheating, costs rise by about 8%.
- Reduce thermostat settings for storerooms, corridors and where there is a high level of activity – workshops should typically be 16°C and stores 10–12°C.
- Set frost thermostats to optimum levels -4°C internal and 0–1°C external.
- Install seven-day time-switches (about £50 each); check settings are correct and correspond to occupancy patterns.
- Remember that radiators can be switched off before the end of occupancy.

- Check that heating and ventilation operate at the minimum recommended settings when the building is unoccupied.

- Check which rooms regularly overheat and correct.

- Fit thermostatic radiator valves (about £15 each), set them correctly and lock them.

- Have heaters and burners cleaned and serviced at least yearly by a qualified contractor.

- Turn off lights whenever possible, especially in toilets, corridors, storerooms and canteens; make staff aware they can save 15% in this way.

- Install slim-line fluorescent tubes which cost the same as normal fluorescent tubes but use 8% less electricity.

- Fit presence detectors for automatic control of lights (about £40 each).

- Fit pneumatic push-button pop-out switches in store cupboards (about £20 each).

- Replace tungsten bulbs with more efficient compact fluorescent bulbs (£10 each).

Environmental measuring and reporting

As the Government's climate change programme proposals make clear, there will be increasing pressure on users of fuel in business and industry to measure and publish their greenhouse gas emissions.

The Department of the Environment, Transport and the Regions, as it then was, published guidance on how to do this, *Environmental reporting – guidelines for company reporting on greenhouse gas emissions*, in June 1999. The top 350 businesses were expected to comply by the end of 2001, to be followed by all organisations with more than 250 employees. Encouragement is also being given, particularly to larger users, to set demanding targets for the reduction of emissions so that they make a proper contribution to the achievement of national targets.

Measuring energy efficiency

By far the most common yardstick for measuring – and managing – energy is by its cost. For a large number of users, interest does not extend beyond the one line on the expenditure budget for heat, light and power. However, if cost is the only yardstick, interest in energy efficiency depends on whether unit costs of fuel are rising or falling. In recent years, prices have steadily fallen, with a corresponding decline of interest in improving efficiency. The Climate Change Levy (CCL) will, of course, help to correct this.

Where energy is used in buildings, a step forward in analysis is cost per unit area. Much information is available on cost standards for offices, schools, hospitals and other types of building, which enable users to compare their performance with best practice. Gas and electricity are sold by the kilowatt-hour (kWh), and this is the most commonly used unit for the analysis. Again, a wide range of information is available, notably through the Energy Efficiency Best Practice Programme, which gives benchmark standards for energy use in various applications.

With increasing attention being given to environmental standards, a performance indicator based on carbon dioxide emissions is becoming more regularly measured and reported. The unit of measurement may be kilograms of carbon dioxide ($kgCO_2$) or kilograms of the carbon content of the carbon dioxide (kgC), where 44 units of carbon dioxide contain 12 units of carbon.

Energy-efficiency improvement programmes

Whilst it is important to be aware of units of measurement, programmes of improvement must inevitably consider ways of actually increasing energy efficiency. Sometimes this is done by making major changes to the way requirements are met, for instance by installing a CHP unit, or replacing a centralised steam boiler by smaller units close to the point of use. These are expensive capital projects which have to be carefully assessed and evaluated, with options such as whether to carry through the project in-house or use a contract energy management company.

Far more often, the improvement programme is achieved gradually. Such a programme might typically aim to improve energy efficiency by 2% per year. This is likely to be measured in terms of a performance indicator, which may be in terms of kWh, kWh/sq m, carbon dioxide emissions, and so forth. If it is measured in cost terms, an adjustment for any changes in fuel prices must be made for the results to have any meaning.

The importance of measuring where energy is used should also be emphasised. For instance, many organisations cannot separate their use of electricity for power and for lighting, nor distinguish where steam and hot water are used after they leave the boilerhouse. Measurement enables energy use to be assessed against standards and its costs to be allocated to users. Adequate metering is essential for good energy management.

In practice, there can be all sorts of variations from year to year. The weather has been different, there are more people and more computers in the office, some parts of the building have been enlarged or refurbished. It is, however, possible to apply normalisation adjustments to certain factors – such as heating degree days – and this helps to allow more accurate comparisons. Another option may be to join an accreditation scheme which relies on more than one performance indicator, enabling a better judgment to be made about good management and progressive improvement.

The value of metering data

All organisations with a maximum electrical demand of more than 100kW will already have metering systems that record consumption every half hour, every day of the week. This Code 5 metering is required under the rules covering the operation of the electricity supply market. Although the data gathered from these meters is primarily intended for use in billing and in balancing supply and demand requirements between generators and suppliers, this data can be a powerful tool in combating the extra liability associated with the introduction of the CCL.

The metering information that is despatched for the purposes of the electricity pool is, however, edited. While this makes balancing supply and demand and billing procedures run more easily, this edited data is of little use for energy management, and it is important to get hold of the raw data. Your data collector should be able to provide this. The supplier's permission should be sought (as, technically, the data belongs to them), but it is now standard practice to allow this.

The figures for consumption will not provide a great deal of information in themselves. Their value lies in comparing them with, for example, trend data, degree day information, and normalised performance indicators. So, the data stream needs to go through some form of analysis.

The results should highlight where energy consumption patterns are exceptional, for example, at night or weekends, or over shutdown periods. They will also indicate any drift from optimum performance and can provide an early warning of serious equipment faults which bring about noticeable drops or increases in consumption over short periods of time.

This information can be made available within a matter of days, rather than the weeks it normally takes the supplier to send a bill. For this reason, it is important to ensure that the contract you make with the data collector provides for the speedy release of this information to you.

Waste water management

Sewerage is an essential service, the exact costs of which are difficult to calculate. There are ways in which businesses can keep track of the amount they pay for waste water. Water charges are tightly regulated and in a constant state of review, with the industry regulator Ofwat protecting customers' interests by setting the overall price limits that govern charges. The 10 sewerage companies in England and Wales are given strict guidelines, but accurately pricing the amount of water the businesses send back into the sewerage system is problematic. Firms can sometimes be paying more than they need to.

Sewerage charges

The *Water Industry Act 1991* allows water companies to levy a single charge for sewerage, although Ofwat recommends costs are broken down into three constituent elements:

- foul drainage (including trade effluent)
- highway drainage (run-off from roads and pavements)
- surface drainage (run-off from properties)

The aim is to ensure charges are related to the services provided. This makes it easier for customers to assess whether they are being correctly billed and to check they are getting the services for which they have paid.

Foul drainage

Foul drainage refers to the dirty water discharged from lavatories, sinks, washing machines, and so on. Charges are based on the volumes of water supplied to the property with adjustments made for non-return to sewer. It is not possible to measure the exact amount of waste returned and it is the responsibility of each water company to decide how it calculates its own system for payment. However, this does not prevent customers from challenging charges. If a query is made, a representative from the water company visits the site and evaluates the situation according to the evidence supplied regarding the ways in which water is used there. The object is to agree allowances (see P307).

Frozen food businesses, which use large amounts of water in production processes, hospitals (where liquids are often disposed of elsewhere) and pharmaceutical companies are examples of organisations which have a relatively low return to sewer and may be eligible for reductions. Even swimming pools can claim a discount for evaporation of water. No foul drainage charges should apply where a property is not connected to the sewerage system. The onus is generally on the consumer to come forward to claim rebates.

Highway drainage

The way water companies charge for highway and surface drainage tends to vary. Some operate a flat fee, others refer to the rateable value of the property or the surface area drained to a public sewer. According to Ofwat's 1998–99 *Report on Tariff Structure and Charges,* Ofwat's director-general believes that as highway drainage benefits all those using roads, directly or indirectly, there is a case for recovering the costs of the service from highway authorities or from users of the highway. Currently, the law prevents this option and these costs are recovered from sewerage customers. This situation is unlikely to change in the near future and it is not currently possible for customers to claim a rebate for highway drainage.

Surface drainage

A charge based on run-off from properties forms a significant part of the total sewerage bill and businesses not using the service, or making only limited use of it, may be able to save money. Again, water companies differ in the way they calculate charges and not all of them differentiate between customers who are connected to the facility and those who are not. Ofwat's director-general wants water companies to provide a clear explanation of the charges on bills and is encouraging them to reduce those charges if the property concerned does not benefit from surface drainage.

Trade effluent

Trade effluent refers to industrial waste, including that discharged at the end of or during manufacturing processes. This covers such things as waste from food factories, dairy product manufacturers, chemical plants and abattoirs. It is also classed as sewerage, but billed separately. Customers pay according to the strength and volume of the trade effluent discharged, both of which have a bearing on the level of treatment needed for the waste. Public swimming pools, for example, may benefit from lower tariffs because of the lower strength of effluent discharged.

Large-user tariffs have been introduced by most of the water companies. These work primarily through the imposition of a high fixed charge and a lower volumetric rate for water supplied – or alternatively one where the standing charge remains the same, but there is a lower volumetric rate for all consumption over an agreed level. The aim is to provide attractive water charges for high users without presenting an incentive to waste water.

Allowances

Water companies may make allowances for customers who can prove that rain water, for example, is drained and taken away by means other than the public sewer. The water may go to a soak-away or watercourse using the customer's own arrangements, or even a trade effluent meter. If significant volumes of water are not returned to the sewer, or if only a small volume of surface water is discharged, it may be worth diverting all the water so that none returns to the public sewer – which is one way to cut charges. Ofwat reckons some businesses may be underpaying for this particular service.

Metering

Some 20% of non-household users, normally small businesses, remain unmetered and in some areas this figure rises to nearly 30%. Since most sewerage charges are based on the volume of water supplied to a property, meters are the best way of ensuring costs relate to usage. The regulator is keen to encourage the use of meters and believes it is the sensible option where economically viable.

Remote reading

Remote reading of meters is gaining favour. Accessing each water meter to take a direct reading is not always easy, and manual readings have to be keyed into the energy management system by hand. To combat such problems, manufacturers have developed remote-reading systems, the main technologies of interest being electronic meter reading and radio reading. For electronic approaches, the meter requires an in-built encoder linked to a touch-pad which passes data to a handheld interrogator. The data is subsequently downloaded to the energy management system. No access to premises is required to take readings. With radio, the meter reader does not have to touch the meter at all. Most remote-reading systems can be retrofitted if required.

Individual water companies will have advisers on commercial and industrial metering issues. Accurate, timely information on consumption patterns can help managers keep water costs under control. If there are cost savings to be made, the water meter could be the key.

EC directives

Meeting EC directives is a requirement for water quality and compliance adds to the cost of treating sewerage and effluent. So how can reduced tariffs be justified? Ofwat reckons reduced charges are based on customers making less use of the reception and conveyance part of the service, consistent with the way tariffs for large users have developed on the water side. The way sewerage companies calculate charges is far from straightforward and structures differ from company to company. General advice from sewerage companies is to contact them if you believe you are not making full use of their services or can prove you are being overcharged.

Preventing water pollution

Point-source pollution – from sewage and industrial effluents, for example – is easily regulated. However, pollution from diffuse sources such as surface water run-off from urban areas is not. Diffuse pollution – from silt and solids in particular – is the most significant pollution being faced today. Surface water can be contaminated by oil, silt, leaves, dog or cat mess, carbon and a mixture of pollutants from the air, roads, industrial yards, car parks and other hard surfaces, such as drives and pavements. Discharges from surface water outfalls have been found with average concentrations of suspended solids over 200mg/litre – almost the same as raw sewage. Discharges have also been found contaminated with sewage debris and high levels of dangerous bacteria.

Main causes of contamination

There are five main causes of contamination:

- contaminants deposited on drained surfaces, such as oil, rubber, chemicals, pesticides and mud
- wrong connections of foul water to surface water drains, by accident or ignorance
- public ignorance of where drains ultimately lead
- spills and deliberate disposal, particularly oil, flushed into surface water drainage systems
- sudden flushing of contaminated water into drains, leading to flooding and subsequent groundwater pollution.

Heavy rainfall accelerates run-off, producing a mixture of pollutants flushing rapidly into drains, then to rivers, causing contamination and flooding. Because the natural settling-out process is bypassed, the common result is widespread contamination of natural watercourses and the public water supply.

Best management practices

The introduction of best management practices (BMPs) means non-point-source pollution and flooding can be effectively and economically prevented and/or controlled. BMPs are ways of minimising diffuse pollution. Two techniques have been developed – procedural and structural – which aim to:

- slow the speed of run-off to allow settlement, filtering and infiltration
- reduce the quantity of run-off collected
- provide natural ways of treating collected surface water before it is either discharged to a watercourse or infiltrated into land

BMP options

A range of BMP options exist from which designers, developers, planners, drainage specialists and civil engineers may choose. These include grass swales and filter strips, infiltration basins, extended detention ponds, retention ponds, wetlands, porous surfaces, and procedural BMPs (aimed particularly at agricultural areas).

- **Swales** – these can utilise the common green space alongside roads or other open areas. Basically a much-improved ditch with a broad bottom and gently sloping sides, a swale gives a low sheet flow, slowing the water and enabling pollutants to settle out. Swales obviate the need for expensive roadside kerbs and gullies. Maintenance costs are much lower and drainage of the road surface is guaranteed.

- **Detention ponds** – these are designed to collect storm run-off, holding it for a few hours to let sediment settle out. Outside of storm periods, most ponds will be dry. The main function is to remove solids – removal rates of 80% are possible. Rates for nutrient and trace metal removal are more modest, however – a retention pond or wetland will improve this performance.

- **Retention ponds** – these retain a significant volume of water all the time. The design can allow for substantial variation in the retained water level and the pond can become an attractive local amenity – as well as an effective filter for nutrients, trace metals, bacteria and organic matter.

- **Storm water wetlands** – these are enhanced wet ponds with shallow areas incorporating a variety of marsh and wetland plants covered in up to 0.15–0.3 metres of water. The algae and plant material filter and remove nutrients to a much greater degree than ponds alone. Storm water wetlands must always be purpose built. Leading surface water into an existing natural wetland can harm aquatic life and is not an acceptable practice.

- **Porous pavements** – these are an alternative to conventional paving and allow water to permeate through, rather than run off, the paving. Rainwater can filter directly into the subsoil or can drain into a reservoir (about 1m deep) before soaking slowly away, discharging to the watercourse or being stored for landscape watering. Porous surfaces are appropriate where run-off is lightly contaminated and close to source. They have been shown to remove up to 80% of sediment, 60%

of phosphorus, 80% of nitrogen and substantial levels of trace metals and organic matter.

- **Infiltration trenches** – these are shallow, excavated trenches, backfilled with stone to create an underground reservoir. From this, the water filters into the subsoil, and can help replenish groundwater resources.

- **French drains** – these are below-ground systems comprising a trench filled with gravel wrapped in a geotextile membrane. Run-off water is led to them directly from the surface or through a system of pipes. French drains are less costly than kerbs and gullies, and are useful where only small watercourses are available to receive run-off water.

Key facts about BMPs

- BMPs are mostly always cheaper than conventional systems, usually by up to 50%.

- Maintenance requirements are generally less than those for conventional drainage systems. BMPs trap pollutants at one point, sparing managers the task of having to clean out many small structures.

- Research conducted in the US shows that pollutants cannot be considered to be hazardous or toxic material.

- Storm water ponds can be designed to be safer for children by adjusting the geometry; slopes to ponds should be gentle, minimising the risk of a child falling into one.

- With sensitive planting and landscaping, BMPs such as swales, ponds and wetlands can be attractive features, as can porous surfaces for car parks and pedestrian areas.

- Benefits include:
    - increases in property values
    - increased wildlife and conservation value
    - sustainable development
    - a cleaner water environment

BMPs in action

Examples of BMP sites in the UK include: porous car parks at Nottingham Trent University; infiltration trenches at Shire Hall, Reading; storm water retention ponds at Lexmark's site, Rosyth; and grass swales at Freeport Leisure, West Calder.

Information on groundwater protection can be obtained from the Environment Agency.

HVAC (heating, ventilation and air conditioning)

Indoor air quality

It is estimated the average person spends up to 90% of their time inside a building. Maintaining air quality is vital to ensuring health and well-being, as well as maximum productivity in the workplace. Yet despite recent air quality initiatives relating to external air pollution and the reduction of emissions, there is currently no legislation and there are no EU directives related specifically to indoor air quality.

When defining air quality, it is important to consider everything from temperature and humidity to air flow and cleanliness, as well as the maintenance of any air conditioning or ventilation equipment used. The Heating, Ventilating and Air Conditioning Manufacturers Association (HEVAC) has set up an initiative specifically on indoor air quality. It is evaluating research on the subject and is keen to create a greater understanding about the problems that may occur if air quality is poor (see PROMOTING CLEANER INDOOR AIR, P317).

Health problems (such as asthma, eye irritations and nausea) are known symptoms of poor air. There have even been cases of legionnaire's disease spread by bacteria in HVAC systems. Poor air quality also impacts on productivity in the workplace.

The effect of equipment on air quality

Factors influencing indoor air quality are the equipment installed in that space. Furniture, carpets, fixtures and fittings, process plant and equipment and general office apparatus such as computers, photocopiers and fax machines all have a substantial effect on air quality, in addition to that of the HVAC equipment.

Temperatures increase with the amount of electrical equipment used, small quantities of toxic ozone can be produced by printers and fax machines, for example, and emissions of volatile organic compounds (VOCs) are possible by-products of soft furnishings, carpets and some furniture. Assessing the equipment and furnishings in a space and choosing equipment with minimum impact on indoor air quality is advisable and can mean smaller and less expensive HVAC equipment is needed as a result.

Saving energy and improving quality

To save energy and improve indoor air quality, HEVAC suggests:

- choosing electrical equipment with a sleep mode where possible to reduce power consumption during inactive periods
- fitting ozone filters to equipment where appropriate
- fitting carpets and furnishings with low emissions of VOCs
- having dedicated extraction equipment to control fumes and emissions
- using solvent-free inks where possible
- checking how easily equipment can be cleaned and following manufacturers' recommendations on cleaning and maintenance

Indoor air quality can be improved simply by removing or limiting as many pollutants as possible, providing a good quality environmental control system (which includes the removal of pollutants) and ensuring adequate ventilation (natural, where possible).

The Chartered Institution of Building Services Engineers (CIBSE) recommends:

- eliminating contaminants at source
- substituting with sources that produce non-toxic or less malodorous contaminants
- reducing the emission rate of substances
- segregating occupants from potential sources of toxic or malodorous substances
- improving ventilation (by local exhaust, displacement or dilution, for example)
- providing personal protection

Choosing equipment

Choosing the correct HVAC equipment is essential. It needs to be appropriate for the space in which it is installed and maintained properly thereafter. Otherwise it could have the effect of reducing air quality. Plant today is smaller and more efficient than it used to be and likewise (new) buildings are becoming more energy efficient. The Federation of Environmental Trade Associations (FETA) emphasises the importance of maintaining equipment and stresses that using top-of-the-range equipment in the wrong place can be just as damaging as older equipment, especially if it is not maintained and cleaned regularly.

Air conditioning which brings fresh air inside may be an excellent idea, but if the unit is sited in the wrong place it could actually be counterproductive, dragging more pollution indoors in the form of traffic fumes, especially if filters are not changed regularly. According to CIBSE, the grade of filtration needed varies according to several factors, including the level of external pollution and the exposure limits set to protect occupants and the amount of protection required for the internal surfaces of the building, air handling plant and air distribution system.

A voluntary system run by Eurovent, the European testing body for HVAC equipment, certifies products. Eurovent tests the equipment's performance and power rating – which ensures that the manufacturers' claims about the amount of energy the product uses are correct. The CCL encourages the use of energy-efficient systems.

Bacteria attack on HVAC systems

Experts first brought bacterial attacks on HVAC systems to London property owners' attention in 1998. In 2001, an increasing number of cases were discovered throughout the UK. The bacteria in question – pseudonomas – attack the inside of systems and ultimately turn them into sprinkler systems. Pseudonomas attack anything that will corrode. London-based systems appear to be well covered but increasing numbers are being discovered elsewhere. It is crucial to assess risk at the testing stage of HVAC systems as problems start as soon as the pipes get wet and are then left with stagnant water. Pseudonomas – which are harmless to humans – can be spread through using dirty hoses for filling systems and unscrupulous companies selling products claiming to eradicate the problem, or giving incorrect or inappropriate advice.

A nine-point plan has been drawn up and facilities managers should check consultants and installers are complying:[1]

1.   The quality of water for filling systems should be monitored and controlled.

2.   Biocide and dispersant should be considered for use with initial fill.

3.   Dose with an appropriate biocide prior to the clean.

4.   Always test water by sampling in the cleaning process.

5.   Ensure all temporary hoses and equipment are chlorinated before use.

6.   Consider the type of filtration to be used carefully.

7.   Consider the type of biocide carefully – its longevity, for example.

8.   Consider the type of inhibitor carefully (nitrite-based units provide bacteria nutrients).

9.   Regularly monitor the micro-biological condition of the water.

Air conditioning

The view of air conditioning as a luxury product is generally being abandoned. Indeed, in a range of locations encompassing offices, shops, restaurants, bars and cars, it has become essential to have an air conditioned environment. The international marketing consulting company Frost & Sullivan believes the rising awareness of the effectiveness of air conditioning systems, linked with their ease of use and low installation costs, is adding momentum to overall market growth. Sales of commercial air conditioning systems in Europe are predicted to reach $4.4 billion by 2006, doubling in size in six years.

The need for air conditioning

Trends toward open-plan offices have witnessed increased demands for air conditioning systems, as the space allocated per employee is more restrictive in an open-plan area than in a conventional office. Add to this the massive amounts of heat generated by the many electronic systems in today's offices and the need for cooling becomes obvious. Opening windows is not always the answer, as in many cases the windows will be sealed units. Where the windows do open wide, the outside environment may be a busy, noisy and dirt-polluted thoroughfare.

A small office with two people and a typical range of office equipment can generate 3,000W of heat per hour, which is more than a two-bar electric fire. Poor air quality is known to reduce or inhibit productivity. The increasing drive towards air quality is expected to spur growth in the air conditioning market, certainly up to 2006. Market research shows that the office segment accounts for 59% of sales.

Market drivers

The commercial air conditioning market in Europe is being driven by five key sectors:

- improvements in air quality
- a decrease in the area for each employee
- increased exposure to air conditioning
- the development of new refrigerants
- the relatively low penetration rate of systems into Europe

Other factors include the increasing reliance on electronic equipment and the use of air conditioning systems as a marketing tool.

The liberalisation of Europe's energy markets is considered to have had some impact, albeit marginally. The argument is that with lower electricity costs, more people could afford air conditioning. However, this has not happened to any appreciable extent and now the CCL might have a restraining effect.

Types of systems

Fixed

The packaged air conditioning market, which consists of packaged split systems and packaged multi-split systems, is expected to increase its share of the total market from 39.7% in 1999 to 47.5% in 2006.

The central-based air conditioning market, which includes the fan coil, air handling unit and chiller segments, is expected to decline from 60.3% to 52.5% during the same period.

There are said to be over 250 manufacturers capable of supplying air conditioning systems. Key players are Toshiba/Carrier, Daikin, Mitsubishi, York and Climaventa-De'Longhi, who between them have 38% of the market. The other 62% includes such names as Sharp, Sanyo, Hitachi, Fujitsu, Biddle, Airwell, Galletti and Jucker Clima. Many companies will sell systems through distributors, specialist dealers or facilities management companies. Central-based systems tend to be distributed directly by the manufacturer because they are fitted to a building's requirements.

Portable

The portable air conditioning market is expected to grow significantly over the next few years. The company Climate Airxpress, which runs a business hiring portable air conditioning systems in both Australia and the UK, expects a turnover of £10 million by 2004. The company estimates the spend on cooling rentals in the UK is "up to £60 million a year" with an appreciable element stemming from the facilities management sector. Other companies in this space include Andrews and Heatbusters.

Andrews claims to have pioneered the concept of hiring portable air conditioners some summers back and offers solutions ranging from small mobile temporary air conditioning units for short-term or emergency use to permanently installed heat pump units – supplying both cool and warm air – suitable for offices of any size which need cooling in the summer and heating in the winter.

Some 65% of Climate Airxpress customers are facilities managers in end-user companies of facilities management companies (such as Haden and Mitie) or heating and ventilation personnel. The market exists all year round. If a computer complex's systems go down, the facilities manager can make one call to bring in suitable equipment. The ranges on offer – from Porta and Bosch-Siemens – handle offices up to server rooms, with rental hires from £30 per week for the smallest system to £220 per week for an 8kW unit. Domestic customers – a small market – would need to spend £800 per room to acquire suitable portable systems.

Climate Airxpress says its business is split 60% for cooling in office environments to 40% for emergency failures of fixed systems – and "80% of the market is London". Typical scenarios have been setting up new offices in buildings which are not air conditioned and relocations within an existing building. Listed buildings figure prominently too, as planning consent to install fixed systems is difficult to obtain.

Close control

The close control air conditioning market comprises data centres, web server farms, internet service provider (ISP) computer rooms and centres for telecom switch gear and computer network management apparatus, where key requirements are for temperature control, humidity and filtration. This segment is valued at some £30.7 million, according to BSRIA (Building Services Research and Information Association), with the major manufacturers being Denco of the UK, Edpac of Ireland and Stulz of Germany. Airedale has a presence in both close control and fixed systems markets. Denco sells directly and through specialist air conditioning and environment services operations such as Middlesex-based LAL.

The telecom market generally needs electrical energy and air conditioning (cooling) in equal measures. Combined cool and power (CCP) claims to eliminate most of the air conditioning power needs, reducing overall energy demand of a 'telehouse', typically by 22–25%. The ratio of cooling and power produced by CCP closely matches the needs of a typical telehouse. Carbon dioxide emissions are reduced by over 20%, securing a number of tax advantages including CCL exemption and enhanced capital allowances (see REDUCING EMISSIONS AND COSTS, P300).

Temperature control

Whatever type of air conditioning system is used, the key objective is temperature control. Office workers like to work in a pleasantly cool, clean atmosphere with adequate levels of humidity (see MAINTAINING ADEQUATE HUMIDITY, P318). With web server farms however, there has to be a positive pressure in the room so that when a door is opened there is no ingress of dirt or other contaminants. Temperature has to be maintained at 21°C, plus or minus 2°C, while the relative humidity needs to be maintained at 50% plus or minus 5%. The machines in these environments (computers, disk drives, network switching equipment, telecom systems, and so on) are particularly sensitive to these two drivers and cannot tolerate any rate of change. While staff in an office might tolerate variations of 10% fluctuations, the machines in server farms and network switching centres cannot.

Refrigerant policy

Since usage of the R22 refrigerant has been banned in all new systems sold, most systems marketed today will be equipped with R407C refrigerants. Advice on CFC (chlorofluorocarbon) and HCFC (hydro CFC) phase-out is available from DEFRA and DTI which reflects the *EC Regulation 2037/2000* on ozone-depleting substances. Two temporary exemptions are 1 July 2002 for fixed systems with cooling capacity of less than 100kW and 1 January 2004 for reversible air conditioning or heat pump systems. For those systems manufactured prior to the relevant ban, no one can use virgin HCFCs from 1 January 2010 and all HCFCs, including recycled materials, will be banned from 1 January 2015.

Recovered CFCs must now be destroyed by an environmentally acceptable technology. Recovered HCFCs can either be destroyed or reused until 2015. There are some rogue companies still marketing equipment with the wrong refrigerant.

Promoting cleaner indoor air

Improving outdoor air quality in terms of lower emissions is a key objective – but what is being done to promote cleaner air indoors?

CIBSE guidelines

While legislation and guidelines on the subject are lacking in the UK, there are standards for indoor air quality set by CIBSE. These are mainly based on comfort levels. In its *Guide A on Environmental Design*, CIBSE states that indoor air quality "may be said to be acceptable" if:

- not more than 50% of the occupants can detect any odour
- not more than 20% experience discomfort
- not more than 10% suffer from mucosal irritation
- not more than 5% experience annoyance, for less than 2% of the time

CIBSE also points out this does not take into account contaminants such as radon gas, which may have serious health effects, but is nevertheless odourless and difficult to detect. Workplaces should therefore be comfortable and ventilated by a sufficient quantity of fresh or purified air.

Getting the balance right is more complex than it sounds. The BRE recommends that natural ventilation is used where possible, but accepts there is a trade-off for many managers. Keeping windows tight, for example, prevents energy from escaping and thus cuts down on energy wastage. It also stops outdoor pollutants such as traffic fumes from coming in. However, with windows sealed, the risk is that temperatures will rise and indoor pollutants increase as a result.

Main pollutants

Air can become polluted in a number of ways, some of which are more obvious than others. HEVAC's indoor air quality (IAQ) initiative cites the following as the main sources of pollution:

- industrial processes producing fumes and air borne contaminants
- bacteria and dust spread by inadequately filtered and poorly maintained HVAC systems
- emissions from building materials, furnishings and equipment
- carbon monoxide produced from gas and paraffin heaters
- tobacco smoke
- pesticides sprayed on potted plants
- mould in damp areas and rotting food, both sources of bacteria
- an excessively humid atmosphere which can help the growth of bacteria

In addition, certain types of rock can release radon gas into buildings through the foundations and air intakes. Domestic pets, dust mites, cockroaches and household plants can release irritants that result in allergic reactions.

Maintaining adequate humidity

The *Health and Safety (Display Screen Equipment) Regulations 1992* provide that employers are to ensure that "an adequate level of humidity shall be established and maintained" in offices where there are visual display unit (VDU) users.[2] Exact levels of "adequate humidity" are not specified, but there is a duty of care to ensure reasonable conditions are maintained. For staff health and comfort, the optimum adequate level of relative humidity is normally considered to be about 50%rH (relative humidity) and certainly not less than 40%. Several optometric organisations (Association of Optometrists, College of Optometrists and EyeCare Information Service) agree with this level, as do professional bodies such as CIBSE, BSRIA, BRE and HEVAC's Humidity Group. The HSE says it is generally considered to be in the interests of worker efficiency that humidity be maintained in the range of 40–70%rH and that in warm offices the relative humidity should ebb towards the lower end of this range. *British Standard 29241* (from 7179) recommends 40–60%rH for office terminals.

Employers' duties

Employers are under a duty to comply with this legislation. This means monitoring humidity constantly to ascertain whether adequate levels are being provided. It is also important for employers to recognise any dry heat symptoms being experienced by staff, in order to identify whether any problems need to be addressed to ensure staff health and comfort. If such problems are not addressed by the facilities manager, the normal course of action would be for employees to complain to their employers, who would take steps to remedy the problem. If the problem continued, the next step would be to involve Environmental Health Officers and, in some cases, the unions. Eventually it could lead to prosecution as with cases of RSI (repetitive strain injury).

Recognising symptoms

Employers are now under an obligation to identify symptoms of low humidity and recognise they have a duty to take corrective measures for staff health and comfort. VDUs produce dry heat and this can cause discomfort to staff who work with computer monitors. Dry air acts like a sponge and absorbs moisture from all surrounding surfaces, such as operators' eyes, nose, throat and skin. Typical resultant dry air symptoms include headaches, dry eyes (particularly for contact lens wearers), dry throats, dry skin, frequent cold and flu-type conditions, and tiredness and lethargy. People with dry skin conditions such as eczema or psoriasis and respiratory or breathing problems such as asthma are often worst affected by the dryness. Static electricity is a conclusive indicator that humidity is too low.

Stress

Stress levels are affected too. A nationwide research study in 2000 by stress expert Dr David Lewis of over 100 workplaces investigated the links between overly dry workplace air and employee stress. Readings showed that the environments of one in five subjects had only 25%rH, making them as dry as the Sahara desert. One in 10 had only 23%rH – as dry as California's Death Valley. In these excessively dry surroundings, employees suffer a rapid loss of water, affecting their physical and mental well-being while increasing vulnerability to workplace stress. Nationally, 83% of workplaces with 35%rH or less were rated as high stress environments by their employees.

Staff discomfort

Although essential for comfort of workers, central heating and air conditioning also dry the air considerably. In addition, lighting and solar gain contribute to the problem.

As early as 1980, the World Health Organisation (WHO) recognised that air conditioning, computers, photocopiers and dust were the scourge of office life. Statistics also show that 6% of staff sickness and absenteeism is due to sick building syndrome (SBS), costing the UK economy between £300 million and £650 million a year (estimated by WHO and a House of Commons environment committee). See HEALTH AND SAFETY LAW: IMPROVING WELL-BEING: SICK BUILDING SYNDROME, P35 for details of buildings at risk of SBS and WHO-recommended solutions.

However, it is possible to monitor and maintain humidity at comfort levels, resulting in a healthier, happier workforce with less sickness absence and increased productivity. This has to be good news for long-suffering employees and employers alike. It makes economic sense too, as the cost of a free-standing retrofit humidifier which plugs into a 13-amp socket is less than two to three days' staff absence due to sickness.

Measuring humidity levels

Free surveys and impartial advice are provided by the Air Improvement Centre. Since 1993, the organisation has carried out numerous humidity and air quality surveys at computerised offices in the London area. In most cases the air was too dry. Feedback from facilities managers led the organisation to design a low-cost, simple to use humidity recording kit.

When workstation risk assessments are carried out, humidity levels should be measured and recorded to ascertain whether there is an adequate level of humidity. The Centre's humidity recording kit comprises a digital thermo-hygrometer with built-in memory, a year's supply of charts showing the adequate humidity band, plus information on the legislation and what practical steps to take if the humidity is too low.

The Centre recommends taking readings in the same location at the same time each day, for example, beside the workstation in mid-afternoon when computer screens have been running for several hours and the worst (driest) conditions are being experienced. On day one, simply read off the relative humidity, record the readings and repeat daily. If readings are below 40%, the air is too dry. In computerised offices, it is most unlikely humidity will be too high. By mid-afternoon humidity can frequently fall to as low as 20–25%rH, which is well below the adequate band.

Managing humidity levels

If humidity is too low, causing staff discomfort, humidity needs to be raised to adequate levels. If the air is too dry, the simple solution is to put just the right amount of moisture back into the air to restore a more healthy and comfortable atmosphere. This usually means aiming for about 50%rH for a normal indoor temperature of about 20°C. It is important to seek specialist impartial advice on the right type of humidifier, and its output rating, for the size of area. Aspects such as hygiene, noise levels and running costs must also be taken into consideration. Some units also combine air cleaning functions and will help filter out dust, traffic exhaust and tobacco smoke, as well as ozone from copiers and printers. The end result will be a healthier – and standards-compliant – workplace.

Waste management

Waste management is an ethical problem that no one can bury. Defined as the unwanted residue of an organisation's activities, waste can include anything from toxic liquids and solids, pallets and packaging, expired light bulbs and printer cartridges, to the contents of the waste paper basket.

Disposal

Three options exist for waste disposal:

- the strict reduction of waste generation – through adjustment, redesign of processes and cooperation with suppliers
- the internal – and responsible – recycling of waste materials to provide new or different products
- getting rid of the waste to someone else and making it their problem

The third option is the most commonly deployed for business; it is an attractive option, particularly as specialist companies move into the waste management field. In the past companies had to pay the local authority or a dedicated contractor to take away unwanted rubbish (to the nearest landfill site or incinerator). Now someone may collect waste for free and use the output as their raw material.

Responsibility over profitability

Of the many millions of tonnes of solid materials, and many more tonnes of consumed water, only 25% is converted into products physically consumed by customers. The balance is the national waste problem. The waste handling industry is understandably booming, worth something like £6 billion in 2001/2.

Many, if not most, of the public want to see that companies are behaving responsibly, something which is increasingly being rated above profitability. Awareness of the impact of waste is at an all-time high. Legislation is following public concern too. Company and product liability is extending into every aspect of the production process from inception to final disposal. The issue embraces a growing emotional draw to environmentalism and the pragmatism of economics. Landfill sites have become a scarce resource and there is not enough space to bury rubbish as has been the practice in the past.

Companies have to implement a coherent waste management strategy, argues DEFRA. The Environmental Protection Agency obliges directors to ensure the waste generated by their businesses is stored, moved and disposed of by approved means (or they face fines of up to £20,000 or six months in prison per offence). The Friends of the Earth organisation reckons the UK has the worst record in Europe for recycling glass and steel, and even paper. Forget the idea of a paperless society – it will never happen. Paper consumption is at least double what it was a decade back.

A sustainable resource

The concept of waste as a sustainable resource has been around for a long time. The idea has been given a boost and recognition through the introduction of European and UK legislation. A recent guide produced by the Environment Council, *A stakeholder's guide to sustainable waste management*, is most useful. The Environment Council firmly believes "environmental problems can be solved by involving, listening to and working with people" and indeed applied that principle in developing the guide.

How do companies turn waste disposal into waste management? The first step is to understand the problem, and the starting point for this is a waste audit. This identifies the materials existing as waste within the company and provides data for subsequent comparison to monitor improvement. A further benefit could be the introduction to a specialist company with which to work in implementing improvements. Kick off with the relevant local authority and/or existing waste contractor.

Savings

In the late 1990s, the Institute of Management and Electrolux UK produced a report which concluded that responsible environmental management is logically consistent with low costs. Savings can accrue through careful housekeeping, but longer-term savings follow investment in research technology or process design.

Waste is set to be the next frontier of competitive advantage. By looking in their dustbins, companies can find new ways to improve internal business performance.

Noise and vibration

The Association of British Insurers says some 80% of claims for occupational disease against employers' liability insurance relate to deafness. This compares with 6% for lung diseases and 4% for upper limb disorders. Hazards of high noise levels at work include:

- incurable hearing damage
- disturbance to work
- interference with communication
- stress

Disablement benefit is paid by the Department of Social Security to people who suffer at least 50 decibels (dB) of noise-induced hearing loss in both ears (that's like trying to listen to the television through a brick wall). Any claimant must have been employed for at least 10 years in a specified noisy occupation.

Statutory requirements relating to noise at work generally are contained in the *Noise at Work Regulations 1989* (see HEALTH AND SAFETY LAW: NOISE AT WORK REGULATIONS 1989, P16). Employers are required to take reasonably practicable measures on a long-term ongoing basis to reduce employees' exposure to noise at work to the lowest possible level, and to lower noise exposure where employees are exposed to levels of 90dB or above. For HSE guidance on controlling noise exposure, see HEALTH AND SAFETY LAW REDUCING NOISE, P29.

There are currently no specific provisions relating to vibration other than those contained in the *Social Security (Industrial Injuries) (Prescribed Diseases) Regulations 1985* and the *Reporting of Injuries, Diseases and Dangerous Occurrences Regulations 1985*.

Damage to hearing

It is natural to lose hearing acuity with age. Loud noises cause permanent damage to the nerve cells of the inner ear in such a way that a hearing aid is ineffective. With prolonged exposure, the region of damage moves to both higher and lower frequencies. Damage begins to extend into the speech range, making it difficult to distinguish consonants, so words start to sound the same. Eventually, speech becomes a muffled jumble of sounds.

Some people are much more susceptible to hearing damage than others. There is the condition of tinnitus (ringing or whistling in the ears and a temporary dullness of hearing), experienced when a person leaves a noisy location. Care should be taken to avoid further exposure (symptoms disappearing with continued exposure actually indicate that the ear is losing the ability to respond to the noise). Medical advice is advised.

The risk of hearing loss is dependent on the noise dose received and on the cumulative effect over time (except from catastrophic circumstances, as with explosions). A procedure for estimating the risk of handicap due to noise exposure is provided in *British Standard BS 5330*. Here, a hearing loss of 30dB is defined as a handicap (understanding of conversations and appreciation of music impaired). But note, to be entitled for DSS disability benefit, a person must suffer a loss of 50dB.

Sound perception

Typically, the quietest sound that can be heard (in other words, the threshold of hearing) is zero decibels (0dB) and the sound becomes painful at 120dB. It should be noted that zero decibels is not zero sound.

Depending on the method of presentation of two sounds, the human ear may detect differences as small as 0.5dB. But for general environmental noise the detectable difference is usually taken to be between 1–3dB, depending on how quickly the change occurs. A 10dB change in sound pressure level (SPL) corresponds, subjectively, to an approximate doubling/halving in loudness.

The SPL of industrial and environmental sound fluctuates continuously. It is possible to measure the physical characteristics of sound with much accuracy and to predict the physical human response to characteristics such as loudness, pitch and audibility. But it is not possible to predict subjective characteristics, such as annoyance, with certainty. A meter can only measure sound and not noise, which is defined as sound unwanted by the recipient. But in practice the terms are often interchangeable.

Sound power level

Sound output of an item of plant or equipment is often specified in terms of its sound power level, measured in decibels relative to a reference power of 1pW (pico-watt). It must not be confused with SPL, which at a particular position can be calculated from a knowledge of the sound power level of the source, provided the acoustical characteristics of the surrounding and intervening space are known. Thus, to provide a picture of the SPL-sound power level relationship, for a noise source which is emitting sound uniformly in all directions close above a hard surface in an open space, the SPL 10m from the source would be 28dB below its sound power level.

Minimising noise through design

Sound travels either via transmission or reflection. Noise transmission is the main problem in cellular offices – especially conversational noise leaking from adjoining cells. This can be especially distracting since there is less background sound in the enclosure to mask it.

In modern offices most cellular space is created by combinations of demountable full-height partitions rather than brick or block walls. The acoustic performance and fit of these partitions is crucial to good sound insulation. Manufacturers' specifications for the noise reduction coefficient of demountable partitions will be for optimum performance.

It is up to facilities managers to get as close as possible to this by ensuring that the partitions are well fitted (special mastics and packing materials can help seal gaps where panels meet uneven floorplates).

Where there is a suspended ceiling and the panels do not pass through and stop at the upper slab, then sound will travel through the ceiling void and compromise the insulation offered by even the best partitioning. Air vents between cells and holes for piping and electrical cabling will also channel noise.

Manufacturers of suspended ceilings should be able to provide a statement of the material's noise reduction coefficient and speech frequency sound absorption.

In open-plan space, noise reflection is more of an issue than transmission. All the office surfaces – flooring, wall coverings, ceilings and furnishings – can combine to reduce or increase noise reflection. Hard, flat surfaces will obviously bounce noise around a space. Soft carpeting with in-built cushioning or combined with underlay will contribute strongly to deadening ambient noise reflection as well as footfalls.

Noise reduction through screening in open-plan space is problematic. The recommended screen height to deaden sound transmission between workstations is 1.65m, but this creates the kind of cellular warren in open space that has become increasingly unfashionable over the last 10 years. Even the most absorbent low-profile screens have little effect on sound transmission.

HSE guidance warns that barriers and screens can provide a limited solution on their own. Near the noise source, most sound is received by direct transmission. A brick or steel sheet barrier can stop this, but even when it is lined with sound absorbing materials, problems with reflected sound further away will remain.

Control noise at source

One of the best ways to cut out noise is to control it at source. Modifying existing equipment to make its mechanisms quieter, for example, will cost only one-fifth of building a box around the piece of equipment.

An even better solution to noisy equipment is not to buy it in the first place. According to HSE guidance *Reducing noise at work*:[3] "Often the single most cost-effective, long-term measure you can take to reduce noise at work is to introduce a purchasing policy for choosing quieter machinery." This avoids the need for "expensive retrofitting of noise control measures".

Another example of controlling noise at source is those call centres which have abandoned the traditional rows of booths in favour of low-screened workstations. Large numbers of employees work in close proximity, avoiding excessive noise by moderating their voices (with the help of sensitive telephone headsets).

Sources of advice

HSE figures have suggested 1.3 million employees in the UK are exposed to noise levels above 85dB. Both short bursts of loud noise and long-term exposure to high noise levels can gradually, but relentlessly, damage the inner ear, according to the Royal National Institute for the Deaf (RNID). Employees may only realise their hearing has been damaged years later.

The BRE says noise is one of the most emotive issues in today's built environment, with the potential to impair health and productivity in the workplace. Once any facilities manager has acknowledged noise reduction is an issue in their workplace, BRE may represent a valuable source of help. Services include:

- accredited measurement of field and laboratory sounds transmission
- product development
- advice on best construction practice
- innovative measurement of building element performance with sound intensity
- environmental noise measurement and assessment

Furniture

There is significant investment in new desks and office furniture. On average, new furniture is acquired every 10 years at a cost of some £1,000 per workstation. It is sobering to realise that office workers constitute nearly 50% of the working population and many of their waking hours are spent at their desks. The functionality, appearance and general cleanliness of the workspace will influence how efficiently staff work, how they interrelate with colleagues and within their teams and how they view the office environment and its ambience.

Selecting furniture

Facilities managers may need to replace existing stock – desks, chairs, storage and office desk accessories. The process of selecting the right products, supplier and manufacturer need not be complex. Most suppliers will agree to lend samples of their furniture for trials. There are many consultants and facilities management contractors willing to take on any aspect of space planning. Some furniture suppliers offer free or low-cost space planning services. Whatever the decision, always seek references or testimonials.

There is also an emerging market for rental furniture. Points in its favour include:

- no capital expenditure
- no cash flow disruptions
- instant flexibility to changing work patterns
- no storage costs relating to redundant furniture
- 'free' space planning services
- immediate disaster recovery

Workspace design

Furniture and storage options integral to a more cost-efficient and flexible workspace design include:

- **Standard workstation** – as with the principle of the universal footprint, the closer you can get to a single desk size and type for all staff, the less likely you are to have to move any desk. Where individuals need larger work surfaces or more storage than the average or are allocated meeting tables, try and provide these through modular extensions to the standard workstations, so that only these extras have to be relocated, leaving the desk undisturbed.

- **Mobile furniture** – if you are likely to have to move complete workstations, choose a system that is robust enough to stand relocation (not all are!) and is ready to move after a minimum of disassembly. Most manufacturers offer desking and filing pedestals with built-in lockable castors to facilitate movement. Check that the wheels are up to the job (again, not all are).

- **Centralised storage** – the more localised the bulk storage, the greater the chance it will have to follow staff in intra-departmental moves. Centralised filing areas on each floor mean moves around the floor shouldn't necessitate moving anything but a small amount of local filing. There may be some trade off with individual efficiency, though, if staff have to walk any distance to refer to documents.

- **Shared worksettings** – the idea that most office space was taken up by desks, each allocated to one employee who would work there all day, went unchallenged until the 1990s. Although this pattern is still dominant, an increasing number of organisations have experimented with alternative models over the past decade, such as reducing personal workspace or removing it altogether and replacing it with a variety of shared worksettings.

The thinking behind shared worksettings was that many white-collar employees were in jobs that took them away from the office for a majority of the time. These workers still claimed permanent desk space which was seldom used. Even those tied to the office were often engaged in types of work which were inadequately catered for by the traditional desk. The latter point has been reinforced by the growing emphasis on knowledge management and teamworking among white-collar workers. Traditional, rigid layouts cannot support collaborative group work or the regular forming and disbanding of project teams. These drivers have produced a variety of new office configurations, all of which have elements in common:

- **teamspace** – in which groups of employees retain a small 'home' desk each and the rest of their space is recycled for shared worksettings such as meeting space and break-out areas
- **hotdesking** – where employees who spend a large minority of their time out of the office have no allocated space but use non-allocated workstations, either on a first-come, first-served basis or by booking in advance
- **hotelling** – where all workspace is bookable by the hour

The most common of these configurations, hotdesking, is covered in more detail in SPACE DESIGN AND MANAGEMENT, PP362–364.

Workstations

Existing workstations can be easily recycled as shared desking. For hotdesking, an 1,800mm-wide desktop is unnecessary and takes up space that could be better used. A surface deep enough to hold a computer monitor – for a shared PC or docking facilities for laptops – and wide enough to spread papers is all that is needed.

Height-adjustable desking

Height-adjustable desking is now more common and should be specified where possible to allow users maximum comfort, however short the stay. When choosing workstations for hotdesking, work surfaces and edgings should be checked for durability. Also ask for references from other users to ensure the products will stand up to more intensive use from multiple users.

Seating

Workstation chairs need to be easily adjustable for height, back support and preferably seat tilt. If more than one person is going to use a chair, the configuration controls need to be easily located and robust. To alert staff to hotdesking chairs, one idea is to colour-code them with vivid fabrics and designs.

Soft seating for break-out areas gives an opportunity to add a splash of colour to the office layout. Sofas and tub chairs should be simply styled and firmly upholstered, designed for comfort but not for curling up on in front of the fire. Fabrics should be hard-wearing and easily removed for cleaning, especially if they are located near catering or vending points.

Aiding correct posture

The type of chair should fit both the task and length of time doing it. Chairs should have a forward tilt mechanism to open the pelvis – similar to the position in standing – and allow the correct concave curve to be maintained in the lumbar spine while sitting. This consequently leads to correct positioning of the other spinal curves. Seating should support the body in a suitable posture – in other words, the 'S' form of the spinal column should be maintained. The purpose of the backrest is to support the whole spinal column effectively, no matter what seating position is adopted.

The user should be able to move and change postures regularly and freely without any constraints from the chair. Cushioning and covering should allow for air circulation over the skin and the surface material must provide sufficient friction to prevent sliding. For details of HSE guidance on seating, see HEALTH AND SAFETY LAW: SEATING, PP28–29.

The cost of back problems

Back problems are the greatest cause of illness amongst people of working age. Most people spend over 70% of their waking day sitting, and this is cited as one of the major factors responsible for back pain and associated injuries. Each year there are 30,000 work-related back injuries, 33,000 work-related back accidents and 500,000 work-related back illnesses. The cost to industry has been estimated at 117 million days of certified sick leave, resulting in at least £5.5 billion in lost production each year. Given all these statistics (even allowing for margins of numerical error) it obviously pays to get the seating right.

Buying furniture

The Office Furniture Advisory Service (OFAS) provides full information on standards and what to look for in purchasing furniture. There are 350 office furniture and seating manufacturers in the UK, and many more suppliers.

Catering

Why should a company have a restaurant? Many large organisations do not. The argument is that there are "many local restaurants, cafes, coffee shops, sandwich bars and fast-food outlets nearby". This philosophy can have an adverse effect: long off-site lunch breaks and stress caused by having to hurry back to the office are two potential pitfalls, and a lack of control over the staff's diet is another – a healthy diet produces a healthy workforce, which means less absenteeism. Furthermore, a company with no restaurant is less

likely to be able to attract staff because of the lack ⸺
subsidised prices, and has nowhere to provide hospitality ⸺

Staff have to be well watered and fed to be content. In res⸺
by Zenith International in 2001, 85% of sample respo⸺
worked more effectively in a smarter workplace and the tw⸺ ⸺orkers
considered most essential to a productive day were natural daylight (93%)
and chilled water (83%).

Drinking water

Workers do not drink enough water. Indeed, nearly 70% said the amount of
water they drink is directly related to where the water cooler is kept, and 80%
of these people were frustrated at coolers being too far away. Lack of water
leads to poor concentration, fatigue, irritability and headaches. It would thus
appear that a key factor in keeping productivity to a maximum is ensuring
staff have access to a water cooler which is integrated into the design of the
workplace. Not everyone wants to eat at work, but everyone needs water.

The company restaurant

Sitting down to eat together at lunch or for a snack is one of the best ways to
break down barriers, discuss problems, thrash out misunderstandings or
share company gossip. To do this, staff typically adjourn to the restaurant,
coffee bar or similar facility. Company size will dictate the type of restaurant
or cafe facilities and levels of services offered. But the driver behind all these
plans is to get staff into a mood where they not only want to come to work,
but enjoy it as well, with eating and drinking central to that enjoyment.

What do the staff want?

Where company catering and restaurants are concerned, facilities managers
must try to understand their customers' needs. Easy-to-organise staff surveys
of what foods and drinks are preferred, what times of day staff would like
them served, reaction to special menus and themed eating days, for example,
can produce extra usage of the restaurant facility.

A focal point

Making the restaurant an attractive, comfortable and interesting place to eat
and socialise, as well as promoting it as the centre to network, meet visitors
or prospective clients and hold impromptu and scheduled meetings, will pay
dividends for the company – and in so doing, for the facilities manager. To
that end, the restaurant should no longer be consigned to the basement or

ed in a remote part of the site, but be easily accessible from all parts of the building and as equally visible. If coupled with one or more branded or franchised coffee bars and/or other outlets – snack counters, salad bars, bank terminals, internet terminals, newsagents, and so on – the restaurant complex should become the focal point of the company. While many of such facilities need to be outsourced, the facilities manager remains in overall control of management.

Fast food

While only operating a fast food-type operation is not recognised as common sense, it may be prudent to offer staff the opportunity to have access to a 'fast' service. The staff survey can help here. Making eating a worthy experience within the company will help boost staff morale and retention.

Vending machines

Many facilities managers eschew vending machines because of the quality of the beverages produced and the image that has built up around them. However, there is still a market for these machines. It is unlikely that the 'tea lady', complete with trolley, buns of dubious freshness and a steaming urn, will ever make a full-scale reappearance. The future of the vending machine would seem assured. But canny facilities managers will approach the area sensitively and provide the staff with what they want. Assuming the board can be convinced, this will help the staff work better, aid staff retention and help percolate money through to the bottom line.

Times

A restaurant should offer a full range of meals and general refreshments – at times the staff want them. Moves to more global trading have resulted in offices being open at what were hitherto deemed antisocial hours. The concept of facilities being offered at practically all hours is not as ridiculous as it used to sound. It is a fact that food still being served fresh at 2.30pm will both encourage a wider spread of diners sitting down for a meal and increase the numbers of staff utilising the restaurant.

Menu

Some people will want to bring in their own food and drink. This should not be discouraged, and space should be made available. Others will increasingly want organic food, or gluten-free products – again the level of demand can be gauged through a staff survey. It is a misnomer to label food 'home-cooked' when it isn't. But this is an expression that has crept into the vernacular and now sits alongside such culinary delights as seasonal specials, cordon bleu cooking, chicken tikka masala, regional speciality days and low-fat cuisine.

Planning the restaurant

Design

The company must select a design strategy (embracing appearance, space planning, lighting, utilities and acoustics) to reflect its culture and image. The physical appearance is important and care will have to be taken to differentiate it from any offerings in the local surroundings. Decisions will have to be taken on whether to provide internet access points, so that staff can plug in their laptops while having a break or talking to customers.

Siting and layout

Siting of the restaurant facility is determined by the availability of utility services and the fact that cooking smells wafting into the reception atrium might not be a good idea for customers waiting there. The restaurant needs to be welcoming and designed so that people can flow freely without obstruction. Key to restaurant layout is throughput, trying to avoid or alleviate queuing problems (one suggestion is to provide a flexible paypoint arrangement – this being the biggest bottleneck). Food should always be on display, tables cleaned regularly and dirty dishes removed efficiently. Clear notices and signs should guide customers through the facility.

Space and costs

If a company opts to serve ready-prepared meals with supporting beverages, sandwiches and soup, its kitchen space requirements will be much less than for an operation providing a gastronomic experience starting from raw ingredients. The amount of space required for food production areas is dictated by the type and range of food offered. Specialist help is needed to design a catering kitchen. If the restaurant is to offer a single-sitting hot meal service only, there needs to be a ratio of three restaurant spaces (that is, areas that can earn money) to every kitchen space (the food preparation area, stores and servery). For two or three sittings this ratio reduces to two restaurant space areas.

The operating costs per employee per year average at about £400 but will increase if the company provides a subsidy.

Ambience

Food is always associated with a feel-good factor. Conducting business, meeting friends, or discussing issues with work colleagues can be carried out more enjoyably over a meal, snack or drink. What adds to the enjoyment is the ambience of the surroundings. This is aided by the décor, sounds, lighting and building infrastructure.

- **Décor** – this concerns colour schemes, furniture, wall and floor coverings, crockery and cutlery design, plants/flowers/foliage and paintings, sculpture and murals, and so on. A good designer is necessary to ensure optimum results. Too garish a colour scheme makes diners feel ill while minimalist white walls call for sensitive incorporation of pictures and plants. Likewise with soft furnishings and furniture generally – too wild a pattern and the diners will be turned off. The type of soft furnishings also impacts on sound absorption and thermal barriers, as well as being decorative. Restaurant staff should wear uniforms of a suitably restrained colour.

- **Sounds** – piped 'muzak' is not to everyone's taste but designers consider noise a pre-requisite. Noise mostly comes from the diners themselves. Noise creates an atmosphere of being busy. Quiet(er) areas need to be supplied – also with 'muzak', such as water features or wind chimes, to mask extraneous noise. What diners do not want to hear is kitchen noise.

- **Lighting** – daylight plays a major part in the restaurant. Lights are used to create atmosphere and good lighting designers are worth employing. The range and type of lamps available means most moods can be catered for and created.

- **Building infrastructure** – the restaurant facility needs to be serviced regularly, with food supplies delivery and waste removal, for example, taken care of. It must also be well served by water, electricity and gas supplies. Heating and ventilation are key requirements, as is humidity control and air temperature. Air filtration to remove particles above 5 microns is mandatory.

Management

Some catering facilities will be staffed and managed in-house, but most will be run by a catering contractor under the management of the facilities manager. The key finding this century is the increasing commercialisation of the sector, where contractors are providing high street-type popular food and beverage offerings, such as good quality coffees, pastries, pizzas and salads. Branded outlets are also being seen alongside, if not instead of, the typical staff restaurant. That this is successful is borne out by contractors' increasing turnovers.

Costing

How to cost a catering facility is difficult. What should be included? All vending machines, for example? Is the service costed per user or per member of staff? Does the company provide a subsidy? Some companies provide a space – a shell – within the building and request a caterer to provide a defined level of service. The caterer pays no rent but must provide the right quality of service to recoup costs. With some of these deals, the company will fit out the kitchens and furnish the restaurant areas, while the caterer provides the staff, meals and beverages. To make a return, it is generally accepted that at least 50% of the staff should utilise the restaurants regularly. Prices should be kept below those of outlets in the local High Street and the ambience, as noted, must be acceptable.

Subsidies

Staff restaurants can be run with or without subsidies. A typical form of subsidy occurs where an employer pays the overheads of the facility – premises and staff, say – and the cost of the food and other items is obtained from the restaurant users. There are subsidies which involve a fixed cash payment from the employer. Average food cost per meal in 2000 was 80p, slightly lower than in 1999 (according to the British Hospitality Association survey) while there are suggestions that prices paid by customers are influenced by whether the contract to provide the meals is run in-house or outsourced.

Choosing caterers

Few companies have the resources to run a catering facility in-house. This means most outsource. Nevertheless, the company still needs to set the pace and define what is wanted of its catering supplier. Facilities managers have pivotal roles to play. The choice of caterer will involve setting up a project team whose members must cover all the points already discussed here. The process of selection of caterer must involve food tasting, layout, menu content and discussions with caterers, their employees and existing customers (including site visits). Will the two companies be able to work together, or is there likely to be some culture clash?

Practical advice on how to go about selecting a catering contractor on the basis of best value for money is contained in a booklet from the Chartered Institute of Purchasing and Supply (CIPS), *How to buy catering services.* Each year the British Hospitality Association surveys the contract catering market in the UK, based on responses from the 16 main companies in the food service management industry. Various statistics are produced by this report, such as average food cost per meal, salary expectations, turnover, number of PPP projects in which contractors have an interest, and types of contract.

Future prospects

More change is expected in the catering sector. Food will become a more potent weapon to attract key workers, with free breakfasts (full English or continental) being offered to entice staff into the office early and beat traffic hold-ups – and to make the workforce more productive. More food options will be available throughout the day, reducing pressure on the restaurant and meaning that a smaller-sized facility is all that is needed.

Cleaning

Cleaning is one of the most outsourced functions. Whilst it is arguably one of the least glamorous, people will always notice if it is not done. It is also a thankless task – a facilities manager might expend an inordinate amount of resources and budget ensuring the wards and corridors of a hospital are clean, for example, only to be judged on how quickly and efficiently they put up a shelf in a sister's office. Cleaning is also an antisocial occupation, most workers in that sector having to work after offices have closed for the day. Late and nightshift working is normal.

Market dynamics

The market comprises everything to do with industrial and commercial cleaning – interior cleaning of office space, leisure facilities, retail units, factories, non-domestic buildings generally, local authority units, and so forth, and exterior cleaning (such as windows, metal cladding), as well as vehicles, industrial equipment – and pest control services. Of late, however, the sector has seen many companies hitherto totally dedicated to cleaning diversifying into offering facilities management services as well as janitorial and portering services, linen, washroom and workwear hire and equipment hire. Given that this sort of diversification makes the contract cleaning market difficult to define, the consensus is that the UK market for contract cleaning services in 2000 was about £3.8 billion.

Market projections show steady year-on-year increases to near £5 billion in 2005. But that must be taken at face value, particularly as no one can specifically define the market. Essentially, cleaning is a job that will survive; there will always be a need for it. Few other professions can make that claim.

With the introduction of the Private Finance Initiative (PFI) and Public Private Partnership (PPP) contracts it has not been uncommon for contracts of 30 years (and more in some cases) to be agreed. But according to the Cleaning and Support Services Association (CSSA), which acts as a marker for the industry, contracts have traditionally been from a few months to five years, and sometimes seven, in duration.

Selecting contractors

Service level agreements (SLAs) need to be marketed carefully. The main objectives are:

- establishing the project objectives
- identifying key players
- securing commitment
- agreeing the scope of services within review

Cleaning in the office environment will be broken down into general cleaning, janitorial services, window cleaning and deep cleans.

When selecting contractors, useful documentation for the facilities organisation includes:

- customer satisfaction surveys
- service utilisation statistics
- job descriptions of services delivery staff
- number and type of complaints
- service specifications
- menu of call-off services
- budgetary information
- contractors' performance information

Once SLAs have been established, they have to be periodically reviewed to ensure they continue to deliver the right services to support the activities of customers. The annual budget preparation should include a review of service levels. The initiation of the SLA project often increases the need to demonstrate the consistency of service delivery. Customers expect the facilities manager to market the services offered, track performance of the services over time and report regularly. This expectation will require the facilities manager to develop better documentation about each service and develop systems that will track the volume of call-offs, frequency of service failures and rectifying measures. Creating an audit trail is part of the overall communications process, but key documents that need to be developed include:

- facilities management services policy
- service directory
- service specifications
- operating procedures
- customer feedback records

SLAs and managing contractors are covered in greater detail in OUTSOURCING, PP238–257.

Costs

How do you cost a cleaning contract? There is no magic formula, although generally, labour, National Insurance contributions, holidays, supervision, materials and equipment would need to be included.

According to the Low Pay Unit, the average wage per hour for a male contract cleaner in April 2000 was £5.35 compared with £4.85 for a female. The national minimum wage hourly rate figures are £4.10 (October 2001) and £4.20 (October 2002). It is understood that over half the cleaning workforce was paid less than £3.60 before the national minimum wage was introduced. When the *Working Time Regulations 1998* (see EMPLOYMENT LAW: WORKING TIME, P75) were introduced, the cleaning sector suffered a double whammy, as to make up income streams to pay the workers at the proper levels, SLAs had to be adjusted and in many cases the frequency with which cleaning was carried out had to be curtailed. The impacts of that were keenly felt in certain quarters, most notably the health service. There are no known statistics yet which might indicate how the total contract cleaning workforce might have been reduced as a result of these initiatives, although the diversification mentioned earlier by some of the key players in the industry could have helped to alleviate any difficulties.

Lighting

Energy efficiency

Lighting accounts for some 20% of total electricity consumption in the UK, and the CCL is affecting the situation. The 0.43p per kW/h levy on electricity used will impact on all sectors, including industry, utilities, transport and local government, and could see electricity bill increases of some 10%. Introducing energy-efficiency lighting schemes is one way businesses can mitigate the effects of the levy. Replacing obsolete installations with more efficient light sources and introducing high frequency control gear and lighting controls are also steps that can be taken. It is often the case that lighting efficiency savings exceed the cost of the levy.

A survey by Frost & Sullivan in 2000 reported how the surge in demand for lighting controls across Europe was attributable to end-users' rising awareness of energy-saving issues and the benefits associated with high quality lighting and effects. The study cited levies of fossil fuel-generated energy as being a principal driver behind growth in the European market for lighting controls.

The market is set to change with the wider use of electronic gear, especially involving digital addressable lighting interface (DALI). According to Frost & Sullivan, the new interface will effectively merge all the superior aspects of the light management systems and control gear markets, allowing complete lighting control and improved light output. How DALI integrates with open systems protocols BACnet, EIB or LONworks remains to be seen (see OPEN SYSTEMS IN BUILDING CONTROL, P294).

Objectives of good lighting

Good lighting should vouchsafe employee safety, acceptable job performance, and good workplace atmosphere, comfort and appearance – a task that is not limited to maintaining correct lighting levels. Of ergonomic relevance are:

- horizontal illuminance
- uniformity of illuminance over the job area
- colour appearance
- colour rendering, glare and discomfort
- ceiling, wall and floor reflectances
- job to environment illuminance ratios
- job and environment reflectances
- vertical illuminance

Sources of light

Natural lighting

The cheapest form of lighting is the most natural – daylight. There is only limited application where production is needed beyond the hours of daylight, at all seasons, and where daytime visibility is restricted by climatic conditions. Windows alone, however, cannot always provide adequate lighting for the interior of large floor areas. The most common source of daylight is through side windows. But large areas of glass can cause uncomfortable thermal conditions in summer within the building.

To maximise the benefits of natural light, low screens and glazed partitions can help allow clear sightlines to windows. Also, 'owned' desks should be closest to the windows, with areas of occasional use, such as meeting spaces, placed further away. Proximity to daylight does bring with it the problem of glare, especially for DSE users. The easiest solution is to introduce blinds, preferably of a venetian or similarly adjustable type, to allow local control. The value of anti-glare filters placed in front of computer screens is debatable and these should only be used if all else fails.

Natural lighting has to be supplemented for most of the time with artificial lighting, for which the most common source is electric lighting. The recommended minimum ratio of artificial light to natural light at any long-term worksetting is 1:5.

Electric lighting

The selection of the sources of electric lighting for particular applications are most often driven by factors such as capital costs, running costs and replacement costs. These costs are as important as the size, heat and colour effects called for from the lighting units. Any lamp's efficiency is measured as light output in lumens per watt of electricity. A lumen is the unit of luminous flux, describing the amount of light received by a surface or emitted by a source of light. Typical values for various lamp types are:

Type of lamp	Lumens per watt
Incandescent lamps	10–18
Tungsten halogen	22
High pressure mercury	25–55
Tubular fluorescent	30–80 (depending on colour)
Mercury halide	60–80
High pressure sodium	100

Common incandescent lamps (that is, coiled filament lamps where the temperature is raised to white heat by the passage of current, so emitting light) are generally inexpensive to install but suffer from relatively expensive running costs. A discharge or fluorescent lighting scheme (where electric current passes through certain gases and in so doing produces an emission of light) has higher capital costs but higher running efficiency, lower running costs and longer lamp life. In larger workplaces, there is often a choice between discharge and fluorescent lamps. The normal mercury discharge lamp and the low-pressure sodium discharge lamp possess restricted colour performance, although recent developments in high-pressure sodium discharge lamps and colour-corrected mercury lamps do not suffer from this disadvantage.

Standards of lighting

The amount of light (standard of illuminance) needed for a given location or activity depends on many variables, such as general comfort considerations and the visual efficiency called for. The unit of illuminance is the lux (Lx), which equals one lumen per square metre. The unit of foot candle is not used – this unit referred to the number of lumens per square foot. To measure the degree of illuminance at a specific workplace, a reliable measuring instrument is called for, such as a pocket light meter, which incorporates a photoelectric cell.

HSE Guidance Note *Lighting at work* (1997)[4] relates illuminance levels to the degree or extent of detail which needs to be seen in a specific task or situation. For example, for work requiring perception of detail in an office, the average illuminance should be 200Lx and the minimum measured illuminance should be 100Lx.

See HEALTH AND SAFETY LAW: LIGHTING, P37, for more on the statutory requirements and health and safety issues relating to lighting.

Lighting output

The lighting output of a given lamp will reduce gradually in the course of its life, but an improvement can be obtained by regular cleaning and maintenance – not only of the lamp itself but also of the reflectors, diffusers and other parts of the luminaire. Good practice for a lamp replacement policy could be, for example, to change a batch of lamps rather than deal with them singly as they wear out, an approach which could be more economical.

Lighting quality

While the quantity (or amount) of lighting assigned to a location or task in terms of standard service illuminance is a key feature of lighting design, it is equally necessary to take in the qualitative aspects of lighting. These have direct and indirect effects on the manner in which people view their work activities and any dangers that could be posed. Quality of lighting is affected by:

- **Glare** – this is the effect of light causing impaired vision or discomfort experienced when parts of the visual field are very bright, compared with the surroundings. It can be experienced in three different forms:

  - *Disability glare* – caused by bright lamps directly in the line of vision, this is visually disabling.

  - *Discomfort glare* – caused by too much contrast of brightness between an object and its background, this is often associated with poor lighting design. Discomfort often occurs without a person's ability to see detail necessarily being impaired.

  - *Reflected glare* – this the bright light reflected off shiny or wet work surfaces, where detail may be completely hidden.

- **Distribution** – this relates to the way light is spread. A standard to classify light fittings has been drawn up called the British Zonal Method which classifies the luminaires according to the way they distribute light, from BZ1 (light passes downwards in a narrow column) to BZ10 (light spreads in all directions). It is important to note that a fitting with a low BZ number does not mean it offers less glare. The shape of the room, reflective surfaces and position are all equally relevant.

- **Brightness** – also known as luminosity, this is very much subjective (so it cannot be measured). One can consider a brightness ratio though, which is the ratio of apparent luminosity between a task object and the surroundings. The correct brightness ratio can be computed by making sure the reflectance of all surfaces in the working area is well maintained. Interior design should take account of reflectance values. If the recommended illuminance level for a particular task (or task illuminance factor) is one, the effective reflectance values ought to be 0.6 for ceilings, 0.3–0.8 for walls, and 0.2–0.3 for floors.

- **Diffusion** – this is the projection of light in all directions with no particular priority. Diffused lighting is popular, and reduces the amount of glare emanating from bare luminaires. Drawbacks stem from the density of shadows caused – these can affect safety standards or even reduce lighting efficiency.

- **Colour rendition** – this refers to an object's appearance under a particular light source, compared to its colour under natural light (a reference illuminant, for example). The colour-rendering properties of luminaires should not clash with those of natural light. They should also be as effective at night, when there is no natural light contributing to the working area's total illumination.

Fluorescent light strips are the cheapest and most common form of lighting in workplaces, but can cause glare and (often imperceptible) flickering.

Indirect light sources such as uplighters (using more powerful halogen or sodium bulbs) provide a warmer, flicker-free light and are popular with building users. Unfortunately, the flat surfaces (on suspended ceilings, for example) required to reflect light to desk level may not be easy to combine with good acoustic absorption.

Computer-controlled lighting systems

The Energy Saving Trust (EST) launched its 'Lightswitch' initiative to provide funding to small and medium-sized UK businesses and individuals to adopt energy-saving measures. As a result there are now a number of consultancies and suppliers who recommend the application of local automatic switching devices, such as standalone presence detectors, as a means of reducing lighting energy costs within the working environment. UK Building Regulations have also recognised the importance of local control in achieving energy savings. It has been stipulated that no switch should be more than 8m from the light fittings it controls.

Lighting specialists, however, believe a more holistic approach, involving the centralised control of all lighting within the working environment, provides a much more powerful solution. Such schemes allow total control of each open-plan area, both from a central control point and locally by staff themselves. They offer a number of ways to achieve high energy savings while simultaneously offering flexible control of lighting schemes to reduce other building operational costs. Automatic control interfaces with the building management system (BMS) can provide energy-saving benefits which go far beyond lighting alone.

Even a simple local management system combining a manual switch-on facility with a 'staff absent' switch-off feature can effectively double energy efficiency. Getting staff to switch lighting on themselves ensures that lighting is only turned on when staff actually need it, and it can then be switched off automatically once staff have left their work area. With a computer-controlled system, the switch-on operation can be achieved in a number of ways, for example by personal infra-red transmitter, desk telephone or an icon on each individual PC screen.

Studies have shown that where staff are able to dim personal lighting, they typically set their lights at a comfort level below traditional guidelines. They thereby accrue additional energy savings while working in their own optimum lighting conditions.

Lighting management systems

Consider a lighting management system (LMS) which provides flexibility through the independent monitoring and control of every luminaire in a building. The key to effectiveness here is the flexibility of the hardware and graphics software which monitors the installation on screen. The system utilises the concept of virtual wiring, where light fittings are 'linked' to switches on other local control devices through software, and where essential and non-essential lighting 'distributions' exist in software only. In a virtual wiring system, changes to light-switching arrangements associated with staff or office layout changes are carried out from the PC graphics.

Such systems combine digital dimming technology with LonWorks interoperability. LonWorks provides a platform for implementing distributed, open, multi-vendor, interoperable control network systems enabling various systems from different manufacturers to communicate and interoperate. Using LonWorks, the integration of a building's lighting control system within the BMS can be achieved. This ensures facilities managers are able to control energy-saving routines which are triggered by factors such as occupancy, external temperatures, solar-heating effects and light levels.

Staff entering offices can be detected by the LMS presence detectors, which broadcast an 'occupation message' over the LonWorks control network. Messages received by the BMS then boost the speed of the heating/cooling unit in the occupied area. Staff who want their lighting on can set the desired dimming level from their desktop.

Motorised window blinds can be centrally controlled (for reducing solar gain), with local control in occupied areas. Once areas are vacated by staff, lighting will be automatically switched off or dimmed to a reduced level and local environmental controls switched to a non-occupancy mode.

LonWorks and LonTalk protocols can be used throughout systems for transmission of data on both vertical and horizontal buses. Systems claim to be able to receive and transmit data to and from other LonWorks systems from any point on the lighting management network.

Emergency lighting

The need for emergency lighting becomes apparent when we consider the resulting panic when suddenly plunged into darkness, particularly in a large multi-floored building with mixed open-plan and closed office arrangements. A reliable and well-maintained emergency lighting system, however, will facilitate a safe exit without causing injury.

Emergency lighting provides a lower than normal level of light and illuminates exit signs to assist in the evacuation of a building. It also provides light on safety equipment, such as fire extinguishers, call points and hose reels.

Emergency lighting luminaires

Emergency lighting luminaires fall into three main types:

- **Self-contained** – the luminaire contains the battery, a control circuit for charging the battery and an inverter for operating the lamp in case of supply failure.

- **Conversions** – almost any type of mains luminaire can be converted for emergency use by the addition of either a self-contained conversion kit (conversion module plus battery) or a slave inverter conversion module.

- **Slave** – the luminaire is powered from a remote central battery cabinet and is interconnected via fire-resistant cable, which should ensure that, if fire affects the wiring, the salve luminaire would continue to operate. The emergency supply can be dc or ac.

Categories of emergency lighting

The different categories or modes of emergency lighting can be described as follows:

- **Non-maintained** – the luminaire only operates when the electrical mains supply fails or there is local circuit failure.

- **Maintained** – the luminaire operates when the supply fails but also operates in a mains-healthy condition using a separate switched mains supply.

- **Sustained (combined)** – the luminaire contains two or more lamps, one being for normal mains operation and the other only for emergency use.

Standards

An emergency lighting scheme must comply with the requirements of the statutory authority and the appropriate standard. The duration of an emergency lighting system is a minimum of one hour. However, most applications in the UK stipulate three hours. In the UK, the latest addition has been the publication of *BS5266 Part 7:1999* (hereafter known as Part 7) which is the UK's adoption of the European Standard *EN1838:1999*. Part 7 forms the standard for emergency lighting applications and replaces the Code of Practice *BS5266 Part 1:1988*. The important changes in the requirements are noted overleaf.

Emergency lighting systems within buildings are required to be verified to the new requirements. The best way to ensure compliance is to seek a product approved by the Industry Committee for Emergency Lighting (ICEL), part of the Lighting Industry Federation, (LIF).

Illuminating escape routes

Part 7 states a minimum level of 1Lx is required on the centre line of the emergency escape route (formerly 0.2Lx). However a deviation is listed – applicable in the UK – for a minimum level of 0.2Lx but is only for "routes which are permanently unobstructed". In practice such criteria would be difficult to guarantee. Points of emphasis, whether on an escape route or in an open area, should be provided with the appropriate illuminance. These points include a change of level, stairs, change of direction, fire-fighting equipment, call points and first aid posts. The ratio between the minimum and maximum level should be no greater than 40:1. In addition, a clause has been added for the limiting of disability glare within the field of view.

Part 7 states the minimum level of illuminance at floor level should be 0.5Lx. Originally it had been an average of 1Lx. The effect of this may result in the requirement for additional luminaires. Similar to the escape routes, the ratio between the minimum and maximum level should be no greater than 40:1.

All these minimum levels must be obtained, even at the end of discharges from aged components, while ignoring the effects of reflections from surfaces such as walls. So with a new installation, in practice, the light output measured should be two or three times the minimum to ensure that the standard is met throughout the full life of the installation.

Illuminating safety signs

Part 7 specifies that the safety signs used to indicate emergency escape routes and first aid areas have to be illuminated and be capable of being seen in all relevant viewing directions. In addition, viewing distances are specified for internally and externally illuminated signs, based on the height of the pictogram on the signs. The European Safety Signs Directorate enforced in the UK by the *Health and Safety (Safety Signs and Signals) Regulations 1996* stipulates a common European pictogram for means of escape from buildings. All worded-only 'exit' signs should have been replaced by December 1998.

Maintenance

Taking care to install reliable emergency lighting is commendable, but the lighting needs to be regularly inspected and maintained. Facilities managers should not fall into the trap of leaving it to the next time a fire officer is expected – by then it could be too late. Batteries fail, charges can stop working and lamps can be faulty. For users, that means an expensive refurbishment and premises closure while remedial work is undertaken.

Testing equipment

Manual testing today is viewed as labour-intensive and expensive. Self-testing systems complying with relevant standards and European directives are available from reputable manufacturers and, despite the higher capital cost, they are efficient and reliable. A key advantage for users is the ability to produce records to the fire authorities which demonstrate that the lighting has been tested and proven to be functional.

Testing of emergency lighting comprises two areas:

- automatic self-testing emergency lights suitable for smaller installations
- centrally controlled test and report systems for large-scale installations

Timers within standalone self-testing systems can carry out tests at weekly, monthly, six-monthly and annual intervals with system failure indicated either visually or audibly. For buildings with more complex emergency lighting, testing units exist which can provide detailed information on fault detection. On these, the exact location of faulty luminaires will be shown and tests can be carried out at times to suit the user.

Some basics, applying equally to manual and automated systems, need to be observed when testing emergency lighting systems. Although automatic systems offer many advantages in saving labour and providing consistency of test format, they must have facilities that are appropriate for the site they are to be used for. The main considerations are to ensure:

- the test duplicates the emergency operation
- the faults indication is clear and retained until rectified
- the tests minimise the risks of the building being inadequately protected while batteries are being recharged

The function test is of short duration and checks that the lamp operates satisfactorily from the battery and that the circuit is healthy. For manual systems this should be done monthly; for automatic systems, weekly. The full discharge test checks battery capacity in addition to circuit operation. The British Standard Code of Practice allows this to be performed twice a year for one-third of rated duration, for the first three years of self-contained battery life. Thereafter an annual full-rated test is needed. Revised draft application standards simplify this, calling for systems to just have the annual full discharge. Whatever system is installed, all tests must be logged and made available at any time.

References

1. For more information visit *www.fhp.uk.com*
2. Copies of HSE guidance on the *DSE Regulations 1992*, ISBN 0–11–886331–2, are available from the Stationery Office.
3. ISBN 0–7176–1511–1
4. HS(G)38

Information

General

BSRIA (Building Services Research and Information Association), tel: 01344 426511, *www.bsria.co.uk*

British Institute of Facilities Management (BIFM), tel: 01799 508608, *www.bifm.org.uk*

Building Research Establishment (BRE), tel: 01923 664000, *www.bre.co.uk*

Chartered Institute of Building Services Engineers (CIBSE), tel: 020 8675 5211, *www.cibse.org*

Facilities Management Association (FMA), tel: 020 7727 5238, *www.fmassoc.org*

HSE, tel: 0870 154 5500, *www.hse.gov.uk*

The Stationery Office, tel: 0870 600 5522, *www.clicktso.com*

Gas and electricity

BACnet, *www.bacnet.org*

CHP Association, tel: 020 7828 4077, *www.chpa.co.uk*

CHP Club website, *www.chpclub.com*

The EIB bus, *www.eiba.com*

The Energy Systems Trade Association's Building Controls Group, *www.esta.org.uk/bcg*

International Alliance for Interoperability (IAI), tel: 020 8660 1631, *www.iai.org.uk*

LONmark Interoperability Association, *www.lonmark.org*

Ofgem, tel: 020 7901 7000, *www.ofgem.gov.uk*

Siemens, *www.siemens-industry.co.uk*

Water management

Parliamentary information relating to water management, *www.defra.gov.uk/environment/water/index.htm*

Ofwat, tel: 0121 625 1300, *www.ofwat.gov.uk*

Climate Change Levy

Energy Efficiency Advice Centres, tel: 0800 512 012

Energy Efficiency Best Practice Programme (EEBPP), *www.energy-efficiency.gov.uk*

Environment and Energy helpline, tel: 0800 585 794

Quantum Partnership, tel: 01923 665080

Water pollution

Environment Agency general enquiry line (for information on groundwater protection), tel: 08459 333111

HVAC

Air Improvement Centre, tel: 020 7834 2834, *www.air-improvement.co.uk*

Eurovent (European testing body for HVAC equipment), tel: +33 1 4996 6980

Federation of Environmental Trade Associations (FETA), tel: 01491 578674, *www.feta.co.uk*

Heating, Ventilation and Air Conditioning Manufacturers Association (HEVAC), *www.hevac.com*

Waste management

The Environment Council, tel: 020 7632 0109

Noise

Association of Noise Consultants, tel: 01763 852958, *www.association-of-noise-consultants.co.uk*

Royal National Institute for the Deaf (RNID), tel: 0808 8080123, *www.rnid.org.uk*

Furniture

Chartered Institute of Purchasing and Supply (CIPS), tel: 01780 756777 *www.cips.org*

Office Furniture Advisory Service (OFAS), tel: 01344 779438, *www.ofas.org.uk*

Catering

Automatic Vending Association of Britain (AVAB), tel: 020 8661 1112, *www.ava-vending.org*

British Hospitality Association (BHA), tel: 020 7404 7744, *www.bha-online.org.uk*

European Point-of-use Drinking Water Association (EPDWA), tel: 01923 833660

Cleaning

Cleaning and Support Services Association (CSSA), tel: 020 7481 0881, *www.cleaningassoc.org*

Lighting

Industry Committee for Emergency Lighting (ICEL), *www.icel.co.uk*

Lighting Industry Federation (LIF), *www.lif.co.uk*

10 Space Design and Management

Louis Wustemann

While most of a facilities manager's functions are carried out behind the scenes, space planning and management is the most conspicuous part of the job. The way that an organisation's workspace is laid out and maintained is a vital part of the corporate image, giving an important message to visiting customers, potential recruits and existing employees.

More fundamentally, providing a comfortable, safe and efficient working environment is essential to enable employees to perform at their best, and ensuring that good use is made of the space available will bring added value to an organisation.

An essential consideration for space planners is the effect the layout and worksettings have on communications and productivity. The chance interaction between staff that generates valuable ideas cannot be made to happen, but research shows that poorly thought-out layouts and the wrong adjacencies make it much less likely.

How can facilities managers plan the workspace to serve its users safely and comfortably and to ensure maximum productivity? This chapter gives advice on successful space planning and the effective management of space changes and office moves ('churn'), setting out both practical design considerations as well as the technological support available for planners in the form of computer-aided facilities management (CAFM) systems.

Space planning

Measuring space

Before beginning to plan or re-plan people into any given space, you first need to know the size of that space. Area is usually estimated in one of the following ways:

- **gross internal area** – the whole internal area of the building measured from wall to wall

- **net internal area** – the gross internal area minus service cores, toilets, lift lobbies and stairways

- **net usable area** – the net internal area minus any areas that cannot be used for the purposes of space planning, such as areas behind doors and narrow gaps between columns and walls
- **net lettable area** – the area on which an organisation pays rent in a leased building – usually somewhere between the net internal and the net usable area

Planning grids

The planning grid is a means of imposing a notional structure to help plan the occupants into the floor space. The most common grid sizes are based on modules of:

- 90 × 90cm
- 120 × 120cm
- 135 × 135cm
- 150 × 150cm

The 90cm module (creating blocks of 0.8 sq m) was the common standard in the office buildings of the 1960s and 1970s, but grids based on 150cm (2.25 sq m) sections have become more common, as the larger grid square allows more flexibility of planning and is more compatible with common distribution patterns of cabling and other services.

Bricks and mortar

Much of the building infrastructure is likely to be handed to the space planner as a fait accompli in many cases. Nevertheless, an understanding of the properties of the fixed elements is useful to make the best use of the space.

While small offices built before the 1920s are likely to have upper stories floored with the boards over timber joists, most space planners will be faced with a concrete floor slab, probably with a raised floor through which cabling is run.

When replacing a raised floor or commissioning one from scratch it is worth considering if the services can be accommodated in a low-profile floor that sits as little as 10cm above the structural floor, rather than the traditional systems that may be up to 50cm above it. The extra height gained will help reduce claustrophobia caused by low floor to ceiling depth.

Suspended ceilings feature in most mid to late-20th-century offices. Hung from the bottom of the floorplate above, they provide a simple distribution system for services such as ventilation, heating and lighting. Modular systems are easiest to match up to planning grids and partitioning systems and best support reconfiguration of the space below. Ceiling materials and coatings can also improve the acoustics in any space.

Partitioning

Interior partitioning in offices ranges from blockwork, through plasterboard and stud walls, to aluminium and monobloc partitions. Which is used depends on various factors, including how long the interior configuration is expected to last. Changing the first two means messy small-scale demolition, while the second two are commonly demountable and offer the opportunity to reconfigure the workplace.

Factors to consider when choosing a partitioning system include:

- compatibility with other structural elements (suspended ceilings, raised floors and so on)
- fire resistance
- acoustic properties
- load-bearing capacity, if you are likely to want to use it to hang shelving
- ease of relocation – some systems are more demountable than others

Cabling

No building over 15 years old was built to cope with the volume of cabling now needed to accommodate information and communications demands at desk level.

In small spaces, cabling is handled adequately by perimeter trunking with wall outlets, but on most deeper floorplates, it is run through a raised floor. In cases where such floors cannot be used, a suspended ceiling is often used for distribution with wiring run down structural pillars or specially installed power poles.

Structured cabling offers a unified alternative to the mess of different wiring types that grew up to serve telephone and data systems. It provides a single system that can be configured to offer telephone, ethernet, multimedia and even CCTV connectivity all at once. The floor void is usually flooded with wiring and outlets provided at every 2–3m throughout the floor grid. This means that wherever the workstations are located or relocated they can simply be plugged into the nearest outlet.

When user requirements alter, the change is enabled by changing the patching configuration in the equipment room without having to touch the horizontal cabling to the floor outlets.

The most common means of connecting equipment to sub-floor cabling is via one of the following:

- **Floor boxes** – these are recesses in the raised floor with standard phone sockets for voice and data plus power sockets, usually covered by hinged lids, which flush to the floor when closed. These provide easy access for plugging and unplugging equipment, but require effort to relocate when layouts change.

- **Grommets** – these are essentially apertures through which cables are passed to connections in the floor void. They look neater and can be easily relocated, but once in place make it more difficult to access the plug-in points below.

Cable management

If a cabling infrastructure is what you have behind the scenes, cable management is the art of dealing with cabling between outlets and equipment. Bad cable management leads to unsightly runs of wiring across the office and, at worst, trip hazards. The simple rule is that the more outlets you have, the closer any workstation will be to one and the less cable you have to manage.

One way to run cables into open space where no local outlets are available is to use screen-based furniture where the cables are run through the screens that hold up adjacent workstations. This makes reconfiguring the layouts very time consuming.

Where cabling has to be run in open space at floor level for short runs, cable bridges that cover and protect the wires forming a shallow bump on the floor are an option, but these should never be run across circulation space.

Space per person

UK health and safety legislation specifies 11 cubic metres minimum workspace per person. This suggests a minimum space allocation of 4.2 sq m, while architects and planners have traditionally used an average of 10 sq m per person when calculating maximum occupancy of the net internal area. This figure attributes a proportion of all support and ancillary space to the individual, not just their work area. The British Council for Offices suggests a good practice range of 12–17 sq m.

These averages give you a rule-of-thumb idea of how many people you can fit into a given net internal area. How you actually fit them into the net usable space depends on the shape of the space and your organisation's space standards. A space standard is the number of square metres allotted to each employee in the organisation as workspace, taking in their desk, chair, local storage and immediate access to the workstation. These can be used as a minimum allocation per person, an ideal to aim for where space permits or as a rigid model for planning large numbers of people into a given area. Space standards vary enormously between organisations, as do the principles for determining them. The most common strategies are:

- **Single standard** – also known as a universal footprint, where every member of staff receives the same space allocation and/or furniture. This makes for very simple space planning, but few organisations carry it through to the most senior management.

- **Space by seniority** – the most common form of space planning since the mid-20th century. The size – and often type – of the individual's space is dictated by their rank. For example, in an organisation where non-managerial staff receive 5 sq m in open space, supervisors might be allocated 7 sq m also in open-plan, while managers would have a 10 sq m cellular office.

- **Space by need** – space is allocated based on an assessment of each individual's job needs. Those who can prove they need extensive personal storage are allotted more room and those whose work is highly sensitive or confidential are placed in cellular space rather than open-plan.

- **Space budgeting** – space is allocated to departments or teams based on a total of their individual notional space, but they are then free to arrange this space as suits them. A team of 10 people with a combined entitlement of 60 sq m could use small workstations and limited personal space to free up more of their team area for shared meeting and break-out space.

Simple standards

For simplicity of planning and managing churn it is best to stick to the smallest set of space standards possible and to make them multiples of each other. For instance, in a status-based system, if the basic standard for staff in open-plan is 4 sq m, junior managers and those with extra space needs might be allocated 6 sq m and middle managers 8 sq m partitioned cells.

Except in the smallest footprints, the space standard does not dictate the orientation or the arrangement of the workstation. Combining the space allocation of a team it is possible to produce regimented bays of desks that can be planned straight across an open floor, variations on a single theme, or, especially using the newer workstation shapes (such as 120° radial desks) seemingly random groupings, all keeping strictly to the relevant space standard.

Workplace options

Even after the advent of steel-framed buildings in the last century, open office floors were still heavily partitioned in many cases. But the influence of open-plan ideas from Germany and the US in the 1950s led to a rapid reduction in the proportion of cellular to open space.

Occupants of open-plan space frequently complain about lack of privacy and environmental control, but a return to highly cellular accommodation is unlikely to come soon. The cost of churn and the new emphasis on knowledge sharing face-to-face as well as electronically means that segregation is not yet on the cards again.

Apart from support and ancillary areas (computer rooms, catering areas and so on) the two most common types of cellular space found in offices are 'owned' offices for one or two people and meeting rooms.

Where individual contained office space is still an entitlement (because of rank or the need for a high degree of privacy or security), such offices are usually planned in blocks, making economic use of shared partition walls, easing the provision of power and voice connections and making planning of the surrounding open-plan areas less complicated.

Open-plan

The principle of offering people different types of workspace apart from their standard workstations to suit different types of work has spread in recent years. More employers are offering facilities in addition to owned desks, by reclaiming wasted space (see SPACE-SAVING TIPS, P359). These facilities include:

- **Break-out areas** – providing break-out areas with soft seating and coffee tables, or even formal meeting furniture, beside inter-circulation in open layouts or beside vending or catering points both creates these nodes and increases local meeting space. If they are located near to workstations, break-out areas should be at least partially screened to avoid distracting those nearby (see QUIET AREAS overleaf for more on this).

- **Touchdown space** – this started as one of the types of workspace offered in hotdesking offices, but the recognition that all office users need ad hoc work surfaces when they are away from their desks has led to their adoption in more conventional offices. The touchdown surface (often a counter fixed to a wall) caters for short stops by employees who need a surface to lean on or spread documents briefly. Wall-mounted touchdown surfaces – which need be no deeper than 450–600mm in most cases – are best placed to the side of foyers or entrances to office floors to maximise their use by staff and visitors. Touchdown surfaces should not have sharp edges or corners. No seating is needed, though bar stools are provided by some organisations. These must be easy to move in and out and adjustable. Power and data connections will allow people to plug in laptops.

- **Quiet areas** – quiet areas or meeting cells should ideally be placed in dead areas of the floorplate (against windowless walls, for example, as they are not designed for long-term use). Where areas of open desking are designated as quiet areas, it seems common sense to put them as far away from the noisier break-out areas as possible. In practice, as long as the two are not next door to each other and there are enough acoustically absorbent surfaces in the workspace, they can be in reasonable proximity (say 10–15m apart) without significant sound leakage. Paradoxically, the lower the screening around quiet areas, the less people will make noise around them because they can see others concentrating.

- **Carrels** – also known as study booths, carrels are hotdesks with some form of screening to provide enclosure for concentrated work in open space. They vary from rows of small 800 × 800mm library-style booths to free-standing desks surrounded by 1,800mm free-standing screens on three sides, and are a flexible alternative to permanent enclosures.

Meeting rooms

Dedicated meeting rooms are often an underused part of the office space, simply because they are over-proportioned. Research by Alexi Marmot Associates found that two-thirds of meetings in a typical organisation involve six people or less, and almost half involve four people or less. This suggests that organisations need very few large meeting rooms. That said, small-scale cellular space, for two to six people, is likely to be well used, especially in organisations where most staff work in open-plan space and may need enclosed space for interviews, important phone calls and short periods of work requiring heavy concentration.

For an administrative department, one small meeting space in the work area for two or three people might be sufficient for every 40 staff. In a consultancy this would rise to one for every 16 staff. Meeting rooms should always be accessible by main circulation routes and, where they are expected to be heavily used by visitors, should be located near lavatories and coat storage if possible.

Using structural glass for doors or walls of cells creates a less blocky appearance and gives passers-by an immediate indication of whether or not the room is occupied. But if more than one wall is fully glazed, etched glass is recommended for some of the expanse to avoid occupants feeling as if they are in a fishbowl.

Circulation

Circulation includes stairs, corridors and routes through open floor space. The first two are usually fixed, but the third needs careful planning. The primary consideration is the legal requirement for 'escape distance' – see HEALTH AND SAFETY LAW: FIRE SAFETY: MEANS OF ESCAPE, P55 for details of maximum escape routes. Beyond the necessity of quick access to fire escapes, it is necessary to consider whether each route will simply be used for getting to individual workspace or to encourage ad hoc communication and how much traffic they might need to cope with in peak periods.

Circulation can be divided into two types:

- primary circulation, including stairs, lift lobbies and corridors
- secondary circulation, providing access within the open floors

The latter can be sub-divided into two types: inter-circulation that takes people from the primary routes through open floors to team areas, vending or storage points; and intra-circulation, which gives immediate access to each workstation off the inter-circulation and is often accounted for partly in the individual space standard.

The recommended width for inter-circulation is 1.5m, which allows three people or one person and another in a wheelchair to pass comfortably. The minimum clearance for one person without turning sideways is around 55cm. Where lifts open straight into offices the recommended minimum circulation space in front of the doors is 3m.

Inter-circulation is usually planned through the middle of the workspace, so that access to workstations is equal on both sides. In cases where a shallow floorplate (under 10m) is wrapped round a large service core, circulation can follow the outside of the core.

With the vogue for less regimented-looking layouts, routes that wind through offset groups of workstations have become more common. These give the office a more pleasant appearance but the designer has to make sure they do not take the travel distance to fire escapes over the legal limit.

Adjacencies

Co-locating team members and staff in the same department is an obvious priority, but co-locating different teams and departments is a more subtle business. Unless you are sure that existing arrangements make for maximum interactivity between parts of the organisation whose work is interdependent, this should form part of your research before planning new space (see COPING WITH CHURN, P361).

Research by BT found that employees interact with those in the same work area as themselves for 10% of their working time, but this drops to 0.4% of their time for employees on different floors. Nevertheless, two departments who need constant interaction may be better served if they are placed on the same end of separate floors near a staircase, than if they are at remote ends of the same floorplate.

Detailed planning

Once you have set your space standards and taken into account the size of the space you have to plan and the desired adjacencies, in the detailed planning your decisions will be affected by a mix of the following factors:

- open-plan vs cellular space
- team vs individual space
- incorporating room for expansion
- flexibility and ease of churn
- aesthetics and staff comfort
- the planning grid

Group planning

When laying out multiples of workstations with similar space standards in open-plan space, it is time consuming and inconvenient to work in single units. Most planners group workstations together in clusters of four or six or more, combining the space standards of the workstations into a larger unit, preferably fitted to the planning grid. These units, often arranged as bays to create some sense of team identity in the open space, can then be replicated across the floor, simplifying the planning. There is no need for this form of cluster planning to produce a monotonous and rigid layout. Once the size and access requirements of a cluster have been set, variations on the theme will break up the appearance of the layout without complicating the plan.

Space records

As the planning process progresses, space planners will need to assemble different types of plan to record information on the proposed layouts, either on paper or on a CAD (computer-aided design) system (see COMPUTER-AIDED FACILITIES MANAGEMENT: SPACE USAGE, P365). They include:

- **Block and stack plans** – block plans can be prepared early on to map the desired adjacencies on a single floor. Where more than one floor is involved, stack plans group all the floors together to show vertical adjacencies as well.

- **Sketches, 3D renderings and mock-ups** – impressions of the planned décor and layouts give the opportunity to try out colour schemes and furniture arrangements and to bring flatplans to life for non-specialists.

- **Detailed space plans** – the final plans will be the blueprint for the new layouts, with all services, circulation routes, storage and workstations marked with details of which teams are based where. These must be updated as soon as and as often as there is any churn.

Office aesthetics

Beyond the essential environmental hygiene factors, other more subtle environmental issues should be considered.

Coloured wall and furniture finishes have become popular. Before deciding on a colour scheme for your workspace, consider the impression and atmosphere you want to create. Reds, oranges and yellows encourage activity and energy but can also cause fatigue, while blues and greens promote contemplation, concentration and creativity. Light colours produce the impression of coolness and spaciousness, while dark colours create a closed-in feeling.

Even in an interior where walls must stay monotone or pale, say to maintain required light levels, bright accent colours can be introduced via chair coverings and storage cabinets – now available from most suppliers in a bewildering choice of hues.

Other ways of softening an office environment are through plants (which are high maintenance but valued by occupants) and by hanging artworks.

Space-saving tips

Every facilities manager wishes to reduce property costs. Making better use of existing space is the easiest way to put off property expansion. One of the most obvious means of space saving is by moving staff who spend a high proportion of their time away from the office to some form of hotdesking or desk-sharing arrangement.

Other ways of reclaiming space include rationalising storage and fewer meeting rooms.

Rationalising storage

Much paper filing is unnecessary or kept in the wrong place. Documents accumulate in piles around workstations through inattention, suggesting the need for more storage cabinets, which are then duly provided. Migrating filing from floor-based units to shelving above desk level on load-bearing walls and partitions where possible will release space.

An increasing number of organisations are now setting a fixed filing allocation (commonly one or two linear metres) for all members of staff except those who can make a strong case for more.

The ultimate in space-free records storage is through the use of document image processing (DIP) systems, which allow all incoming documentation to be scanned and stored electronically. DIP systems may one day be the norm, but they are currently expensive to install and suffer from the popular lack of confidence in IT systems as the sole repository of important information.

Fewer meeting rooms

Meeting space in most organisations is usually oversized (see MEETING ROOMS, P356) and underused. Dedicated meeting rooms can be downsized. There are usually plenty of underused spaces that can be recycled as meeting space. Company restaurants are the obvious example. Chairs and tables in catering areas remain unoccupied for most of the working day and the simple provision of a couple of mobile whiteboards to be wheeled in outside mealtimes will allow a cafeteria to double as non-bookable meeting space. Corners of reception spaces and lobbies are other candidates for touchdown tables.

Third-party planners

For those who feel they lack the expertise or time to carry out space planning, consultants and facilities management contractors offer external assistance with anything from individual moves to the whole property management operation.

Independent specialists or the planning services offered by larger architects, surveyors and even removal companies, will almost certainly bring experience and ideas for space efficiency that most facilities managers would not have access to otherwise. More specifically they may be able to provide benchmarking data to help managers compare standards with other organisations.

When choosing a contractor, look for someone who understands your organisation, can provide references from other satisfied clients, will keep your plans secure and will commit themselves to a detailed service level agreement (for more detailed information on procuring and managing contractors, see OUTSOURCING, PP238–257).

Coping with churn

Churn is defined as the number of people who relocate within a workspace in a year, divided by the total number of occupants and multiplied by 100 to give a percentage figure. If 20% of your staff move once, you have a churn rate of 20% for that year, but if 10% of the staff move twice you still end up with 20%.

Benefits and costs

In fact, 20% would be an enviable rate for many facilities managers, who have to cope with levels well in excess of 50%, giving the impression of perpetual motion in the workspace. But the rate of churn – which seems to be rising in most industries – is not necessarily a cause for concern. As more organisations adopt project management principles, high churn that reflects the grouping and regrouping of staff to deal with time-limited tasks and projects is a sign of dynamism and a healthy response to constant change in the wider world.

What facilities managers should concentrate on is making churn less disruptive and, above all, less costly. A recent study by Cornell University in the US found that office moves cost an average £119 for a simple 'briefcase' move with no disturbance to the layout, rising to over £430 where furniture and storage is shifted, and jumping to £1,270 where any alterations (such as moving partitions or reconfiguring wiring) are needed. Cutting the cost of churn is a matter of building as much flexibility as possible into space plans, building services and fixtures, in order to maximise the number of briefcase moves.

Building in flexibility

Where managers have any influence over the fit-out of a space, the specification of some of the following features will add to the initial cost but generate savings in churn expense year after year:

- **Open-plan** – the fewer fixed partitions there are in the space, the more easy it is to move people round and the lower the risk of structural alterations when people do move. Where partitioning is used, take care to choose a system that is truly demountable.

- **Structured cabling** – the flood distribution of wiring through a floor (see CABLING, P352) and the 'plug and play' facility offered by structured cabling systems means that ICT (information and communications technology) needs a minimum of reconfiguration.

- **User-configurable phones** – a telecoms set-up (available for all but the oldest systems) that allows users to relocate their extension number to any handset makes moves easy, especially short-term relocations of days or weeks.

- **Space standards** – the closer you can get to a single standard or universal footprint (see SPACE PER PERSON, P353), with the same space allocation for most employees, the less often you will have to rearrange a layout or move furniture to accommodate individual or group moves.

Furniture and storage

Standard workstations, mobile furniture and centralised storage are all-important features of an adaptable workspace and are covered in more detail in WORKPLACE FACILITIES: FURNITURE, P327 (see also HOTDESKING: FURNITURE, P364).

Hotdesking

Hotdesking is when workspace is not parcelled out to individual employees but shared between a department or team. The arguments in its favour are compelling on paper. Although most organisations accept the costs of maintaining and servicing buildings that are only open around one-third of the available hours in the year (allowing for nights and weekends), occupancy rates can be reduced to as little as 10% of the available time due to the needs of many nominally office-based staff to leave the office on research, client or supplier visits, and with homeworking on the increase.

Making it work

But simply taking away 'owned' workstations and replacing them with fewer, shared desks is not likely to be greeted with any enthusiasm by those affected by the change; they simply lose the status of fixed workspace and gain a new set of responsibilities, including tidying up after themselves. Where hotdesking has succeeded it has been accompanied by a wider change to working practices that brings benefits to the hotdeskers themselves.

The most common quid pro quo for employees giving up their desks is to offer them more pleasant workspace for the times that they are in the office. Some of the space saved from removing 'owned' desks is commonly recycled for new types of worksettings (see WORKSPACE OPTIONS: OPEN-PLAN, P355), such as touchdown points, soft-seating areas and study booths, as well as standard desks. Even with these provisos, hotdesking schemes commonly generate space savings of 30% or more.

How many hotdesks?

There is no rule of thumb for the correct ratio of desks to employees in hotdesking arrangements. Ratios in existing schemes vary from 3:4 (hotdesks:employees) to 1:10. The level of provision will depend on a number of factors, including:

- the proportion of an average week staff spend in the office
- whether they are equipped to carry out desk work elsewhere (at home, for instance)
- whether it will be appropriate for employees to use empty desks in other departments if hotdesks are all full

The best pointer to a correct ratio is an occupancy study, carried out over several days, probably spread over a fortnight or more, to gather data on how many of the existing desks are used by peripatetic staff on an average day and at peak usage.

The perennial question about hotdesking is how to cope with the eventuality of all the employees wanting to come in on the same day. Though this overload almost never occurs in practice, providing the range of space-efficient worksettings suggested above (touchdown counters and so on) can make it possible to cope with unexpected spikes in demand for workspace.

Efficient hotdesking

The aim of introducing hotdesking is to save space, but not at the expense of staff productivity. If employees have to spend much more time finding a desk, configuring their phones or connecting to the company network, any gains will be wiped out. The following points will help ensure a smooth operation, though some may be unnecessary for small hotdesking schemes.

Layout

Place the worksettings designed for the shortest stops nearest the entrance to the hotdesking space, with desks for longer, concentrated periods of work nearer the back. By the same token, any 'owned' workstations for staff who are not hotdesking should be furthest from the entrance, away from the comings and goings of the hotdeskers.

Managing shared space

Although there should be adequate provision for employees dropping in and out without notice, hotdesks and meeting rooms should be bookable by telephone, in person and, ideally, over an intranet. Staff should be discouraged from booking the same space for days and other territorial habits, such as leaving material at workstations. A clean desk policy is essential for success. A dedicated concierge or receptionist may be useful to take bookings, maintain facilities (replenish stationery, log IT faults and so on) and, located near the entrance to the hotdesking area, can provide added security in a space with a transient population.

Communications and IT

Telephones must be configured so that hotdeskers can receive calls wherever they are sitting. Most PABXs allow temporary reassignment of extension numbers already. The more expensive addition of a 'follow-me' phone facility is the best solution. Access to sockets for voice, power and data must be easy for laptop users. Desktop power pods will avoid making visitors scrabble under workstations. Desks earmarked for longer stays should be equipped with screens and keyboards to which users can hook up to their laptops, since portable computers are unsuitable for prolonged use.

Furniture

Though permanent storage at hotdesks is inappropriate, as built-in storage at desk level encourages people to territorialise them by leaving things in the drawers, employees must have some means of moving files between bulk storage and their workspace. Most furniture systems now include wheeled storage pedestals which can be pushed or pulled round.

Chairs may have multiple users every day and must be easily adjustable. For more on seating, see WORKPLACE FACILITIES: FURNITURE: SEATING, P329.

Stationery

Stationery supplies, which should be easily accessible and sited somewhere near the common areas, are best located near communal printers and photocopiers and pigeon holes/post boxes – another feature facilities managers need to allow for where employees do not have post delivered to a desk.

Computer-aided facilities management (CAFM)

The rise of the networked PC has coincided with the establishment of facilities management as a recognised profession and has led to a rush by software companies to provide tools designed to make paper plans redundant and to help managers keep track of the organisation's assets and model changes with ease.

The programs available range from the simplest space-planning software, available free from many office furniture suppliers, which can be used for planning small spaces, to full-blown CAFM systems that support any or all aspects of the facilities manager's job. For the purposes of this chapter, computer-aided systems have been divided into five basic types. However, any one package may contain some of the functions and tools listed under each category.

Infrastructure – buildings, space and asset management

Property-based CAFM holds the data needed to ensure property and its contents are properly catalogued and monitored. Property databases hold details of all topics associated with construction, ownership, lease and occupancy and can aid routine tasks by, for example, flagging up lease renewal and refurbishment dates or calculating multiple occupancy costs so they can be re-charged to groups of occupants.

Space usage

Space usage is a prime function of this type of CAFM system. Object-oriented databases link to CAD space-plan drawings to provide a complete picture of space usage down to workstation level. Detailed information, both textual and graphical, can be produced on current space usage, and space needs can be planned for. Churn decisions regarding structural alterations and moving equipment and people can be made online, resulting in work orders being issued and CAD drawings being updated automatically.

Networks and cabling

The telecoms and cable infrastructure can be managed effectively within CAFM. Network connectivity can be tracked, an electronic inventory can be created of the physical cabling and telecom network connections and network plans drawn up.

Health, safety and environmental management

Health and safety CAFM

Health and safety CAFM helps the facilities manager ensure a safe working environment and demonstrate compliance with legislation and best practice. Systems come ready loaded with health and safety legislation guidance on topics such as the European 'six pack', *RIDDOR* and *The Control of Substances Hazardous to Health Regulations 1999*. These can link to the asset register or a human resource database, and suggest and diary appropriate actions such as checking first aid provision or organising manual handling training. Hazard registers can be compiled and maintained on topics such as asbestos, actions can be scheduled and worksheets created. Relevant health and safety data can be appended to work orders, and the resulting health and safety-related actions recorded. Many health and safety CAFM systems include DSE (display screen equipment) workstation self-assessment software.

Environmental CAFM

Environmental CAFM allows you to monitor, compare and manage the consumption of energy, and to monitor emissions and flag up hazard levels by integrating all energy-related data from existing building control systems and meters across sites and existing energy-related databases, plus all entered data. Energy usage is recorded and compared with pre-entered industry norms. The facilities manager can then identify areas for improvement, and once energy-saving measures are in place, continue monitoring. Reports can then be produced to demonstrate energy saving.

Pollution levels can be monitored across sites and over time, and staff can be alerted automatically if levels exceed pre-set values. Similarly, indoor air quality can be monitored for inadequate ventilation, improper temperature and humidity or excessive carbon monoxide.

Maintenance, repairs and contract management

With a maintenance CAFM system you can keep a full maintenance history of every piece of equipment or plant held on all sites, and the entire fabric of every building. Users can establish total downtimes and ongoing cost of ownership, which subsequently helps in assessing performance and planning replacements and refurbishments. Maintenance CAFM also enables a preventive maintenance schedule to be planned and implemented, so that essential services are maintained and equipment is ready when needed. Equipment such as heating systems can be interfaced so they can flag up their own faults, or trigger maintenance works orders after an optimum number of operating hours. And day-to-day maintenance repairs can be requested and recorded.

Online purchase requisitions, material requests and work requests can be submitted directly to internal departments or external partners. Scheduling, work assignments, shop assignments, work weeks, personnel histories, department assignments and relocation histories can all be stored and interrogated.

Helpdesk, service desk and security management

Help and service desk CAFM

Helpdesk CAFM helps the facilities management team to provide a responsive fault reporting and resolution service to building occupiers, and to fulfil occupiers' requests for routine services. Data can be collated to show which equipment or parts of a building generate the most faults or complaints. CAFM allows you to automate some of the helpdesk functions within service desk CAFM by allowing occupiers to access services such as room bookings, vehicle servicing or catering online.

Security CAFM

Security CAFM enables the facilities manager to monitor all the physical, personnel and electronic aspects of security – access control, CCTV, movement detectors, intruder systems, security staff routines – and manage them as an integrated system from a single control room. Access control systems can be interfaced, enabling the online issuing and cancellation of tokens and photo-ID visitor passes, and alterations to access times and levels, while if necessary occupants can be located within a site on screen. Alarms can be monitored remotely and fire safety can also be integrated, with heat and smoke detection and break-glass call points automatically alerting staff to the location of any suspected fire. These in turn can activate fire alarms and automatic voice evacuation messages.

Financial, budget and inventory management

Financial and inventory CAFM allows you to track and manage costs associated with capital assets, operations, consumables, work orders, training – anything in fact which impinges on facilities management work. At strategic level, these systems enable accurate measurement and forecasting of the cost of all activities undertaken by the facilities management function, and the control of its budgets.

Facilities staff can requisition spares from inventory or order them directly from suppliers according to pre-set agreements and price structures. This enables the close management of facilities management-specific inventory of equipment, spares and consumables, such as cleaning materials.

Specifying CAFM

It is essential to specify the 'owner' of the CAFM project. Who has ultimate responsibility for ensuring the system meets the objectives set? And who therefore has the authority to make sure necessary resources and support are available when required? Primary contacts within individual departments or divisions need to be pinpointed, as they will be the people who you will ultimately rely on to feed through information on any changes, whether it be a layout modification or change of occupancy.

Choosing a CAFM system

With so many CAFM products on the market, how do you ensure you are choosing the best system for your needs? Be rigorous in studying a CAFM system portfolio and take up references from existing users.

In planning a CAFM system, the best place to start is probably with the space management aspect, since space is the second largest business cost after salaries. As most CAFM systems take a modular approach, it therefore makes sense to plan the first phases of the project to incorporate the space management requirements, and bolt on other applications later.

Ask the right questions

To select the right CAFM product, you will need to ask the right questions. Some examples of questions, and the reasoning behind them, are listed below:

Is the system standalone or are there any extra software packages to buy?

Does the system need additional database software, or is this integral to the CAFM system and not, therefore, an extra expense? Recommended add-on databases are typically Oracle, Sybase or SQL, but these require licences. Check compatibility as well; many systems have to be mounted on a CAD system. For example, a system working with AutoCAD would work on release 14 at the end of 2000 but not be able to function with AutoCAD 2000 – a special software fix was needed to enable the CAFM system to function.

What is the scope of the CAFM system?

Check that the CAFM portfolio will deliver on all requirements. For example:

- For **management information** there should be information on publishing on the web, planning, benchmarking and performance measurement.

- For **business support** there should be data on finance and contract management.

- For **property management** there needs to be information on property portfolio control, estate diary and real estate development.

- For **space and asset management** there needs to be information available on design, costs and inventory, recharge, moves and changes and visualisation of space usage. Can the system be used to place assets, and then list them and data points by space ID, floor, building and so forth? Can the CAFM system also contain scanned or typed contract information regarding buildings, floors or equipment? Can it be used to create zones for cleaning, security, occupancy, and so on?

- For **call handling** the information must relate to the helpdesk, vendor tracking, maintenance procedures, purchasing and vendor invoicing.

- For **building management**, information needs to be available on environmental monitoring, HVAC, plant management, energy inventory, and reports and actions.

- For **security** there needs to be information on access control, alarm monitoring, fire monitoring and incident reporting and tracking.

Will it be difficult to integrate existing data into the new system?

Any package must interface with existing systems to avoid expensive data re-entry. Check that the system has an open architecture that can complement, integrate and/or support existing systems. For example:

- Can you import and export between databases?

- Does the system support open database connectivity (ODBC) with, for example, dBASE, Microsoft Access and Paradox?

How can I access the information?

Depending on your needs, on-site access may not be sufficient. You may wish to access the data remotely, via an internet browser or 'thin-client' scenario, whereby you can run small programs running on your PDA (personal digital assistant) or laptop to access the CAFM system remotely.

Will an off-the-shelf package do?

Off-the-shelf products will be cheaper than customised ones. Check, however, that the product really will be able to meet your needs, and be aware that project-scope creep and sales pressure can change the boundaries.

Is it future-proof?

There is always a worry that existing technology will soon become obsolete. Be clear about your current and future specifications from the outset, to ensure that the product will be able to grow with your business needs. Ensure also that the system has developing procedures and continual development in place so that databases can be upgraded easily as technology changes.

How are graphic images handled?

Facilities management automation will often involve linking some kind of graphic image with a database. Check what types of image files can be accommodated and whether the system can scan and digitise existing paper images.

How is the information presented?

- Is the database information available in both tabular and graphical formats?
- Can you change between view formats easily and are changes entered into one format automatically updated in another, or do you have to go back to the master database?
- Can reports integrate data and graphics for professional-looking reports?

Are there any user groups?

Hopefully you will have talked to other purchasers of the CAFM system when going through the selection process. But contact should not end here – keep in touch with them. If your provider has a user group, join it.

Choosing a CAFM provider

Once the system has been shortlisted, careful attention should be paid to choosing the right provider to implement it. It is a serious piece of software with a long, seemingly never-ending list of modular but interlinked applications. The quality of the provider is therefore key to both the successful implementation of CAFM, and to ensuring that it meets your precise business needs.

Suppliers should be able to offer all of the following services:

- project management consultancy
- software installation and customisation

- data management and capture
- software support and training

Consultants worth their salt should offer to perform an information audit and needs analysis prior to any implementation. They should agree with you exactly what is required to be input into the system, what outputs are required, and what, how many and how often reports are required.

Data entry and protection

Accuracy is crucial in the setting up of original databases and where banks of data are to be transferred across from current legacy systems. If you engage temporary clerical staff to enter raw data, take the time to explain the context of what they are doing, and check their work thoroughly, especially in the early stages.

Thought should be given to exactly what needs to be captured in order to achieve the desired results. What will the resultant data analysis be used for and how much depth is required? Who is the target audience and what kind of reports will they expect to see? It is important to identify your exact needs for the initial phase, as it is complicated to insert or delete columns into the database design once data entry has begun.

Where data already exists, do not transfer it to the CAFM database until you have cleansed it, otherwise errors and miscounts will be replicated. For instance, a desktop copier may appear two or three times on a paper-based asset register because it was moved from office to office.

Accuracy is also needed when entering ongoing data. Free-form text is useful for informative notes shared by users, but if data is to be sorted and collated, events must be described in the same words every time. This means having only relevant fields on screen, and pick-lists for which the choice of entry is unambiguous.

Early in the project explore with your provider the levels of security offered by the CAFM system. Firewalls and encryption will be necessary where data is available to third parties. Internally you need to set up appropriate user access levels, good password practice and clean screen policies. Be aware also of your responsibilities under the *Data Protection Act 1998*. If your system holds details of identifiable individuals, such as staff, within a space plan or access control system, you need to register with the Data Protection Registrar.

Planning the transition

In the run up to switching to CAFM, the following will help ensure a successful transition:

- Identify exactly what needs to be achieved with CAFM to justify the investment. Take time to develop a series of measurables – and also the process for tracking them to ensure the project is on target. These could range from the logistics of a particular process to quality of data. The project plan should also have a time frame with target dates to ensure everyone involved has clear objectives to focus on.

- Plan and make provision for the ongoing management and maintenance of the system. From the moment CAFM is up and running, you will need to keep the system updated with every change that takes place on the ground.

- Check that you have people available in-house who are willing to train on the computer system. Who will be in overall charge of maintaining the database?

- Do you have the appropriate hardware and software to run the system? Check if current terminals are powerful enough and what, if any, modifications to other programs or the network will be needed to share data.

Implementing the system

By the time it comes to implementation, the project plan should be fairly well advanced. You will have defined your data capture requirements, and the processes developed for ongoing maintenance should include a change management methodology to capture changes during the initial implementation period. The next steps are:

- Obtain existing CAD plans and ensure their format is compatible for linkage to the database. Take some time to verify the floor plans are accurate and up to date before commencement of the data entry. Although the processes put in place will deal with changes as they occur, it is worthwhile kicking off the project with pristine data.

- Identify common space and allocate ambiguous space to the relevant departments or cost centres.

- Commence data entry and CAD updates, whilst adhering to the agreed standards.

- Submit individual building reports and floor plans to the relevant contact for verification.

- Produce your first set of reports for your target audience, using the agreed data requirements and reporting format.

Review your measurables and the original cost-benefit analysis at the end of the initial implementation phase. Can you prove the CAFM system's financial viability by showing that actual savings have reached what was originally estimated? Is it providing the data that was expected? Before making it your default system, are there processes that can be tightened up or improved?

The initial implementation of CAFM may be complete, but additional situations where this powerful use of data can be applied will quickly become apparent. You will most likely find that a continual stream of requests will require the future implementation of several more modules in the system.

11 Access and Security

Frank Booty

There is a noticeable increase in the willingness to threaten or use violence for limited gain; statistics from the Home Office and Metropolitan Police have shown how the incidence of armed raids increased during the 1990s. Applying an integrated security strategy to reduce the incidence of aggression in the workplace can help reduce violent crime. Other security risks which must be addressed include the risk to stock, equipment and data. What options are available to the facilities manager seeking to maximise security? Closed circuit television, access control, and staff training are among the practical measures which can be taken.

Closed circuit television (CCTV)

The purpose of a closed circuit television (CCTV) system is to deter and detect crime and unauthorised actions. The reasons for facilities managers to consider installing CCTV systems arise typically from threats to property and people. Such threats could be real (a burglary, for example) or perceived (the outcome of a security audit that has unearthed potential risk areas). There are also other applications for CCTV that many people are not aware of, such as monitoring a premises' environment in order to meet health and safety requirements for both the public and staff, staff training, site traffic control and process monitoring.

Threats

Threats can affect both premises and their contents and those who work in them. Threats to premises, particularly external areas, are reasonably easy to identify (exits, entrances, perimeters, and so on). Internal threats are more subtle and are often influenced by the function of the space – shoplifting and staff pilfering are two examples.

Identifying threats is a pre-requisite when planning a CCTV project. Past experience is seen as the best guide, with the best people to consult being staff, as they are most likely to have spotted potential security breaches or suffered threats. Areas which will need surveillance are: areas where valuable items are stored, including cashiers departments where money is kept or handled; areas where staff may face dangerous situations; and all public areas.

The guiding principle is to achieve a balance between crime prevention and protecting personal privacy. It is therefore important to ascertain not only that CCTV is necessary, but also exactly what its purpose and key objectives are.

Security audits

For most CCTV projects it is advisable to conduct a security audit. Such an audit should assess:

- who, what and where needs monitoring or protecting
- procedures for cash movement and tills
- the location of sensitive or valuable equipment
- types of cameras and other security systems such as alarms, access control and facial recognition
- siting the cameras to cover designated areas and avoid blind spots
- on-site and remote monitoring
- evacuation procedures

Security consultants can play an important role in planning a CCTV project. Aside from being independent, they should have a wider experience and knowledge of security issues and situations. Indeed, one of the many major factors to consider when choosing a security consultant is the background and expertise of their team. Another criterion should be membership of industry or professional associations (such as the British Security Industry Association), although not all reputable consultants and suppliers are necessarily members (it is not mandatory to join such a body).

Overall security measures and systems should be audited once or twice a year, paying close attention to reported incidents and the response. All employees must be made aware that, whatever their job or status, they have collective and individual responsibility for security in their workplace.

Choosing cameras

The choice of cameras and accessories depends largely on the application and location for which they are intended. External cameras may need supporting lighting for night-time use, and weatherproof housing. The choice of lens is vital to cater for such factors as focal length, depth of view and variable lighting levels. For internal locations, less obtrusive cameras might be required, to avoid affecting the interior décor. This type of demand has led to the development of cameras such as dome models.

Every site and building is unique and facilities managers will need to translate the purpose and key objectives of the project into a technical specification to arrive at the best CCTV installation. The following factors should be borne in mind when identifying objectives and technical needs:

- Colour is appropriate for indoor surveillance, since colour aids identification, but externally the level of lighting present will dictate whether black and white or colour cameras are appropriate.

- If the budget is limited, a smaller number of higher resolution cameras will be more effective than a large number of low specification devices.

- Various levels of control over cameras are possible: pan, tilt and zoom can cover a far larger area. Dome cameras conceal the direction in which the camera is pointing, making it impossible for individuals to tell whether actions are being surveyed.

- Criminals will eventually find out whether a camera is dummy or operational and the cost differential is usually minimal, making dummies an unwise purchase.

- External cameras need weatherproof, robust housings and may need demisters, washers and wipers.

- When specifying equipment, consider how future demand might change and try to make expandability and upgrade possible.

Cameras should be sited carefully and mounted low enough to give a clear picture, but high enough to prevent vandalism. CCTV can be integrated with other elements of company security – cameras can be triggered by alarms from intruder or access control systems, for example.

Operation

For layout and operation of the CCTV control room, refer to *British Standards 7499* and *5979* (a security consultant will be able to advise the level of control and sophistication necessary). Do consider the following:

- Do not overspend on unnecessarily sophisticated equipment – it should be easily operable by the minimum number of staff in the control room.

- Multiplexers enable continuous images to be viewed and recorded from up to 16 cameras.

- Images from several cameras can be shown sequentially, or on a split screen simultaneously.

- Restrict access to the control room to authorised personnel.

If live surveillance is considered necessary, be aware that a person's typical concentration span when viewing monitors is only 20 minutes. Sufficient staff will be necessary to build in breaks and constant rotation. Cameras can be triggered by movement detectors in normally quiet areas, with an alarm to prompt a guard to monitor the screen. Alternatively, remote monitoring is available by an alarm-receiving centre.

The integrity and success of any scheme is only as good as the staff who operate it. Staff should understand the purpose and objectives of the system, be familiar with the code of practice, procedures and incident response protocol, and be thoroughly trained. The operation of the scheme should be monitored regularly and a longer-term independent audit put in place.

Remote monitoring

One CCTV security company specialising in the remote monitoring of commercial property claims savings of up to 75% over traditional manned guarding security. From a central remote monitoring facility, the company controls barriers to allow a vehicle through a site to a chosen building, monitors (un)loading of the vehicle and allows the vehicle to exit the site.

Such an arrangement also enables remote control of lighting, air conditioning and pumps, especially in emergency situations. The software provides visual perimeter protection using complex programmable dome cameras combined with live audio facilities. This enables verbal communication between monitoring-centre operators and unauthorised people picked up on camera, or to verify visitors' identification.

Other companies offer remote desktop video surveillance over any distance to enable monitoring of remote or unmanned premises with a PC or notebook computer. Costs of such systems put them within reach of shops, garages, offices, workshops, and so forth.

Low-light CCTV cameras can be used to identify vehicle number plates near remote facilities where there can be problems from vehicle headlights dazzling conventional cameras, or there are poor light levels. The use of advanced digital signal-processing circuitry within the cameras enables number plates to be read under any conditions, even against full-beam headlights.

Security review

Any CCTV installation should be treated as part of an overall security review. Apart from any security systems, this should also include:

- integration of CCTV with any manned security
- establishment of correct security and safety procedures
- promotion of an organisation-wide security culture
- the training to achieve these objectives

Recordings

Recordings can be stored on videotape, disk or other electronic media to be viewed offline or in case of an incident. Information recorded must be adequate, relevant and not exceed what is necessary to fulfil the agreed objectives. If recordings are to be used as evidence in the case of criminal action, they must have been handled in accordance with Home Office guidelines.[1]

Guidelines for handling recorded media include the following:

- Recordings must be indelibly marked with date, time and camera, and be labelled.
- All record-keeping must be accurate and complete.
- Tapes should be kept for 31 days before being wiped clean and reused.
- Tapes should not be reused more than six times.
- Storage of tapes and disks must be secure, especially where they contain incident data, both for protection of potential evidence, and for the protection of individuals' privacy.
- Access to storage must be controlled.
- Ensure good practice in the use of tapes and disks, and release of tapes to third parties. Destruction of tapes should be secure and controlled.

Data protection

The *Data Protection Act 1998* covers CCTV recordings of individuals who can be identified and where the system can be programmed to search for a specific part of a recording if it is known that an image of a suspected individual is recorded. If your system is capable of this you are obliged by law to register with the Data Protection Registrar. Do this as soon as you decide on such a system – to stay within the law you will have to take into account the principles behind the Act when designing the scheme.

Violence and aggression in the workplace

The objective of an aggressive act is typically the attainment of some material benefit, such as cash or high value goods. Aggression, expressed as violence, is essentially an issue between the people involved, comprising the aggressor, the aggressed, colleagues of the aggressed and bystanders who happen to be in the area. The consideration here is where aggression is perpetrated by a person who does not form part of the workplace staff.

At-risk areas

Aggression often takes place in areas accessible to the public. Typically these include:

- shops, post offices and petrol stations
- retail finance services
- DSS and local government enquiry offices
- transport ticketing areas
- hospitals and schools

The common thread is the interface between the public and members of staff. All these environments exist for the purpose of serving the public and accessibility is therefore a necessary part of that service. The thrust of management effort has been to provide a better service to customers. The dilemma is that unrestricted access is the antithesis of good security.

Studies by criminologists have shown that crimes, particularly those involving violence, take place in environments where the aggressors believe that:

- they are unlikely to be seen by the public, police or security officers
- if seen, there is little likelihood of being identified
- there are few people to report the crime in time for there to be an effective reaction
- there are many good escape routes by foot and vehicle

The people involved

What of the people involved?

- **Staff** – staff at transaction counters are mainly under 30 years old and most are female. Their objectives and reactions are predictable in that their objective is minimum injury and their reaction can be trained and managed.

- **Raiders** – raiders are also mainly under 30 years old, most are male and are aware of the risks of being apprehended and the various penalties that will be suffered if caught following a raid, with or without injury. The raider, operating alone or as part of an organised group, relies on the ability to dominate the situation by surprise, threats and violence. To stay and take a hostage will incur delay – to delay is to invite capture and to injure will intensify the police hunt and increase the penalty.

- **Public** – customers or members of the public who are present when a raid occurs are wholly unpredictable. However, in most cases people are initially shocked and take no action during the raid.

Nature and effect of aggression

The consequences of aggression on those involved are both physical and psychological. The incidence of physical injury from violent attacks can often be healed. However, the psychological effects of actual or threatened violence can leave long-lasting and sometimes irreparable damage.

Protecting staff at the workplace should not just involve physical protective measures, but also protection against fear and all its implications. There are many cases of victims of aggression who suffer intermittent periods of illness and are unable to return to their former work, or any other work, for fear of a repetition. The worst times can be the anniversaries of the attack, or the days of the week or dates of the month of the attack. Colleagues of an attacked victim also suffer in terms of frustration at having been unable to assist a colleague.

The number of illegal firearms, ammunition and quality replica handguns in circulation increases the chances of attack. No one can know whether a weapon is loaded. The knowledge that a raider has no intention of discharging the weapon is no comfort against the sight and sound of a raider making verbal and physical threats.

The objective of the security design of premises and equipment must be to create disincentives to the raider so aggression and violence are not attempted. Provision of active security measures that involve staff can also remove the guilt complex of impotence.

Personal safety – training and counselling

Courses in personal safety in the workplace seek to train staff how to recognise and remedy confrontational behaviour in others, examine their own attitudes and eliminate areas that can spark aggression. Typical course content would include: planning safety in travel to, from and during work; controlling stress and tension; and non-verbal communication. Importance should be placed on taking control in the event of an attack, getting away and the consequences of fighting back. Assertiveness and the law on self-defence needs to be discussed and risks should be put into perspective, backed up by statistics.

The human resource issue is critical in the event of trauma. A crisis management team needs to be put in place which accepts that there will be a human aftermath. Response to any incident must be proactive and assistance offered to the whole organisation; this may lead to short-term disruption, but will be for the long-term good. Management must identify external sources of assistance, accept a philosophy and model of intervention. With adequate crisis intervention, there should be fewer individual long-term needs.

Principal strategies for defence

The theoretical strategies for effective defence against crime are generally accepted and can be adopted on their own or in any combination. Adopting all strategies in different facets of the overall security is seen to offer the best strategy. The theory lists the principal strategies of hardening the target, removing the target, removing the means, reducing the pay-off and surveillance.

- **Hardening the target** – cash transaction counters can be equipped with armoured doors, walls and windows, akin to a bank vault. However, this can be unwelcoming to the customer and there are weak points of visibility at the windows and of access through the doors.

- **Removing the target** – removing the cash into an armoured enclosure as above is one solution, but is not available to most transaction counters where there is a tradition of open access across the counter.

- **Removing the means** – raiders rely on the tactic of surprise to achieve immediate and total dominance of the area by fear and aggression. Conventional transaction counters have no active defence. This advantage should be removed. Some counters are equipped with bullet-resistant glazing and offer a degree of passive protection, but still no active defence.

- **Reducing the pay-off** – good cash management by the use of teller-assist units and time-locked mini-safes can reduce the amount of money lost to a raider.

- **Surveillance** – this serves no purpose unless there is a practical action that can be taken as a result of the surveillance revealing a threatening situation. CCTV is sometimes incorrectly claimed to protect premises. It is only a passive deterrence against violence and can help identify offenders.

Practical anti-aggression measures

CCTV

CCTV has three possible functions:
- deterrence of aggression for fear of being observed
- notification that an incident is occurring
- identification of aggressors before, during and at the end of an incident

Cameras should be visible to members of the public. In entrance lobbies, miniature monitors should be mounted so the public can see their own image – no one has a way of knowing whether the CCTV image is being recorded.

Access restriction

Access restriction serves to deter attempted entry and prohibit actual entry. The restriction of access to an area that any member of the public needs to enter will inevitably be a compromise between security needs and the business needs of the organisation. With staff-controlled door systems, staff can be actively involved in deciding who they allow to enter their premises and exclude any suspicious characters.

Personal attack alarms

Personal attack alarms serve to summon assistance in the event of an incident. They can be interfaced to other systems to attract a security officer's attention at a CCTV console to start a recording sequence, sound a siren or start a strobe light. The alarms, of course, cannot stop the aggression, but may deter the raider.

Rising screens

Rising screens are designed to protect personnel against actual and threatened violence (both physical and psychological). They have a track record of successfully defeating violent raids in a number of countries, environments and cultures. Rising screens are installed into the service counter where staff and public have direct contact, and provide a physical, opaque barrier to projectiles, syringes, physical contact, sight and sound at the touch of a button. Aggression is restricted to the fraction of a second between realisation of a raid and the action of raising the screen. Staff are able to remove the threat the moment the presence or threat of a raider is perceived or suspected.

Screens are housed in a steel body shell which is built into and supports the counter. The screen is a telescopic arrangement of two sheets powered pneumatically to rise from the counter to the ceiling – body and lower screen panels can resist bullet penetration from powerful handguns (.44 Magnum and sawn-off shotgun with solid ball shot). Upper panels – not generally required to be bullet resistant – are made of sheet aluminium and impenetrable to sight, sound and thrown objects. Special situations can have panels resistant to 7.62mm armour-piercing ammunition.

Whilst security measures can go a long way towards reducing violent crime, it should be noted that violent raids will still occur, and improved security in some sectors can have the knock-on effect of driving raiders to tackle targets that appear to offer the next best risk to reward ratio.

Access control, asset protection and guarding

Access to the workplace should achieve a balance between convenience for employees and bona fide visitors, and the denial of access to areas where people do not have a need or right to be. Access control must not interfere with escape in case of emergency or fire. Advice is available from security consultants, approved security retailers, the police and the local fire service.

Access risk analysis

Access must be a basic consideration at the risks analysis stage – every workplace is different, with variations in the business activity and risks. Risks will range from opportunistic or organised crime to the ignorance and carelessness of staff. When assessing access risk:

- Start at the perimeter of the property and work in to the main door(s) of the building, other external doors and windows, the reception area, and on to all internal doors.
- Decide who is to be allowed free or controlled access at these various points and at what times.
- Consider how to secure and allow entry and egress through access points.
- Consider how to identify people who are authorised to be on site.

Security measures

Perimeter boundary

Certain – sometimes obvious – matters need to be considered when specifying a perimeter boundary:

- Invisible barriers can be created by infra-red beam systems.
- Fences or walls have to fit design criteria and be aesthetically appropriate – but check planning permission.
- Power fencing conforming to health and safety standards can be used to deliver a low voltage electric shock to intruders.
- Tunnels, culverts and manholes giving access to the premises should be secured.
- Perimeter entry points need to be kept to a minimum, but should allow for smooth flow of traffic at peak times.
- Gates should be high and strong enough to deter entry when locked.

Building exterior

Consider the following:

- How vulnerable is the building exterior at quiet times or at night when the premises are empty?
- Keep entrance doors to a minimum, and locked when not in use.
- All windows should have locks.
- How easy is access from roads, footpaths, flat roofs, roof lights and fire escapes?
- Secure ground-floor windows with steel bars or wire mesh.
- Ensure goods in and out are always manned during opening hours.
- Good external lighting is a deterrent to intruders in areas with good natural surveillance.

For external doors and doors leading to vulnerable areas, fit as a minimum thief-resistant mortise deadlocks conforming to *British Standard 3621*. Specialised advice on locks should always be sought. Always buy from a member of the Master Locksmiths Association.

Authorised entrants

ID badges can form part of an access control strategy, and need to be unique to the facility and not easily copied. Electronic access control systems can combine security with convenience. They allow doors to remain locked, giving continuous security, but automatically unlock them when authorised employees or visitors are identified by their unique codes. Individuals can be identified by voice entry, pin pads into which numbers are keyed, contact systems such as magnetic swipe systems, non-contact systems where cards or tags pass within range of readers, or new technologies such as biometric fingerprint or eye retinal reading systems.

Intruder alarms

Intruder alarms are a good visible and audible deterrent. They should conform *to British Standard 4737*. Do get advice from insurers first, and only use installation companies who are members of, or approved by, an appropriate body. There are two basic types of intruder alarm: audible-only or monitored, where the system is connected to a 24-hour alarm-receiving centre (ARC) by telephone or radio link.

Over 90% of alarms are triggered by events other than genuine break-ins. The Association of Chief Police Officers has reached an agreement with NACOSS (National Approval Council for Security Systems), BSIA (British Security Industry Association), ABI (Association of British Insurers) and the British Retail Consortium to reduce the number of false alarms by 10% each year.

The police have identified three levels of response:

- level 1 – immediate
- level 2 – response may be delayed due to higher priorities
- level 3 – no police response, key holders only

Newly installed and properly monitored systems, or where the presence of an intruder is suspected, receive response level 1. If four false alarm calls are reported within 12 months, response drops to level 2. If seven false calls are reported in the next 12 months, response drops to level 3. Restoration to a higher level will only be achieved when an organisation can prove that no false alarms have been made for three months.

Asset protection

Cash, stock and equipment are prime targets for thieves – both internal and external. Large items of electrical equipment and any easily portable equipment, such as tools, laptops and mobile phones, are vulnerable to theft and burglary, on and off the business premises. The following good practice tips should help minimise the risk:

Company cash and valuables

- Consult insurers and train staff in cash handling.

- Payment of wages by cheque, credit transfer or giro reduces the need to carry cash.

- Department petty cash should be monitored and managed by accounts staff.

- Cash should be banked frequently.

Stock

- Do not carry high levels of inventory.

- Employ trustworthy people.

- Access control should only admit authorised personnel.

- Check goods issued and receipts.

- Issue standard quantities for specific use.

- Perform regular spot stock checks.

Equipment

- Encourage employees to carry laptops inside a bag – business people carrying laptops are frequently mugged.

- Clear security marking of assets is a simple way to deter thieves and identify items if stolen.

- Security guards can check parcels or equipment being taken off the premises.

- Consider having spot checks of staff leaving the premises to deter internal thieves; a code of practice should be drawn up and clauses written into staff contracts which authorises the procedure (search is only possible with the agreement of the individual).

Manned guarding

If manned guarding of the premises is to be part of an overall security system, a decision must be made to employ staff directly or to outsource the service to an external supplier. This will be determined by the size and nature of the organisation and other measures, such as CCTV. Outsourced guarding can either be static – on the premises continuously as in-house staff would be – or mobile – a patrol which tours a number of premises out of hours, calling in to check the premises at intervals.

Private Security Industry Act

The *Private Security Industry Act 2001* became law in May 2001. For the first time, the security industry in the private sector in England and Wales will be subject to a regulatory system, as in other EU member states. Under the Act, the Security Industry Authority has been created. All individuals (employees, directors and partners of security firms) will have to be licensed and all companies approved. Licences will last three years, providing conditions are not broken.

In-house security departments are exempt from the legislation. As licensing and associated costs are certain to be borne by the contract guarding company, the exception of licensing requirements for in-house personnel could mean a move away from contracting. But key figures in the manned guarding and security business point out that this could defeat the object of the Bill and result in a two-tier system with the quality of personnel working in-house deteriorating.

Staff

In-house staff should be employed for security work. It is not realistic or fair to expect existing untrained maintenance or reception staff to take on security duties. All employers are obliged to adhere to the *Working Time Regulations 1998*. Security personnel need detailed job descriptions, called "assignment instructions". These should cover all duties and responsibilities, which may include access control, issue and control of ID badges, record-keeping, CCTV monitoring, and incident and emergency response. Guards may also need to make regular premises patrols.

Training of security staff is available through the Security Industry Training Organisation. Security staff need an understanding of the limits of their powers of search and arrest – refer to the *Police and Criminal Evidence Act 1984*. Security staff should also be trained and certified as first aid providers and in fire safety. All training should be regularly updated.

Information protection

The continuity and survival of a business depends increasingly on its information. Risk analysis should take into account:

- production processes and design drawings
- proprietary software programs
- customer lists, marketing plans and tender information

- financial data
- legal records
- personnel records

In addition, business documents need to be protected against disclosure, copying, theft, fire and vandalism.

With electronic information, networks can be hacked into, e-mails read, information copied or corrupted, and virus infections introduced. An information security policy should be formulated following the risks analysis and with reference to business objectives.

All companies should be aware of the provisions of the *Data Protection Act 1998* which sets out rules for handling personal data about any living, identifiable individual, which is automatically processed by computer or other technology.

Fire risk

Fire poses a devastating risk to any business. Minimising the risk of fires is fundamental to any business continuity plan.

Causes of fire

Fires generally start as a result of people's actions or conversely their lack of action. If the following list of the commonest causes of fires is examined, it will be seen that fires are caused by people doing something they should not or by not doing something that they should:

- fire raising and arson
- careless disposal of cigarettes or matches
- combustible material left near a source of heat
- accumulation of easily ignitable rubbish or paper
- carelessness on the part of contractors and maintenance workers
- electrical equipment left switched on when not in use
- misuse of portable heaters
- obstructing ventilation of heaters, machinery or office equipment

Fire is a chemical reaction, requiring three fundamental elements to be in place: oxygen (always present), fuel (the combustible substance which can be a solid, liquid or gas) and an ignition source of heat energy. As all three points of the fire triangle must be in place to cause a fire, it follows that managers

Minimising fire risk

Poor housekeeping is the greatest single cause of fire. This checklist of best practice guidelines is recommended to minimise risk:

- Where smoking is permitted, suitable deep metal ashtrays should be provided. Ashtrays should not be emptied into combustible waste unless the waste is to be removed from the building immediately. It is recommended that smoking ceases one hour before close of work, so that if smouldering occurs it will be detected before staff leave the premises.

- Combustible waste and contaminated rags should be kept in separate metal bins with close-fitting metal lids.

- Cleaners should preferably be employed in the evenings when work ceases. This will ensure that combustible rubbish is removed from the building to a place of safety before the premises are left unoccupied.

- Rubbish should not be kept in the building overnight or stored nearby.

- No smoking areas should be strictly enforced, especially in places which are infrequently used, such as stationery stores and oil stores. Suitable 'No smoking' notices should be displayed.

- Where no smoking is enforced due to legal requirements (areas where flammable liquids are used or stored, for example) or in areas of high risk or high loss effect, it is recommended that the notice reads 'Smoking prohibited – dismissal offence'.

- Materials should not be stored on cupboard tops, and all filing cabinets should be properly closed and locked at the end of each day.

should attempt to prevent this from happening. Both managers and employees should strive to prevent sources of fuel and ignition from coming together.

Anything that burns can be regarded as fuel. A premises' structure may be made of materials which will readily burn when exposed to fire or flame. Some potential sources of fuel commonly found in premises are:

- upholstered furniture, carpets and curtains
- office storage, filing and other storage cabinets
- wood and paper
- packaging materials
- paints and adhesives
- petrol and paraffin
- liquefied petroleum gas

A good housekeeping approach assists in reducing risk to an acceptable level.

Statutory requirements

Note that in the wealth of fire legislation, premises are not policed by enforcing authorities. Employers are required to find out for themselves how to comply with the legislation. Consequently many companies buy in fire safety advice as and when needed from an independent fire safety consultant. A list of consultants is available from the Institution of Fire Engineers. See HEALTH AND SAFETY LAW: FIRE SAFETY, P52 for statutory requirements relating to fire risk assessment.

Reference

1. See the Home Office booklet on using and storing tapes as evidence: *CCTV – Looking out for you*, available from the Stationery Office on tel: 020 7873 9090

Information

Association of British Insurers, tel: 020 7600 3333

Association of Security Consultants, tel: 07071 224865

British Computer Society, tel: 01793 417417, *www.bcs.org.uk*

British Security Industry Association, tel: 01905 21464, *www.bsia.co.uk*

CCTV User Group, for model code of practice and model procedural manual, tel: 01252 627970

The Centre for Crisis Psychology, tel: 01756 796383

Data Protection Registrar, tel: 01625 545745, *www.dataprotection.gov.uk/summary.htm*

Institution of Fire Engineers, tel: 0116 255 3654, *www.ife.org.uk*

International Institute of Security, tel: 01803 663275

International Professional Security Association, tel: 01495 757153, *www.ipsa.org.uk*

Master Locksmiths Association, tel: 01327 262255, *www.locksmiths.co.uk*

NACOSS (National Approval Council for Security Systems), tel: 01628 637512, *www.nacoss.org.uk*

National Security Inspectorate, tel: 0870 2050000

Roger Worth Training Ltd, tel: 01924 217111

Security Systems and Alarms Inspection Board, tel: 0191 296 3242

The Stationery Office, tel: 0870 600 5522, *www.clicktso.com*

12 Maintenance and Repair

Frank Booty

All properties and facilities need maintaining. For many concerns, maintenance is at the core of the facilities management role. Organisations are beginning to realise that planned preventative maintenance is more economical than ad hoc replacement of parts when they fail. As well as ensuring a planned maintenance schedule is effective, facilities managers must be careful to comply with statutory requirements relating to both electrical systems' testing and workers' safety.

Facilities managers also need a strategy in place for maintaining critical IT equipment. Whereas vendor-specific service agreements offer excellent service and assurance, such provision is compromised by the number of products from different vendors existing within one workplace. What solutions are available to the facilities manager, concerned with keeping the administrative burden of dealing with contracts to a minimum and ensuring that downtime does not affect the bottom line?

Plant and property maintenance

Statutory requirements

Construction (Design and Management) Regulations

A growing number of larger companies, local authorities and other public bodies have been pursuing increasingly formalised procedures for checking the health and safety standards of contractors wishing to work for them. This process has been accelerated by the introduction of the *Construction (Design and Management) Regulations 1994* which require organisations to satisfy themselves that potential principal contractors are capable of dealing with the health and safety issues associated with projects relating to their premises (see HEALTH AND SAFETY LAW: MAINTENANCE AND REPAIR, P47).

Statutory maintenance tests

Do note the important issue of statutory maintenance tasks. Failure to check your equipment, system or process and record the results at the prescribed frequencies is serious. There are also certain areas where there is an insurance implication, such as lifts or elevators, where the relevant official has to inspect the system during the maintenance process.

Costs

Costs for maintaining different types of building range from £2,700 per 100 sq m per year for air conditioned offices down to £950 per 100 sq m per year for warehouses.[1] Annual maintenance expenditure typically covers areas such as decorations, fabric, services, cleaning, utilities, administrative costs, overheads and external works.[2]

In maintaining properties, fabric costs relate to the floor to wall ratio, the density of partitioning, the standards of fittings and frequency of use. Any services maintenance programme will depend on the quality, age and condition of the heating, ventilation and air conditioning systems installed. The amount of churn within a company will also affect maintenance costs.

The wages paid to maintenance operatives will have a key effect on the overall maintenance cost. Base or average hourly wage figures for maintenance workers for 2001 were calculated as:[3] £6 per hour for labourers, £6.60 per hour for semi-skilled labourers, £8 per hour for electricians, £8.33 per hour for general fitters and £8.31 per hour for plant maintenance fitters. It must be noted that these costs are unlikely to decrease.

Types of maintenance

According to British Standards, maintenance is a combination of all technical and associated administrative actions to retain an item or system in – or restore it to – a state in which it can perform its required function efficiently and as expected. Essentially there are two types of maintenance:

- **planned** (programmed, preventative and cyclical)
- **unplanned** (reactive, normal response, and emergency response)

Planned maintenance is maintenance organised and executed with forethought, control and application of records. It encompasses condition-based maintenance, which is progressed following information received about a system or structure's condition from routine or continuous monitoring processes.

Unplanned maintenance includes breakdown, corrective and emergency maintenance. A repair is the restoration of an item or system to an acceptable state through renewing, replacing or mending worn out or damaged parts. It is typically considered that the ups and downs of unplanned maintenance work should be run alongside planned work schedules. The reaction to unknown and unplanned events can thus be offset against meeting statutory obligations and service needs.

Managing maintenance contracts

All critical systems and response times should have been detailed in a particular service level agreement (SLA) (see OUTSOURCING: SERVICE LEVEL AGREEMENTS, P245). Facilities managers can measure the performance of a specific service against actual happenings in the SLA through utilising a helpdesk or computer-aided facilities management (CAFM) system (see SPACE DESIGN AND MANAGEMENT: **CAFM, P365**).

Voucher systems

The maintenance systems run as a part of a helpdesk or CAFM system typically utilise job ticketing or voucher systems. A job voucher or ticket will be issued to relevant tradesmen or contractors, providing them with information such as the location of the fault, description, agreed response time and estimated time for the work to be completed. Planned maintenance vouchers often include service routine details to assist personnel to process the required work. Cost codes track labour costs and all spare parts and consumables utilised during the work. A method of recharging is employed. This involves knowing all the consumable items used in the service; typically these will have been drawn up in the SLA or maintenance contract.

Software features

Many modern maintenance software packages utilise barcoding to enable efficient collection of data and costings on particular jobs, which saves a lot of time and effort through from not having to handle manual data entry tasks. Such systems can also be used to chart the history of items of plant, systems and schedules, as well as to make records of maintenance frequencies and issuing of spares. They can also assist in the processes necessary to perform statutory maintenance tests required on certain systems (electrical installations, for example).

Number and frequency of visits

There will be occasions when a planned service will have to be rescheduled and such a state has to be recorded. Companies will always want to know that the precise number of planned maintenance calls agreed in the SLA or contract have been actioned or delivered. Recording an event that has been pushed forward or back aids that process.

The frequency of maintenance visits has to be agreed, usually according to manufacturers' service requirements or recommendations. Maintenance software packages often feature the ability to plan workloads over defined periods to enable the best possible fit with the resources available to perform tasks. Unplanned activities can also be accommodated.

Managing the maintenance schedule

- Check to see if any statutory obligations have to be complied with.
- Find out exactly what plant and equipment there is within the estate and produce a detailed asset register (most likely this will be computerised), which should be checked and updated regularly.
- Ensure all heath and safety regulations are being followed.
- Conduct a risk assessment on all systems and tasks.
- Make sure all systems and components essential to the company's business continuity plan are known and that they are properly included in maintenance priorities.
- Develop a planned preventative maintenance schedule for all essential items of equipment, systems and fittings.
- Make sure an accessible maintenance and test-result recording and documentation system is operational.
- Set up a helpdesk (or at least a work request system) which links to all other procedures and systems within a company.
- Anticipate unplanned maintenance work and agree relevant charging structures.
- Make friends with the finance director, as capital investment budgets will need to be drawn up and life cycle costing exercises undertaken.
- Keep your team informed.
- Talk to your customers. Ask them what they think of your services (by conducting regular surveys), and find out what they want.

Employee safety

Effective maintenance is key to ensuring a healthy and safe workplace. Managers who control premises have a legal duty to ensure the safety of employees (see HEALTH AND SAFETY LAW: MAINTENANCE AND REPAIR, PP47–52). Facilities managers have to be satisfied any contractors working on site (which is most of the time for most facilities managers) are complying with health and safety guidance and regulations, and that they have conducted risk assessments. Most bodies will insist on regular two-way communication on health and safety matters. Compliance with health and safety should typically be embedded in specifications or SLAs from the outset.

Risk assessments

Workplace injuries (or worse) are substantially reduced through the adoption of rigorous risk assessment practices, which highlight areas where maintenance is necessary. Risk assessment processes can be conducted through software systems or minimally through a paper form-based approach. When considering workplace tasks or activities, what should the facilities manager be looking for? Typically it is things such as:

- air quality, humidity and temperature
- manual handling
- DSE-related issues – checking closeness to screens, rest breaks, and so on
- first aid facilities
- static on carpets
- cleaning
- adequate lighting
- cable runs and any 'rogue' trailing leads
- control of substances hazardous to health
- noise

In compiling a risk register, the facilities manager will forge deeper relationships with the finance department. Insurance companies will give reduced premiums against companies where known risks can be ranked from low to high and insured accordingly. Turning the argument somewhat, there are insurance companies who insist companies produce a risk register. The facilities manager who acts proactively in this case will be fondly welcomed by the finance department.

Preventative maintenance programmes

Preventative maintenance is maintenance carried out at predetermined intervals or according to prescribed criteria, with the intention of reducing the probability of failure or performance degradation of a system or structure. A preventative maintenance programme allocates specific maintenance tasks to particular periods in a timetable.

Preventative maintenance programmes save money and eliminate downtime. Maintenance programmes range from the basic, bare essential checks to comprehensive tests run according to manufacturers' specifications. Generally, full maintenance programmes are carried out at the end of a season when systems are shut down after several months of operation. This ensures readiness for the next period of operation. Ideally, a system should also be checked out immediately before start-up to make sure it is ready when needed. This applies particularly to heating systems in hotels but is equally valid in industrial premises.

A large proportion of the work carried out by maintenance companies involves sorting out problems for owners who do not implement planned preventative maintenance programmes. In other words, these companies are called in only when customer systems become defective. This way of operating is undoubtedly more costly than implementing a planned preventative maintenance programme.

Providing site owners authorise a full inspection and maintenance programme, with replacement of parts where required, they should be able to rely on this system for the forthcoming season of operation. However, some owners are tied by budgetary constraints and are forced to reduce expenditure. Although maintenance may be budgeted for, contingency funds for repairs are not, nor are the new parts needed to prevent breakdowns. Saving money is one thing, but a lack of maintenance can often compromise safety.

Reading the signs

Maintenance engineers should be trained to spot the tell-tale signals from ionisation probes and ultraviolet cells which indicate the condition of parts of a system. They should also take full-load current and bearing temperature readings from system motors, which verify their state of health. These indicators flag up when something is wrong. Certainly, they can be ignored and the system could continue to operate for a few more weeks, but without exception, it fails – and usually at the most inconvenient time.

Companies new to this process are recommended to have a full inventory check or technical audit of the heating, plumbing and ventilating plant at a site. A planned preventative maintenance schedule can then be worked out to cover all the equipment.

This might, for example, require inspection of oil burners every three months. If the planned maintenance schedule complies with the manufacturer's specifications, the system is unlikely to malfunction.

However, any deviation from these specifications – any cutting corners or cost savings – will inevitably result in unplanned maintenance problems and increased costs. System operating costs will increase with the age of the system, as will maintenance costs and system downtime.

Faults with new installations

There can be major problems with new installations. Age of the system is no guarantee of trouble-free operation. New systems also require planned maintenance. The frequency of major failures due to poor installation or inadequate design is surprisingly high. This is where a site survey procedure often highlights system faults and design defects, which can be rectified economically early in the life of the system. Before the end of the first year of operation, it makes sense to have all the building systems checked for defects, while the installers remain liable for rectifying any installation faults. It is common to find access control panels that are not wired correctly, and missing thermostats.

Spare parts holding

To support the maintenance programme, a minimum spares holding is recommended. This would include belts for motor drives – inexpensive items but nevertheless essential for the system to operate correctly.

Air conditioning

Preventative maintenance is equally valid for air conditioning systems. Filter elements need replacing regularly or the consequence can be costly.

One company had a unit with a badly blocked filter element, which had been pulled out of its track and was resting on the drive belt. Friction burn marks were evident on the element. This might have caused a serious fire but was, fortunately, spotted in time. The antidote is to maintain a spare parts holding of filter elements, costing £200. A spare parts holding of under £1,000 guarantees minimal maintenance costs, and assures minimal downtime and system reliability – insurance which is well worth considering.

Test instrumentation

Sophisticated monitoring equipment is essential. All engineers should carry flue gas analysers and be able to interpret the results to achieve safety and maximum efficiency. This can often save money over time. Engineers have been known to encounter boilers which are operating at efficiency levels as low as 40%, when they should be operating at about 80%. This increases the fuel consumption of the system but more importantly can lead to blocked and sooted-up flues, which, in turn, can lead to carbon monoxide emission hazards.

Cost of inadequate maintenance

- Many costly problems can be avoided with a little forethought. Consider this typical scenario: an engineer visits a site and finds an extractor motor is running hot. High bearing temperatures and full-load current readings indicate an imminent failure. The engineer recommends fitting a replacement but for one reason or another this is not done. Two weeks on, late in the evening, the motor dies. As a consequence of the overheating, the fire alarm goes off and the building has to be evacuated. The engineer is called back to provide an emergency repair service. The cost of replacing the motor when the faults were originally diagnosed would have been around £400, installed and running. Instead, the cost of the remedial work, involving late night call-out rates and an overnight motor rewind service is over £2,000.

- Sometimes customers ignore advice and refuse to sanction the necessary expenditure. This can have dire consequences. For example, some weeks after receiving spares holding recommendations, one company experienced a drive belt failure on its gas boosters at 9pm on a Saturday, resulting in a major loss of service until a new belt could be located on the following Monday. The cost of a spare belt drive belt is £6 and, had the spare been available as advised, there would have been minimal loss of service.

Staff training needs

Frequently there are basic maintenance procedures that managers are unaware of, which can be carried out by staff without the need for a maintenance engineer. This ranges from the act of pressing a boiler reset button to restarting the system. For example, replacing filter elements at prescribed intervals is a relatively simple task which can realistically be carried out in-house, provided the necessary instruction has been provided. Even with complex computer-based building management systems, the property manager needs to be able to interpret the mass of information they are provided with. Training is, therefore, a key requirement.

Environmental issues

Some of the latest sites have been designed for operation with low nitrous oxide emission systems. This is to reduce the emission of gases which are known to affect the composition of the ozone layer. Awareness of nitrous oxide gas emissions will be a concern for the future and is something everyone in the industry should be increasingly concerned with. There may also be future standards for the operation of energy controls, including those applying to building management systems (BMS). However, there are still many buildings today running conventional systems at very low efficiencies and burning vast amounts of fuel unnecessarily.

Turnkey service management

When buying a new electrical appliance, key to the decision-making process is whether to take out a service management agreement. With technology advancing at exponential rates, and appliances now supporting more and more critical applications, the thought of downtime is unacceptable. Despite manufacturers' claims, nothing is infallible. There will be occasions (albeit infrequent) when problems arise and repairs are necessary. This is when the service engineer becomes your best friend.

Manufacturers offer numerous after-sales packages to provide users with the assurance that, should a product suffer from a failure of some kind, a service engineer will be on standby to offer assistance. Domestically speaking, such service management agreements (usually defined as extended warranty packages) may initially appear costly, but when weighed against an independent engineer's call-out and hourly charges, they could bring benefits after only a single use.

Within the corporate arena, service management agreements play a more integral role in the initial purchase of a product. When committing to purchase a new piece of equipment, assurance is necessary that not only is the organisation purchasing at the best price available, but also that the equipment is accompanied by a comprehensive service package. In the event of failure, the cost to the organisation in loss of productivity alone could easily outstrip the initial capital outlay for the equipment.

Managing multiple vendors

With so many organisations looking for the best deals each time they buy new equipment, it is unlikely that every appliance will be supplied by the same vendor – which has ramifications for the service manager. Organisations looking to manage multiple electronic devices, for example, should consider a single maintenance contractor.

Each individual vendor may offer a uniquely tailored service solution for its own range of products, which means an organisation could realistically hold multiple agreements for multiple vendors. For example, consider the possibility that 'brand-X' operates six different products within a particular company, as do four other vendors, each in turn offering a tailored service agreement for each product (e-mail server, network printer, uninterruptible power supply (UPS), PCs, and so on). In the event of one of these products failing and an engineering call-out being required, the host organisation must sift through numerous contracts in order to find the correct one for the correct piece of equipment. The amount of time taken simply to identify the appropriate service department or contact may have potentially cost the organisation thousands of pounds in lost productivity. This begs the question – why hasn't someone devised a better methodology for multiple product servicing?

The complete service solution

An organisation needs rapid reaction to any technical problem that it may face, but cannot necessarily afford the time to deal with multiple service contracts. To address this issue, a select number of organisations have begun to look at how a new service model can be executed. This has been particularly prevalent within the power and electronics industry.

Within this sector, the implications caused by downtime can be catastrophic. Take, for example, the ramifications of an internet service provider (ISP) suffering a power outage, and all of its servers being down for a period of time. The consequences to its business, and the business of its users, could be costly.

As with any other organisation, when purchasing equipment, companies in this sector look for the best specification and price, regardless of the brand, so it is likely that multiple brands are in use side by side. However, this is a niche market, and while different brands may offer similar performance (and be purchased on this basis), the exact mechanics are individual and require experts to maintain them. This brings us back to the premise that many brands generally means many contracts. However, this is no longer necessarily the case: enter the complete service solution.

Expert technical assistance

In essence, the complete service solution is a simple idea – one organisation provides the complete service management for all devices. In practice, it is not quite that simple – it is unlikely that a photocopier engineer could provide technical support for a server fault, for example.

Behind the complete service solution lies the fundamental premise of service management – expert technical assistance. As such, the complete service solution offers expert assistance for a specific set of products, be they photocopiers or UPSs. Consider the UPS as the example in this case. The

UPS is a niche product (particularly in the high-end segment where a single unit may involve a five figure capital outlay), and each unit can be fundamentally different. It is hard to directly compare the UPSs of two manufacturers, as each unit integrates inherently individual technology and specifications around a common design – that of offering power protection and assurance 24×7.

Within this marketplace, an immediate response to any service need is imperative. This is why certain manufacturers in the industry have paid close attention to the traditional service management problems, and have devoted time to evolve this practice into a complete one-stop service solution.

The UPS industry has devised two modes of service management:

Third-party service management

Within this model, a single manufacturer operates as the sole service provider to the customer, thus providing direct service and support to every brand within the host organisation. In the event of a failure, the user contacts the manufacturer, and it will send one of its service engineers to address the technical problem. Despite the apparent advantages of this method (one contract for all servicing needs), the manufacturer must be able to service all brands of UPS to a high level. As mentioned already, all UPSs encompass individual specifications and technologies, so it would be essential for the managing organisation to employ expert engineers in all of the UPSs currently in the marketplace.

Outsourced management ('total support')

Operating along similar lines to the model above, the outsourced management solution is executed through a single manufacturer acting as a service facilitator (or agreement host). In the event of a failure, the user contacts the chosen host manufacturer for technical support. Once the call has been received, it is analysed to discover which particular brand of UPS is at fault and whether the agreement host is equipped to support the device in question. Instead of sending the host manufacturer's own service engineer to service all manner of units, this service model means the host manufacturer will (where necessary) outsource the maintenance of a particular unit to the specific vendor. Through this practice, the user is benefiting from cost-effective, vendor-specific service management while enjoying a centralised support contact process.

Of the two models above, the outsourced management method offers the user the advantages of a focused service management agreement without the aggravation of having to deal with multiple contracts. Within the high-end UPS sector, total support has been recognised as the optimum service management method and has received recognition from many well known organisations, such as Tesco and Bank of Scotland. But should this practice be restricted to just the high-end electronics industry?

Needs of smaller organisations

Due to the critical nature of the UPS and its importance within an organisation, users are demanding total support across an entire range of organisations (from small networks to enterprises). Traditionally, smaller units have not been covered by service management agreements such as total support, but with advancing technology allowing smaller and smaller units to support larger systems, users are demanding the same level of service management as their larger counterparts.

As such, manufacturers have adapted the model to cater for this sector. An example of how the applications for such a service model may operate is in supermarkets, where the organisation-wide EPoS (electronic point-of-sale) cashier system may be supported by a large UPS, but individual tills have their own separate UPSs. Larger UPSs may require specialised support (from the host organisation or outsourced vendor), but in most cases surrounding smaller UPSs, immediate support can be offered by the host organisation as the majority of failures in these units are due to the natural lifespan of the internal batteries. In cases such as these, the host is able to 'hot-swap' the batteries on site no matter what brand of UPS is being operated. In this way, the supermarket could call on technical support for all sizes of UPSs, thus assuring power protection for all of its systems.

E-business solutions for support

The potential now exists for manufacturers to combine thousands of pages of maintenance manuals, parts illustrations, service bulletins and parts catalogues on a web-based system into intelligent, extensible software applications, providing their customers and channel partners with an e-business platform that improves equipment maintenance and drives additional spare parts sales. The combination of solutions gives manufacturers and operators of high-value equipment shared access to the product support information that enables them to service their revenue-producing assets more effectively and efficiently, resulting in less downtime and improved field staff productivity. Such a combined solution also provides collaboration and transaction capabilities that support post-sale business processes such as order management, warranty management, channel management, shop-floor task execution and inventory management.

References

1. Costs computed for 47 different types of building by Building Maintenance Information (BMI) in its Special Report 299 – *Review of Maintenance Costs March 2001*.

2. The Building Cost Information Service (BCIS) provides a map of the UK detailing the costs of carrying out a maintenance contract, showing regional pricing levels, available in the appendices of the above report.

3. The Reward Group, 2001

Information

Building Maintenance Information (BMI) and Building Cost Information Service (BCIS), tel: 020 7695 1500, *www.bcis.co.uk*

CORGI (Council for Registered Gas Installers), tel: 01256 372200, *www.corgi-gas.com*

NICEIC (National Inspection Council for Electrical Installation Contracting), tel: 020 7564 2323, *www.niceic.org.uk*

Appendix 1

1987 No 764

Town and Country Planning (Use Classes) Order 1987

Made - - - 28th April 1987

Authority: Town and Country Planning Act 1990, ss 55(2)(f), 333(7)

NOTES

Continuation

Authority: following the consolidation of the Town and Country Planning Act 1971, ss 22(2)(f), 287(3), this Order now has effect as if made under the Town and Country Planning Act 1990, ss 55(2)(f), 333(7).

1 Citation and commencement

This Order may be cited as the Town and Country Planning (Use Classes) Order 1987 and shall come into force on 1st June 1987.

2 Interpretation

In this Order, unless the context otherwise requires:

'care' means personal care for people in need of such care by reason of old age, disablement, past or present dependence on alcohol or drugs or past or present mental disorder, and in class C2 also includes the personal care of children and medical care and treatment;

'day centre' means premises which are visited during the day for social or recreational purposes or for the purposes of rehabilitation or occupational training, at which care is also provided;

. . .

'industrial process' means a process for or incidental to any of the following purposes:

404

(a)   the making of any article or part of any article (including a ship or vessel, or a film, video or sound recording);

(b)   the altering, repairing, maintaining, ornamenting, finishing, cleaning, washing, packing, canning, adapting for sale, breaking up or demolition of any article; or

(c)   the getting, dressing or treatment of minerals;

in the course of any trade or business other than agriculture, and other than a use carried out in or adjacent to a mine or quarry;

'Schedule' means the Schedule to this Order;

'site' means the whole area of land within a single unit of occupation.

NOTES

Amendment

Definitions omitted revoked by SI 1992/657, art 2(1).

3 Use Classes

(1)   Subject to the provisions of this Order, where a building or other land is used for a purpose of any class specified in the Schedule, the use of that building or that other land for any other purpose of the same class shall not be taken to involve development of the land.

(2)   References in paragraph (1) to a building include references to land occupied with the building and used for the same purposes.

(3)   A use which is included in and ordinarily incidental to any use in a class specified in the Schedule is not excluded from the use to which it is incidental merely because it is specified in the Schedule as a separate use.

(4)   Where land on a single site or on adjacent sites used as parts of a single undertaking is used for purposes consisting of or including purposes falling [within classes B1 and B2] in the Schedule, those classes may be treated as a single class in considering the use of that land for the purposes of this Order, so long as the area used for a purpose falling [within class B2] is not substantially increased as a result.

(5)   . . .

(6)   No class specified in the Schedule includes use:

(a)   as a theatre,

(b)   as an amusement arcade or centre, or a funfair,

[(c)   as a launderette,]

(d)   for the sale of fuel for motor vehicles,

(e)   for the sale or display for sale of motor vehicles,

(f)   for a taxi business or business for the hire of motor vehicles,

(g)   as a scrapyard, or a yard for the storage or distribution of minerals or the breaking of motor vehicles,

[(h)   for any work registrable under the Alkali, etc. Works Regulation Act 1906],

[(i)   as a hostel]

[(j)   as a waste disposal installation for the incineration, chemical treatment (as defined in Annex IIA to Directive 75/442/EEC under heading D9), or landfill of waste to which Directive 91/689/EEC applies].

NOTES

Amendment

Para (4): words in square brackets substituted by SI 1995/297, art 2(1).

Para (5): revoked by SI 1992/657, art 2(2).

Para (6): sub-para (c) substituted by SI 1991/1567, art 2(1).

Para (6): sub-para (h) inserted by SI 1992/610, art 2(1)(b).

Para (6): sub-para (i) inserted by SI 1994/724, art 2(1).

Para (6): sub-para (j) inserted by SI 1999/293, reg 35(2).

Date in force: 14 March 1999: see SI 1999/293, reg 1(1).

4 Change of use of part of building or land

In the case of a building for a purpose within class C3 (dwellinghouses) in the Schedule, the use as a separate dwellinghouse of any part of the building or of any land occupied with and used for the same purposes as the building is not, by virtue of this Order, to be taken as not amounting to development.

5 Revocation

. . .

NOTES

Amendment

This article revokes SI 1972/1385 and SI 1983/1614.

SCHEDULE

Part A

Class A1. Shops

Use for all or any of the following purposes:

(a)   for the retail sale of goods other than hot food,

(b)   as a post office,

(c)   for the sale of tickets or as a travel agency,

(d)   for the sale of sandwiches or other cold food for consumption off the premises,

(e)   for hairdressing,

(f)   for the direction of funerals,

(g)   for the display of goods for sale,

(h)   for the hiring out of domestic or personal goods or articles,

[(i)   for the washing or cleaning of clothes or fabrics on the premises,

(j)   for the reception of goods to be washed, cleaned or repaired,]

Class A2. Financial and professional services

Use for the provision of:

(a)   financial services, or

(b)   professional services (other than health or medical services), or

(c)   any other services (including use as a betting office) which it is appropriate to provide in a shopping area,

where the services are provided principally to visiting members of the public.

Class A3. Food and drink

Use for the sale of food and drink for consumption on the premises or of hot food for consumption off the premises.

NOTES

Amendment

Words in square brackets substituted by SI 1991/1567, art 2(2).

Part B

Class B1. Business

Use for all or any of the following purposes:

(a)   as an office other than a use within class A2 (financial and professional services),

(b)   for research and development of products or processes, or

(c)   for any industrial process,

being a use which can be carried out in any residential area without detriment to the amenity of that area by reason of noise, vibration, smell, fumes, smoke, soot, ash, dust or grit.

Class B2. General industrial

Use for the carrying on of an industrial process other than one falling within Class B1 above … .

Class B3. Special Industrial Group A

. . .

Class B4–Class B7.

. . .

Class B8. Storage or distribution.

Use for storage or as a distribution centre.

NOTES

Amendment

In entry relating to Class B2 words omitted revoked by SI 1995/297, art 2(2)(a).

Entry relating to Class B3 revoked by SI 1992/610, art 2(b).

Entries relating to Classes B4 to B7 revoked by SI 1995/297, art 2(2)(b).

Part C

Class C1. Hotels

Use as a hotel or as a boarding or guest house where, in each case, no significant element of care is provided.]

Class C2. Residential institutions

Use for the provision of residential accommodation and care to people in need of care (other than a use within Class C3 (dwelling houses)).

Use as a hospital or nursing home.

Use as a residential school, college or training centre.

Class C3. Dwellinghouses

Use as a dwellinghouse (whether or not as a sole or main residence):

(a)   by a single person or by people living together as a family, or

(b)   by not more than 6 residents living together as a single household (including a household where care is provided for residents).

NOTES

Amendment

Class C1: substituted by SI 1994/724, art 2(2).

Part D

Class D1. Non-residential institutions

Any use not including a residential use:

(a)   for the provision of any medical or health services except the use of premises attached to the residence of the consultant or practitioner,

(b)   as a creche, day nursery or day centre,

(c)   for the provision of education,

(d)   for the display of works of art (otherwise than for sale or hire),

(e)   as a museum,

(f)   as a public library or public reading room,

(g)   as a public hall or exhibition hall,

(h)   for, or in connection with, public worship or religious instruction.

Class D2. Assembly and leisure

Use as:

(a) a cinema,

(b) a concert hall,

(c) a bingo hall or casino,

(d) a dance hall,

(e) a swimming bath, skating rink, gymnasium or area for other indoor or outdoor sports or recreations, not involving motorised vehicles or firearms.

Appendix 2

1995 No 418

Town and Country Planning (General Permitted Development) Order 1995

Made - - - 22nd February 1995

The Secretary of State for the Environment, as respects England, and the Secretary of State for Wales, as respects Wales, in exercise of the powers conferred on them by sections 59, 60, 61, 74 and 333(7) of the Town and Country Planning Act 1990, section 54 of the Coal Industry Act 1994 and of all other powers enabling them in that behalf, hereby make the following Order:

SCHEDULE 2

Article 3

Part 2
Minor Operations

Class A

Permitted development

A. The erection, construction, maintenance, improvement or alteration of a gate, fence, wall or other means of enclosure.

Development not permitted

A.1 Development is not permitted by Class A if:

(a) the height of any gate, fence, wall or means of enclosure erected or constructed adjacent to a highway used by vehicular traffic would, after the carrying out of the development, exceed one metre above ground level;

(b) the height of any other gate, fence, wall or means of enclosure erected or constructed would exceed two metres above ground level;

(c) the height of any gate, fence, wall or other means of enclosure maintained, improved or altered would, as a result of the development, exceed its former height or the height referred to in sub-paragraph (a) or (b) as the height appropriate to it if erected or constructed, whichever is the greater; or

(d)   it would involve development within the curtilage of, or to a gate, fence, wall or other means of enclosure surrounding, a listed building.

Class B

Permitted development

B. The formation, laying out and construction of a means of access to a highway which is not a trunk road or a classified road, where that access is required in connection with development permitted by any Class in this Schedule (other than by Class A of this Part).

Class C

Permitted development

C. The painting of the exterior of any building or work.

Development not permitted

C.1 Development is not permitted by Class C where the painting is for the purpose of advertisement, announcement or direction.

Interpretation of Class C

C.2 In Class C, 'painting' includes any application of colour.

Part 3
Changes of Use

Class A

Permitted development

A. Development consisting of a change of the use of a building to a use falling within Class A1 (shops) of the Schedule to the Use Classes Order from a use falling within Class A3 (food and drink) of that Schedule or from a use for the sale, or display for sale, of motor vehicles.

Class B

Permitted development

B. Development consisting of a change of the use of a building:

(a)   to a use for any purpose falling within Class B1 (business) of the Schedule to the Use Classes Order from any use falling within Class B2 (general industrial) or B8 (storage and distribution) of that Schedule;

(b)   to a use for any purpose falling within Class B8 (storage and distribution) of that Schedule from any use falling within Class B1 (business) or B2 (general industrial).

Development not permitted

B.1 Development is not permitted by Class B where the change is to or from a use falling within Class B8 of that Schedule, if the change of use relates to more than 235 square metres of floor space in the building.

Class C

Permitted development

C. Development consisting of a change of use to a use falling within Class A2 (financial and professional services) of the Schedule to the Use Classes Order from a use falling within Class A3 (food and drink) of that Schedule.

Class D

Permitted development

D. Development consisting of a change of use of any premises with a display window at ground floor level to a use falling within Class A1 (shops) of the Schedule to the Use Classes Order from a use falling within Class A2 (financial and professional services) of that Schedule.

Class E

Permitted development

E. Development consisting of a change of the use of a building or other land from a use permitted by planning permission granted on an application, to another use which that permission would have specifically authorised when it was granted.

Development not permitted

E.1 Development is not permitted by Class E if:

(a)   the application for planning permission referred to was made before the 5th December 1988;

(b)   it would be carried out more than 10 years after the grant of planning permission; or

(c)   it would result in the breach of any condition, limitation or specification contained in that planning permission in relation to the use in question.

Class F

Permitted development

F. Development consisting of a change of the use of a building:

(a)   to a mixed use for any purpose within Class A1 (shops) of the Schedule to the Use Classes Order and as a single flat, from a use for any purpose within Class A1 of that Schedule;

(b)   to a mixed use for any purpose within Class A2 (financial and professional services) of the Schedule to the Use Classes Order and as a single flat, from a use for any purpose within Class A2 of that Schedule;

(c)   where that building has a display window at ground floor level, to a mixed use for any purpose within Class A1 (shops) of the Schedule to the Use Classes Order and as a single flat, from a use for any purpose within Class A2 (financial and professional services) of that Schedule.

Conditions

F.1 Development permitted by Class F is subject to the following conditions:

(a)   some or all of the parts of the building used for any purposes within Class A1 or Class A2, as the case may be, of the Schedule to the Use Classes Order shall be situated on a floor below the part of the building used as a single flat;

(b)   where the development consists of a change of use of any building with a display window at ground floor level, the ground floor shall not be used in whole or in part as the single flat;

(c)   the single flat shall not be used otherwise than as a dwelling (whether or not as a sole or main residence)—

(i)   by a single person or by people living together as a family, or

(ii)   by not more than six residents living together as a single household (including a household where care is provided for residents).

Interpretation of Class F

F.2 For the purposes of Class F—

'care' means personal care for people in need of such care by reason of old age, disablement, past or present dependence on alcohol or drugs or past or present mental disorder.

Class G

Permitted development

G. Development consisting of a change of the use of a building—

(a)   to a use for any purpose within Class A1 (shops) of the Schedule to the Use Classes Order from a mixed use for any purpose within Class A1 of that Schedule and as a single flat;

(b)   to a use for any purpose within Class A2 (financial and professional services) of the Schedule to the Use Classes Order from a mixed use for any purpose within Class A2 of that Schedule and as a single flat;

(c)   where that building has a display window at ground floor level, to a use for any purpose within Class A1 (shops) of the Schedule to the Use Classes Order from a mixed use for any purpose within Class A2 (financial and professional services) of that Schedule and as a single flat.

Development not permitted

G.1 Development is not permitted by Class G unless the part of the building used as a single flat was immediately prior to being so used used for any purpose within Class A1 or Class A2 of the Schedule to the Use Classes Order.

Appendix 3

Property portfolio checklist

(*delete as appropriate)

Identification of property

(a)   [*provide full postal address including post code*]

(b)   The ordinance survey map reference is [ ].

(c)   The deeds are stored at [*insert address and reference*].

Planning matters

(a)   The permitted planning use is use as [*insert details*] within class [*insert use class*] of the *Town and Country Planning (Use Classes) Order 1987*/sui generis use not within the *Town and Country Planning (Use Classes) Order 1987** [see APPENDIX 1].

(b)   There are no conditions attached to any planning permissions/The following conditions are imposed by planning permissions*:

Planning permission ref.	Nature of condition	Has condition been satisfied?

(c)   There are no enforcement or stop notices affecting the property/The following enforcement or stop notices affect the property*:

Type of notice	Date of service of notice	Compliance date specified in notice	Has notice been complied with?

(d)   There are no pending planning applications/The following planning applications are pending*:

Planning application ref.	Nature of planning application	Date planning application lodged	Expected decision date

(e)   There are no planning decision appeals outstanding/The following planning decisions have been appealed*:

Planning application ref.	Nature of planning application	Deadline for lodging appeal	Date appeal lodged	Appeal being dealt with by written representations or inquiry

(f)   All planning permissions have been implemented/The following planning permissions remain to be implemented*:

Planning permission ref.	Nature of planning permission	Details of outstanding works	Deadline for implementation

(g)   The property is/is not* within a conservation area.

(h)   The property is not a listed building/is a listed Grade [*insert grade*] building*.

Title matters

(a)   The title to the property is freehold/leasehold*.

(b)   The title is registered at HM Land Registry under title number [*insert title number*]/The title is unregistered*.

(c)   (if registered) The registered proprietor is [*insert name*].

(d)   (if unregistered) The legal owner is [*insert name*].

(e)   The property is not subject to a mortgage/The property is subject to the following mortgages*:

Name of mortgagee	Date of mortgage

(f)   There are no restrictions relating to the use of the property/The following covenants restrict the use of the property*:

Date of restriction	Beneficiary of restriction	Nature of restriction

(g)   There are no restrictions relating to building works at the property/The following covenants restrict building works at the property:

Date of restriction	Beneficiary of restriction	Nature of restriction

(h)   There are no restrictions relating to disposals of the property/The following covenants restrict disposals of the property*:

Date of restriction	Beneficiary of restriction	Nature of restriction

Terms of occupation

(a) The property is held under a lease/licence* dated [*insert date*].

(b) The parties to the lease/licence* are [*insert names and address of parties*].

(c) The term of the lease/licence* is from [*insert commencement date*] expiring on [*insert expiry date*].

(d) The premises demised by the lease/licence* is known as [*insert description of premises from lease or licence*] and is shown edged [*red*] on the attached plan(s) [*attach lease plan(s)*].

(e) The lease/licence* can be terminated on [*insert date of termination in break clause*] by giving the following notice [*insert the length of notice required*]/The lease/licence* cannot be terminated early*.

(f) The lease is/is not* protected by the *Landlord and Tenant Act 1954*.

(g) There is no option to renew/there is an option to renew on [*insert date of option*] by giving the following notice [*insert length of notice required*].

(h) The annual rent is [ ].

(i) The rent is not subject to review/The rent is reviewed upwards only/upwards and downwards* on [*insert rent review dates*]*.

(j) VAT is/is not* charged on the rent.

(k) The rent is payable on the usual quarter days (25 March, 24 June, 29 September, 25 December)/[*insert dates if not quarter days*]*.

(l) The following sums are payable in addition to the annual rent:

    (i) service charge   Y/N

    (ii) insurance premiums   Y/N

    (iii) outgoings   Y/N

    (iv) rates   Y/N

(m) The lease/licence* contains the following provisions relating to disposals:

    (i) assignment of whole: Y/N permitted Y/N landlord's consent required

    (ii) assignment of part: Y/N permitted Y/N landlord's consent required

(iii) subletting of whole: ☐Y/N permitted ☐Y/N landlord's consent required

(iv) subletting of part: ☐Y/N permitted ☐Y/N landlord's consent required

(v) sharing of occupation: ☐Y/N permitted ☐Y/N landlord's consent required ☐Y/N group companies only

(vi) parting with possession: ☐Y/N permitted ☐Y/N landlord's consent required

(n) The lease/licence* contains the following provisions relating to alterations:

(i) structural alterations: ☐Y/N permitted ☐Y/N landlord's consent required

(ii) non-structural internal alterations: ☐Y/N permitted ☐Y/N landlord's consent required

(iii) non-structural external alterations: ☐Y/N permitted ☐Y/N landlord's consent required

(iv) minor partitioning works: ☐Y/N permitted ☐Y/N landlord's consent required

(o) The lease/licence* contains the following provisions relating to insurance:

(i) The landlord/the tenant* is responsible for insuring the premises.

(ii) policy number:
     insurer:
     sum insured:
     renewal date:

(iii) The landlord/tenant* is responsible for insuring plate glass.

(p) The tenant is responsible for the following repairs:

(i) internal repairs ☐Y/N

(ii) external repairs ☐Y/N

(iii) structural repairs ☐Y/N

(iv) inherent/latent defects ☐Y/N

(q)   The landlord is responsible for the following repairs:

    (i)   internal repairs   Y/N

    (ii)   external repairs   Y/N

    (iii) structural repairs   Y/N

    (iv) inherent/latent defects Y/N

(r)   The tenant is responsible for the following decorations:

    (i)   internal decorations   Y/N

    (ii)   external decorations Y/N

(s)   The landlord is responsible for the following decorations:

    (i)   internal decorations   Y/N

    (ii)   external decorations Y/N

(t)   The lease can be forfeited in the following circumstances:

    (i)   if any sums due under the lease are not
         paid within [*insert number*] days of due date   Y/N

    (ii)   upon a breach of the tenant's covenants   Y/N

    (iii) upon insolvency of the tenant   Y/N

    (iv) inherent/latent defects   Y/N

Appendix 4 Facilities service cost benchmarking protocol

Category	Sub-categories (Contract bundle items)	Principal examples/Cost elements	Items included in costs	Items excluded
Services maintenance and repair	Heat and ventilation	boilers radiators chillers ductwork filters fire extinguishers humidifiers	handy-men supervisors blue-collar staff specialist services cleaning tenants areas service charge element water treatment PPM, emergency, ad hoc, etc. smoke tests statutory testing	catering equipment new installations alterations improvements grounds lighting general management time security systems cleaning equipment computer installations
	Plumbing	sprinklers sanitary fittings water supplies drainage	emergency inspection and testing PAT tests legionnaire testing	data cabling churn line management
	Electrical	switchgear wiring internal lighting small power floor outlets fire alarms generators building management systems energy management systems UPS	hardwire testing testing and inspection of earth bonding	
	Lifts	lifts escalators		

Building maintenance and repair	Fabric	structural roofing partitions doors	handy-men supervisors blue-collar staff maintenance equipment tools	new installations alterations improvements management time churn office equipment grounds maintenance furniture
	Decorations	finishes	materials tenants areas service charge element	
	Fixtures and fittings	fixtures fittings	signage essential spares plantroom cleaning gutter clearance	
Grounds maintenance and repair	Maintenance	services (including drain clearance) hard landscaping (fences, pavings) soft landscaping (planted areas, lawns)	gardening horticulture tree surgery fences	internal landscaping
	Cleaning	power washing	service charges snow clearance car park areas	
	Utilities	lighting	road maintenance (including gritting)	
	Security	special grounds patrols/guarding specialist grounds security system maintenance		
Furniture maintenance and repair	Maintenance	chairs desks	service charge element	additional purchases moves special aids and adaptations
	Repairs			
	ISOLATED replacements	(only considered if uneconomic to repair)		
Equipment maintenance and repair	Maintenance	loose electrical appliances	service charge element	additional purchases blinds and curtains IT equipment photocopiers
	Fitting out	AV equipment		
	Repairs	rental costs		
	ISOLATED replacements	(only considered if uneconomic to repair)		

continued

Appendix 4 – continued

Category	Sub-categories (Contract bundle items)	Principal examples/Cost elements	Items included in costs	Items excluded
Alterations and fitting out	Churn Fitting out Improvement Adaptations	moves and changes costs	construction project management professional fees statutory fees furniture and fittings	major refurbishment statutory improvement
Cleaning	Windows and cladding	windows external walls	deep clean toilets carpet shampoos	deep clean kitchens catering area cleaning
	Internal areas	floors internal walls ceilings sanitary fittings toilet area surfaces	stain removal cleaning materials supervisors tenants' areas service charge element graffiti removal atria glazing roofs and integral gutters	contract management time cleans due to churn plantroom cleans grounds cleaning
	Supplies	janitorial supplies		
	Furniture and equipment	furniture, fittings and business equipment	litter picking	
	Special cleans	exposed services catering special cleans computer special cleans lighting special cleans ductwork special cleans lift shaft special cleans	cleaning equipment maintnenance health and safety requirements (eg. slippery surface signs)	
	Pest control	pest control	wires, nets, poisons (eradication contract)	
	Waste disposal	general office waste disposal waste recycling service hazardous/environmentally sensitive waste disposal secure waste disposal	equipment maintenance (eg. shredders) hire of containers	
Laundry	Laundry services	uniforms pillows sheets towels	consumables dedicated staff costs contract costs linen hire	tablecloths chefs' whites new linen/towels, etc.

Security & reception	Reception	reception door guard/commissionaire	staff costs day guards (external and internal)	fire alarms new installations alterations improvements management time changes due to churn
	Guarding	external guarding internal guarding	night patrols (external and internal) uniforms radios security cards camera operators	
	Surveillance	external surveillance internal surveillance	tenants' areas service charge element	
	Duties	visitor escorting lost property	barriers swipe cards CCTV pass issue key management	
	Security system maintenance	car parking control card readers CCTV equipment		
Utilities	Energy	electricity gas oil	tenants' areas service charge element	telephones management time environmental testing
	Water and sewerage	water sewerage		
Internal décor	Horticultural	trees cut flowers planters	contract charges cleaning costs	
	Objets d'art	objets d'art	insurance premiums	
Archiving		physical documents electronic media film-based media document/file disposal specialist filing systems	contract charges maintenance contracts	
Reprographics	Machines	convenience copiers central black and white photocopying central colour photocopying origination/DTP controller	paper management maintenance leases	utilities
	Consumables			

continued

Appendix 4 – continued

Category	Sub-categories (Contract bundle items)	Principal examples/Cost elements	Items included in costs	Items excluded
	Dedicated staff	off-site printing laminating equipment binding equipment and consumables		
Stationery	Departmental	standard paper products	envelopes office equipment other: cards/diaries/files flip-charts/foils/pens line management	paper for photocopiers writing materials
	Personal	bespoke paper products (headed paper, etc.) non-paper consumables		
	Storage materials			
	Management			
IT Communications	Switchboard	switchboard service operation switchboard service maintenance	staff costs equipment maintenance line management	
	Equipment maintenance	telephone/fax equipment maintenance radio pagers/DECT mobiles maintenance audio-visual conferencing equipment maintenance telephone cable maintenance		
	Call charges	mobile phone charges national line charges inter-site leased line charges international line charges bureau services charges		
IT Computers	PC equipment	PC equipment maintenance	equipment/hardware costs lease costs ISDN/other line costs ISP subscriptions domain subscriptions consultancy costs maintenance contracts	new purchases (hardware and software)
	Software	software maintenance line charges website management		

Distribution (Mail/Post room)	Mail processing/delivery	processing and delivery of incoming mail	dedicated staff
		collection and preparation of mail for external distribution	uniforms
			equipment maintenance
		processing and delivery of internal mail/messages	dedicated IT
			scanning/X-ray
	Charges	post office charges	postal charges
	Couriers	local couriers' charges	courier charges
		national couriers' charges	packaging (ie. jiffy bags, bubble wrap, etc.)
		international couriers' charges	
	Equipment	post room equipment maintenance	
Text preparation	Typing services operation	Typing services operation	staff costs
			equipment costs
	Bureau charges	Bureau charges	
Transport/fleet management	Pool cars	pool cars maintenance	staff costs
		pool cars cleaning	equipment costs
		pool cars operation/chauffeurs	uniforms
	Delivery vans	pool delivery van maintenance	overalls
		pool delivery van cleaning	
		pool delivery van operation/drivers	
	Service vehicles	service vehicle maintenance	
		service vehicle cleaning	
		service vehicle operation/drivers	
Catering	Staff dining	staff dining: breakfast menu	subsidy costs
		staff dining: lunch menu	chef, cooks, supervisors, waiters, servers, till staff
		staff dining: sandwich bar	specialist cleaners
		staff dining: snacks and beverages	preparation
	Vending	vending: sandwiches	food cost
		vending: confectionery and snack products	drink cost
		vending: canned/bottled drinks	alcohol
		vending: beverages	sandwiches
			fitting out
			general cleaners
			utilities
			purchase
			finance

continued

427

Appendix 4 – *continued*

Category	Sub-categories (Contract bundle items)	Principal examples/Cost elements	Items included in costs	Items excluded
	Hospitality	hospitality: sandwich lunches hospitality: beverage service hospitality: cold buffet lunches hospitality: hot buffet lunches	leases, rental crockery disposables linen	
	Private dining	private dining rooms: breakfast menu (silver service) private dining rooms: lunch menu (silver service)	laundry consumables	
	Special functions	special functions: seated dinners (silver service) special functions: buffets (silver service) special functions: cocktail parties	deep cleaning/specialist cleaning income from till receipts catering contractor management fee	
	Bar	bar: coffee lounge bar: alcoholic and soft drinks	consultants	
	Maintenance and repair	catering equipment maintenance		
Porterage		workplace removals general services	supervision staff uniforms trolleys	waste disposal moves
Helpdesk/MIS		helpdesk operation booking services equipment/software maintenance	supervision staff uniforms specialist equipment/software maintenance	
Travel		booking service operation travel charges		
Fitness centre		fitness centre management fitness centre equipment maintenance		
Nursery/crèche		nursery/crèche management nursery/crèche equipment maintenance		

General management	intelligent client function (ICF) management agency	senior/strategic management salaries benefits overheads contract management (in-house and outsourced contracts) expenses equipment course fees professional subs	blue-collar workers task supervisors
Professional services	health and safety management project management estate management space management conference/meeting room management	facilities consultants	blue-collar workers task supervisors

Notes

All categories to include outsourced contracts and in-house staff

In-house staff costs to include benefits and overhead allowances

All costs to be exclusive of VAT

Costs of space occupied by category to be excluded but may be shown separately

Depreciation and amortisation costs are not included within the categories but may be shown separately

Table of Legislation

Index

The names of cases and titles of publications are in italics.